CHANNELS OF PROPAGANDA

J. MICHAEL SPROULE

San Jose State University

San Jose, California

ERIC Clearinghouse on Reading, English, and Communication

EDINFO
PRESS

Published by
EDINFO Press
and
ERIC Clearinghouse on Reading,
English, and Communication
Carl B. Smith, Director
Indiana University
P.O. Box 5953
Bloomington, IN 47407

Editor: Warren Lewis
Design: Lauren Bongiani Gottlieb
Cover Design: David J. Smith

Cover photos courtesy AP/Wide World Photos.

This publication was prepared with funding from the Office of Educational
Research and Improvement, U.S. Department of Education, under contract
no. RR93002011. Contractors undertaking such projects under government
sponsorship are encouraged to express freely their judgment in professional and
technical matters. Points of view or opinions, however, do not necessarily
represent the official view or opinions of the Office of Educational Research and
Improvement.

Library of Congress Cataloging-in-Publication Data

Sproule, J. Michael
    Channels of propaganda/J. Michael Sproule
        p. cm.
    Includes bibliographical references and index.
    ISBN 0-927516-34-9 (cloth)
    ISBN 0-927516-61-6 (paperback)
    1. Propaganda. I. Title
HM263.S647   1994
303.3'75—dc20
                                            94-6131
                                              CIP

ERIC/REC ADVISORY BOARD

TABLE OF CONTENTS

COMMITTEE ON PUBLIC INFORMATION
DIVISION OF ADVERTISING
1 MADISON AVE., NEW YORK CITY

E3

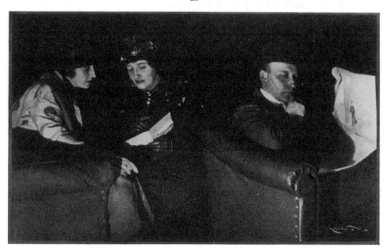

Spies and Lies

German agents are everywhere, eager to gather scraps of news about our men, our ships, our munitions. It is still possible to get such information through to Germany, where thousands of these fragments—often individually harmless — are patiently pieced together into a whole which spells death to American soldiers and danger to American homes.

But while the enemy is most industrious in trying to collect information, and his systems elaborate, he is *not* superhuman—indeed he is often very stupid, and would fail to get what he wants were it not deliberately handed to him by the carelessness of loyal Americans.

Do not discuss in public, or with strangers, any news of troop and transport movements, of bits of gossip as to our military preparations, which come into your possession.

Do not permit your friends in service to tell you—or write you—"inside" facts about where they are, what they are doing and seeing.

Do not become a tool of the Hun by passing on the malicious, disheartening rumors which he so eagerly sows. Remember he asks no better service than to have you spread his lies of disasters to our soldiers and sailors, gross scandals in the Red Cross, cruelties, neglect and wholesale executions in our camps, drunkenness and vice in the Expeditionary Force, and other tales certain to disturb American patriots and to bring anxiety and grief to American parents.

And do not wait until you catch someone putting a bomb under a factory. Report the man who spreads pessimistic stories, divulges—or seeks—confidential military information, cries for peace, or belittles our efforts to win the war.

Send the names of such persons, even if they are in uniform, to the Department of Justice, Washington. Give all the details you can, with names of witnesses if possible—show the Hun that we can beat him at his own game of collecting scattered information and putting it to work. The fact that you made the report will not become public.

You are in contact with the enemy today, just as truly as if you faced him across No Man's Land. In your hands are two powerful weapons with which to meet him—discretion and vigilance. *Use them.*

COMMITTEE ON PUBLIC INFORMATION
8 JACKSON PLACE, WASHINGTON, D. C.

George Creel, Chairman
The Secretary of State
The Secretary of War
The Secretary of the Navy

Contributed through Division of Advertising

United States Gov't Comm. on Public Information

This space contributed for the Winning of the War by

The Publisher of

Officially-sponsored Tattling

CHAPTER 1

THE REALM OF PROPAGANDA

Do we need a term such as propaganda to focus attention on the manipulative dimensions of communication? If one had asked this question of most students of communication in 1955, the answer would have been an emphatic "no!" The previous decade had seen the disappearance of propaganda as a significant theoretical term in American social science and its replacement with the more euphemistic concepts of communication and persuasion. Verbal neutrality of this latter kind seemed to fit the post-World War II era when social researchers aspired to the value-free status attained by those scientists who studied physical phenomena.

A few scholars, such as sociologist Alfred McClung Lee, did continue to use propaganda in the sense in which the term was commonly understood during the 1920s and 1930s, that is, as a descriptor for efforts at self-serving mass persuasion by institutions and groups. Most social scientists of the 1950s and early 1960s, however, recoiled from a term that carried the inherently negative connotations of covert manipulation.[1] How could researchers accept grants from the U.S. government and from business organizations to study mass persuasion under a label that cast aspersions not only on the messages themselves but also on the communicators and their purposes?

Yet, now in the 1990s, we are in the midst of a revival of propaganda as a serious term for understanding social influence.[2] What is going on? Why this return to a theoretical formulation which, however neutrally it is defined, ever reminds us of the self-serving behind communications that organizations and interest groups present to the public? The answer seems to lie in certain moral ambiguities inherent within

1

methods of twentieth-century mass persuasion. During times of social stability, such as were the 1950s, the relative consensus abroad in society may dull concerns about the orchestration of public opinion. No matter how hard we try to rationalize or evade them, however, the tactics of propaganda raise troubling questions for a society that wishes to retain not merely the forms of democracy but also its realities.

In Chapter 1, I invite you to begin with me an odyssey into the ebb and flow of contemporary mass persuasion and the dangers that propaganda's siren songs pose for a democratic people. Beginning with a view of the "propaganda problem," the journey takes us to several vantage points from which American writers and opinion leaders have tried to reconcile mass persuasion with the democratic way of life. Chapters 2-6 act as our vehicles for spying propaganda in today's society and public life. After this view of propaganda's modern haunts, I pose some questions in chapters 7 and 8: What action ought a democratic people take to safeguard intelligent discussion and free choice from the taint of devious communication? To what extent does propaganda cast a shadow over our public life? Can large-scale, engineered persuasion ever be squared with the ideal of democratic public deliberation, and if so, how?

THE PROPAGANDA PROBLEM

The expression *propaganda* has a checkered history. Although propaganda lacks a negative connotation in Romance languages, the English language treats the term as a sinister sister to legitimate persuasion. This linguistic anomaly is attributable to the early connection of the term propaganda with the Roman Catholic Church. The word originates from the Congregatio de propaganda fide (Society for the Propagation of the Faith), an organization having charge of the missionary work of the Roman Church. Given the antipathy toward Catholicism in seventeenth- and eighteenth-century England and among the English residents of the American colonies, it is not surprising that the term became, in the English-speaking world, a synonym for suspicious and disreputable persuasion, or worse.

The *Oxford English Dictionary* logs many nineteenth-century instances wherein propaganda was used, for instance, as "a term of reproach to secret associations for the spread of opinions"; however, it was not until World War I that political commentators found a context for using propaganda as a pointed theoretical concept to understand modern society.[3] During the war, Americans discovered the covert persuasive efforts of the Central Powers (Germany and Austria) and, after the war, those of the Allies (Britain and France) also came to light. These exposures of hidden persuasion shaped the context in which propaganda entered general parlance. During the 1920s, a variety of further conditions transformed propaganda into an especially apt concept for understanding the march of modern society. Propaganda, with its focus on the strategic cultivation of persuasion by organizations, seemed a term particularly suited to explain social influence, given the rise of radio, the solidification of powerful governmental and commercial institutions, the increasing activities of organized interest groups, and the spread of transnational political ideologies, such as fascism and communism. Further, propaganda was a useful concept in an era that saw the decline of the great orator, the persuasive power of great speeches, and the direct-influence effect of pamphleteering, three vehicles characteristic of social suasion in the early nineteenth century. Propaganda fit the new phenomenon of mass persuasion whereby large groups and institutions seemed newly able to surround the public with symbols conveying synthetic, made-up meaning.

To say that propaganda fit a new situation of institutionalized persuasion, however, does not convey a suitably specific definition for our purposes in this book. Nor is it sufficient to point out that definitions have varied and continue to differ. While the task of constructing a definition of propaganda is not easy, it helps to begin with the idea that most conceptions of propaganda present the term as having inevitably negative connotations. Most uses of propaganda emphasize the manipulative power of mass persuasion by causing us to recognize four conditions frequently found in questionable efforts at social influence. The first is manipulation through covertness; second is the overpowering of people with a massive and self-serving outpouring of symbols; third is distortion through tricky language; fourth is the pursuit of a special interest as opposed to pursuing objectives of wider public good.

Covert Manipulation

Propaganda is an attempt to persuade people without seeming to do so. Whereas the direct persuasion of a speech alerts our critical faculties that someone is trying to win us over, propaganda's covertness hides the manipulative element in mass communication. Ivy Lee, a founder of the field of public relations, recognized the connection of covertness and propagandistic communication when he argued that "the essential evil

3

of propaganda is failure to disclose the source of information."[4] Lee put the responsibility for detecting covertness on the nation's editors who, he argued, should demand to know the exact sources of what they printed. Lee's emphasis on the possibility of manipulation through covertness was widely shared during the 1920s and 1930s, culminating in the Foreign Agents Registration Act of 1938. This law required that agents in the United States who work for a foreign nation must register their activities with the U.S. government.

Warriors in U.S. government psychological warfare employ the idea of covertness as one basis for distinguishing among three kinds of propaganda. White propaganda is the open dissemination of essentially accurate information and clearly-marked opinion. When the Voice of America broadcasts an official announcement of the U.S. government, it is spreading white propaganda. Gray propaganda contains more of a biased slant in its treatment, and gray sources either are partially concealed or are only vaguely suggested. A case in point is when the Central Intelligence Agency arranges with a commercial publishing house to subsidize publication of a book that the agency views as useful. For instance, the CIA once supported publication of *The Dynamics of Soviet Society*, by Walt Rostow, a social scientist.

Black propaganda, more often known now as "disinformation," is the product not only of a considerable effort to conceal the source of the information but also employs a significant number of distortions or outright falsehoods. For instance, the CIA manufactured a variety of bogus leaflets that were presented as having been written by Vietnamese communists during the time when Americans fought in that country. A visiting American newspaper columnist, Joseph Alsop, once picked up such a leaflet which stated that many South Vietnamese were to be sent to China to work on the railways there. Believing that the CIA's leaflet had been written by the communists, Alsop used it as a reference point in his newspaper columns.[5]

Massive Orchestration

If covertness is the first defining characteristic of propaganda, a second essential feature is the massive orchestration of communication. The importance of size and scope flows naturally from today's tendency for important communications to originate in institutions and organized groups instead of from individual speakers and essayists. Modern conditions seem to demand that we characterize propaganda as large-scale

4

symbolic orchestration to distinguish it from persuasion, a term which is easily applicable to single speeches and essays.

The massiveness of propaganda is what turns its self-serving and unreflective character into a problem. All persuasion tends toward self-advantage and, therefore, contains an inherent bias. Aristotle long ago observed that rhetoric was the art of emphasizing what favors our case and of minimizing what is unfavorable to our purposes.[6] Where minimizing and maximizing occur among advocates of equal strength, and where the public is treated to more than one side of a question, the self-serving nature of rhetorical communication cannot only be tolerated but, from the point of democracy, deserves encouragement.

When coupled with symbolic giantism, however, the self-serving nature of communication can become dangerous. One-sided communication threatens the ability of the public to decide wisely whenever an advocate marshalls huge symbolic resources through control of a large institution, access to tremendous funds, support of a powerful interest group, or preponderance in mass media. For this reason, propaganda tends to be associated with communications from government, from business, and from large pressure groups, especially as diffused through giant media channels.

Tricky Language

A third defining characteristic of propaganda is its tendency to emphasize tricky language designed to discourage reflective thought. Any persuasive devices that help short-circuit logic are associated with propaganda. This notion is reflected in the classic seven propaganda devices developed by the Institute for Propaganda Analysis:

- name calling
- glittering generalities (use of good/bad words such as "freedom" or "injustice")
- transfer (use of prestigious symbols, such as the flag)
- testimonial (endorsements from prestigious persons)
- plain folks (propagandists representing themselves as "next door"-type of people)
- card stacking (minimizing and maximizing)
- bandwagon (the idea that everybody is doing it or thinking it).[7]

5

The danger of bias through tricky language is particularly worrisome in propaganda as compared to speeches. Aristotle and other classical rhetoricians believed that orators, however pleasing and attractive their claims were, nevertheless needed to support their conclusions with a train of reasons. Speakers required good arguments not only because they stood before their fellow citizens to ask for public action but also because they risked challenge from opposing advocates. In contrast, propagandists can cast their conclusions widely, sometimes modifying the basic message to fit different groups in an atmosphere that, as often as not, neither calls for a particular public decision nor brings direct point/counterpoint debate.

Therefore, one way to characterize propaganda is to note that it typically purveys conclusions, packaged in attractive language, often entirely without support of developed reasons or arguments. The emphasis of propaganda upon conclusions, and its concomitant deemphasis of developed reasons, became the basis on which early theorists distinguished propaganda from education. For instance, sociologist Frederick Lumley argued that educators try to teach people to seek out evidence, whereas propagandists dampen critical facilities by feeding people conclusions. According to Lumley's line of thinking, even a competition of propagandas still means that the public is malnourished by an empty diet of prepackaged conclusions. Educator William Biddle argued, therefore, that propaganda inherently acts to "diminish independent, critical intelligence."[8]

The idea of hollow but glittering symbols as typical of propaganda probably accounts for why many people refer to advertising as propagandistic. On the other hand, advertising as it is usually pitched directly touts a named product, and the audience is correspondingly aware of the effort to sell. According to the criterion of covertness, therefore, advertising ought not to be classified as communication universally falling into the category of propaganda. Yet, as I observe in chapter 6, advertising can become highly propagandistic when a plug for a product is embedded as part of the ostensible content of an entertainment program. When, between 1982 and 1989, Coca-Cola owned 49 percent of Columbia Pictures, Coke attempted to profit by inserting into Columbia films not only close-up shots of its drinks but actual dialogue that mentioned them.[9]

Particular Interests

In the late 1940s, a number of scholars developed the concept of pro-tolerance propaganda to signify their hopes that what scientists had learned about large-scale social influence might be harnessed to good social purposes. Although these researchers recognized that attitudes were hard to change, they were optimistic that communication research might help alleviate anti-Semitism and other forms of social prejudice. They were hopeful that mass media might be employed to spur grass roots efforts by local volunteers who would nudge their fellow citizens into patterns of greater religious and social tolerance.[10]

If propaganda can be used to combat unsavory prejudices, does this mean that some varieties of symbolic orchestration are good? I once posed this question to George Seldes, dean of American media critics and longtime political journalist. Seldes has spent a lifetime crusading against commercial and political pressure artists who frequently gain a stranglehold over important media channels. In *Lords of the Press* (1938), his classic expose, Seldes explained that wealthy media owners sometimes abused their power, for instance, to trample the Consumers Union, which was refused the right to advertise in mainstream publications of the era.[11] In more recent times, Seldes has expressed the opinion that the American press exhibits far greater honesty than when he was a young man during the Roaring Twenties; however, he has continued to crusade against such special interests as the tobacco industry which, he argued, exerts pressure to prevent accurate presentations of the adverse effects of smoking on health.

Given Seldes's career as an exposer of pro-business and pro-conservative propagandas in journalism, I questioned him about propaganda emanating from the liberal side of society. The Left, Seldes responded, consists of "all the writers and artists, and liberals and all like that"; in contrast, "on the right you will find all the corporations, and all the big money." In this context, Seldes explained, "if both engage in propaganda, one is, you might say, [promoting] social service or general welfare." Seldes set the propaganda of the Tobacco Institute which aims at enriching this particular industry in contrast to the propaganda of labor unions which aspire to a more general utopia. In Seldes's estimation, these two propagandas "are not equal." "One is on the general welfare side and the other is anti-general interest and pro-special interest."

Pressing Seldes on the matter of special versus general interests as a test of propaganda, I asked him to comment on the argument made by critics of affirmative action that such policies had become a special-interest reverse discrimination disguised as a general social good. No, Seldes responded, although affirmative action disadvantaged some people, these policies provided a general benefit by promoting social equality. In this view, promotions favoring affirmative action would represent an honest propaganda toward a general interest, even if the immediate benefits were not available to everyone.[12]

This colloquy took place in 1984, six years before the "political correctness" controversy emerged as a major topic of discussion in America. By 1990-1991 (see discussion in chapter 5), a number of conservative and liberal critics began to raise alarms about what they alleged were quasi-totalitarian pressures exerted to force college faculties and students into "politically correct" (P.C.) speech on social issues pertaining to race, gender, and homosexuality. Debate about whether or not the P.C. controversy bespeaks a general or special-interest propaganda probably will remain a topic of heated discussion throughout this decade.

The P.C. debate suggests that it is no simple matter to separate general interests from special interests and, in turn, good propaganda from bad propaganda. However, Seldes's essential point rings true that society exempts propaganda from condemnation when social influence is perceived to be in the general interest. For this reason, few complained when Hollywood began to produce films in the early 1940s that glorified military service. What kind of slacker would presume to naysay John Wayne in *The Fighting Seabees* (1944) for dramatizing the heroism of the Navy's dedicated and tough construction crews who risked life and livelihood near Japanese lines. Moviedom's turn to martial themes was regarded as quite appropriate in the context of a world-wide struggle against fascism.

Channels of Propaganda

What emerges from the foregoing discussion is a general definition of propaganda. Propaganda represents the work of large organizations or groups to win over the public for special interests through a massive orchestration of attractive conclusions packaged to conceal both their persuasive purpose and lack of sound supporting reasons.

No treatment of propaganda is complete, however, without explicitly attending to the major channels through which the public is introduced to lullabies of biased persuasion. We may, therefore, elaborate our definition to clarify the process by which symbolic orchestration reaches the public. Specifically, propaganda takes place when influencers attempt to win over the public by infiltrating messages into various channels of public expression that are viewed as (ordinarily or ideally) politically neutral. The characteristic propaganda channels are government agency action, scientific research, religion, news, educational classrooms, and entertainment. This roster of the channels of propaganda sets our agenda in chapters 2 through 6 in which we explore each in detail.

The tendency for propaganda to work through ostensibly neutral public forums means that much propaganda is an attempt to diffuse an ideology rather than to articulate a specific socio-political position. Put another way, propaganda does not always explicitly advance an argument; often its aim is to sell a general system of ideas (an ideology) or a visual background (an image) that implicitly supports an action or policy. To take two representative cases, neither *Top Gun* (1986) nor *Born on the Fourth of July* (1989) explicitly argued a position on military spending or on war; yet, these movie dramas respectively purveyed ideologies and images of militarism and pacificism. In depicting the heroism of the Navy's top fighter pilots, *Top Gun* suggested that combat is honorable and necessary. In contrast, *Born on the Fourth of July* was pacifistic, suggesting that war's aims are futile and that the warrior ideal has been manipulative.

Perspectives on Propaganda

Various participants in society's debate over mass persuasion offer differing perspectives on the propaganda problem. The oldest and most widely diffused position on propaganda in America is that of reform-minded progressives. Around the turn of the century, the muckrakers, progressive reform journalists, became the first to argue that propaganda represents a danger to democracy. After World War I, Walter Lippmann gained a reputation as a leading newspaper columnist and political commentator through his books and articles arguing that propaganda imperiled democracy. Lippmann argued that a free nation could not survive in an urban mass society unless the major channels of public communication were protected from self-serving manipulation.

The culmination of progressive sentiment on mass persuasion was the Institute for Propaganda Analysis, chartered in 1937, which widely diffused materials on propaganda education throughout America's schools. Progressive propaganda critique waned during the twenty years after World War II, but it has enjoyed a revival in the years following the Vietnam War.

While the progressive position underlies most contemporary criticism of propaganda, it has never enjoyed a monopoly in the literature on mass persuasion. From the time of the muckrakers up to the present, practitioners of mass communication have staked out a competing position that propaganda represents a relatively harmless offshoot of traditional American boosterism and the go-getting spirit. Major practitioner defenses of propaganda may be found in the fields of public relations (Ivy Lee and Edward L. Bernays), advertising (Rooser Reeves), survey research (George Gallup), and broadcasting (Frank Stanton). Similarly, when Harold Lasswell, Paul Lazarsfeld, and other academic social researchers began to conduct statistical and experimental communication research for government and private industry, they developed what we may call a scientific perspective on the political impact of propaganda. Communication scientists defend their work for society's large persuaders on the basis of the practitioner's notion that the competition of propagandas in the marketplace renders propaganda socially neutral.

Another group of academicians who joined the communication scientists in departing from progressive propaganda critique were members of the critical-thinking movement such as John Dewey and Edward Glaser. The critical-thinking, or rationalist, school of thought looks for ways to remedy what its adherents believe is a characteristic inability of members of the public to think reflectively. Rationalists believe that the public's cognitive incapacity is a greater threat to democracy than are efforts by powerful organizations and groups to play upon public credulity. Finally, a polemical school of propaganda critique emerged in the twentieth century when politicians and political activists began to monitor the channels of public communication to make sure their ideological enemies enjoyed no advantages there. The paradigm case of polemical propaganda critique may be seen in the work of the notorious Un-American Activities Committee of the U.S. House of Representatives (HUAC). In furtherance of its charter, HUAC did sometimes focus on fascist or communist subversion directed from abroad; however, the intellectual impetus of the Committee was in the direction of what today is known as McCarthyism (although Joe McCarthy, a member of the U.S. Senate, never served on HUAC). HUAC was dominated by right-wing politicians who tried to discredit domestic liberals and progressives by connecting the political Left to communism.

To take a contemporary case in point, in 1992 a number of Governor Bill Clinton's political opponents suggested that he might have come into contact with Russian secret agents during an educational trip to Moscow taken while he was a Rhodes Scholar. Democrats quickly branded this innuendo as McCarthyism in view of the vague and undocumented nature of this political slander that desperate opponents were hurling against the front-running presidential candidate.

The debate by progressives, practitioners, scientists, critical thinkers, and polemicists over the meaning and implications of mass persuasion is, then, a longstanding one. To form a judgment about the impact of propaganda on democratic life, it is crucial to understand how these various schools of thought on propaganda emerged and how they have competed. I expect that readers of this book will want to formulate their own position on the propaganda problem by combining aspects of one or more of these five standard schools of American thought on propaganda.

THE MUCKRAKERS AND THE DISCOVERY OF PROPAGANDA

The early nineteenth century was an era of the great orator. Before poetry and novels became America's literature, the popular political speakers provided the nation with a body of printed pamphlet works that expressed the social and political aspirations of the people. By 1870, however, the social influence of speechmaking and pamphleteering was giving way to that of news reporting. The nation's leaders realized that they could more effectively reach the public through newspaper coverage than by oratory.[13] Political theorists and social commentators did not at first apprehend the implications for democratic life of replacing the direct persuasion of oratory and pamphlets with the indirect commercial medium of the newspaper.

Writers on American society were slow to apprehend how the American political landscape was changing due to newspapers, with their large circulations and sensational stories, and press agents, who strove to slant the news in favor of their clients. James Bryce, British Ambassador to the U.S. and leading political theorist of the 1890s, described American politics as consisting of an informed electorate able to make known its wishes directly to public officials.[14] Orthodox political theory of the late-nineteenth century did not explicitly take into account news control and orchestrated campaigns, despite evidence that institutional persuaders were using propaganda to channel public thinking before the public could formulate an opinion on key issues.

Ivy Lee and Public Relations

Turn-of-the-century political movements by rural agitators (populists), middle-class reformers (progressives) and urban radicals (socialists) began to undermine the dominant view of Lord Bryce and others that American politics was founded on an intelligent and democratic consensus. Business leaders were particularly concerned by demands of reformers and radicals for government regulation of the economy. Accustomed to doing business with behind-the-scenes lobbying and pressure, leaders of America's businesses increasingly saw a need to speak directly to the general public in order to forestall demands for aversive legislation.

One of the first to recognize the need for new communication practices by business was Ivy Lee, an enterprising, erstwhile newspaper reporter. Lee founded one of the first modern public-relations firms on the basis of his faith that journalists could make a good living serving as advisers to business organizations. Lee recognized that newspapers were becoming rational economic organizations, and that reporters were increasingly interested in professional standards. Lee was able to persuade a number of major corporate leaders that the newspaper business was becoming increasingly professionalized such that corporations no longer could assume that bribery and threats would net them the best press coverage.

In an early application of his new approach to press relations, Lee induced the coal operators to abandon the policy of public silence that they had maintained during the 1902 strike. By acting as liaison between the coal industry and the press, Lee was instrumental in making sure that management, rather than the strikers, would have a greater influence over the public's perception of the strike. Lee also persuaded the Pennsylvania Railroad to abandon its policy of blocking news coverage of railroad accidents. Instead, Lee put in place a system of press-friendly relations whereby reporters not only enjoyed access to good facilities but also received news handouts ready for publication.[15]

The Muckrakers Respond

The incipient craft of public relations, exemplified by Ivy Lee, drew criticism for being insidious. Muckraking journalists wondered whether the public really benefitted from a cozy relationship between newspapers and society's power brokers. The muckrakers were reform-oriented journalists who popularized the progressive reform movement with their factual exposés of corrupt practices particularly in American government and business. Because their works appeared in the popular press, their often truculent critiques won a wide general audience. As practicing journalists, the muckrakers were conversant with the habits of powerful institutions and groups alternately to bully and court the press in the interest of receiving favorable newspaper coverage.

Ray Stannard Baker's essay on "How Railroads Make Public Opinion" (1906) represented one of the first in-depth muckraking investigations that revealed how the propaganda employed by the powerful could stand as an enemy to reform. This article, culmination of a five-part series on railroad corruption, exposed details of the behind-the-scenes public relations campaign launched against regulatory legislation then pending in Congress. Baker reported that a group of railroads hired a public-relations firm to keep track of newspaper coverage and to visit editors in the belief that "the fountainhead of public information is the newspaper." The firm also sent out self-serving articles, noting when they were printed as news. Avoiding direct bribery, the railroad campaign nevertheless employed economic pressure on newspapers by encouraging local business people to write letters or sign petitions against further regulation of railroads.[16]

Taking the typical muckraker's view of institutional persuasion, Baker argued that public-relations practices represented a threat to democratic social influence. Baker argued that the covert nature of public relations prevented practitioners from likening themselves to lawyers in a court of public opinion. Moreover, public relations, by its very nature, served particular, as opposed to general, interests.

Muckraker Will Irwin, in a series of articles on the newspaper industry, later identified two overt dangers posed to the accuracy of the news caused by cozy relations between propagandist and journalist. The first of these dangers was the implicit, and often explicit, tendency of

13

newspapers to color the news to avoid offending major advertisers. Newspapers were part of the general business environment which, Irwin observed, required "mutual favors."[17] A second temptation to biased journalism was rooted in the habit of editors and publishers to associate more with the wealthy and powerful than with the working class. As a result, newspapers were likely to reflect upper-class views. Irwin recommended increased professionalism among newspaper people as the route to reform in journalism.

The collision of corporate public relations and reform journalism produced the climate of intellectual ferment out of which emerged the earliest two schools of American thought on propaganda, the practitioner school, represented by Ivy Lee, and the progressive school, advanced by the muckrakers. The two schools concurred that twentieth-century social influence increasingly would take the form of cooptation of such ostensibly neutral channels of public information as the news. The practitioner school treated institutional social influence as a non-controversial outgrowth of democratic free speech. Further, practitioners believed that their own emerging professional codes of ethical practice would prevent covert social influence from threatening society.

In contrast to practicing persuaders, progressive reformers held public-relations practices to be inherently unfriendly to democracy. Progressives believed that public opinion was innately corrupted—tainted at the source—when it came under the sway of propaganda. Progressives believed that vigilance by reformers was the only real antidote for twentieth-century propaganda. In their view, democracy depended on alert critics who were ready to lay bare the evidence that powerful interest groups subtly insert their self-serving partisan material into the channels of public expression.

THE GREAT WAR AND FUROR OVER PROPAGANDA

Until 1915, the topic of propaganda was a subject of discussion chiefly among progressive reformers and the nation's intellectuals. During World War I, however, the propaganda struggles of the Allies and the Central Powers acted to bring news control and covertly orchestrated persuasive campaigns to the attention of the general public.

War Propagandas

At the outset of World War I, both the Allies and the Central Powers developed propaganda campaigns to advance their respective

14

causes among citizens of the United States, the world's most powerful neutral. Desirous of securing arms, and hopeful of a full-blown military alliance, Britain set up a propaganda operation in the U.S. directed by novelist Gilbert Parker.[18] Parker's propaganda bureau began by providing America's opinion leaders with a variety of pamphlets and publications defending the Allied position and attacking Germany for its brutality and alleged war atrocities. Parker's group further identified Americans sympathetic to the Allied cause, encouraging these individuals to make statements and take action in support of the Allied cause. The British were so successful in covering the tracks of their propaganda operation that pro-Ally Americans did not realize, until after the war, that they had participated in an orchestrated program of political warfare.

Supporters of Germany's cause chiefly included German-Americans and Irish-Americans, the latter not caring who won the Great War so long as Britain lost. Those favorable to Germany recognized the virtual impossibility of the United States ever entering the war in support of the Central Powers, so the pro-Germans set their sights on cultivating neutralist sentiment. Parallel to the secretly organized British propaganda campaign in the U.S. was a pro-German propaganda cabinet consisting of German and Austrian officials together with pro-German Americans. Like the British, the pro-German propaganda cabinet mounted a campaign of pamphleteering and efforts to get opinion leaders to speak out either in sympathy with Germany or in favor of neutrality.[19]

The sinking of the passenger liner, *Lusitania*, by a German submarine in May 1915 ultimately deprived German propagandists of an open-minded public; however, the decisive blow to the German propaganda campaign in the U.S. was its close administrative connection with espionage and sabotage. Unlike the English, who kept their propagandists well-separated from their espionage agents, the German propaganda cabinet in the U.S. kept close links to covert bribery, espionage, and sabotage. In a series of articles, the *New York World*, August 15-18, 1915, published documents exposing the covert efforts of leading pro-German propagandists.

The *World's* series showed that the pro-Germans worked "to establish newspapers and news services, finance professional lecturers and moving picture shows, and to enlist the support of American citizens and publish books for the sole purpose of fomenting internal discord among the American people to the advantage of the German Empire."[20] As a result of this series, George S. Viereck, editor of *The Fatherland*, as well as other spokespersons for the German cause, appeared to be purveying propaganda rather than exercising the right of free expression. German activities, as revealed by the *World*, set the tone for how Americans first understood modern propaganda. Americans saw propaganda in simple partisan terms, as expressed in the phrase "The German Propaganda." Propaganda was understood as the use by enemy agents of secret subsidies and bribery to corrupt public opinion through tainted publications.

Postwar disillusionment in the United States set the context for a broadening of the idea of propaganda. The opening of the war archives of the defeated Central Powers provided a flood of secret diplomatic correspondence that contradicted the wartime Allied gospel that the war had been the result of a German/Austrian plot. Accompanying revisionism on the matter of war guilt, the postwar years saw a blurring of the previous dichotomy between presumably truthful Allied persuasion and false German propaganda. Postwar exposés showed that many tales of German war atrocities were exaggerated, mythical, or even faked by Allied propagandists.[21]

The Committee on Public Information

With the end of the war came also a tendency to rethink the wisdom of America's own wartime propaganda. American propaganda had been centered in the Committee on Public Information, established by President Woodrow Wilson, and headed by progressive journalist, George Creel. Established in April 1917, the CPI not only centralized government communications on the war but also mounted an unprecedented campaign of persuasion to wean the public away from neutrality and toward Woodrow Wilson's vision of the war as a crusade to spread democracy around the world.

The range of the CPI's campaign was extensive, including not only direct pamphlets and speakers but also encompassing official handouts ready for printing as news, catchy magazine advertisements, striking posters, entertaining and informative war expositions at state fairs, and enterprising uses of the newly-emerging medium of film.[22] While the fighting raged, the CPI's vast undertaking was seen chiefly in terms of the practitioner view of propaganda. With the nation's economy mobilized for war, what could be wrong with an all-out mobilization of public opinion? After the war, Creel continued to defend his work as a wartime propagandist by relying on the practitioner's position on social influence. Creel argued that the CPI program was factual and socially beneficial. Not only did the Committee ignore hate material and atrocity stories, Creel maintained, but also the CPI campaign proved that "propagandists do *not* have to lie."[23]

While Creel gave an administrative or technician's view of propaganda operations, the dominant tendency of progressives was to rethink wartime persuasions. Progressives were troubled by the subtle infiltration of hate and atrocity material into governmental communication. Particularly culpable were lurid posters that portrayed Germans as murderers and rapists. "Remember Belgium," headlined one CPI advertisement that was accompanied by an artist's conception of German arson, pillage, and implied rape. Also troubling were the CPI's paranoia-producing advertisements and news features that enjoined Americans to turn in neighbors who made utterances construable as unfavorable to the war. One particularly popular CPI advertisement, entitled "Spies and Lies," asked readers to "report the man who spreads pessimistic stories."

Another condition prompting Americans to rethink the wartime persuasions was the growing recognition that the Allied communication campaigns inherently undermined a traditional assumption of democracy in the United States. If propagandists freely influenced the content of news and monopolized the channels of public communication, how could citizens independently obtain the necessary information to make rational political decisions?

Progressives who had worked in the wartime propaganda campaign were concerned about what the new climate of massive, and often covert, symbolic inducement meant for postwar democratic life. Walter Lippmann, who served with the Army's fledgling psychological warfare unit in France, was one of the first to reactivate the old progressive critique of propaganda.[24] Based on his observations of Allied censorship and propaganda, Lippmann concluded that the chief problem of modern democracy was protecting the channels of public communication from propaganda. Lippmann believed that unless public opinion was protected against propaganda, the public's mind could be tainted with prejudices and thus exploited by powerful social groups and institutions.[25]

Will Irwin, the progressive press critic, had served with the CPI during the war and, like Lippmann, worried about the future of public communication in an "age of lies." Irwin admitted that "we never told the whole truth—not by any manner of means. We told that part which served our national purpose."[26] Upon returning to private life again as a journalist, Irwin found evidence that propaganda was continuing to infiltrate the news in peacetime as it had done during the late war. Propagandists practically had tugged on the sleeves of every journalist covering the Versailles Treaty negotiations while, on another front, pro- and anti-communist sources spread conflicting accounts of the Revolution in Russia.

THE COMMUNICATION INDUSTRY AND PROGRESSIVES' CRITIQUE

Progressive propaganda critique was impelled not only by a rethinking of wartime persuasions but also by a worry that the war's pattern of orchestrated social influence would become a permanent fixture of the cultural landscape.

The Communication Industry: Overt and Covert

Progressives turned their attention to signs that a mass-communication industry was taking shape that had an unprecedented power to reach the public mind. Signs that CPI-style persuasion would become the norm included boasts by advertisers about their work for the CPI and the Treasury Department. Advertising agencies regaled prospective clients with visions of how they could raise business profits just as they had successfully marketed war bonds.[27] The Great War also acted as a spur to the new field of business public relations when the CPI discharged scores of trained publicists. In government, the CPI pattern of official press spokesmen and official handouts became standard.[28]

The postwar period saw the growth of radio as a vital new channel of the communication industry. With its audience of millions, radio became a medium of mass communication whose power was open not only to advertisers but also to politicians. While radio was opening up the public ever more directly to the voices of key commercial and political persuaders, new methods of survey research offered the potential for both predicting and assessing the effects of mass communication. In particular, because radio audiences were otherwise invisible, market and opinion research firms sprang up to help advertisers identify the size and composition of their listening publics. By the 1930s, market research firms began to apply their tools to problems of politics. The administrative utility of polls was not lost on President Roosevelt, who used George Gallup's data to help steer the nation toward policies of assistance to Britain in the war against Hitler.[29]

Progressives believed that mass communication through advertising, radio, and audience research would give institutions and interest groups a symbolic leverage that would capture people's imaginations before they could formulate and articulate a reflective public opinion. While propaganda critics were concerned about developments in the direct channels of mass persuasion, they were particularly alarmed that mass persuaders would increasingly insert their messages covertly into a wide variety of contexts in which people did not expect to be persuaded.

During the 1920s and 1930s, progressive critics of mass persuasion collectively produced a body of literature generally known as "propaganda analysis." Propaganda analysts focused less on overt advertising and political speechmaking in order to pay more attention to covert manipulation of the public mind. Emphasis was given to the diffusion of self-serving commercial and political ideologies into ostensibly neutral arenas of public communication, including news, religion, government agency action, entertainment, and education.

News Propaganda

During the 1920s, progressive critics picked up and widened the old muckraker's theme of tainted news. Led by progressive journalist Heber Blankenhorn, Lippmann's cohort in Army psychological warfare, the Interchurch World Movement published an influential report criticizing steel-industry leaders for their effort falsely to characterize the steel strike of 1919 as an outbreak of domestic bolshevism.[30] At the same time, Upton Sinclair, the muckraking novelist, published *The Brass Check* (1919), his personal narrative about domestic reformers' being ignored or given prejudiced press treatment. Sinclair's book had a significant impact on many journalists of the period, such as George Seldes, who had chafed under the rampant ideological censorship of the time but who, thus far, had lacked the sense of professional consciousness necessary to combat it. For his part, Seldes took up Sinclair's challenge and embarked upon a career as a press critic. Beginning with his first book, *You Can't Print That!* (1929), Seldes assessed censorship and propaganda overseas. Among his other works was the aforementioned *Lords of the Press*, in which Seldes described sundry ideological alterations of the news resulting from the commercial ownership of newspaper chains.[31]

Four Other Covert Channels

While progressives criticized news propaganda as the chief cause of corrupted public opinion, they also investigated how propaganda operated in four other channels of expression: religion, government, entertainment media, and education. Religion was vulnerable as a channel of propaganda in view of the easy ability of preachers to vest secular political views with the appearance of absolute divine sanction. Sociologist Ray Abrams provided the definitive account of how preachers had abused their role of spiritual adviser in the interest of reinforcing official views of the war. Abrams described how most American clergy, many of whom had been pre-war pacifists, quickly jumped on the wartime bandwagon and contributed much to the hysteria of the period. Abrams also echoed what would become a common sentiment among propaganda critics, that extremes of patriotic utterance and action often belied self-serving motives. For instance, Abrams explained, mainstream Protestant churches were able to use their pro-war positions as a device for weakening smaller pacifist sects.[32]

Even though the CPI was quickly disbanded after the Armistice, certain wartime practices of public relations remained in government. While propaganda analysts of the inter-world-war era were most concerned about propaganda in news and by big business, these critics also found in the actions of government agencies the tell-tale signs of manipulation under the guise of public education. For instance, Robert Wohlforth criticized the War Department's citizenship courses given at high schools, colleges, and training camps to an estimated 260,000 young men. Worrisome to Wohlforth was the anti-progressive ideological line of the Army's educational materials. Students were cautioned about the evils of pacifism, socialism, and the dangers of rule by the masses—"mobocracy." Wohlforth believed that while the Army's program pretended to strengthen citizenship, the courses actually stuffed the nation's youth "with the sawdust of reactionary platitudes, tin-whistle ideals and big business morality."[33]

A related and more extensive argument about propaganda in government was put forth by critics who probed the links between arms manufacturers and the Executive Branch. *Merchants of Death*, an expose by Engelbrecht and Hanighen, caused a considerable stir that prompted action in Congress. The authors argued that arms merchants were an important, but often unrecognized, part of the system of war. This was because twentieth-century arms manufacturers employed public-relations techniques to stir up war scares, thereby insuring increased sales of armaments.[34]

The accelerating popularity of the movies and the rise of radio as a mass medium caused progressive propaganda critics to explore whether entertainment was en route to becoming a particularly dangerous channel for the subtle spread of partisan ideologies. Harold Larrabee described two ways in which film could inculcate attitudes in the movie-going public. First, films promoted "conventional moral standards." One instance of this covert, cultural dimension of film propaganda was the tendency of films to present villains as being wealthy persons, and to show criminals as great consumers of liquor. Films presented a background picture of social life, and where they directly confronted real social situations, films also had the potential to "convince the audience of the right or wrong of a particular cause."[35]

Another form of direct cinematic propaganda could be seen in the small number of films that took positions in favor of religious groups, relief campaigns, and political proposals. Further in the way of direct propaganda, progressives demonstrated ways that commercial persuaders inserted plugs for their products into entertainment and educational films. Darwin Teilhet exposed the new phenomenon of "sponsored films," movie shorts that, under the guise of providing information, actually touted such specific products as perfumes.[36]

Direct propaganda in films was probably less of a concern to most progressives than was the general cultural impact of the popular entertainment media. Underscoring the importance of the issue, Professor of Education Edgar Dale pointed to data showing that every week more than 11 million children under age 14 attended the movies.[37] Critics worried that children were being exposed to a vast amount of material, originally prepared for adult audiences, that was oriented to crime and sex and contained high levels of vulgarity. Dale discovered that a larger percentage of movies in 1930 focused on crime and sex than in 1920. Not only that, Dale argued, movies distorted the viewers' sense of social life. From a detailed probing of movie content, he found that characters in films overwhelmingly pursued personal, as opposed to public, objectives. Dale reported that only nine percent of the goals of leading film characters pertained to improving general society.[38]

In another Depression-era study of the movies, Herbert Blumer, a sociologist, used data from the testimonies of children to argue that movies exerted a negative impact on the young. From his examination of the daydreams reported by children, Blumer argued that movies exerted a powerful "emotional possession" on young people. [39]

Finally, in their scrutiny of the diffusion of propaganda, progressive critics turned to educational material. In a retrospective on the atmosphere of the war years, H. L. Mencken included in his *American Mercury* magazine two articles about educators as wartime propagandists. Charles Angoff reviewed the sorry record of college teachers being fired for criticizing the wisdom of the war. C. H. Grattan focused on the lack of critical judgment exercised during the war by historians who abandoned scholarly methods and embraced the then-popular view that the war was a simple matter of democratic good versus authoritarian evil. Not only did progressive critics point to the educational propaganda of the war years but also they worried about the future of education in an era of propaganda. Historian Charles Beard expressed concern about the propaganda he found in a syllabus issued to school principals by the New York City Department of Education. According to Beard, the syllabus both distorted the history of the Great War and advocated the controversial political proposal of universal peacetime military service. Beard concluded that "if this syllabus is what we are to expect from the public schools in the coming age, then we must look elsewhere for education."[40]

Educators against Propaganda

Concerns about propaganda accelerated during the 1920s and 1930s. Americans learned that the National Electric Light Association had been subsidizing textbook authors to write favorably of privately-owned power plants. Investigations of the NELA campaign by the National Education Association (1929) and the American Association of University Professors (1930) widely publicized the general problem of propaganda in the schools. During the 1930s, educators were confronting problems of propaganda inherent in various educational materials and prize contests that public schools accepted from outside organizations and groups.[41]

Educators of the 1920s and 1930s worked to build propaganda analysis into the curriculum in order to help students function in a world of ideological diffusion. Propaganda became an important theoretical term as well as a significant pedagogical concept in many fields of the humanities and social sciences.[42] Further, exercises in propaganda analysis became important in secondary school teaching. [43]

The chartering of the Institute for Propaganda Analysis marked the high point of the anti-propaganda movement of the 1920s and 1930s. Supported initially by a grant from progressive philanthropist Edward A. Filene, the Institute was able to mount a monthly bulletin, *Propaganda Analysis*, that was widely read by educators and opinion leaders around the nation. The bulletin employed such microscopic tools of analysis as the seven propaganda devices (see p. 5 above). Issues of *Propaganda Analysis* also presented case-study articles, analyses of the propagandas of government, interest groups, public-relations professionals, and foreign governments. In another phase of its work, the Institute almost succeeded in becoming self-supporting by selling innovative educational materials for use by schools and by adult education groups. By 1941, the Institute estimated that its curricular materials were being used by 1,000,000 students.[44] The Institute's program represented the archetype of the progressive philosophy that educating the public about propaganda is the most appropriate response to the manipulative dimensions of modern mass communication.

Between 1919 and 1941, American progressive propaganda critics developed an extensive literature analyzing episodes of propaganda in news, religion, government, entertainment, and education. Not only did progressives reprise the propagandas of the war years but also they focused on contemporary efforts at ideological diffusion by domestic and foreign groups. Progressives believed that propaganda was a new and intrinsically worrisome tool of social competition that posed dangers for democracy. For this reason, they did not give attention to the efforts of disparaged groups only, such as the communists or fascists. Instead, propaganda analysts aimed most of their critical barbs at mainstream institutions and aggregations who were transforming the marketplace of ideas into a supermarket of packaged images.

The progressive view of propaganda became so widely diffused into general public consciousness during the inter-war years that Americans began to view propaganda as having been arguably the major cause of World War I.[45] However, progressives were not the only ones writing about propaganda during the 1920s and 1930s. Competing schools of thought emerged that provided alternate perspectives on social competition through mass persuasion.

THE PRACTITIONERS RESPOND

Under fire for tainting public opinion, and thereby undermining American democracy, public relations practitioners, pollsters, advertisers, and radio and film producers felt impelled to respond to their critics. The practitioners were people of action; they therefore produced fewer reflective books and articles than did the progressive propaganda critics. Nevertheless, the practitioners were proud of their emerging professions, and they developed a significant body of theoretical literature during the 1920s and 1930s.

Professional Codes and Practices

Ivy Lee became a speaker for the incipient practitioner approach to propaganda. Lee denied that the public-relations activities of powerful institutions in any way upset the balance of forces in society. First, according to Lee, the essential impact of public relations was to attune business practices more to public opinion, and therefore to enlighten the world of commerce. Furthermore, by keeping to their own ethical codes, public-relations practitioners would prevent corrupt practices of persuasion. Lee's personal ethic of public relations included never sending out a "deliberate lie." Lee argued, however, that social truth is always relative; no one could ever completely ascertain the facts pertaining to an issue. In like manner, Lee contended that no one could determine in advance what is in the best interests of the receiver of a communication. In a world of intellectual relativism, Lee's remedy for problems of propaganda was to have editors and publishers demand to know the sources of the information and of facts they printed.[46]

The Democracy of Persuasion

Edward L. Bernays, independent public-relations counsel and alumnus of the CPI, became the leading inter-world-war spokesperson of the practitioner perspective on social influence. Bernays contended that the increasing importance of public opinion made the public-relations counselor invaluable to institutional persuaders as a mediator who "interprets the client to the public, which he is enabled to do in part because he interprets the public to his client." Taking the view that the public is frequently impervious to reason, Bernays borrowed from crowd psychology to conceive of the public as suggestible and imitative. However, Bernays explained, modern propagandists do not view the public according to a mechanistic stimulus-response psychology; instead they understand that members of the public experience diverse group loyalties. Here the role of the public-relations counselor is to identify appeals that tap the often conflicting stereotypes held by the public.

One important innovation in Bernays's approach to public relations was the effort to "create news" rather than merely to court publishers, editors, and reporters. As an example, Bernays explained how he manufactured a news event to save a New York hotel that was losing business because of rumors of its imminent closing. Bernays arranged for the establishment's well-known maitre d'hotel to receive a five-year contract. The national press picked up the story, thereby ending the epidemic of cancelled reservations.[47]

Bernays was a communications practitioner with liberal inclinations who worked to reconcile his profession with America's democratic traditions. Yet, his observations and reflections threw up a challenge to progressive critics who argued that covertly manufactured news marks a manipulative threat to democracy. Not so, countered Bernays, because there is nothing so characteristically American as special pleading. From the standpoint of democracy, Bernays reflected, organized competition in propaganda is superior to having decisions made by "committees of wise men." When critics deplored unseen efforts to organize mass opinion, they were, according to Bernays, asking "for a society such as never was and never will be." He maintained that modern politics would be impossible without propaganda as a link between leaders and the masses.

In the Bernaysean social universe, the public-relations counselor acted more as mediator than manipulator. Here effective public relations is not simply a matter of inducing the public to accept a pre-ordained institutional point of view; rather, public relations also acts on persuaders as well, making them more socially responsible. Further, public-relations techniques are always available to dissidents in society, thereby enabling minorities to obtain an audience. Finally, just as any other professional group, public-relations firms necessarily develop codes of ethical practice to function in a world of ambiguity and conflict. "Therefore, the public relations counsel must maintain an intense scrutiny of his actions, avoiding the propagation of unsocial or otherwise harmful movements or ideas." Having a social conscience is an essential basis of good business, Bernays said, since consumers would easily discover for themselves any distortions. Business could not long deceive the public without losing its ability to persuade.[48] Less-grounded but equally committed defenses of professional polling and broadcasting research and programming were provided by George Gallup, the pollster, and Frank Stanton, research director and later-to-be president of CBS.[49]

THE SOCIAL-SCIENTIFIC APPROACH

Centered outside of the academy, practitioners such as Bernays were unable to dislodge the progressive school of thought on propaganda that reigned supreme in academe. During the late 1930s, however, communication practitioners began to form alliances with a new kind of entrepreneurial social scientist. Out of this collaboration sprang the "communication research" school of thought in higher education which eventually displaced progressive propaganda critique.

During the 1930s, quantitative social scientists embraced the chance to hone their theories and methodological skills by working on the practical communication problems of business and government organizations. Social scientists first realized significant opportunities for institutionally-supported research during the Great War, notably in the work of psychologists to develop intelligence tests for the Army. As a result of the wartime cooperation between scientists and administrators, certain aspects of social science became profitable. For example, soon after the war, a group of psychologists formed The Psychological Corporation, an organization that offered personnel testing, market research, and advertising testing for hire.[50]

Harold Lasswell, a young political scientist who came of intellectual age in the heady days when social researchers first were recruited to harness science to practical objectives, expressed the basic tenets of the scientific approach to propaganda. Lasswell agreed with communication practitioners that the competition of propagandas precluded mass persuasion from becoming a social danger.[51] Not only that, argued Lasswell, propaganda should be viewed as a benign alternative to force. By embracing the belief that propaganda is socially neutral, social scientists interested in communication were able to justify why they abstained from critically scrutinizing the purposes and strategies of communications. Instead, they were free to study such law-like aspects of social influence as "under what conditions do words affect power relationships?"[52]

Content Analysis

Lasswell himself was able to demonstrate the practical value of his quantitative approach to propaganda when he offered his services to the

U.S. government during World War II. Lasswell's group, located in the Library of Congress, provided useful interpretations of phrases and themes in enemy propaganda, supplying this information to various federal agencies. For instance, Lasswell's findings enabled the Department of Justice to prove that certain extremist publications in the U.S. were deliberately disseminating Nazi propaganda. Further, by demonstrating what topics were most prevalent in Nazi propaganda, content analysis supplied evidence for predictions about impending Nazi actions.

As a result of this wartime demonstration of the power of quantitative content analysis, this research technique became part of the standard repertoire of the academic social scientist. The effort was to be strictly scientific, to use analysis precisely to determine the effects of communications, rather than to engage in critical speculations about those messages.[53] Lasswell wrote hopefully of a new era of postwar "policy science" in which researchers would use their expertise to inform and improve policy decisions.[54]

Survey Research

Survey research "polling" was a second building-block of the emerging communication research perspective on propaganda. Gallup's earliest polls were surveys based on postcards but, later, his investigators gathered data over the telephone and through door-to-door interviews. By the early 1930s, George Gallup had left academe to found a firm that applied polling to problems of market research, political advertising, and assessing broadcast audiences. Gallup's staff became best-known for conducting polls on political topics for newspapers; however, his firm earned lucrative commissions from businesses by surveying attitudes of consumers toward products.

An emerging alliance between private and academic survey researchers became important in the development of the communication research school of thought on propaganda. Princeton psychologist Hadley Cantril borrowed Gallup's methods and his data to spread the gospel of scientific polling among college social scientists. Cantril also organized the Princeton Radio Project which cemented the early alliance of commercial broadcasters and academic researchers. Tapping sociologist Paul Lazarsfeld to direct the project, Cantril was able to make Princeton's radio research program (later moved to Columbia University) into a successful cooperative project among academic social scientists, the Rockefeller Foundation, and Frank Stanton's broadcasting research department at the Columbia Broadcasting System. Early Princeton studies helped broadcasters understand why listeners tuned to particular shows. Lazarsfeld's think-tank, later christened The Bureau of Applied Social Research, soon produced landmark studies of how both media and interpersonal conversation influenced decisions to vote and to purchase products.[55]

Experimental Studies

In addition to content analysis and survey research, communication scientists turned to experimental studies. At the onset of World War II, the Army set up a Research Branch to bring social science knowledge to bear on problems of military organization. Drawing its personnel both from academe and from leading commercial research organizations, the Research Branch conducted surveys and experimental studies of the troops, as well as descriptive analyses by researchers trained in methods of observation.[56] On behalf of Army commanders, Research Branch personnel pursued a host of objectives that included discovering which brand of cola the GIs preferred and what the troops believed was the likely date of victory.

A particular innovation of the Research Branch was the Experimental Section, directed by Carl I. Hovland, that conducted controlled studies of message effects. For example, Hovland's researchers tested the impact of various films shown to the troops during basic training. Tests revealed that whereas soldiers were likely to forget specific facts, they were less likely to forget general interpretations. Further, in studies using the Program Analyzer, audiences of GIs pushed buttons to indicate their like or dislike of what they watched. One specific finding was that Army audiences disliked close-up shots of people talking or giving speeches.[57]

Which Direction for Academe?

By the end of World War II, American academicians could draw upon two research traditions for the study of propaganda. The older school of thought was progressive propaganda analysis, a humanistic framework of critique that had been popular during the 1920s and mid-1930s. On the other hand, the successes of American social science in aiding the war effort enhanced the prestige and power of the emerging scientific approach based on quantitative content analysis, survey research, and experimentation. How would the two traditions sort themselves out?

After the war, the social scientists of the Research Branch were eager to share the fruits of their extensive program with the general scientific community. Accordingly, the Carnegie Corporation (a private agency that granted funds for various projects) supported publication of a three-volume series, *The American Soldier*, summarizing the work of the Army's Research Branch. The impact of this large, coordinated, and sustained program of empirical survey and experimental scholarship was to accelerate the acceptance and use of quantitative methods in the academic social sciences. The volumes chronicling the Army's research became the "paradigm of the new social science."[58] The work of Hovland's Experimental Section served as the precursor of the Yale attitude change studies published during the 1950s.[59]

Not all social scientists joined in approving the move from humanistic social science to the new-style empirical social research. Humanistically oriented scholars were concerned about the abandonment of critical analysis that accompanied the kind of large-scale, grant-supported research that was designed to help policy makers. Would social scientists lose the capacity for independent analysis and judgment when they executed whatever studies that society's leaders were inclined to commission?

Robert S. Lynd and Alfred McClung Lee, two sociologists grounded in the historical-critical tradition, expressed reservations about new-style, ultra-quantitative social research. Lynd saw the Army's research program as 1,600 pages of work designed "to sort out and control men for purposes not of their own making." Lee was troubled by "assembly-line research" carried out to make the Army's authoritarian framework more palatable to citizens. The two humanist sociologists wondered if government and industry would now dictate what problems would be studied by social researchers. Despite concerns of this kind, however, most social scientists seemed to view the work of the Army's Research Branch as heralding an unprecedented new era in which social science would play a leading role in national progress.[60]

Between the late 1930s and the early 1940s, major social scientists in the communication field gained the institutional support they needed to advance experimental and survey approaches to propaganda. The Rockefeller Foundation's support for radio research at Princeton/ Columbia and the Army's Research Branch both helped to legitimize scientific studies of propaganda as social science's unique contribution to understanding social influence. Lazarsfeld, in particular, spoke of the importance of replacing critical propaganda analysis with statistically-grounded studies of media effects. Lazarsfeld and his colleague, Robert K. Merton, announced that wartime imperatives demonstrated why "impressionistic" critical studies of propaganda were of less social value than were quantified data about which parts of a message induced what effects in an audience.[61] Hard data about media effects were necessary, they wrote, so that national leaders could promote morale and combat enemy propaganda. As with the Army's studies of soldiers, Lazarsfeld's surveys of voters called attention to the exciting possibility of basing institutional decisions on certified information about how people responded to media messages. Concerns that messages from large governmental and business institutions might constitute propaganda received less attention in the postwar period.

After the war, advertisers and broadcasters redoubled their efforts to defend mass communication as something consistent with American democracy. For instance, Rooser Reeves articulated the position of advertisers that their persuasive powers were severely limited by resistant audiences. Not only was advertising unable to engender desires in an unwilling public, said Reeves, but also advertising was shaped by the preferences of the public. Frank Stanton of CBS argued that TV was not pure escapism, and that the increased public interest in excellent music, art, and drama was attributable, in part, to mass media.[62]

The "Value-Free" Orientation

While evangelizing for hard-headed statistical and experimental research, Lazarsfeld, Lasswell, and many other important social scientists nevertheless harbored liberal reformist sentiments. Communication scientists might have discounted the dangers of propaganda, but many became involved in studying how communication could promote tolerance and, more generally, how science might be used to solve social problems.

Although interested in social reform, communication scientists were wont to keep their value-tinged interests in social change separate from their scientific agendas. Researchers straddled science and reform by dedicating themselves to discovering how the process of communication worked. Communication researchers emphasized their disinclination to get involved in direct action on social problems. However, they claimed, their findings about how messages influenced listeners could serve as the basis for positive social change, for instance, better radio programs to promote tolerance of ethnic groups. The effort to keep reform separate from academic research resulted partly from the fact that science always has carried more prestige than service. The tax laws further encouraged this separation by requiring that foundations and grant agencies not support research that directly agitated for government action.

Also relevant in dampening the ardor of communication researchers for active participation in social debates was the U.S. government's increasing mania about internal security. Even the most unrevolutionary people found themselves caught up in the web of accusations and mindless guilt by association. For instance, Lazarsfeld found himself beleaguered by questions from internal security personnel about his having once been listed as attending a program of the American Writers Congress, a group later cited as a Communist-infiltrated organization. Lazarsfeld responded by noting the presence of many military men at the wartime event, and by mentioning that President Roosevelt had sent his greetings to the gathering. Lasswell became enmeshed in the paranoia of the government's security apparatus apparently as a result of an automobile accident during his move from Chicago to the East Coast. His truck caught on fire, scattering around the countryside various communist propaganda leaflets which he had collected as part of his early content research.[63]

Not only did the new methods of content analysis, survey research, and experimentation represent the cutting edge of social science but also they were safer than gathering propaganda leaflets or critically scrutinizing the persuasive efforts of governmental or industrial leaders. With tax officials and internal security personnel alert to any hint of controversiality, academic researchers found it prudent to moderate their participation in social affairs, and to keep their research safely removed from troubling social issues.

When post-war communication researchers approached inflammatory political content, they did so with a studied scientific neutrality. A case in point was work by Joseph Klapper and Charles Glock, researchers in Lazarsfeld's Bureau of Applied Social Research, who analyzed newspaper stories about a dispute between the House Un-American Activities Committee and Edward U. Condon, chief of the National Bureau of Standards. HUAC charged that Condon was "one of the weakest links in our atomic security" because of his political associations, although the Department of Commerce Loyalty Board had cleared him of any charges.

Klapper and Glock argued that, as communication scientists, they could take no position on "the truth or falsity of the charges brought against Dr. Condon." Instead, these researchers conducted a content analysis (based on 23 dimensions of content) of 4,589 news stories taken from nine newspapers over a period of eight months. The (unsurprising) findings were that the content of some newspapers was more favorable to HUAC, and that other newspapers were more approving of Condon. For all this effort, the researchers expressed no conclusion about the substantive merits of the HUAC/Condon dispute. The fairness and accuracy of coverage was simply "a matter of interpretation which is beyond the scope of this analysis." Yet, researchers did note that newspapers paid more attention to HUAC's promise to give Condon a hearing than they did to the Committee's actual failure to do so.[64]

During the 1950s, the objective scientific approach to propaganda became standard in higher education. A visible sign of the shift from a critical to a statistical-experimental orientation could be seen in a substitution of terminology. Until the late 1940s, researchers on social influence customarily adopted the lingua franca of post-World-War-I humanists, and described their studies as inquiries into "propaganda." By the mid-1950s, however, the terms "communication" and "persuasion" had replaced the earlier, more value-laden expression. During the 1950s, communication critics such as Gilbert Seldes, Alfred McClung Lee, and Vance Packard received attention for books in which they analyzed media trends, and Harold Innis's historical-interpretive works had some influence.[65] But the dominant tendency was for social scientists to study communication as a "value-free" process rather than as one that laid bare the nation's social ethics. Illustrative of the determined focus on communication process were studies contrasting the role of mass media and personal contacts in producing attitude change, and studies that showed how innovations were introduced and spread throughout society.[66]

THE RATIONALIST APPROACH

Beginning in the late 1890s, John Dewey, a philosopher at the University of Chicago, worked to reconcile traditional logic with both modern society and the scientific method.[67] The result was to help initiate a critical, or straight-thinking, school of thought on modern persuasion.

The Public: Manipulated or Incompetent?

Scholars who worked from the perspective of straight thinking were interested less in how groups and institutions might manipulate the public and more in how the public mind was inherently susceptible to emotion and suggestion. The critical-thinking perspective aimed to make readers and listeners more rational by focusing their attention on the logical requirements of observation and inference. Stemming from Dewey's early work on scientific and reflective thinking, the rationalist approach, like propaganda analysis, gained currency with post-war disillusionment over the propagandas of the Great War.

Both propaganda analysis and the straight-thinking movement shared an origin in social stresses rampant during the years of World War I; however, the two schools of thought reflected differing views of exactly how American public opinion had failed. For most progressives, the major lesson of the war was that institutions could manipulate public opinion through hate appeals and self-serving claims that short-circuited critical logic. This view served as warrant for the focus of propaganda analysis on the alliance between powerful institutions and the communication industry. Whereas propaganda analysis focused on institutional manipulation, proponents of critical thinking focused their attention on wartime spy paranoia and hatred of all things German. Did not these manifestations of the dark side of the modern mind indicate that society was basically irrational? Academicians such as Dewey, who were committed to a rational or scientific view of life, felt called to help the public overcome its sinister tendencies. Believing that Americans could not be trusted without explicit education in how to think, rationalists developed a curriculum, called "straight thinking" and, later and more popularly, "critical thinking."

Although sharing the concern about degraded public action during the war years, the propaganda-analysis and straight-thinking approaches to public communication gradually diverged during the 1920s and 1930s. The shift of some progressives away from confidence in the reasoning power of the public is well illustrated by contrasting the earlier and later works of Dewey and Lippmann. Until the mid-1920s, Dewey and Lippmann expressed considerable concern about the institutional purveying of propaganda; however, their later works revealed an increasing emphasis on the innate limitations of the public's reasoning power.[68] Consistent with this emerging view of the incompetent public, psychologists, logicians, and educators began during the 1920s and 1930s to make important contributions to the literature of straight thinking. The result was a curriculum designed to combat the allegedly untrustworthy social intelligence of the people.[69]

The educational methods of straight thinking differed considerably from those of propaganda analysis. As illustrated by the materials prepared by the Institute for Propaganda Analysis, propaganda critics alerted students to such issues as these: Whose interests are being served by communication? How are messages diffused? What effect does propaganda have on society?[70] In contrast, the pedagogies of straight thinking assessed the logical quality of message texts. Typical exercises in straight thinking included relating premises to conclusions, testing assumptions, and restraining emotions that might act as barriers to rational decision-making.

Given today's calls for more education in critical thinking, it is almost surprising to observe that, before World War II, the straight-thinking movement was a relatively minor school of thought in American educational circles. Where straight thinking came into the curriculum, it was frequently an offshoot or a supporting dimension of propaganda analysis. However, by the early 1940s, the critical-thinking approach to propaganda became dominant in the American school curriculum. Political as well as pedagogical reasons underlay this shift from progressive propaganda criticism (focusing on institutional manipulation) to straight thinking (focusing on public irrationality).

The Wartime Decline of Propaganda Analysis

Propaganda analysis was a method well attuned to post-World-War-I disillusionment as well as to rampant Depression-era criticism of major social institutions. In contrast, political conditions of the early 1940s favored more attention to the failings of the public than to manipulative intentions of society's leading institutions and groups. First, the outbreak of war with Germany and Japan caused progressives to become less interested in the machinations of domestic elites and correspondingly more concerned about external threats. In other words, the American political Left now joined the Right in emphasizing national solidarity. Progressives now began to share the concern, which conservatives had long expressed, that propaganda analysis might induce a dangerous level of skepticism in students. Perhaps a generation of propaganda critique might have the effect of keeping Americans from rallying to the anti-fascist call to arms.[71]

Not only did the outbreak of war cause progressives to emphasize social unity over social criticism but also progressives began to rethink what seemed to be the quasi-isolationist tendency of propaganda analysis. Clyde Miller, founder of the Institute for Propaganda Analysis, believed that the Institute might continue to give useful service during American involvement in a world war. Most progressives, however, saw nothing but trouble ahead for any organization that tried to analyze competing domestic propagandas during a time of national emergency. Already strapped for cash, the Institute suspended operations on October 29, 1941, on the expectation that it would be unable to secure sufficient operating funds during the anticipated war.[72]

Within two months of the Institute's suspension, the crusade against fascist Germany and Japan was in full swing. The outbreak of war caused many progressives to criticize the Institute's relatively detached approach which earlier they had praised. Sociologist William Garber and social critic Lewis Mumford both excoriated the Institute for what they contended was a mindless objectivity that ignored the moral differences between England and Nazi Germany. The Institute had labeled equally as propaganda the pre-1941 efforts of both Britain and Germany to sway Americans. Garber and Mumford complained that the Institute's inclination to lump together English and Hitlerite war propaganda ignored the social purposes of the two sources of symbolism. Supposedly at fault was the methodology of propaganda analysis which they criticized for allegedly treating only the surface content of language.

The Garber/Mumford accusations focused on the Institute's seven propaganda devices which did, in fact, take a linguistic view of propaganda. The criticism overlooked, however, the Institute's many case studies of such propagandists as Father Charles Coughlin, a right-wing radio orator, and the Associated Farmers who worked against organized labor in California. Nevertheless, Garber's and Mumford's argument was widely accepted, thus contributing to the discrediting of 1930s-style propaganda analysis among progressives.[73]

The Quasi-Neutrality of Straight Thinking

In contrast to propaganda analysis, with its explicit attention to the arguments made in social disputes, the pedagogy of straight thinking brought with it less in the way of a controversial political content. The subtle shift from propaganda analysis to straight thinking is clear from a comparison of the 1937 and 1942 yearbooks of the National Council for the Social Studies. The 1937 volume was explicit in identifying specific propagandists in society, for instance, recommending that teachers become alert to such agencies of propaganda as the National Electric Light Association which treated the public according to a "sucker philosophy." Similarly, in a discussion of the channels of communication, the 1937 volume was specific in presenting the Hearst and Gannett newspaper chains as large businesses likely, therefore, to reflect the big-business point of view. The 1937 volume was written to enable teachers to help students deal with contemporary issues. In this view, students lived in a world of competing propagandas; therefore, schools should help them understand how to evaluate various sources of information.

The 1942 yearbook of the Social Studies Council marked an interesting contrast to the 1937 volume. While both collections expressed the importance of helping students understand the contemporary world, the 1942 edition faulted its predecessor for employing a too narrow approach. Readers of the period would have understood that this was a reference to the former focus of educators on linguistic elements such as the propaganda devices that, some now argued, ultimately failed to make students immune to propaganda. In contrast, the 1942 yearbook proclaimed that it provided a broader perspective by following the principles of the scientific method that began with observation and ended with the confirmation or disconfirmation of a hypothesis about society.

In actual practice, what the 1942 volume recommended was not particularly different from its predecessor. Both collections encouraged teachers to help students evaluate the sources of information, and to make their own reasoned judgments about social issues. Yet, the 1942 volume was much less likely to mention any home-grown propagandist villains, and was wont to focus on cognitive problems internal to the citizen, for instance, emotional thinking. Similarly, the 1942 volume gave increased attention to forms of deductive and inductive thinking and to logical fallacies. Using Dewey's method of reflective thinking, the newer yearbook emphasized relating evidence to conclusions. Topics of analysis were more likely to be bland: the growth of Buffalo, New York, the actual speed of canal travel, and student reaction to the school cafeteria. This stood in contrast to the 1937 volume whose examples of classroom exercises included evaluating the political slant of newspapers and listening to broadcasts about labor-management disputes.[74]

During the years after World War II, propaganda analysis was increasingly overshadowed by the pedagogy of straight thinking. Curricular exercises increasingly dealt with logical rules and forms, and they were focused upon hypothetical arguments rather than on-going social struggles. Illustrative is Max Black's classic book on critical thinking in which Black emphasized deductive forms of logic along with the requirements of the scientific method. At the same time, the widely-used Watson-Glaser test of critical thinking (which had originally been prepared in cooperation with the Institute for Propaganda Analysis) emphasized such exercises as recognizing the assumptions implicit in hypothetical arguments.

The legacy of formalism and hypothetical argumentation in the pedagogy of critical thinking continues to the present day. A survey of critical-thinking instruction in the 1980s showed that these programs typically took a message-based approach that, like the 1942 yearbook cited above, passed over wider issues, such as propagandists' inserting their own ideologies into the channels of public communication.[75] This shift in classroom focus from propagandists to logical rules paralleled the transition in scholarly research from propaganda critique to communication process. Both these transformations reflected the conservative political turn during World War II and the Cold War.

THE POLEMICAL APPROACH

The polemical approach to propaganda, a fifth major school of thought on modern social influence, originated after World War I, and it became powerful in the late 1940s and 1950s. Polemical propaganda critics scrutinize public communication for the purpose of keeping important social forums free from influence and control by their ideological opponents.

Polemical writers on propaganda tend to fall into two camps. "Hard" polemicists are active politicians who use criticism as a weapon to discredit opposing partisans, thus to change the political world. "Soft" polemicists are intellectuals whose more carefully reasoned essays and books are nevertheless closely affiliated with political movements.

As contrasted to progressive propaganda critics, "soft" polemicists are less likely to advocate education and professional self-restraint as solutions to propaganda; they more often favor direct political action.

Hard Political Polemics

The polemical school of thought first became significant during World War I with the effort of the government to suppress anti-war communications. The CPI developed a campaign to combat rumors illustrated by its popular advertisement, "Spies and Lies." This advertisement had the Creel Committee requesting that citizens avoid serving as a "tool of the Hun" by circulating "the malicious, disheartening rumors which he so eagerly sows." What to do? "Report the man who spreads pessimistic stories, divulges—or seeks—confidential military information, cries for peace, or belittles our efforts to win the war."[76] Postwar Senate investigations of German and Bolshevik propaganda by the Overman Committee similarly showed that American politicians were concerned by the apparent successes of ideologically-anathematized groups in spreading their messages. The Overman Committee used a one-dimensional polemical attack to tar all pre-1917 peace efforts with the brush of German propaganda because Germans had encouraged various neutralist sentiments.[77]

The paradigm case of the "hard" polemical pursuit of propaganda was the infamous House Un-American Activities Committee. HUAC was activated as a temporary committee in 1934 in response to a consensus of Congress that fascist and communist propagandas were a danger to social stability. Rechartered in 1938, HUAC was captured by an anti-Roosevelt coalition of Republicans and anti-New Deal Democrats led by Congressman Martin Dies of Texas. Dies transformed HUAC from a body receiving testimony about extremist propaganda controlled from overseas (fascist and communist) into a forum to legitimize charges against the New Deal and organized labor.

In its efforts to weaken the Roosevelt presidency, the Dies Committee focused on such relatively trivial issues as the possible presence of communists in the Federal Theater Program. The FTP had been chartered to offer free public theater by tapping the talents of unemployed playwrites, directors, and actors. Dies's attack on FTP plays was part of a general effort to purge the executive branch of liberals and progressives. Because many of the FTP's plays did give a critical treatment of American economy and social structure, Dies had a legitimate

38

point in questioning whether the government should be sponsoring politically-tinged drama; however, Dies exaggerated the point in the interests of sensationalizing it, calling FTP plays "straight Communist propaganda."[78]

"Hard" polemical propaganda critique briefly became a socially significant force during the 1940s and 1950s with headlines generated by various House and Senate internal security committees. Notable were the HUAC hearings on communist infiltration of Hollywood as evidenced by favorable treatment of Russia in films produced during World War II.[79] Joseph McCarthy became the linchpin of polemical propaganda analysis in the 1950s with his efforts to portray the U.S. government as riddled with communists. After the demise of McCarthy, polemical propaganda critique lost its patina of official respectability. However, competitive politics insures that distorted polemical attacks on ideological enemies will never disappear entirely.

Soft Polemical Critique

Distinct from "hard" polemical propaganda analysis, with its flimsy and distorted evidence, is the "soft" polemical critique produced by politically-minded intellectuals of the Right and Left. For instance, during the 1930s, Rightist intellectuals opposed progressivism's tendency to favor big government and to limit capitalist enterprise by regulation. Conservative "soft" polemicists exposed and attacked progressivism's ability to gain important footholds in the national government as well as in education and journalism. Conservatives such as Elisha Hanson, attorney for the American Newspaper Association, complained of the New Deal's expansion of governmental persuasion. Later, William F. Buckley, Jr., gained national visibility with his charges that the Yale University faculty purveyed an agnostical, collectivist ideology. Since that time, other conservatives, such as Richard Weaver, William Bennett, and Allan Bloom have given critiques of progressive education as something undermining social stability. Rightist critics today also argue that progressive tendencies in journalism turn the news into propaganda against political conservatism. Some of the earliest charges of this kind were advanced by Herman Dinsmore, Edith Efron, and Ernest Lefever.[80]

Contemporary polemical works come not just from Rightist intellectuals but also from thinkers on the political Left. The polemical tangent to progressive propaganda analysis has existed since the days of the more-extreme muckrakers, such as David Graham Phillips, and since the post-World-War-I attacks on advertising by proponents of consumer cooperatives. Leftist soft polemical analysis has taken on renewed significance since the Vietnam years. Prominent instances include Vietnam-era teach-ins, Ralph Nader's attacks on misleading business practices, and Chomsky's and Herman's thesis of a post-Vietnam conservative effort to reestablish the interventionist Cold-War ideology that was weakened by the Indochina debacle.[81]

THE RETURN OF PROGRESSIVE PROPAGANDA ANALYSIS

The upheavals of the 1960s weakened the value-free ideal that underlay communication research, prompting academicians to rediscover the importance of social criticism and the potential dangers of powerful institutional manipulation. Following a decade of civil rights, womens' rights, and anti-war protests came a new literature of progressive propaganda critique. Examples include Joe McGinniss's *Selling of the President 1968* and David Wise's *The Politics of Lying*.[82] Books of this sort were focused chiefly on governmental or political machinations. Following the pattern of the 1930s, however, the new literature of propaganda analysis soon took off in varying directions. The most powerful vector of the new wave of critical propaganda studies has been that focused on news reporting, a matter also pursued by Rightist polemical critics.[83] In addition, the new school of progressive critique has taken up such subjects as dangers posed to democracy by opinion polling and the propagandistic dimensions of entertainment, education, and marketing—all issues that I pursue in chapters of this book.[84]

In *Channels of Propaganda* I take chiefly a progressive critical line on the phenomenon of propaganda. In other words, the thesis pursued here is that covert manipulation and massive orchestration of persuasion both threaten democratic public opinion. In my view, the practitioners and communication scientists exaggerate the extent to which a competition of propagandas neutralizes the danger of covert orchestration of opinion. Democracy always is imperiled when the communication channels covertly induce people to adopt ideas and policies that serve special interests.

Although in much of this book I focus on analyzing and exposing hidden propaganda in various channels of expression, the solution to propaganda offered here is not chiefly that of education. Because I give more emphasis to political participation than to education, *Channels of*

Propaganda is somewhat of a deviation from the type of propaganda analysis prevalent during the 1930s. In chapter 7, I argue that the present quality of American political discourse is not yet sufficient to check the growth of dangerous propaganda. In chapter 8, I recommend putting in place electronic public forums so that open debate among advocates could render propaganda less injurious to democratic public opinion.

Channels of Propaganda is part of a general reemergence of propaganda analysis in the 1980s and 1990s. The post-Vietnam rediscovery of manipulation as a factor in social influence has prompted the rehabilitation of the venerable term "propaganda."[85] The value of this concept as a tool for analyzing the communication industry is well-put by Alfred McClung Lee, who noted that the term "propaganda" reminds us that communication always occurs in an atmosphere of social struggle.[86] The renewed, progressive school of propaganda criticism during the 1980s and 1990s includes both curricular materials for use in the schools as well as a literature with appeal to popular audiences. New materials of propaganda education have once more brought matters of ideological diffusion and manipulation into mainstream textual-rational pedagogies of critical thinking.[87] As in the inter-world-war period, popular books of progressive propaganda critique by McGinniss, Wise, and others have attained large audiences.

American thinking on propaganda revolves around five approaches that have deep roots in the social and intellectual history of the U.S. in the twentieth century. Since 1900, the progressive propaganda critics, the communication practitioners, the critical-thinking rationalists, the scientific communication researchers, and the polemicists all have enjoyed periods of significant social and intellectual influence, as well as experiencing times of relative dormancy. One effect of these five schools is that today one can neither assume that mass persuasion is harmless nor take for granted that propagandists have brought an end to real democracy. Students of propaganda must not only examine contemporary instances of institutional persuasion, as in chapters 2-6, but also must enter the historical conversation about whether and how mass persuasion may coexist with democracy, as in chapters 7 and 8. Further, by becoming familiar with the history of propaganda, students have a basis for developing their own vantage point to probe the health of our democracy, the worthiness of society's chief persuaders, and the contributions of our communication media.

In this chapter I have focused on the question "What is propaganda?" In the next chapters, our attention shifts to contemporary evidences of propaganda in government action, scientific research, religious ministrations, the news, the classroom, and in our contemporary modes of entertainment.

ENDNOTES

1. J. M. Sproule, "Propaganda Studies in American Social Science: The Rise and Fall of the Critical Paradigm," *Quarterly Journal of Speech*, 73 (1987), 60-78; Alfred McClung Lee, *How to Understand Propaganda* (New York: Holt, Rinehart, 1952), pp. 6ff.

2. J. M. Sproule, Review of *Propaganda and Communication*, by G. S. Jowett and V. O'Donnell, *Quarterly Journal of Speech*, 73 (1987); 517-520; Garth S. Jowett, "Propaganda and Communication: The Re-Emergence of a Research Tradition," *Journal of Communication*, 31, No. 1 (1987), 97-114.

3. *The Compact Edition of the Oxford English Dictionary*, 2 vols. (Glasgow: Oxford University Press, 1971), 2:2326.

4. Ivy L. Lee, *Publicity: Some of the Things It Is and Is Not.* (New York: Industries Publishing, 1925), p. 23.

5. Victor Marchetti and John D. Marks, *The CIA and the Cult of Intelligence* (New York: Knopf, 1974), pp. 163-175.

6. *Rhetoric*, I.3, II.19.

7. [Clyde R. Miller], "How to Detect Propaganda," *Propaganda Analysis*, 1, No. 2 (November 1937), 5-7.

8. Frederick E. Lumley, "The Nature of Propaganda," *Sociology and Social Research*, 13 (1929), 319; William W. Biddle, *Propaganda and Education* (New York: Teachers College, Columbia University, 1932), p. 7.

9. Mark C. Miller, "Hollywood: the Ad," *The Atlantic*, April 1990, pp. 42-43.

10. Samuel H. Flowerman and Marie Jahoda, "Can We Fight Prejudice Scientifically? Toward a Partnership of Action and Research," *Commentary*, 2 (December 1946), 583-587; Paul F. Lazarsfeld, "Some Remarks on the Role of Mass Media in So-Called Tolerance Propaganda," *Journal of Social Issues*, 3, No. 3 (Summer 1947), 17-25; Flowerman, "Mass Propaganda in the War Against Bigotry," *Journal of Abnormal and Social Psychology*, 42 (1947), 429-439.

11. George Seldes, *Lords of the Press* (New York: Julian Messner, 1938).

12. Interview with George Seldes, Hartland-4-Corners, VT, May 12-13, 1984.

13. Barnet Baskerville, *The People's Voice: The Orator in American Society* (Lexington: University Press of Kentucky, 1979) and Thomas C. Leonard, *The Power of the Press: The Birth of American Political Reporting* (New York: Oxford University Press, 1986).

14. James Bryce, *The American Commonwealth* (3rd ed.; 2 vols.; New York: Macmillan, 1899), 2:247-374.

15. Ray E. Hiebert, *Courtier to the Crowd: The Story of Ivy Lee and the Development of Public Relations* (Ames: Iowa State University Press, 1966).

16. Ray S. Baker, "How Railroads Make Public Opinion," *McClure's Magazine*, 26 (1906), 535-549.

17. Will Irwin, *The American Newspaper* (Ames: Iowa State University Press), p. 52. (Original work published 1911)

18. James D. Squires, *British Propaganda at Home and in the United Sates from 1914 to 1917* (Cambridge: Harvard University Press, 1935).

19. George S. Viereck, *Spreading Germs of Hate* (New York: Liveright, 1930).

20. "How Germany Has Worked in U.S. to Shape Opinion, Block the Allies and Get Munitions for Herself, Told in Secret Agents' Letters," *New York World,* August 15, 1915, p. 2.

21. Arthur Ponsonby, *Falsehood in War-Time* (New York: E. P. Dutton, 1928); Viereck, 1930.

22. James R. Mock and Cedric Larson, *Words that Won the War* (Princeton, NJ: Princeton University Press, 1939); Stephen L. Vaughn, *Holding Fast the Inner Lines* (Chapel Hill: University of North Carolina Press, 1980).

23. Respectively, George Creel, *How We Advertised America* (New York: Arno, 1972; original work published 1920), p. 56; Creel, "Propaganda and Morale," *American Journal of Sociology*, 47 (1941), 345.

24. Walter Lippmann, "The Basic Problem of Democracy, I," *Atlantic Monthly*, 124 (1919), 616-627; Lippmann, "Liberty and the News," *Atlantic Monthly*, 124 (1919), 779-787; Lippmann, *Public Opinion* (New York: Macmillan, 1922); Will H. Irwin, "An Age of Lies," *Sunset*, 43 (December 1919), 23-25, 54, 56.

25. Lippmann, "Basic Problem," p. 626.

26. Irwin, "Age of Lies," p. 54.

27. Alfred McC. Lee, *The Daily Newspaper in America: Evolution of a Social Instrument* (New York: Octagon, 1973; original work published 1937).

28. Will H. Irwin, *Propaganda and the News* (New York: Whittlesey, 1936).

29. Donald L. Hurwitz, *Broadcast "Ratings"* (Doctoral dissertation, University of Illinois, 1983) and Hadley Cantril, *The Human Dimension* (Princeton, NJ: Princeton University Press, 1967).

30. Commission of Inquiry of the Interchurch World Movement, *Public Opinion and the Steel Strike* (New York: Harcourt, Brace, 1920) and Commission of Inquiry, *Report on the Steel Strike of 1919* (New York: Harcourt, Brace, 1921).

31. Upton Sinclair, *The Brass Check: A Study of American Journalism* (Pasadena: The Author, 1919); Judson Grenier, "Upton Sinclair and the Press: *The Brass Check* Reconsidered," *Journalism Quarterly*, 49 (1972), 427-436 and George Seldes, Interview with author, Hartland-4-Corners, VT, May 12-13, 1984. See Seldes, *You Can't Print That!* (Garden City, NY: Garden City Publishing, 1929); Seldes, *Lords of the Press* (New York: Julian Messner, 1938).

32. Ray H. Abrams, *Preachers Present Arms* (New York: Round Table, 1933).

33. Robert Wohlforth, "Catch 'em Young—Learn 'em Rough," *New Republic*, 64 (1930), 258.

34. H. C. Engelbrecht and F. C. Hanighen, *Merchants of Death: A Study of the International Armament Industry* (New York: Dodd, Mead, 1934).

35. Harold A. Larrabee, "The Formation of Public Opinion through Motion Pictures," *Religious Education*, 15 (1920), 147.

36. Darwin Teilhet, "Propaganda Stealing the Movies, *Outlook and Independent*, 158 (May 27, 1931), 112-113, 126.

37. Edgar Dale, *Children's Attendance at Motion Pictures* (New York: Macmillan, 1935), p. 73.

38. Edgar Dale, *The Content of Motion Pictures* (New York: Macmillan, 1935), pp. 21, 185.

39. Herbert Blumer, *Movies and Conduct* (New York: Arno, 1970; original work published 1933).

40. Charles A. Beard, "Propaganda in the Schools," *The Dial*, 66 (1919), 598-599; Charles Angoff, "The Higher Learning Goes to War," *American Mercury*, 11 (1927), 177-191; C. Hartley Grattan, "The Historians Cut Loose," *American Mercury*, 11 (1927), 414-430.

41. National Education Association, *Report of the Committee on Propaganda in the Schools* (National Education Association, 1929); E. R. A. Seligman, "Propaganda by Public Utility Corporations," *Bulletin of the American Association of University Professors*, 16 (1930), 349-368; William McAndrew, "French Wine-Growers and American School Children," *School and Society*, 32 (1930), 96-97.

42. Harold D. Lasswell, Ralph D. Casey and Bruce L. Smith (Eds.), *Propaganda and Promotional Activities: An Annotated Bibliography* (Minneapolis, MN: University of Minnesota Press, 1935).

43. For example, Benjamin Rosenthal, "Teaching the Recognition of Propaganda in the Social Studies Classroom," *The Social Studies*, 30 (1939), 268-272.

44. Benjamin Fine, "Propaganda Study Instills Skepticism in 1,000,000 Pupils," *New Yori Times*, February 21, 1941, pp. 1, 14.

45. George Gallup (Ed.), *The Gallup Poll: Public Opinion, 1935-1971* (3 vols.; New York: Random House, 1972), 1:192.

46. Lee, *Publicity*.

47. Edward L. Bernays, *Crystallizing Public Opinion* (New York: Boni & Liveright, 1923); Bernays, *Propaganda* (New York: Liveright, 1928). Quotations respectively from Bernays, 1923, pp. 14, 183.

48. Quotations respectively from Bernays, *Propaganda*, pp. 11, 18, and Bernays, *Crystallizing*, p. 215.

49. George Gallup and Saul F. Rae, *The Pulse of Democracy: The Public Opinion Poll and How It Works* (New York: Simon and Schuster, 1940); Frank N. Stanton, "Psychological Research in the Field of Radio Listening," in *Educational Broadcasting 1936*, ed. C. S. Marsh (Chicago: University of Chicago Press, 1937), pp. 365-377.

50. J. McKeen Cattell, "The Psychological Corporation," *Annals of the American Academy of Political and Social Science*, 110 (November 1923), 165-171.

51. Harold D. Lasswell, "Propaganda," *Encylopaedia of the Social Sciences*, 12 (1933), 521-528.

52. Harold D. Lasswell and Nathan Leites, *Language of Politics* (Cambridge: M.I.T. Press, 1949), p. 18.

53. Bernard Berelson, *Content Analysis in Communication Research* (Glencoe, IL: Free Press, 1952), p. 15.

54. Harold D. Lasswell, "The Policy Orientation," in D. Lerner & H. D. Lasswell (Eds.), *The Policy Sciences: Recent Developments in Scope and Method* (Stanford, CA: Stanford University Press, 1951), pp. 3-15.

55. Representative research in this genre includes Paul F. Lazarsfeld, "Radio Research and Applied Psychology," *Journal of Applied Psychology*, 23 (1939), 1-7; Lazarsfeld (Ed.), "Progress in Radio Research" [Special issue], *Journal of Applied Psychology*, 24 (1940), 661-859; Hadley Cantril, *The Invasion from Mars* (New York: Harper, 1940); Cantril, *Gauging Public Opinion* (Princeton, NJ: Princeton University Press, 1944); Paul F. Lazarsfeld and Frank N. Stanton, *Radio Research: 1942-1943* (New York: Duell, Sloan and Pearce, 1944).

56. Samuel A. Stouffer, E. A. Suchman, L. C. DeVinney, S. A. Star, and R. M. Williams, *The American Soldier* (2 vols.; Princeton, NJ: Princeton University Press, 1949), 1:37-40.

57. Carl I. Hovland, A. A. Lumsdaine, and F. D. Scheffield, *Experiments on Mass Communication* (Princeton, NJ: Princeton University Press, 1949), pp. 108ff, 167ff.

58. Daniel Lerner, "The *American Soldier* and the Public," in R. K. Merton & P. F. Lazarsfeld (Eds.), *Continuities in Social Research* (Glencoe, IL: Free Press, 1950), p. 220.

59. Carl I. Hovland, Irving L. Janis, and Harold H. Kelley, *Communication and Persuasion* (New Haven, CT: Yale University Press, 1953); Carl I. Hovland, *The Order of Presentation in Persuasion* (New Haven, CT: Yale University Press, 1957); Irving L. Janis and Carl I. Hovland, *Personality and Persuasibility* (New Haven, CT: Yale University Press, 1959).

60. Robert S. Lynd, "The Science of Inhuman Relations" [Review of *The American Soldier*, Vols. 1-2, and *Experiments on Mass Communication*], *New Republic*, 121, No. 9 (1949), 22-25 and Alfred McC. Lee, Review of *The American Soldier* (2 vols.), *Annals of the American Academy of Political and Social Science*, 265 (September 1949), 173-175.

61. Paul F. Lazarsfeld and Robert K. Merton, "Studies in Radio and Film Propaganda," *Transactions of the New York Academy of Sciences*, 6 (1943), 58-79.

62. Paul F. Lazarsfeld, Bernard Berelson, and Hazel Gaudet, *The People's Choice* (3rd ed.; New York: Columbia University Press, 1968; original work published 1944); Rosser Reeves, *Reality in Advertising* (New York: Knopf, 1961), pp. 138ff, especially; Frank Stanton, "Mass Media and Mass Culture," Lecture at Dartmouth College, November 26, 1962.

63. Paul F. Lazarsfeld, "Memorandum," File 002/8, Series 1, Box 2, Lazarsfeld Papers, Rare Book and Manuscript Library, Columbia University, c. 1954; Harold D. Lasswell, Affidavit, October 23, 1951, Army-Navy-Air Force Personnel Security Board File, Lasswell Papers, Manuscripts and Archives Division, Yale University Library.

64. Joseph T. Klapper and Charles Y. Glock, "Trial by Newspaper," in D. Katz, *et al.* (Eds.), *Public Opinion and Propaganda* (New York: Dryden, 1954; original work published 1949), pp. 16-21.

65. Gilbert Seldes, *The Great Audience* (Westport, CT: Greenwood Press, 1970; original work published 1950); Harold A. Innis, *The Bias of Communication* (Toronto: University of Toronto Press, 1951); Lee, *How to Understand Propaganda;* Vance Packard, *The Hidden Persuaders* (New York: McKay, 1957).

66. Representative works include Elihu Katz and Paul F. Lazarsfeld, *Personal Influence*T (New York: Free Press, 1955); Everett M. Rogers, Diffusion of Innovations, 3rd ed. (New York: Free Press, 1983; original work published 1962.)

67. John Dewey, *Studies in Logical Theory* (Chicago: University of Chicago Press, 1903); *How We Think* (Boston: D. C. Heath, 1910); *Essays in Experimental Logic* (New York: Dover, 1953; o (Original work published 1916).

68. Compare John Dewey, "The New Paternalism," *New Republic,* 17 (1918), 216-217, and "Highly-Colored White Lies," *New Republic,* 42 (1925), 229-230 to *Liberalism and Social Action* (New York: G. P. Putnam's, 1935). *The Public and Its Problems* (Chicago: Swallow Press, 1927) shows within itself Dewey's ambivalence about whether to root social problems in the competence of the public. Also compare Walter Lippmann, "Basic Problem," "Liberty," and *Public Opinion,* to Lippmann, *The Phantom Public* (New York: Harcourt, Brace, 1925), *The Good Society* (Boston: Little, Brown, 1937), and *Essays in the Public Philosophy* (Boston: Little, Brown, 1955).

69. Examples include Edwin L. Clarke, *The Art of Straight Thinking* (New York: Appleton, 1929); Robert H. Thouless, *Straight and Crooked Thinking* (New York: Simon and Schuster, 1932); Edward M. Glaser, *An Experiment in the Development of Critical Thinking* (New York: Teachers College, Colmbia University, 1941).

70. For instance, Violet Edwards, *Group Leader's Guide to Propaganda Analysis* (New York: Institute for Propaganda Analysis, 1938).

71. Bruce L. Smith, "Propaganda Analysis and the Science of Democracy," *Public Opinion Quarterly*, 5 (1941), 250-259; Max Lerner, *Ideas for the Ice Age* (New York: Viking, 1941).

72. See minutes of executive committee for October 29, 1941 in Papers of the Institute for Propaganda Analysis, privately held by Alfred McClung Lee, Short Hills, NJ; letter of Clyde Miller to Clyde Beals, November 19, 1941, in Papers of Kirtley F. Mather, Harvard University Archives. See also Alfred McClung and Elizabeth B. Lee, "The Fine Art of Propaganda Analysis—Then and Now," *Etc.*, 36 (1979), 117-127.

73. William Garber, "Propaganda Analysis—To What Ends?" *American Journal of Sociology*, 48 (1942), 240-245; Lewis Mumford, *Values for Survival* (New York: Harcourt, Brace, 1946). Cf. unsigned articles published by the Institute for Propaganda Analysis: "Father Coughlin: Priest and Politician," *Propaganda Analysis*, 2 (June 1, 1939), 61-68; "The Associated Farmers," *Propaganda Analysis*, 2 (August 1, 1939), 89-100.

74. Contrast Howard R. Anderson (Ed.), *Teaching Critical Thinking in the Social Studies* (Washington, D.C.: National Council for the Social Studies, 1942) and Elmer Ellis (Ed.), *Education Against Propaganda* (National Council for the Social Studies, 1937).

75. Max Black, *Critical Thinking* (2nd ed.; New York: Prentice-Hall, 1952); Raymond S. Nickerson, David N. Perkins and Edward E. Smith (Eds.), *The Teaching of Thinking* (Hillsdale, NJ: Lawrence Erlbaum, 1985).

76. "Spies and Lies," Advertising Copies and Layouts, CPI 1-C6, Records of the Committee on Public Information, National Archives, 1918.

77. U. S. Senate, *Brewing and Liquor Interests and German and Bolshevik Propaganda* (3 vols.; Washington: U.S. Government Printing Office), 1919.

78. U. S. House of Representatives, *Investigation of Un-American Propaganda Activities in the United States* (17 vols.; Washington: U.S. Government Printing Office, 1938), 4:2729-2873 and Martin Dies, *The Trojan Horse in America* (New York: Dodd, Mead, 1940), p. 300.

79. U. S. House of Representatives, *Hearings Regarding Communist Infiltration of the Motion Picture Industry* (Washington: U. S. Government Printing Office, 1947).

80. Elisha Hanson, "Official Propaganda and the New Deal," *Annals of the American Academy of Political and Social Science*, 179 (May 1935), 176-186; William F. Buckley, Jr., *God and Man at Yale* (Chicago: Regnery, 1951); Richard M. Weaver, *The Ethics of Rhetoric* (Chicago: Regnery, 1953); William H. Bennett, "To Reclaim a Legacy," *Chronicle of Higher Education*, November 28, 1984, 1, 6-21; Allan Bloom, *The Closing of the American Mind* (New York: Simon and Schuster, 1987); Herman H. Dinsmore, *All the News that Fits* (New Rochelle, NY: Arlington House, 1969); Edith Efron, *The News Twisters* (Los Angeles: Nash, 1971); Ernest W. Lefever, *TV and National Defense* (Boston, VA: Institute for American Strategy, 1974).

81. David G. Phillips, "The Treason of the Senate [1906]," in A. and L. Weinberg (Eds.), *The Muckrakers* (New York: G. P. Putnam's Sons, 1964). pp. 71-83; Stuart Chase and F. J. Schlink, *Your Money's Worth: A Study in the Waste of the Consumer's Dollar* (New York: Macmillan, 1927); Howard H. Martin, "The Rhetoric of Academic Protest," *Central States Speech Journal*, 17 (1966), 244-250; Donald K. Ross, *A Public Citizen's Action Manual* (New York: Grossman, 1973); Noam Chomsky and Edward S. Herman, *After the Cataclysm* (Boston: South End Press, 1979).

82. Joe McGinniss, *The Selling of the President 1968* (New York: Trident, 1969); David Wise, *The Politics of Lying* (New York: Vintage, 1973).

83. Timothy Crouse, *The Boys on the Bus: Riding with the Campaign Press Corps* (New York: Ballantine, 1973); Herbert J. Gans, *Deciding What's News* (New York: Vintage, 1979); Todd Gitlin, *The Whole World is Watching: Mass Media in the Making & Unmaking of the New Left* (Berkeley: University of California Press, 1980); Ben H. Bagdikian, *The Media Monopoly* (Boston: Beacon, 1983).

84. Benjamin Ginsberg, *The Captive Public* (New York: Basic Books, 1986); Herbert I. Schiller, *The Mind Managers* (Boston: Beacon, 1973); J. Fred MacDonald, *Television and the Red Menace* (New York: Praeger, 1985); Todd Gitlin, *Inside Prime Time* (New York: Pantheon, 1985); Neil Postman, *Amusing Ourselves to Death: Public Discourse in the Age of Show Business* (New York: Viking, 1985).

85. See Garth S. Jowett and Victoria O'Donnell, *Propaganda and Persuasion* (2nd ed.; Newbury Park, CA: Sage, 1992); Anthony Pratkanis and Elliott Aronson, *Age of Propaganda: The Everyday Use and Abuse of Persuasion* (New York: W. H. Freeman, 1992); James E. Combs and Dan Nimmo, *The New Propaganda: The Dictatorship of Palaver in Contemporary Politics* (New York: Longman, 1993).

86. Alfred McC. Lee, *Sociology for Whom?* (New York: Oxford University Press, 1978), p. 130.

87. Howard Kahane, *Logic and Contemporary Rhetoric* (Belmont, CA: Wadsworth, 1971); Craig A. Hosterman, "Teaching Propaganda," *Communication Education*, 30 (1981), 156-162; Hugh Rank (Ed.), *Language and Public Policy* (Urbana, IL: National Council of Teachers of English, 1974); Rank, *The Pitch* (Park Forest, IL: Counter-Propaganda Press, 1982); Rank, *The Pep Talk* (Park Forest, IL: Counter-Propaganda Press, 1984).

NASA National Aeronautics and
Space Administration   **Lunar Outpost**

Lunar Outpost

Establishment of a permanently inhabited lunar outpost is a crucial step toward fulfilling the national space policy goal of expanding human presence into the solar system. The Moon is an ideal laboratory for learning to live and work on the space frontier. Planning for such an outpost is in the early stages. A few more years of concept studies will precede the choice of a final lunar outpost design.

This artist's concept shows what a lunar outpost might look like, based on the results of studies conducted thus far. Actual lunar surface systems may be different from those shown in the picture. A site for the lunar outpost will be selected by evaluating factors such as closeness to surface features of scientific interest, Earth's visibility, soil chemistry, and roughness of terrain. The outpost could expand into a network of lunar bases and ultimately a lunar settlement.

In this scenario, the construction "shack" (2) shown in the picture would be built before a permanent lunar habitat. Crews on early scientific missions could live in their landing craft and use the shack to support their surface exploratory missions. Crews on these missions would bring with them all of the air, water, and food that they need for their stay on the Moon. The shack could also support the construction of other elements of the lunar outpost.

The experimental six-legged robotic "walker" (8) is an example of the kind of machine that could assist people with surface exploration. Beyond the horizon, at the end of the road in the middle of the picture (10), is a landing site for lunar vehicles, located 2.2 kilometers away from the outpost for safety reasons.

One design option for a permanent lunar habitat is an inflatable structure (1), erected in a crater or an excavation and shielded with bags of lunar surface material, known as regolith (4), to protect crews against solar and cosmic radiation. Regolith would be bagged by machine (5). The habitat in this picture is 16 meters in diameter, with 2,145 cubic meters of volume, four levels of living and working space, and 594 meters of floor space. Accommodating 12 people, it would be pressurized and thermally controlled. A pressurized tunnel (3) could connect the construction shack with the habitat.

Research could be conducted in fields such as geology, astronomy, astrophysics, and life sciences at a lunar outpost. In addition, technologies required for human missions to Mars could be demonstrated on the Moon. The use of extraterrestrial resources could be demonstrated as well; for instance, a pilot plant could be built to test various methods of extracting oxygen from lunar surface materials. The oxygen would be used for spacecraft fuel and breathable air.

Power needs at a lunar outpost could be met by solar photovoltaic power systems (7,9,11). Thermal radiators (6) would dissipate excess heat.

For the Classroom

1. Why must people be shielded from radiation on the Moon?
2. How long is the lunar day? How long is the lunar night?
3. What is the chemical composition of lunar regolith?
4. Why is the Moon a good place for astronomical observations?
5. What might we learn by studying geology on the Moon?

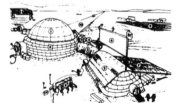

1. The inflatable habitat
2. The construction equipment structure
3. Connecting tunnel
4. Continuous, coiled regolith bags for radiation protection
5. Regolith bagging machine, coiling bags around the habitat while bulldozer scrapes loose regolith into its path
6. Thermal radiator
7. Solar panel
8. Experimental six-legged walker
9. Solar power system for the outpost
10. Road to landing pad
11. Solar power system for the lunar oxygen pilot plant

NASA Stokes the Imagination

CHAPTER 2

PROPAGANDA IN GOVERNMENT

When people think about propaganda, they often also think of government. This is no accident. As we observed in chapter 1, America's first major bout of propaganda consciousness sprang from discovery of German propaganda operations in the U.S.A. and, later, from second thoughts about the U.S. Committee on Public Information. In like manner, one effect of the Johnson Administration's Vietnam-era credibility gap was that it prompted a return of popular propaganda consciousness. These vast persuasive campaigns undertaken by public administrative agencies provide us with a useful starting point for a survey of contemporary government propaganda.

Propaganda represents an inherent instrument of twentieth-century government. This principle is well recognized, not only by muckraking progressive critics but also by conservative political opponents of big government. But to say that propaganda is inevitable is not to dismiss mass persuasion as harmless. We are driven to ask whether government propaganda might be an obstacle to democratic life.

Turning to distinctions drawn earlier by Bernays, the practitioner, and Lasswell, the scientist, we may take heart that propaganda not only is an alternative to force but also that it sensitizes leaders to the will of the public. Nevertheless, the twentieth century's turn to propaganda presents certain irrepressible dilemmas for the democratic way of life. Propaganda is a form of persuasion that is strongly rooted in principles of manipulation. When political officials choose the route of propaganda, they adopt a course of covertness that discourages citizens from direct participation in public life. Further, governmental propaganda blankets people with attractive partisan conclusions that limit the peo-

53

ple's chances either to perceive issues clearly or to discuss them fruitfully. The result is a backwards kind of democracy in which the citizens speak but often through the voices of officials who act as ventriloquists.

GOVERNMENT BY PROPAGANDA

On September 5, 1989, President George Bush delivered his first prime-time television speech to the nation. Bush used the occasion to announce new measures in his war on drugs. Bush's speechwriters thought that a perfect visual nugget in the speech would be for Bush to show a package of crack that had been confiscated in the neighborhood of the White House itself. However, obtaining this needed visual aid turned out to be a difficult assignment for agents of the Drug Enforcement Administration (DEA). Eventually, some agents were able to lure a suspected Washington drug dealer to Lafayette Park, across from 1600 Pennsylvania Avenue, where they captured his illegal wares. As a result of his minions in the DEA, Bush obtained the desired visual tool, allowing him to demonstrate how the drug problem had spread to the president's own back yard. Ironically, the suspect did not even know where the White House was. According to DEA agent William McMullan, "We had to manipulate him to get him down there. It wasn't easy."[1] In Bush's speech, therefore, crack cocaine was not the only thing that was packaged. When Bush used his visual prop, he strengthened his speech, but at the price of insinuating administratively-packaged propaganda.

Presidents tend to prefer the soft sell of propaganda to the harder task of constructing strong verbal arguments of the kind that Aristotle recommended to his students of public speaking. During the 1992 campaign, Bill Clinton honed the tactic of speaking to groups of ordinary citizens. Although this bypassing of the press enhanced direct communication with the public, the tactic was open to manipulation as when Clinton later substituted children for adults in these "forums." In the estimation of one critic, the president's televised meeting with 40 children on February 20, 1993 allowed him to "radiate empathy" and, at the same time, promote his programs without the tough questions that reporters or adult citizens might ask. As White House correspondents watched from the sidelines, Clinton's aides exulted over how their boss had come across to the viewing public. The soft-ball questions and answers that punctuated Clinton's session with the kiddies was a spontaneous performance but not of a type that the public might use to judge real character and competence.[2] What, we worry? Did not these mechanics make for a better product in the spirit of show business and public-relations politics?

Recent Presidential Styles of Propaganda

Few chief executives have begun their presidency with as much glitz as William Jefferson Clinton. Seemingly, the Democrats went out of their way to pack in as much celebrity power as Washington would hold during the week-long festivities attending the inaugural. Aficionados of the rich and famous were treated to frequent glimpses of Barbra Streisand, Goldie Hawn, Sally Field, Christie Brinkley, Aretha Franklin, Sigourney Weaver, to name but a few. The gala MTV Ball on inauguration night represented a logical extension of the Clinton-Gore ticket's earlier usurpation of the youth audience with appearances on MTV.

Six months into the new administration, the invasion of the celebs continued seemingly unabated. Streisand had become so familiar a visitor to Washington that even the *Wall Street Journal* began to interview the singer on politics. The marriage of Hollywood and the White House in 1993 continued to solidify because the union helped ease the insecurities of both sides of the partnership. As one commentator observed: "The Hollywood elite wants to be seen as serious, and the Washington elite wants to be seen as glamorous."[3] However, the Clinton Administration's pursuit of a politics of glamor smacked of the kind of propaganda that, to me, harked back to circuses of the Roman emperors. Citizens may have been intrigued by press attention to visits by Judy Collins, Liza Minnelli, Billy Crystal, Christopher Reeve, John Ritter, Lindsay Wagner, Paul Newman, Joanne Woodward, Michael Douglas, and others. But what did the visits of the Beautiful People contribute to the welfare of citizens?

Bill Clinton might have wondered the same thing when his administration's focus on the economy became blurred as a result of his early attention to issues uppermost in the minds of Hollywood's liberal set: gays in the military, AIDS funding, and abortion rights. If good political propaganda transforms special interests into the perceived general welfare, the early Clinton presidency was remarkable for its failure to succeed in engineering such transformations. Barely one month into the new presidency, Clinton's aides were privately bemoaning the fact that their administration's signature issue seemed to be gays in the military, a result that appeared not only to play into the hand of opponents but also to confuse many supporters. Clinton suffered the fate of having the Pentagon's brass raise alarms about military morale at the same time that gay leaders raged at compromises hindering their hoped-for permissive policy on homosexuality in the military.

By April 1993, the Clinton Administration was apologizing both privately and publicly for going "off-message," that is, for pursuing so many objectives at once. The failure to focus on the overall tax-and-spending issue reinvigorated Republican opposition. Where Ronald Reagan had bowled over the Democrats in Congress to enact his deficit-producing combination of a military build-up coupled with tax cuts, Clinton was defeated in his modest proposal for stimulus spending. Later, by the narrowest of margins (51-50 in the Senate), Clinton did win passage of his package of relatively-modest tax increases and spending cuts. However, in a stark reversal of the formula for good political propaganda (making special interests appear general ones), Clinton's tax increases were rated as troubling by about half of those contacted in opinion polls. This, despite the Clinton program's raising the tax burden only about 1% on incomes of less than $200,000 (versus 17% on those above this high income level).[4] Here the Republicans proved the better propagandists, making their defense of the wealthiest one percent of tax-payers appear, in the estimation of many Americans, to embody the general public interest.

In many ways, the Reagan presidency (1981-1989) represented the high point of successful executive-branch propaganda. This conclusion follows not only from a comparison of how Clinton and Reagan packaged and sold their respective budget plans but also from how George Bush and Ronald Reagan variously controlled the national agenda of visual imagery and verbal commentary. During the 1980s, Reagan was recognized widely as the master of a media-oriented, public-relations government. For instance, Reagan was out in front personally to welcome hostages released from Lebanon in 1985 after an airplane hijacking incident. As a result of revelations from the Iran/Contra Congressional hearings of 1987, we now know that the Reagan Administration was so preoccupied with hostages as to even exchange arms with Iran to secure their release. Having paid so dearly in political risk to rescue hostages, it only made good sense to use the news cameras as a tool for associating Reagan with the successful liberations. Welcoming events for former hostages were well choreographed for maximum political glitz. For instance, as 30 former captives and their families arrived at Washington, Reagan was on hand to welcome them. In the crowd gathered at the airport, one could spot signs saying "Thank you Ron and Nancy" and "USA is No. 1." Operatives had distributed the signs earlier to a group of about 400 well-wishers gathered to meet the hostages.[5]

Taking the Reagan Administration as a standard, during the early days of the Bush presidency less news coverage about the executive branch was focused on the person of the president. Under Bush, the cabinet secretaries and other spokespersons received relatively more attention, making for a less focused government communication. "The White House is no longer setting the tone for the news as much," said Robert Lichter of the Center for Media and Public Affairs. Some supporters of Bush became concerned that the president was missing the chance to control the tenor of public deliberation by capturing the attention of the news. L. Brent Bozell complained that Reagan's press czar, Michael Deaver, "knew how to use the media, how to manipulate it. Bush doesn't." Spokespersons of the TV Networks resisted the idea that the Reagan Administration ever enjoyed a free reign to manipulate the media. But Paul Friedman, executive producer of ABC News "World News Tonight," acknowledged that the recent tendency not to cover every presidential action might mean that "we finally may be getting a little more sophisticated."[6]

Not that Bush's people were innocent of propagandistic posturing. If their standard bearer seemed to have a more mercurial screen presence than that of Reagan, the genial ex-actor, they compensated by having Bush chat up reporters informally and also treat journalists to visits in the White House. Early in his presidency, Bush permitted more off-the-record private lunches, dinners, and White House chats than had Reagan. Bush gave some reporters a personal tour of the White House. One such favored reporter was Jessica Lee, White House correspondent for *USA Today*, who reported that it felt "thrilling" to see the Gettysburg Address in the Lincoln bedroom.[7]

The promotional strategies pursued by all recent executive administrations have prompted criticism about propaganda; this generalization applies to Reagan's staged events, to Bush's private smoozing of reporters, and to Clinton's celebrity kibitzing. All these ploys of indirect persuasion share the common feature of using an ostensibly neutral channel of public communication (official events, news, and entertainment) as vehicles to clothe political policies with the garb of unquestionable virtue. All these ploys, from orchestrated welcoming ceremonies, to pep sessions with journalists, to celebrity hobnobbing, act to reduce the chances that the public witnesses a competitive clash of political positions.

Propaganda and Government, One and Inseparable

While the presidencies of Clinton, Bush, and Reagan provide us with recent examples of official propaganda, we must keep in mind that none of these presidents pioneered official propagandizing. In chapter 1, we commented on the Wilson Administration's various ploys to steer the nation through World-War-I-era propaganda. Later, under Franklin D. Roosevelt, the executive branch honed the arts of peacetime mass persuasion. When, during the early twentieth century, Washington agencies took on new powers to act independently of the Congress, the rise in propaganda by government became inevitable.

One observer of Roosevelt's New Deal remarked that every democratic government needed to maintain "at least passive approval"; therefore, no elected Administration having wide powers to act would ever hold back from cleaning and sharpening its establishment tools for persuasion. In 1940, for example, the U.S. Department of Agriculture issued 1,500 press releases, sent 280 stories to editors, prepared 2,300 articles for magazines, and sent out 32 million publications.[8] Not only that, but the Department enjoyed the survey research services of a leading social scientist, Rensis Likert. Likert's researchers charted attitudes in farm communities to help the Department successfully implement its policies.

Jacques Ellul, French intellectual and leading propaganda theorist, denied that propaganda can ever be completely consistent with democratic life, even though elected governments reflexively turn to it. Ellul argued that propaganda, however well intentioned, inevitably debased free public opinion. He explained that propaganda sows confusion and, therefore, leaves the public less competent to make decisions.[9]

Ellul presented an interesting paradox. Western governments experience an urge to use propaganda that is accompanied by guilt about seeming to manipulate the public. Ellul's paradox may be discerned in the ambivalence of Americans towards official pronouncements about war. On the one hand, postwar disillusionment with World War I (and, later, the Vietnam War) brought recriminations about manipulation through propaganda. By the 1930s, for instance, Americans generally viewed propaganda as having been a major cause of the U.S.'s decision to aid King George and fight Kaiser Wilhelm. On the other hand, Americans frequently have exhibited a strong inclination to accept official communications about war. This desire for national solidarity held sway during World War II and during the Cold War. More recently, the deep-seated thirst of Americans to identify with their national leaders produced great support for the Administration and the Pentagon during the Persian Gulf War of 1991. Later, the public's reflexive suspicions about manipulation probably contributed to the rapid drop in Bush's opinion poll ratings during the year following the war.

Events of the day seem able to trigger feelings either of national unity or of suspicion about wartime communication. In 1941, the shock of Pearl Harbor conjured up a mood of national solidarity that overwhelmed the previously rampant Depression-era skepticism about government propaganda. In like manner, events of the 1960s, notably the U-2 spy plane affair (described below) and the communist Tet Offensive in Vietnam (1968), reactivated latent suspicions about government that had been repressed during World War II and the Cold War. The American national psyche has been conditioned by alternating periods in which propaganda has been accepted here, rejected there. As a result, events of the day may induce Americans to draw either from their will to believe governmental communication or from their impulse to doubt it.

Nothing illustrates the twentieth-century public's ambivalence toward government propaganda more clearly than the U-2 affair of 1960.

The U-2 Affair

The U-2 spy plane incident of 1960 marked a pivotal point in the public's recognition of the propaganda paradox. The U-2 affair showed that even though the U.S. government had lied, it seemed to have had a noble motive for doing so. This crisis of mid-1960 supplied a particularly stark demonstration that, although propaganda was efficient in defending the nation, it also could be injurious to democratic governance.

The U-2 was a technologically advanced U.S. spy plane. Because the U-2 was designed to operate at 70,000 feet, it was able to evade the air defenses of the Soviet Union. In a top-secret operation, the

Eisenhower Administration regularly mounted espionage flights that violated the national borders of the USSR. While Soviet radar detected the overflights, the Soviet government kept quiet about the incursions. The Kremlin was unwilling to publicize the embarrassing fact that Russia lacked fighter planes or missiles capable of downing a U-2. In April 1960, President Eisenhower reluctantly acquiesced to the insistence of his advisers that another U-2 flight was necessary. Not wanting to antagonize the Russians, Ike had hesitated before approving the new spy flight which was scheduled to take place only two weeks before his summit meeting with Soviet leader Nikita Khrushchev.

On May 1, 1960, in a scenario that exceeded the worst fears of the president, a U-2 plane, having taken off from Pakistan, was downed by a Soviet missile some 1,300 miles within the borders of Russia. The pilot, Francis Powers, was captured alive. When the CIA lost contact with Powers's plane, the agency cranked up the prepared cover story. According to initial announcements from Washington, the flight amounted to a NASA weather plane innocently straying over the Soviet border. The false story was necessary because, up to that time, the U.S. government had never admitted engaging in deliberate spying against the USSR. The U.S. press gave scant attention to the first story put out from Washington to the effect that a NASA weather plane flying over Turkey was missing. The CIA felt confident of its deceptive cover story in the belief that it was impossible for the pilot to have survived the Soviet missile. The agency further assumed that the light U-2 plane would have disintegrated during its fall. Nevertheless, preparing for contingencies, the CIA was ready to charge that the Russians had moved the plane further inland to effect an appearance of U.S. spying.

While the CIA was deciding exactly how to put an acceptable public face on Powers's failed flight, Soviet leaders also were debating how to handle the affair. Khrushchev decided to announce to the Supreme Soviet simply that the plane had been shot down, withholding for the moment any reference to the surviving pilot. In response to Khruschev's claim of having downed an American spy plane, presidential press spokesman, James Hagerty, reported that Eisenhower had ordered an investigation by NASA and the State Department. NASA thereupon issued a statement elaborating on the character of the U-2 weather mission. A number of U.S. Congressmen, who were in the dark about the U-2 program, demanded that the Russians apologize for downing an innocent American plane. Certain U.S. reporters, such as James Reston, had learned earlier about the U-2 spy flights, but Reston and the others carefully safeguarded the secret. In his newspaper column, Reston merely wondered aloud why the U.S. had sent a weather plane so close to the Soviet border a scant two weeks before the scheduled Eisenhower/Khruschev summit meeting.

Meanwhile, Ambassador Llewellyn Thompson in Moscow sent an urgent cable to the State Department reporting that he had overheard a Soviet diplomat refer to interrogations of the pilot. Two days after his initial report to the Supreme Soviet, Khrushchev announced that, indeed, the pilot of the spy plane had been captured alive. He derided the Americans for the "silly things they have said" to cover up the spy incident. He exhibited for the press spy photos captured from the U-2. Khruschev's dramatic announcement put Eisenhower in a dilemma. Either Ike could admit that he had authorized the provocative U-2 spy flights, or he could deny knowledge of the flights with the effect of appearing ignorant of events in his own Administration.

Subsequent announcements revealed that the U.S. government was strung out between the two horns of Eisenhower's dilemma. State Department spokesman Lincoln White, who earlier had categorically denied a deliberate attempt to violate Soviet air space, now had to read a new press release claiming that Washington authorities gave "no authorization" for an espionage flight, but that, nevertheless, a flight of this kind somehow had taken place. A few Administration officials worried about what the public might think of their government if some low-level officer had the power to authorize an important espionage flight. Nevertheless, Secretary of State Christian Herter believed that denying Eisenhower's involvement was necessary to keep the president untainted by the incident. Later, the U.S. announced that spy planes had operated under Eisenhower's general orders to obtain information on the USSR, although the U.S. government continued to deny that specific missions were subject to presidential authorization.[10]

Naturally, the American public did not pick up every nuance of the U-2 episode, and most expressed their support for Eisenhower and the spy operation. For alert citizens, however, the incident revealed the full panorama of Cold War propaganda that involved secrecy (even from Congress), covert operations, official lies, and tacit press support for the whole operation. The ill-fated U-2 mission of May 1960 conjured up lessons about government propaganda that had been largely forgotten by America's opinion leaders for nearly a generation.

GOVERNMENT AND THE PRESS

The U-2 episode showed that government can sometimes prevail upon news people to withhold information in the interest of not undermining official policy. It is not difficult to find instances where government officials have used any number of ploys both to court and to bully the press in the interests of favorable news coverage.

Courtship: The Carrot

The press-relations policies of the National Aeronautics and Space Administration (NASA) illustrate how an administrative agency may court and co-opt news reporters. Before the *Challenger* space-shuttle disaster of 1986, the national space program was generally presented as a shining model of American ingenuity, bravado, and achievement. NASA became accustomed to maintaining friendly relations with reporters assigned to the space beat. Since NASA's relatively few failures seemed to result from unavoidable technical problems, reporters felt little impulse to dig behind the scenes for news stories. It was enough to rely upon NASA's press releases, official tours, and authoritative briefings. When, in January 1986, NASA's image of invincibility was tarnished by the *Challenger* disaster, relations between the space agency and the press went sour. Reporters found that their formerly friendly sources in the space program were suddenly unavailable. In the days after the *Challenger* explosion, NASA officials withheld such routine information as launch-time temperatures.

While the space agency's new unapproachability did not unduly disturb the regular NASA press corps, the *Challenger* disaster also had attracted a new cadre of reporters who had few previous links to the space agency. Not having to worry about maintaining long-term friendly relations with the NASA officials, aggressive outside reporters uncovered startling information by talking to lower-level employees. For instance, the *Orlando Sentinel* reported concerns at Morton Thiokol, Inc. about the impact of low temperatures on the O-rings of the shuttle's solid-fuel rocket boosters. Other news agencies quickly followed with disclosures about internal debates among space engineers concerning the advisability of shuttle launches during times of low temperature.

By early 1986, the tradition for the press to give NASA reverential news treatment was coming to an end. Two years after the disaster, stories were still appearing alleging that NASA was pursuing a variety of self-serving ploys. For instance, the *New York Times* reported that Robert B. Hotz, a member of the presidential commission on the *Challenger* disaster, believed that NASA tried to cover up evidence that shuttle crew members had been alive during the two minutes between the explosion and the impact in the Atlantic. Hotz argued that NASA could not bring itself publicly to acknowledge that routine safety equipment such as oxygen and parachutes might have saved the astronauts.[11]

Pressure: The Stick

If courtship of the press by NASA shows how to numb the media's nose for news, the Nixon Administration gives us a model of how to minimize negative press coverage by brandishing a big stick. Nixon's predecessor, Lyndon Johnson, had been known for making direct phone calls to media executives; at the same time, LBJ's aides harassed the lower-level media folk.[12] No Administration more systematically attempted to influence media coverage, however, than that of Richard Nixon. Convinced that "the media" had brought down Johnson's presidency, the Nixon people worked from the start to mount an aggressive press-relations policy. The objective of the Nixon White House was to cast a pall on the credibility of the major news institutions so as to reduce the public impact of any criticism of the Administration that might be shown on TV or published in newspapers.

On November 13, 1969, in a speech before the Midwest Republican Conference in Des Moines, Iowa, Vice President Spiro Agnew attacked the television networks for coverage of the Vietnam War. This address provided an early signal that Nixon-style press relations would be even frostier than those of Johnson. Earlier, Nixon and the White House staff had been pointedly angered by the critical commentary given by reporters and guest analysts after Nixon's national TV address about Vietnam policy on November 3, 1969. In response, the White House speech-writing team prepared remarks for delivery by Vice President Spiro Agnew scolding the press for lapses in objectivity and good sense.[13]

Agnew's address began with complaints about network commentary on Nixon's earlier speech concerning Vietnam. The Vice President contended that the TV networks not only subjected Nixon's important Vietnam address to a superficial "instant analysis" but also that they sought out comment from avowed opponents of the Administration's Vietnam policy. The result, Agnew complained, was "to guarantee in advance that the President's plea for national unity would be challenged." Agnew continued with a general critique of the people and practices of TV news. The news networks were powerful, Agnew argued, able to elevate obscure people to great influence. In addition, by means of a skeptical tone of voice or an elevated eyebrow, commentators could "raise doubts in a million minds" about the government's wisdom or truthfulness. Not only that, TV pundits comprised a small clique residing on the East Coast, who allowed their biases to influence the presentation of news. Agnew faulted the networks generally for emphasizing violence and controversy in order to maximize profits.[14]

Agnew's speech was a harbinger of the testy style of press relations preferred by the Nixon Administration. Further, Nixon's White House was emboldened in its attack upon the press by the success of Agnew's address in building upon certain public resentments of media methods. Pressured by the Nixon Administration's subtle war of nerves with broadcasters, Richard S. Salant, head of CBS News, observed that "there has never been anything like this before." NBC President Julian Goodman added that "I think the tension between the media and the government is now perhaps at its strongest."[15] Ironically, conditions eventually became even more adversarial when media coverage of the Watergate scandal brought the Nixon Administration's conflict with the press to a head. Midway into the Watergate crisis, CBS News anchor, Walter Cronkite, commented that "Every administration has made attempts to check the press. But the current administration has gone further in its efforts to suppress free speech and cast doubts on the efficacy of the press than any other."[16]

Frank Stanton, President of CBS, speculated as early as 1971 that the anti-press efforts of the Nixon Administration were part of an orchestrated behind-the-scenes campaign. Documents later showed that Stanton's surmise was correct.

Even before the White House sent Agnew to Des Moines with his anti-media speech, the idea was growing in the Nixon Administration that the best press-relations approach was not to fire back at irritating news coverage with one-shot responses, but rather to mount a major propaganda campaign against TV journalists. On October 17, 1969, Jeb Magruder, a White House staffer, relayed to H. R. Haldeman, Nixon's chief of staff, a summary of "21 requests from the President in the last 30 days requesting specific action relating to what could be considered unfair news coverage." Magruder contended that piecemeal action on these many requests probably was "wasteful of our time." He proposed instead a comprehensive approach that involved the following: (1) establishment of a section in the Federal Communications Commission to monitor press coverage, (2) subtle threats to media corporations about possible anti-trust investigations, (3) threats about IRS investigations, (4) an effort "to show favorites within the media", and (5) letter-writing campaigns stimulated by the Republican National Committee.[17]

Eventually Jeb Magruder was designated project manager of a White House effort to attack the press with charges of bias. Illustrative of Magruder's covert strategy for weakening media criticism was his plan to "plant a column with a syndicated columnist which raises the question of objectivity and ethics in the news media" and then to have "Dean Burch [Chair of the Federal Communications Commission] 'express concern' about press objectivity in response to a letter from a Congressman." Even though the White House settled on the campaign approach to dealing with the media, the Nixon people did not entirely abandon the one-shot treatment of particular media enemies. A case in point was detailed in a note of July 16, 1970 from L. Higby to Magruder suggesting that "we need to get some creative thinking going on an attack on [Chet] Huntley for his statements in *Life* [magazine]."[18]

Nixon's anti-press campaign may shock, but it should not surprise. News coverage is the mother's milk of democratic governance. Most citizens are no longer in the position directly to observe the daily doings of their elected officials, even on the local level. Much of what people know about their socio-political world is indirect; in this atmosphere, elected leaders can be expected to take whatever action possible to skew news coverage in their favor. Government of the people presumes propaganda to the people in the form of a press that is alternately courted and clouted.

Governing *versus* Campaigning

Communicating with the public is a normal function of government, a fact that partly obscures the propaganda dimensions of governmental press relations. In this connection, however, political campaigns bring to light certain distinctions between routine government communication and covert partisan propaganda. For instance, acting as the ceremonial Head of State, a U.S. President routinely welcomes distinguished guests to the White House, and it is normal to expect news coverage of these events. During election season, however, it becomes evident to the discerning viewer that a covert, partisan propaganda is at work when celebrities, interest-group leaders, and sports figures call on the president. Here, journalistic attention to White House ceremonies allows the president to campaign without seeming to do so.

The press frequently complains about becoming a knowing but unwilling partner in the campaign propaganda of public officials. A case in point was when Jerry Roberts, political editor of the *San Francisco Chronicle*, scrutinized George Bush's presidential campaign of 1988. According to Roberts, "George Bush is trying to copy Ronald Reagan's 1984 political strategy of ducking tough questions from the press in favor of carefully orchestrated media events."[19] Complaints by Roberts and others about propagandized public events raise important questions, but these critiques still have a pathetic and futile whimper to them. Public and partisan interests are closely connected in government, so neither the press nor anyone else will be able to prevent *creative* propaganda techniques from putting a partisan spin on civic occasions.

An illustration of creativity in ceremonial propaganda may be seen in how the White House handled Paul Simon, U.S. Representative from Illinois, when President Reagan signed into a law an act authorizing a national center for tracing missing children. Simon, an Illinois Democrat, had been the original sponsor of the law; however, he was overlooked when it came time to invite members of Congress to the White House for the ceremonial launching of the center. At the time, Simon was challenging a vulnerable Republican in the 1984 contest for a Senate seat (Simon won the election anyway), hence omitting him seemed politically expedient.[20]

Because of the great size and scope of the executive branch, those who control the White House may call upon the resources of many administrative agencies in seeking to make propaganda points. A case in point occurred when the Reagan White House used NASA to help boost Vice President George Bush's election campaign in 1988. In October, 1988, NASA mounted the first flight of the space shuttle since the *Challenger* disaster of 1986. George Bush showed up in person to be seen as first to welcome the returning crew members of the shuttle, *Discovery*.

Reporters remarked how NASA departed from standard press practices in conspicuously helping news people cover this particular shuttle landing. For instance, journalists normally had been kept a mile away from the disembarking shuttle crew, but on this occasion, reporters were allowed within 125 feet of the spacecraft. Bush's behavior was somewhat out of the ordinary, too. Not only did *Discovery's* flight mark the first time that Bush (Vice President for eight years) ever had greeted a shuttle but also Bush waited patiently for an hour to deliver his brief greeting to the astronauts. Bush explained that his Democratic rival in the 1988 presidential campaign was not invited to the shuttle ceremony because this would "politicize" the event.[21]

During the '88 election, it sometimes seemed as though the whole executive branch had enlisted as behind-the-scenes handlers to help Bush get favorable attention in the news. For instance, as part of his campaign message, Bush had proclaimed his commitment to the environment. Complicating this political appeal was the reputation of the Reagan Administration for indifference or hostility to legislation protecting the environment. Hence, it was helpful to Bush that during the election campaign the Environmental Protection Agency and Department of the Interior were busy announcing new measures to deal with the ozone depletion problem and strip mining. White House officials denied a partisan purpose in their amazing ability to release information strategically, and to time official actions for the best news coverage. Privately, however, Administration officials conceded that "people across the Government are trying to be helpful to the Vice President."[22]

DARKER SIDES OF GOVERNMENT PROPAGANDA

Up to this point, we have considered government propaganda as chiefly a matter of subtle emphasis, something difficult to separate from the administrative responsibilities of ceremony, action, and information. Many of the governmental press practices cited to this point represent relatively benign kinds of propaganda. Courting news reporters, staging events for the cameras, releasing information strategically, and timing official actions to coincide with campaigning—all these represent what our military services would term "white" or "gray" propaganda. However, four tactics of a more dangerous disposition make up another side of the executive branch's propaganda operations. These tactics include secrecy, leaks, disinformation, and silencing opponents.

Secrecy

Keeping secrets—and spilling them—is not only part of human nature but also is inevitable in government. Unfortunately, the keepers of official information often invoke the national interest to justify stretching the blanket of secrecy over things that are merely inconvenient or embarrassing for government officials. In government work, the risks of releasing sensitive information are far greater than for keeping it hidden. Lower-level officials may find their careers damaged if they fail to place a sufficiently high security classification on information, but there is no corresponding penalty for overclassifying data. True, the Freedom of Information Act allows citizens to request relevant information from government, but, freedom-of-information requests frequently elicit only heavily-censored documents. President Jimmy Carter undertook some efforts to restrict the practice of labeling routine or political documents as "secret," and to limit the number of government agencies with power to classify information.[23] Carter's policies represented an anomaly, however, since the tendency after the onset of the Cold War was to increase government secrecy in America.

Because the Carter years had seen some small efforts to relax governmental secrecy, the Reagan Administration's effort to tighten secrecy practices revived the perennial conflict between official secrecy and participatory democracy. In 1982, the Reagan Administration broadened the amount of information subject to classification as "secret." The Administration put more economic, technical, and scientific data under the limits of official secrecy than ever before. In March 1983, the Reagan Administration implemented National Security Decision Directive 84. This executive order required all government officials with access to "sensitive" information to agree to a lifetime obligation to submit anything they wrote for public consumption to government clearance prior to publication. Previous requirements of this type had applied only to intelligence officials, such as those in the CIA. The Administration also required government officials to agree to submit to any order for a lie detector test.

Because many people in Congress objected to this sweeping censorship of secrecy, the Reagan White House officially suspended implementation of its controversial security directive; nevertheless, many public employees continued to sign the oath required by the order. Still, the White House became more cautious about asking for new secrecy laws from Congress, fearing that these requests would be denied. Despite this reticence, the Administration prosecuted a Navy employee, Samuel L. Morison, for turning over a photograph of a Soviet aircraft carrier under construction to the publication *Jane's*

Fighting Ships. The prosecution of Morison evidently was intended to set in place a new legal precedent. Formerly, Congress had long made a distinction between sending information secretly to a foreign power and simply leaking information for general publication. This and other instances of the Reagan-era mania with security was ironic, however, because, as I observe below, leaking secret information to gain favorable coverage had become a routine practice by the Pentagon and the White House itself.[24]

Secrecy practices inevitably pose the danger that legitimate security efforts may default as propaganda serving the special political interests of those in power. Members of the press contended, however, that most of the Reagan Administration's complaints about disclosures involved mere political embarrassment and not the release of actual military information. Further, odd situations sometimes have resulted from the impulse to overclassify information. Just such an instance took place when William Safire, speech writer for the Nixon Administration, once worked on an important presidential address on Vietnam policy. Safire decided to mark the document with secrecy classification abbreviations:

> To keep every staff aide and his brother from fiddling with my prose, I typed across the top the impressive-looking words and acronyms that so frequently are used in the national security world: 'TOP SECRET SENSITIVE.' To give that a little authentic zip, I added 'NOFORN, NOCONTRACT,' which has to do with restricting the distribution from foreign allies and defense contractors.[25]

Three days later, Safire called President Nixon's chief of staff, Bob Haldeman, to ask about the speech. Haldeman said that the draft needed more work, "but we can't let you have it—you're not cleared for Top Secret/Sensitive/Nocontract/Noforn."

Safire raised this instance to reveal the dilemma of secrecy. On the surface, calls to "protect our secrets" seem reasonable and are politically popular, but secrecy prohibitions can be, and are, misused to prevent criticism of government actions. For this reason, secrecy has a powerful life of its own. In 1989, the Bush Administration considered a major heightening of the power of secrecy procedures. The Administration proposed to eliminate the right of persons denied security clearance for reasons of "exploitable vulnerabilities" (such as alcohol abuse or sexual conduct) to learn of the exact nature of the charges.[26] Were such a proposal to be enacted, four million government and defense industry employees would be denied their ability to answer charges for which they had been deemed ineligible for a job due to security reasons.

It is not difficult to find troubling episodes of governmental secrecy in U.S. administrative agencies. One significant example may be found in the development of nuclear power and weapons plants. During Congressional hearings in 1988, the U.S. Department of Energy conceded that government agencies had kept secret numerous nuclear accidents at the Savannah River nuclear weapons plant in South Carolina over a 28-year period. Energy Department officials stated that the failure to disclose accidents stemmed from practices dating back to the early Cold-War-era production of nuclear weapons. At the outset of the Cold War, U.S. officials believed that safety disclosures would arouse public fears that, in turn, would interfere with the development and production of nuclear arms.[27]

In a similar story, documents released in 1990 showed that the U.S. government hid radiation leaks at the Hanford, Washington, nuclear weapons plants during the 1940s and 1950s. Government officials kept closely guarded the secret that more than 10,000 Washington residents were exposed to harmful levels of iodine-131 spewed by the weapons plants' smoke stacks between 1944 and 1947.[28] In both South Carolina and Washington, safety was sacrificed in the interest of the smooth production of weapons.

Even during the Cold War thaw of the 1970s, the U.S. government apparently tried to block research that pointed up significant harm to their health suffered by workers at nuclear weapons plants where people were routinely exposed to very low levels of radiation. In the early 1970s, Dr. Alice Stewart was conducting research supported by the Atomic Energy Commission on the health effects of radiation. She found evidence that workers at the government's Hanford nuclear weapons plant suffered a third more than the expected level of various cancers, even though the workers were exposed to half of the radiation allowable under existing safety limits. Stewart warned her superior, Dr. Thomas Mancuso, of the alarming findings, and he, in turn, briefed the AEC on what was the first documented evidence of higher cancer rates for adults regularly exposed to low levels of radiation. Within weeks, the AEC took *bold* action. Instead of pursuing the intriguing and alarming new findings, however, the agency promptly cut off funding for Mancuso's research team which had held a research contract with the AEC for the previous 13 years. When the incident was investigated by

70

Congress, U.S. government officials insisted that the dismissal had nothing to do with the revolutionary research findings that were eventually published in 1977.

One problem that nuclear safety researchers long have faced is that the health records of government nuclear-plant workers were classified as secret and therefore unavailable to general scientific researchers not under official control. Only in March 1990 did the Department of Energy open nuclear plant health records for public scrutiny.[29] Throughout the nuclear era, government agencies have exerted themselves to withhold any information contradicting the official view that nuclear power plants were wonderful and safe. This was a message comforting to policy makers in government and industry, making it easier to build nuclear weapons plants, conduct nuclear tests, and develop private nuclear power plants. Secrecy in relation to nuclear plants not only helped government but also was favorable to the private nuclear power industry which certainly did not want to raise alarming questions about plant safety.

Other instances may be found in which federal officials used information strategically to help outside business interests or ideological groups. One episode concerned the Federal Government's tread-wear grading program that, in 1984, had been saved from abolition only by court intervention.[30] The utility of the tire-wear statistics for consumers was evidenced in 1988, when a private auto safety group reported on the relative longevity of automobile tires using information collected (but not publicized) by the government. In this connection, the Reagan Administration's effort to curtail the tire-testing program seemed to cater to tire manufacturers. Executives believed that tread-wear statistics complicated their advertising efforts.

Another case in which federal data collided with Washington politics took place in 1984, when the Federal Centers for Disease Control stopped comparing the death rates of pregnant women who aborted and those who carried a birth to term. Data gathered up to that point indicated that women were between 7 and 25 times more likely to die from childbirth than from abortion. The House Government Operations Committee later charged that the executive branch had dropped the statistical comparison for political reasons because the data upset abortion foes.[31]

Leaks

Given the preoccupation of the Reagan Administration with secrecy, it is not surprising that few things rattled the Reaganites more than unauthorized leaks of official information to the press. In fact, the Administration required employees to take lie detector tests as part of an effort to track down who was leaking what to whom. Concern for the security of information is understandable because leaks can make it difficult for the executive branch to consider policies and take action. Further, leaks of information get in the way of diplomatic efforts, and they make it more difficult for the U.S. to counter aggressive foreign intelligence agencies. Notwithstanding these legitimate reasons for preventing disclosure of official information, we may observe certain propagandistic qualities in the Reagan Administration's attack on unauthorized disclosures.

Leaks can become an official propaganda of government when the leakers are not renegade employees but rather are high-level Administration officials. "Official leaks" tend to take one of two forms. First, an administrator may have high-level authorization to release sensitive information in the interest of promoting official Administration policy. For example, Lt. Col. Oliver North, who helped mastermind covert military operations in Nicaragua (expressly prohibited by U.S. law), justified his lies to Congress on the ground that the legislators would leak the true situation had he informed them of it. At the same time that North complained of leaks by members of Congress, the colonel himself was busy leaking information to the press. In fact, one Administration ploy to overthrow the Nicaraguan government was to discredit the *Sandinistas* of Nicaragua by leaking selected CIA data to the U.S. press.[32]

In addition to official leaks timed to promote executive branch policy, a second kind of official, government leak occurs when a high-level policy maker distributes data with the aim to affect a dispute raging in the executive branch. By making a policy conflict public, an official may be able to gain advantage over another member of the Administration or to nip a controversial policy in the bud by generating adverse public reaction. Reagan's CIA Director, William J. Casey, was suspected of employing the latter tactic. Casey was thought by the White House to be leaking stories that he was under attack by other government officials. White House staffers suspected that the leaks were a ploy by Casey to prompt a public endorsement from his friend, Ronald Reagan.[33]

Disinformation

Occasionally, governments use outright disinformation or "black propaganda." "Disinformation" is a term coined by the Russians to designate self-serving lies spread by their security services to discredit such enemies as the U.S.A. As an example of Soviet disinformation, we may turn to the work of the KGB secret police in 1987 to plant rumors that the U.S. was kidnapping handicapped South American kids for use as donors in organ transplants in the U.S.A. Other KGB-planted stories included the tale that AIDS began as germ warfare by the USA and that the U.S. was developing a bomb that killed only Arabs and another that killed only persons of African descent.[34]

Just as the U.S. used disinformation during the Vietnam war, the Reagan Administration employed black propaganda in a peacetime campaign against Libyan leader Col. Moammar Khadafy. In August 1986, an article appeared in the *Wall Street Journal* reporting that the U.S. and Libya were on a collision course. The article asserted that U.S. officials were planning more military action against Libya (of a type similar to the previous bombing strike against that nation). Journalists at the *Wall Street Journal* later believed that the Administration officials who leaked the information had vastly hyped the likelihood of more U.S. military action. This raised the possibility that the *Wall Street Journal* story had been part of a disinformation campaign to rattle the Libyans.

A couple of months later, in fact, Bob Woodward of the *Washington Post* revealed that John Poindexter, Reagan's national security adviser, had planned a disinformation campaign against Libya. Poindexter's idea was to make Khadafy believe that the U.S. was preparing to move against Libya.[35] Administration officials defended their disinformation effort, contending that the campaign was designed to mislead Libyans, not the U.S. press. In other words, the CIA was to place fake stories in foreign newspapers so as to preoccupy Khadafy with visions of U.S. military action and with tales of internal opposition to his government. However, some sources contended that the Reagan Administration also provided misleading information to U.S. reporters, thereby prompting false news reports at home. The resulting flap prompted Bernard Kalb, State Department chief spokesman, to resign.[36]

Silencing Opponents

In addition to worries about executive-branch secrecy, leaks, and disinformation, critics express concern about covert tactics for intimidating political opponents. Allegations periodically surface that the Internal Revenue Service is being used as a weapon against government critics. For instance, IRS harassment was a part of the Nixon Administration's anti-media campaign.[37] More recently, in 1988, a peace group called Pledge of Resistance held a large demonstration in front of San Francisco's federal building to oppose U.S. government policy in Central America. Within days, agents of the Internal Revenue Service arrived at the organization's headquarters in Oakland to ask questions about the group's payroll and other financial records. Civil liberties groups criticized the action as having a chilling effect on demonstrators. However, Larry Wright, a spokesperson for the Internal Revenue Service, called the probe a "routine" inquiry that was unrelated to the demonstrations. He said that the IRS was simply following up a report from a "usually reliable source" to the effect that the protesters were being paid $50.00 each to demonstrate.[38]

The executive branch has made various uses of legal tactics originally designed to weaken opponents of America's Cold War-era foreign policy. For instance, the McCarran-Walter Act of 1952 allows the government to deny entry into the U.S. to persons deemed dangerous. This act was used 734 times in 1984 as the basis for turning down requests for entry visas. On close examination, however, many of those persons denied entry seem to have been barred not for reasons of subversive action but rather for controversial advocacy.

An example of someone denied entry to the U.S. on account of her statements and writings was Margaret Randall, a Marxist professor. Randall clearly represents the kind of person who will be weeded out if political tests are applied to those seeking entry to the United States. Not only had Randall lived in Cuba but also she wrote poems about the Kent State massacre characterizing the U.S.A. as an enemy to humanity. Randall, who earlier had renounced her American citizenship, decided that she wanted to return to the U.S. After examining her writings, the U.S. Immigration and Naturalization Service concluded that Randall had too many ties to communists and to revolutionaries and that her offenses went "far beyond mere dissent." Randall herself claimed that she was merely a "middle-aged college professor who writes about dissent" and that she "never advocated the overthrow of the American government, never engaged in terrorism or sabotage."[39]

The American Association of University Professors filed a brief against the Immigration and Naturalization Act because it allowed for "ideological exclusion." The AAUP contended that the act permitted officials to exclude entry into the U.S. of thousands of "eminent artists, scholars, scientists, and intellectuals invited to address or meet with United States citizens."[40] The McCarran-Walter Act resulted from Cold War-era fears about allowing propagandistic agitators into the U.S.A. Ironically, the act seems to have become, at least in part, a tool of government propaganda when our own officials use it to silence persons who merely advocate controversial positions.

Another law designed to combat propaganda that itself ironically has become a tool for propaganda is the Foreign Agents Registration Act enacted by Congress in 1938. The act was implemented to counter Nazi and Soviet propaganda materials which during the late 1930s were being smuggled into the U.S.A. from Europe. One provision of the act required the Justice Department to affix the label "propaganda" to any qualifying film originating outside of the U.S and then to keep records of which groups requested the film to be shown. The provision for labeling a film as propaganda received attention in 1983 when officials of the Justice Department branded three Canadian films as "propaganda." Two of the films dealt with acid rain allegedly originating in the U.S., and one was a cinematic treatment of anti-nuclear themes.[41]

In a related case, critics complained about a policy of the U.S. Information Agency to evaluate educational films for "propaganda" content before issuing tax-exempt certificates for export purposes. If labeled as "propaganda," a film could not receive a certificate that allows U.S.-made educational films a duty-free exemption for distribution overseas. A group of American film makers brought suit in 1985 to challenge the USIA rules, alleging that the agency systematically discriminated against films with themes critical of U.S. government policies or American life-styles. The film makers complained that the warning label—"propaganda"—effectively prevented the distribution of educational films disapproved by the USIA.[42]

If government officials are wont to use anti-propaganda laws as tools of propaganda, we may have reason to be skeptical about a decision of the State Department in 1986 to establish an Office on Disinformation Analysis and Response. The office was presented as being necessary to counter Soviet propaganda that discredits the U.S. abroad.[43] While the Soviet propaganda operation has been vast and unsavory, American history raises the possibility that the U.S. Disinformation Office might itself become an instrument of official administrative propaganda used on Americans.

THE BIG TWO AGENCIES

Any number of government agencies are able covertly to diffuse partisan views under the guise of conducting routine administrative action. The two government agencies most often accused of propaganda are the FBI and the Defense Department (the latter known also as DoD or the Pentagon). Because these agencies conduct necessary security duties, they also have the power covertly to advance the partisan positions favored either by the current occupant of the White House or by the leadership of the agencies themselves. For its part, the FBI, during the era of J. Edgar Hoover, exhibited a willingness to mix crime-fighting with ideological service to the executive branch and to leaders of Congressional internal security committees. Similarly, the Defense Department not only serves the Administration but also has catered to branches of the armed services (Army, Navy/Marine Corps, and Air Force) and even sometimes to the interests of defense contractors.

The FBI

Bill Moyers, journalist and former press aide to President Lyndon Johnson, recalled that LBJ both feared and used J. Edgar Hoover, long-time director of the FBI. Hoover was able to tantalize Johnson with information about political enemies. For instance, Hoover once dropped by to fill in LBJ about a particularly juicy report of an FBI informant. According to Hoover's source, the Republican National Committee might have been responsible for setting up a sex scandal involving one of Johnson's aides. Johnson thereupon ordered the FBI to follow up on the story, which turned out to be an unsubstantiated rumor. While Johnson saw the FBI as politically useful, he recognized that the agency also could be a threat. LBJ knew that Hoover could exert political leverage by leaking information to members of Congress as well as to the President.[44]

For a time, the FBI actually did become a systematic fountain of propaganda as a result of Director Hoover's alliance with the House Un-American Activities Committee and with various anti-communist writers. Hoover's FBI would leak information to favored members of Congress who were making an anti-communist reputation via HUAC or Joe McCarthy's Permanent Subcommittee on Investigations.

The Bureau also would leak information to journalists and columnists, sometimes directly or on other occasions by mailing anonymous envelopes stuffed with memoranda. Columnists receiving the material included Drew Pearson, Paul Harvey, David Lawrence, and Westbrook Pegler. The program continued well into the 1970s, as indicated by information released in 1978 under the auspices of the Freedom of Information Act. For instance, the FBI kept links with "reliable" reporters and editors of the *San Francisco Chronicle* and *Examiner*, leaking material to these journalists so that they would prepare stories that either discredited or defamed anti-Vietnam war activists and organizations. The FBI's mass-media program involved newspapers in many cities, giving the Bureau many outlets for its positions on social issues.[45]

An example of the FBI's alliance with the political Right may be seen in efforts to rein in and weaken liberal Protestant clergy. Hoover was interested in detecting and publicizing any radicalism in the American clergy because many church people not only expressed theological liberalism but also participated in left-wing social activism. Informants kept the Bureau alerted to unconventional expressions from the clergy as well as to any direct or indirect links between American clergy and groups that also included individuals having Communist Party connections. HUAC then came into play by employing public hearings and reports to publicize the FBI's information (not all of it completely accurate) about alleged communist influence in American churches. Sometimes, however, the publicizers of FBI data went too far. For instance, J. B. Matthews, Senator Joe McCarthy's chief aide (and former HUAC chief investigator), drew fire for publishing a controversial article in which he asserted that communists were using Protestant clergy as dupes to subvert America. The resulting pressure from the Eisenhower Administration led McCarthy to fire Matthews.[46]

The FBI also gave HUAC the information that led to the famous investigation of communism in Hollywood. The gist of HUAC's complaint about Hollywood was that leftist writers were infiltrating Red ideology into film scripts. On the surface, HUAC's attack was plausible. A number of Hollywood's leading writers undoubtedly either were currently, or had been formerly, members of the American Communist Party. Further, during World War II, Hollywood had produced films that glorified Russia and/or excused Soviet policies. For instance, in Warner Brothers' *Mission to Moscow*, Stalin's notorious purge trials were presented as necessary to counter the Nazi threat to Russia.

In retrospect, nevertheless, the charge of communist infiltration in Hollywood was based on some rather naive notions of how Tinseltown operated. First, the allegedly pro-communist wartime films had been approved by the U.S. government as necessary to bolster public support for aiding the Soviet Union, an important World-War-II ally. Jack Warner, president of Warner Brothers, wondered why HUAC complained about his films when Congress itself had authorized tons of military equipment for Russia at the very same time.[47] Further, scriptwriters were controlled by a tight corporate system in which their work was closely edited and monitored. In this commercial operation, individual writers could hardly function independently as freelance propagandists.

The leaders of Hollywood's major studios were initially alarmed and offended by HUAC's inquiries; but film moguls accepted HUAC's interference, once it became clear that charges would center on individual writers rather than the studio system itself. Hollywood's hierarchy thereupon circulated a blacklist, agreeing not to hire writers or actors who were marked as refusing to cooperate in the anti-Red purge. The FBI provided much of the information (exhibiting varying degrees of accuracy) to support the blacklisting of writers and actors who were associated with political groups or causes that earlier also had attracted communists as members.[48]

The FBI's link with the political Right was an entente made in heaven. The FBI had vast powers of investigation but no official mission to publicize its findings. The Congressional committees and independent journalists, on the other hand, had only feeble resources for investigation, but they had vast opportunities to circulate for political advantage the FBI's findings (and speculations). With information leaked by Hoover, HUAC and others were able to grab headlines in the nation's newspapers and thereby promote successfully a partisan brand of anti-communism.

The result of the FBI's alliance with right-wing politicians and writers seems to have been that of nudging American politics into a more extreme Cold War position than might otherwise have been the case. The FBI's view was that communists were running rampant in America, posing such an immediate threat of internal subversion as to constitute an national emergency. In this atmosphere, right-wing politicians and writers used the FBI's covert information to discredit not only communists but also to undermine anti-communist liberals who did not accept the premise that the Red Menace necessitated dispensing with American principles of free speech and equal protection of the laws.

Not only did the FBI covertly supply information for right-wing political attacks but also the Bureau's counter-intelligence efforts in the 1960s against domestic dissidents exhibited an aura of propaganda. J. Edgar Hoover set up a program—called "Cointelpro"—to infiltrate and disrupt dissident organizations. Free speech and advocacy rights came under routine attack as part of the program. For example, FBI agents prepared a fake letter to one dissident, Muhammed Kenyatta, that was purportedly from other students at Tougaloo College in Mississippi. The letter threatened violence if Kenyatta did not absent himself from campus. Kenyatta subsequently left the state, and the FBI agents took credit for driving him away.[49]

The death of FBI Director Hoover brought a lessening of the FBI's role as a secret partner in political propaganda. Nevertheless, the agency's propagandistic proclivities lingered in the form of the Bureau's Squad 47 which conducted illegal break-ins, mail interceptions, and wire taps during the early 1970s. The FBI's new director, L. Patrick Gray, denied approving any such measures, although his top men said that they believed they had the director's approval. Later, under the Carter Administration, the Justice Department investigated, and began prosecution of, FBI agents for illegal work. When the prosecutions commenced, FBI agents conducted a public demonstration to dramatize their charge that lower-level employees were being punished while higher-ups, who either had authorized the illegal activities or winked at them, were going scot free.[50]

As a result of Watergate-era exposures of unethical or illegal FBI programs, many believed that this sort of activity had come to an end. When the Reagan Administration's covert operations against Nicaragua were disclosed during the mid-1980s, however, charges surfaced that the FBI had returned to its old habits of covertly harassing dissident persons and groups. In this case, the targets were citizens and organizations active in opposing the Reagan Administration's efforts to aid the *Contra* rebels in Nicaragua. Documents obtained through the Freedom of Information Act revealed FBI surveillance of such mainstream organizations as the National Council of Churches, the Maryknoll Sisters, and the National Education Association.

These FBI investigations started as part of an apparently legitimate effort to discover whether the Committee in Solidarity with the People of El Salvador (CISPES) had links to any terrorism against the U.S.-backed government of El Salvador. However, rather than close down the operation when no illegal activities turned up, the FBI's leadership allowed the investigation to take a propagandistic turn. The Bureau widened its dragnet to include various individuals and groups that took public positions in opposition to the Reagan Administration's policies in Central America. The program got out of hand, arguably becoming a *de facto* harassment of persons and groups for exercising their Constitutional right to oppose government policy.

Many of the individuals investigated were college teachers or students who came to the Bureau's attention through news stories reporting the public expression of anti-Administration positions. These individuals found it intimidating to learn that the FBI was interrogating their friends as part of an investigation of "terrorism." The FBI drew particular fire for opening a file on Samantha Smith, a Maine schoolgirl. Smith had traveled to the USSR in 1983 after writing a letter to the Soviet leader, and she briefly became an international celebrity.[51]

When investigation is routinely triggered by mere advocacy, it can become an official propaganda against that selfsame advocacy. No one would question the right of the FBI to probe criminal activity by means of methods sanctioned by the courts. However, citizens rightly have complained about break-ins and mail interceptions conducted without permission from the courts. Further, it is appropriate for a democratic society to question whether harassment of dissidents by government agencies inhibits free speech and free advocacy. Even more troubling is the FBI's switch from investigation to agitation when the agency aimed to weaken dissent by planting intelligence with sympathetic journalists. These actions are neither directly connected to law enforcement nor to prosecution of criminal activity.

The Pentagon

Although progressive critics of the 1920s and 1930s occasionally looked at propaganda from the military establishment, not until the Vietnam era did the Defense Department, now grown gargantuan, come under serious scrutiny by propaganda analysts. In 1970, Senator J. William Fulbright published *The Pentagon Propaganda Machine* in which he ranged over the whole public-relations machinery of the Defense

Department. Fulbright estimated that during the preceding ten years, the Pentagon had spent $44 million for a mighty "mind-shaping machine," a sum which did not include the cost of "military aircraft, aircraft carriers, and other naval vessels used for junkets by 'civic leaders' and other VIPs." Fulbright argued that the military was overstepping its bounds by promoting an ideology of militarism combined with an "obsession about communism." For instance, he cited the DoD's sending out military officers to give speeches to the public, speeches that, often as not, purveyed a "simplistic, often outdated, and factually incorrect view of complex world problems." Fulbright also complained that the Pentagon treated its captive audience of G.I.s to censored news through the Armed Forces Radio and Television Service.[52]

Fulbright wrote his book during the height of the nation's Vietnam-era skepticism about government. The late 1960s and early 1970s was characterized particularly by a rampant disillusionment with what was called "The Military Establishment." By contrast, in 1992, the public seemed more inclined to tolerate Pentagon press relations on the basis of the practitioner's view of public-relations self-promotion as normal in organizational life. Yet, the DoD continues to come under fire for two propaganda practices: (1) official secrecy and (2) a self-serving control of information.

At what point does secrecy shift from being a necessary practice for national security to a self-serving effort to minimize criticism of military policy? The line between secrecy for national security and secrecy for public-relations purposes is a finely drawn one. Human nature being what it is, we can expect a certain amount of self-serving secrecy from any organization, especially one that sees itself as guardian of the nation's very existence. We may take as representative of the controversy between military secrecy and the public's right to know a case that occurred in 1984 when NASA's Space Shuttle deployed a sophisticated spy satellite. When news reporters began to ask about this particular shuttle mission, the Air Force prevailed upon the Associated Press and *Newsweek* to withhold reporting about the launch. When the *Washington Post* later printed a story that NASA would be launching a spy satellite, Caspar Weinberger, Secretary of Defense, branded the *Post*'s story as a case of "giving aid and comfort to the enemy." Since the Soviets probably already had as much information about the launch as was contained in the sketchy article printed by the *Post*, journalists scratched their heads about Weinberger's strong reaction. *Newsweek* magazine speculated that the Pentagon may have leaked the information for the article and later attacked the *Post* for printing the story, all as part of a ploy to embarrass NASA and win support for a new fleet of military satellite launchers.[53]

Secrecy policies in military affairs frequently mean that information about significant events comes out in dribs and drabs. A representative case in which secrecy produced gradual disclosure of information may be seen in connection with a Navy nuclear accident that occurred in 1965. An A-4E Skyhawk jet, armed with a nuclear bomb, toppled overboard during a weapons drill on a U.S. aircraft carrier, the *Ticonderoga*. The event was sensitive because the Japanese do not like U.S. ships carrying nuclear weapons to enter their ports. In 1981, the Navy had stated that the bomb lost in 1965 fell into the ocean 500 miles from land, whereas the 1989 reports located the A-bomb accident a mere 70 miles off the coast of Japan.[54]

As the *Ticonderoga* incident shows, issues of military secrecy are closely related to the military's capacity to manage information. One familiar tactic here is the self-serving way that the Pentagon deploys statistics. For instance, in 1975, the communist government of Cambodia seized a merchant ship, the *Mayaguez*. The Defense Department, mounting an operation to rescue the crew, sent in U.S. Marines and the Air Force to attack the island where the ship was being held. Casualties? The Pentagon released casualty figures slowly, each time with a slightly higher total. Eventually, DoD acknowledged that 15 men had been killed in battle. But this total did not include an additional 23 soldiers who died in a helicopter crash while en route to joining the combat team.[55] It was well for the Pentagon to keep the two figures separate because the total of 38 soldiers killed might look unfavorable in connection with an operation to rescue 39 crewmembers.

The Department of Defense often is in a position advantageously to combine its control of information with its ability to make policy proposals. In 1989, Senator Sam Nunn of Georgia, chair of the Senate Armed Services Committee, accused the Pentagon of using outdated information about Soviet military strength to justify requests for new arms appropriations. Apparently, the DoD wanted to stem calls for major military cuts that were coming in response to the fall of communist regimes in eastern Europe, the breakdown of the Soviet-led Warsaw Pact, and the decline of communism in the USSR itself.[56]

Not only has the Pentagon used information to defend its actions and requests but also it has been accused of deploying data to intimidate critics. Critics claim that the Defense Department threatens to close military bases as a means for intimidating opponents in Congress. In 1986, for instance, the Pentagon proposed closing bases in the districts of three prominent Democratic members of Congress, including House Speaker Thomas P. O'Neill, who were attacking the Reagan Administration for excessive military spending.[57]

Another arrow in the Pentagon's quiver of propaganda ploys is the power to give or withhold support for entertainment programs focusing on military themes. The 1986 movie *Top Gun* pleased the Defense Department brass and accordingly received considerable cooperation from the military. This movie starred Tom Cruise in the role of a hot-shot Navy pilot who excelled in the Top Gun training school for fighter aces. The dramatic moment of the film comes when Cruise saves the day by shooting down Russian fighter planes menacing a U.S. aircraft carrier in the Indian Ocean. After reviewing the script, the Navy pledged its assistance to the *Top Gun* film project, charging nominal fees for the use of two aircraft carriers, a naval base, a large number of F-14 jets, and other facilities.[58] When the Pentagon has been less pleased with a script, DoD has proved less helpful to film makers. In 1973, for example, the military refused to cooperate with producers of *The Cinderella Liberty* and *The Last Detail* allegedly because the brass disapproved of how the military life was portrayed in those pictures—even after the producers made certain changes requested by liaison officers.[59]

Nowhere do national security and propaganda mingle more freely than in news coverage of actual military engagements. The Pentagon seems to have convinced itself that news coverage was the major cause of U.S. military and political failures during the Vietnam War. According to this line of thinking, the military establishment erred in Vietnam by allowing news people great freedom to range over South Vietnam, filming where they wanted and interviewing whom they pleased. The problem, in the military's view, was not that the news coverage revealed any military "secrets," but, rather, that news cameras helped undermine the national will to carry on the struggle by showing a close-up view of the unglamorous gore of combat.

Academic studies of Vietnam war coverage present a somewhat different picture from the perception held in military circles. According to researchers Epstein and Hallin, American news coverage actually favored the military early in the war when journalists, few of whom spoke Vietnamese, based their reports on official briefings in Saigon and on battlefield tours conducted by the brass. Given this military-managed approach to war news, the U.S. appeared to be in control of the situation and to be making steady progress against enemies unseen except for evidences of their atrocities. Further, before the communist Tet Offensive of 1968, only 22% of film reports showed actual combat—and much of this consisted of incoming mortar rounds or distant sniper fire and bombing.

Another factor that helped keep television news from conveying a negative view of the Vietnam conflict was the editing in New York performed on film footage sent by news teams in the field. Having no direct contact with the war, and tending to accept the Johnson Administration's interpretation of Vietnam as a Cold War struggle of good *versus* evil, the news editors were not disposed to present combat action in a critical light. Editors routinely cut out scenes that were particularly gruesome, and they agonized over presenting film that even implied a criticism of America's conduct of the war. For this reason, the consternation at CBS News was considerable before that network eventually aired a filmed report by Morley Safer showing G.I.s burning peasant huts. CBS duly balanced Safer's film with expressions by spokespersons of the Johnson Administration; nevertheless, LBJ called Frank Stanton, CBS president, to protest.

The tendency to rely on official sources, to frame stories according to the prevailing Cold War assumptions, and to edit film footage closely, was broken only during the Tet Offensive of February 1968. On this occasion, the Viet Cong's attacks occurred suddenly and simultaneously all over South Vietnam, causing a chaotic situation. The rapid pace of events meant that news directors had less time either to edit the footage sent from Vietnam or to place film images in the standard Big Picture that "we're winning the war." After Tet, however, the old news patterns reasserted themselves. In fact, when the Paris peace negotiations began, news editors in New York told their Vietnam correspondents not to send combat footage. According to Robert Northshield, an NBC producer, negotiations were now the featured slant, so "combat stories seemed like a contradiction and would confuse the audience."[60]

What are we to make of academic studies claiming that Vietnam war coverage was generally presented in a framework that favored the government? Relevant to this point was a Harris poll of 1967 in which respondents indicated (64% to 26%) that TV coverage made them *more* favorable to the Vietnam War.[61] Do such studies and numbers invalidate the Pentagon's view? Not entirely, it would seem. True, the Pentagon's perspective on wartime news coverage may be overdrawn and self-serving, but the military's suspicions that combat footage reduces the public's enthusiasm for war may also be accurate. We cannot dismiss the possibility that closeup views of human beings killing each other casts a negative pall over warfare. From an administrative perspective, news coverage of war is better when combat comes across as technological rather than human, and when fighting is made to seem remote rather than close-up. To these ends, Pentagon practice since Vietnam has been to steer war coverage in directions that make the fighting appear remote and, in so far as possible, technologically antiseptic and, as the word was used during the Persian Gulf war, "surgical." This pattern clearly emerged in the Grenada operation of 1983. The Pentagon prohibited reporters from entering the island of Grenada until days after the U.S. invasion, yet the Reagan Administration denied that it had acted to interfere with news coverage. Spokespersons said that reporters were kept out of Grenada to safeguard their own security and that of the troops. The managing editors of the Associate Press took a differing view, condemning the Administration for actions that forced a news blackout. Edward Joyce, president of CBS News, testified before a House Judiciary subcommittee that the Administration's guidelines for press coverage of Grenada constituted "censorship" unprecedented in U.S. history.[62] Journalists observed that reporters might have accompanied the troops with the understanding that they would not file stories until after the Grenada operation was completed.

In a similar vein, columnist Eric Boehlert termed news coverage of the U.S. invasion of Panama (December 22, 1989) as more akin to "an army recruiting film" than to actual news.[63] Pitched street fighting went unphotographed, although the cameras of pool reporters were allowed to show helicopters in the sky and soldiers patting Panamanian youngsters. G.I.s were shown recuperating in hospitals, but less attention was given to the dead. The Pentagon was quick to provide figures on the numbers of Panamanian soldiers killed, but it had no information to share on civilian casualties.

The Pentagon's vision of the perfect TV war implies news coverage in which combat comes across as brief, remote, successful, mechanized, and relatively bloodless. These principles certainly applied to the War in the Persian Gulf. From a public-relations point of view, the war began well for President Bush when he ordered the air attack on Iraq and Kuwait on January 16, 1991. News coverage alternated between *Top Gun*-style scenes of airplanes lifting off, and optimistic (if vague) official briefings. While the hired war-experts of the networks were somewhat less euphoric than reporters stationed in the Middle East, viewers nevertheless were treated to rampant speculation on January 16 that the war might be over in a day, given the massive successes reported by the military. A favorite statistic seemed to be the claimed 80% success figure for bombing attacks, which turned out to mean nothing more than that 8 out of 10 planes had released bombs somewhere in the vicinity of the target. Favored camera shots were those selected photographs released by the military depicting laser-guided bombs precisely finding and destroying their targets. President Bush's popularity ratings soared to levels as high as the ostensible accuracy of the bombing.

Unlike the weekend wars in Grenada and Panama, however, the Persian Gulf conflict was of sufficient duration and scope to call into question the press-relations techniques favored by the Pentagon. Reporters complained that the military selected the soldiers, sailors, and airforce personnel to be interviewed, and that military censors altered stories to improve the image of the armed services. When one news reporter described the mood of pilots returning from bombing raids as "giddy," the censor substituted "proud" when dispatching the story. Another censor refused to send a report unless the film clip were altered to remove an obscenity uttered by a pilot.

While censorship rankled reporters, the American public could hardly have been described in spring 1991 as clamoring for more dogged coverage. In fact, many citizens not only expressed resentment about the attention paid by the press to war protesters but also expressed worries that live reports were betraying important military secrets. One survey taken early in the war found that 57 percent of the public wanted firmer control over media coverage of the war. This plurality found its wishes soon made manifest when the Pentagon's restrictions imparted a surreal and distant character to ground combat portrayed on American television. When 4,000 Iraqis made an unsuccessful foray into Saudi Arabia, television presented the fighting strictly as something over yonder or that was already completed.[64] Later, during the 100 hours of full-scale ground fighting, televised combat scenes showed artillery and tanks lobbing their shells toward remote targets.

Nothing could be more natural than for administrators to put the best possible face on their actions. The FBI and the Pentagon are two agencies that have special reasons for, and techniques of, image-polishing propaganda. The problem for the public is to separate what is in the long-term interest of the nation from what serves the convenience of those temporarily in charge of government. Questions of propaganda surround all governmental communication.

TWO ILLUSTRATIVE CASES

The FBI and the Pentagon stand as models of how administrative policy can become propaganda when cast in the form of doctored or controlled news. Government propaganda also may take the form of coordinated propaganda campaigns; two illustrative cases of this style of official propaganda are the Iran-*Contra* affair and the push for the Star Wars missile defense program.

Aid for the *Contras*

In 1979, a revolutionary government was established in Nicaragua by the Sandinista insurgents who overthrew the right-wing dictatorship of Anastasio Samoza. Taking a left-wing, socialistic orientation, the *Sandinista* government began to nationalize industry and to establish friendly relations with communist regimes. *Sandinista* rule prompted opposition that included old supporters of the Samoza dictatorship, prominent business people, and former anti-Samoza insurgents who had become dissatisfied with *Sandinista* policies. Some of these opponents of the *Sandinista* government banded together to begin a military rebellion. This anti-*Sandinista* military wing became known as the *Contras*. Unhappy with the left-wing policies of the *Sandinista* government, the Reagan Administration used the CIA to provide military aid to the *Contra* rebels in order to strengthen and expand the rebellion.

American aid for the *Contras* might have remained a routine Cold War operation of the CIA except for a decision of Congress to intervene. On December 21, 1982, Congress approved legislation (called the Boland Amendment after its author, Rep. Edward Boland) that barred the CIA and the Department of Defense from spending money to overthrow the government of Nicaragua. Nevertheless, the CIA proceeded with its program, irritating Congressional oversight committees with hazy and tardy notifications about various covert operations, for instance, the mining of Nicaragua's major harbor. Another sign that the

87

CIA seemed to be out of control was an agency manual prepared for the *Contras* recommending "neutralization" of highly-placed Sandinista police and judges. Former CIA director Stansfield Turner observed that "the term 'neutralization' is generally understood to mean 'assassination.'"[65]

So, in October 1984, Congress tightened the limits on *Contra* aid, adding a provision to the Fiscal Year 1985 DoD Appropriations Act prohibiting expenditure of any funds to aid the *Contras* either directly or indirectly. However, continuing its push for *Contra* aid in 1985, the Reagan Administration finally was able to secure some non-military humanitarian funds for the *Contras*. After a subsequent round of Administration lobbying, Congress completely reversed itself in June 1986; military assistance to the *Contras* was permitted anew.

Although Congress had prohibited military aid to the *Contras* in 1984-85, a covert program to provide weapons continued during this period under the auspices of the National Security Council. Rumors and unconfirmed reports about the secret pro-*Contra* campaign began to surface in fall 1986. Shortly after the 1986 elections, the Reagan Administration acknowledged that, in fact, high officials had worked to supply military aid to the *Contras* during the months when this aid was prohibited by law. By a twist worthy of a James Bond thriller, the *Contra* aid program became connected to secret U.S. arms-for-hostages deals with Iran when Reagan Administration operatives worked to shift the proceeds from these sales to the *Contras*.

Official and unofficial disclosures about the tangled Iran-*Contra* affair prompted Congress to hold hearings on the matter during summer 1987. Subsequently, Col. Oliver North and others implicated in the scandal were indicted and tried for illegal activities. Yet, even by 1993, matters of moral responsibility and legal guilt remained murky in regard to America's dealings with Iran and Nicaragua in the mid-1980s. By analogy with the U-2 episode, we may expect that the full story of the Iran-*Contra* operations will not be known until all of the key participants have retired from active politics. For their parts, both President Ronald Reagan and Vice President George Bush had denied any involvement in the planning and execution of the illegal arms shipments. When evaluated along the lines of the U-2 affair, however, available circumstantial evidence suggested that history may eventually connect officials at the highest level of the Administration to the covert *Contra* aid program.[66]

The *Contra* affair is interesting from a propaganda perspective because the covert arms shipments were surrounded with various forms of covert government persuasion. One tangent of propaganda in the *Contra* affair was the constant effort by the Reagan Administration to pressure Congress to reverse the prohibition on military aid to the *Contras*. To this end, the Administration worked to foment events that would prompt favorable news coverage of the *Contras*. Polishing the *Contras'* image was necessary because of certain blemishes attending to the group's history and conduct. The *Contras* were tarred by reports not only that many of their fighters were soldiers of the former dictator but also that the *Contras* engaged in atrocities against civilians. To promote a favorable image of the *Contras*, the Reagan Administration prompted this organization to write a constitution, portions of which guaranteed human rights and free elections. Having an official constitution made the *Contra* rebels appear more like a real government, based on civilian control, and not tied to the old dictatorship of Anastasio Samoza.[67]

The Administration's efforts to squeeze *Contra* aid from Congress also included the use of such familiar propaganda tactics as leaks and secrecy. Part of the lobbying effort to secure a $100 million aid package was to show members of Congress a secret document that detailed a Nicaraguan campaign of disinformation to defeat *Contra* aid. This tactic backfired when some members of Congress argued that it was inappropriate to circulate classified materials as part of a partisan lobbying campaign. Senator David Durenberger charged that such a ploy jeopardized intelligence sources.[68]

Not only did the Administration employ leaks and secrecy but also officials occasionally used lies to protect the operation. When Nicaraguans shot down a CIA supply plane in October 1986, CIA officials joined Reagan Administration political appointees in a conspiracy of silence during testimony before Congressional oversight committees. Asked whether the U.S. government was directly or indirectly involved in the air shipment, government officials implied that the plane had nothing to do with CIA aid for the *Contras*.[69]

Still another propagandistic ploy in the Reagan Administration's arsenal was to use Red-baiting as a weapon to weaken opponents of *Contra* aid. For example, Patrick J. Buchanan, White House aide, wrote an article in the *Washington Post* arguing that opponents of *Contra* funding would stand "with Daniel Ortega [Sandinista leader] and the communists." Members of Congress objected to the tactic. Sen. Nancy L.

Kassebaum (R., Kansas) labeled the Administration's phraseology of "good freedom fighters and evil Marxists" as a "simplistic reasoning" that was "highly offensive." Rep. Michael D. Barnes (D., Maryland) charged that the White House had been committing "the moral equivalent of McCarthyism."[70] Barnes's complaint harkened back to the effort by the late Senator Joe McCarthy of Wisconsin to tar and intimidate opponents by hurling extreme charges based on fuzzy generalizations and guilt by association. As practiced in the 1950s, McCarthyism represented a self-serving effort to cut off debate by claiming that opponents were disloyal, perhaps in league with the communists. This strategem of hurling "-ist" accusations remains distressingly familiar today in the rhetoric of contemporary rightist and leftist groups.

Part of the effort to gain government aid for the *Contras* came from right-wing pressure groups. For instance, the American Conservative Union sent out 100,000 letters alleging extreme cruelty on the part of the Sandinistas, and the ACU arranged for anti-Sandinista Nicaraguan refugees to visit members of Congress.[71] Opponents of *Contra* aid also were active on the propaganda front. For instance, the Washington Office on Latin America published a report accusing the *Contras* of atrocities. This report was prepared with assistance of the law firm that represented the Nicaraguan government in the U.S.[72]

Star Wars

Beginning in 1983, the Reagan Administration pushed for the Strategic Defense Initiative (SDI) program on the basis that this anti-missile system would be the ultimate solution to problems of national security. Popularly known as Star Wars, the space-based defense system was controversial from the first. Was the SDI system workable? Was it good policy? Whatever one's position on SDI, it was clear that the propaganda features of the program flew high and were all but impenetrable.

It is common in modern political life for leaders to conduct debate on the basis of information provided by specialists in various fields. These specialists offer advice, but they do not normally control political debate. The American tradition is to have the expert *on tap* but not *on top*. The technical complexities of the Star Wars debate, however, seemed almost to require reversing the normal order of politician and expert. Space-based missile defense systems were not simply matters of how many troops to call up or how many airplanes to build. Because the issues were more high-tech and remote, politicians seemed to lack clout in debating the merits of SDI. Elected leaders seemed wont to defer to scientists and engineers. Due to the technical character of the Star Wars debate, politicians sometimes seemed irrelevant. With the debate centering on criteria of technology rather than politics, the main issue increasingly became the question of whether Star Wars would work, not whether the new weapons system might destabilize the balance of world power or whether it would needlessly militarize outer space. Even the issue of cost could be pushed aside, for the initial research expenses for Star Wars were relatively small compared to other weapons programs. Finally, it was easy for Star Wars supporters to weaken political opponents with the charge that they were crazy to oppose research on a system that, although not currently feasible, just might work in the future.

For many reasons, therefore, the technical perspective on SDI made questions of "how to do it" seem more important than "why to do it." The dream of a high-tech security system in the heavens brought the American can-do attitude and movie-based notions of space weaponry to bear on traditional ideas of national security and contemporary fears of missile attack. This mental juggernaut transformed even equivocal information about the program into seemingly logical and persuasive arguments for it. In this spirit, Caspar Weinberger, Secretary of Defense, defended the program with these words in October 1985: "We do not yet know whether a thoroughly capable defense system can be established; so prudence demands that we not allow the dangerous gap between our triad [land-, air-, and sea-based weapons] and the growing Soviet nuclear force to widen."[73]

When Star Wars became less a matter for political debate and more a matter of technical efficiency, an opening was made for propagandistic communication. Much of the Star Wars propaganda took the form of the Administration transforming (seemingly) objective research into a partisan weapon. For one thing, the Reagan forces were in a good position to influence debate on SDI through lucrative defense contracts to researchers. When a program is promoted under such terms as "national defense" and is backed by big research money, the endeavor becomes hard to oppose. By 1986, more than 10,000 engineers and scientists were researching the Star Wars system. Spending included $2 billion for research projects and around $3 billion for weapons development and testing. At this time, the government was projecting expenditures of $26 billion over four years.

91

Although the Star Wars program provided considerable money for researchers, opposition grew in the scientific community against this controversial program. Many scientific skeptics viewed the SDI system as a boondoggle, at best, and, at worst, as a dangerous militarization of outer space. Comments by John Gourlay, computer science faculty member at Ohio State University, are representative: "It's so pitifully obvious to a computer scientist that the computer concept of the system is beyond the reach of our foreseeable science." Some researchers began to air their questions about the program, prompting a true public debate among scientists and engineers. Scientists at the University of Illinois and at Cornell began to circulate a petition in which signers pledged not to participate in Star Wars work. By March 1986, the anti-SDI petition campaign had gathered 3,200 signatures from professors in math, computer science, physics, and engineering, as well as 2,200 more from graduate students.[74]

Notwithstanding the enthusiasm and sense of mission of the anti-Star Wars researchers, it was unreasonable to expect that more than a small number of scientists would risk opposing a government-sponsored research program. In fact, during the year 1985-1986, the Office of Innovative Technology and Science, which administered the Strategic Defense Initiative, received over 3,500 research proposals from professors interested in Star Wars work. From a scientist's point of view, why hurt one's career by abstaining from exciting, well-funded, cutting-edge research? Why get a reputation for being picky about research money? Even pacifist scientists wondered why they should rock the boat when the SDI program was years away from the direct deployment of weapons. Another rationalization for pacifists was the possibility that Star Wars would prove unworkable, in which case the scientists would have conducted only basic research that might in other ways benefit humanity.

James A. Ionson, director of the SDI Office of Innovative Technology and Science, nicely summarized the lure of Star Wars work to upwardly mobile scientists: "Our goal is to search for concepts and technology perceived to be in the 21st century and then to perform the fundamental research to pull that into the 20th century." But John Pike of the Federation of American Scientists countered by saying that the Administration merely was buying support among scientists by parceling out small grants to researchers at schools across the country.

For a number of reasons, therefore, Star Wars contracts seemed to be a safe gravy train for researchers, whereas opposition appeared alternately risky and useless. After all, thousands were already at work, and the Reagan Administration was deeply committed to the program. From a psychological point of view, the SDI program appealed to the American go-getting spirit. Further, for scientists who publicly opposed Star Wars there was the danger of McCarthyism. Julie Franklin, an Ohio State University physics graduate student, believed that many scientists who refused her requests to sign the anti-Star Wars pledge held back due to fears of being attacked in a new wave of Red-baiting.

Even if most academic engineers and scientists had refused involvement in Star Wars, the research program would have proceeded apace in the private sector. The government was letting out a high percentage of SDI contracts to private companies and research corporations. In the private sector, which depends heavily on federal contract funds, sentiments to oppose research for national defense were almost choked off from the start. Joe Brown, manager of the Battelle Institute's Defense Systems Department, acknowledged the strong arguments against the feasibility of the SDI program, but, he added, "We take our defense work as a matter of course and of normal business. We certainly don't have any sentiment against defense here."[75] Another advantage to the government in using private research companies was that the private sector has little compunction against classifying research findings as secret. Academic scholars resist secrecy as a matter of principle and also because they desire the fame that comes with their discoveries and research.

Participants in Star Wars research risked becoming propagandists if, in the interest of securing grants, they hid their doubts about the program and provided secret research data to sponsors. The key question of propaganda in the SDI operation was the tendency for research to make the scientific debate artificially one-sided. Proponents of Star Wars had direct access to research findings; further, they had freedom to use classified information at will to promote the program in public debate. In contrast, opponents of SDI were in a riskier position in discussing the program. Sen. Charles Mathias (R., Maryland) observed that "many scientists who question the significance of the results [of SDI X-ray laser tests] are afraid that they will be accused of compromising national secrets if they speak out, while those in charge of pushing the program are free to do so."[76] Mathias suspected that the much-promoted successes of SDI's lasers were inflated or even staged. Wanting another opinion, members of Congress asked the General Accounting Office to investigate the whole matter.

Fears in Congress about a propagandistic use of Star Wars research had arisen in 1985 when accusations were launched about efforts to hype the results of weapons tests. Frustrated at what they viewed as the covering up of weapons test failures, two high officials at the weapons labs at Livermore and Los Alamos resigned. One of them, Ray Kidder, a Livermore physicist, was quoted as complaining that "the public is getting swindled" by the way information was released. He explained that the pro-SDI side "has access to classified information and can say whatever it wants and not go to jail, whereas we [the skeptics] can't say whatever we want. We would go to jail."[77] John S. Herrington, Secretary of Energy, denounced Kidder and the other scientist skeptics for harming national security through their complaints about SDI research.

The controversy over Star Wars research may outlive the Reagan/Bush era, given that major military programs seem to have a life of their own. For his part, Reagan held out hopes for an impenetrable shield in the sky to guard against the ultimate nuclear nightmare. The Bush Administration scaled back the program, envisioning a system that would protect against small nuclear strikes mounted by a country like Iraq rather than a super power. Vice President Dan Quayle went so far as to characterize the original Star Wars plan as including much unrealistic "political jargon."[78] Live TV coverage of missile attacks against Saudi Arabia and Israel during the Persian Gulf War may help maintain the political appeal of a high-tech missile defense program.

GOVERNMENT PROPAGANDA *VERSUS* PUBLIC INFORMATION

The right to govern presupposes the duty to inform. Government's need to act in the public interest carries the obligation to help citizens understand their socio-political world. Yet, propaganda lurks in the fissures between action and information. The possibility for official policy and communication to propagandize the public applies to all Washington agencies, not just to the FBI and the Pentagon, and to all campaigns of information, not merely those pertaining to the *Contras* or Star Wars. Coupled with the seeming inevitability of propaganda issues in governmental communication is the seductive character of some official propagandas. It is not difficult to find cases in which many citizens support what might otherwise be labeled as a questionable propaganda by government.

Anti-Smoking Propaganda?

Nowhere is the seductive character of propaganda more in evidence than with regard to federal efforts to reduce the incidence of smoking. Many, if not most, Americans would see an executive-branch effort to reduce smoking as nothing more than enlightened public service. However, James J. Kilpatrick, conservative Virginia newspaper columnist, was one of a small group of others who termed the federal anti-smoking campaign "Big Brotherism." Does the popularity of a government information program mitigate a propagandistic effect?

Kilpatrick's objection to federal anti-smoking efforts dated back to the early policy of the Federal Trade Commission to require warning labels listing the tar and nicotine levels of tobacco products. Kilpatrick argued that the government had already publicized the health impact of smoking. Hence, he believed, the FTC proposals were an unjustifiably redundant effort that represented questionable persuasion more than neutral information.[79]

The question of whether federal anti-smoking efforts amounted to propaganda became more pronounced during the Carter Administration. Joseph Califano, Carter's Secretary of Health, Education, and Welfare, established the U.S. Office of Smoking and Health with $4.5 million budgeted for anti-smoking educational efforts. While this federal anti-smoking effort was gearing up, a researcher at the National Cancer Institute, Dr. Gio B. Gori, released a report indicating that smoking a relatively small number of low-tar cigarettes was "tolerable" from a health standpoint.[80] Gori's conclusion applied only to the extremely low-tar products (2% of all cigarettes sold); however, the tobacco companies took up this analysis, arguing that Gori's findings justified the industry's position that "the scientific evidence does not prove that smoking causes human disease."[81] Since Gori's conclusion was inconsistent with the Carter Administration's general anti-smoking effort, his data were attacked by HEW and by the American Cancer Institute. For his part, Gori claimed that his superiors at the National Cancer Institute were under pressure from Califano to fire him, although Institute officials denied feeling any pressure.

Was Califano's anti-smoking program a useful program of public health education or was it one-sided propaganda? Many citizens might not bother to ask such a question; after all, people today feel free to interrupt perfect strangers to remind them about the health hazards of smoking. Nonetheless, even though the U.S. government's anti-cigarette campaign enjoyed considerable public support, popularity did not exempt this governmental information program from questions of propagandistic practices. Even so, judged from the criterion of general public interest, anti-smoking efforts seem benign even in the light of Kilpatrick's complaint of overzealous federal paternalism and Gori's charges of behind-the-scenes administrative finagling. Nonetheless, the accusations of Kilpatrick and Gori are warnings that citizens need to remain alert to the possibility that a public service initiative might become a one-sided propaganda vehicle for true believers.

Propaganda in Civil Defense?

If propaganda issues suffuse popular information programs, they also accompany such routine official programs as civil defense. Granted that many people today view anti-smoking efforts as noncontroversial education, would not most intelligent citizens during the 1950s have made the same judgment about the federal atomic fallout safety program? In the case of civil defense in the Eisenhower era, however, both an absence of perspective and a lack of information retarded the ability of Americans to detect possible veins of propaganda in this mountain of government action.

Government films of the 1940s and 1950s gave information about nuclear war combined with soothing reassurances on the subject of successful civil defense. Americans were advised to duck and cover, to wash what was contaminated, and then simply to continue with their ordinary lives. In one film, a father reassured his children after a nearby nuclear blast that "there's nothing to do now but wait for the authorities and relax."[82]

Today, it is common for intellectuals to dismiss the federal civil defense efforts of the Cold War as a form of propaganda to support nuclear weapons. The argument goes something like this: By making citizens believe that they could survive a nuclear war, the U.S. government subtly put across an overly optimistic view of nuclear war as something rational and manageable. The endeavor to present atomic war as acceptable was a useful propaganda to reinforce a military strategy based on nuclear deterrence. Hence, the argument runs, civil-defense rhetoric helped policy makers to preclude any ban-the-bomb sentiments that might have disrupted the Pentagon's contingency preparations for World War III.

How might citizens of the 1950s have acquired either sufficient information or the angle of perception necessary to view civil-defense efforts as a propaganda for nuclear weapons? Many nuclear experts of the day themselves underestimated the dangers of radiation. Ordinary citizens could hardly have risen above the common wisdom of the period enough to have branded the civil-defense films as propaganda rather than education. Even today, not everyone would accept the interpretation that official optimism about nuclear war represented a kind of propaganda. In fact, the U.S. government continues to express reassuring views about a post-thermonuclear world. For example, a 1982 working paper of the Federal Emergency Management Agency argued that American agriculture would be able to call upon sufficient land and workers to supply the needs of the population. Some of this optimism, as columnist Ellen Goodman pointed out, stemmed from the assumption that "those who are doomed to die will be consumers for [only] part of that time."[83]

The Difficulty of Detecting Government Propaganda

Another case illustrating the difficulty in separating government propaganda from public education may be seen in the Cold War-era policies of the Atomic Energy Commission. The AEC concealed both the occurrence of radiation leaks at government nuclear plants and the health records of nuclear workers. Relatively few citizens challenged the AEC's policy of secrecy, which was calculated to prevent public alarm during the Cold War. Further, the atom agency was able to report the general unavailability of specific studies of the health effects of radiation. In retrospect, it seems callous for the AEC to have allowed citizens to be exposed to radiation without at least giving more of a warning. Nevertheless, since the nativity of nuclear arms came during the crisis years of the early Cold War, citizens faced a double obstacle to securing necessary information to challenge official policy.

Similar questions about detecting propaganda may be raised in connection with Secretary of State Alexander Haig's accusation in 1981 that the Vietnamese government was using biological weapons in its invasion of Cambodia. Even in 1983, when Thomas Seeley of Yale, an independent scientist, publicized contradictory findings, it was far from clear where the truth lay. Seeley argued that the government's chemical samples were not residues of the chemical agent called "yellow rain," but rather represented the excrement of wild honey bees. The Reagan Administration was able to scoff at this seemingly bizarre finding. It took four more years for the issue to come to any closure. In 1987, scientists obtained through the Freedom of Information Act certain declassified documents showing that the Reagan Administration had made its charges about biological warfare on the basis of flimsy evidence. Apparently, Army chemists themselves were unable to validate Haig's charges about the use of chemical weapons against Cambodia.[84] "Yellow rain" may well have been bee droppings.

It is relatively easy to summon up the moral outrage to condemn governmental propaganda, especially years after the events have taken place. We must keep in mind, however, that propaganda probably is inevitable in a representative democracy where government enjoys a wide latitude to act but is periodically held accountable to voters. The democratic requirement that governments communicate with citizens also may imply a rhetorical right for officials to make the strongest possible case in favor of their positions. After all, when citizens elect a government, they expect it to take action. If our national administrators have any vision or spunk, we expect them to use the available resources to win support for their policy initiatives. If we expect leaders to take action, then is it unreasonable to believe that they will behave naively in communications with the public. Making the most of one's situation is basic to human nature. Unless we select public servants for their piety and saintly qualities, we should expect to find propaganda serving as an arm of administrative government. For reasons of institutional mission and human inclination we must expect that distortion—accentuating the positive and minimizing the negative—will continue to be a part of the (dis)informational environment even of democratic societies.

Detection and analysis of government propaganda demand more than moral vehemence and intellectual vigilance. When we reflect over the Carter-era anti-smoking campaign, the civil defense programs of the 1950s, the Cold War-era policies of nuclear plant secrecy, and Secretary Haig's charges about "yellow rain," we realize that in each case necessary information was unavailable at least to ordinary citizens and probably to experts. In these episodes, successful propaganda analysis would have required not only heightened levels of information but also the will to challenge official policies that either were popular or were widely viewed as necessary.

Given that propaganda analysis requires both high-level information and heroic outspokenness, citizens may find their interests better served by transforming chronic indignation and suspicion into regular participation in public life. It may prove the case that effective propaganda analysis requires less of a detached critical analysis and more of a regular involvement in political and social life. Alert citizens active in voluntary associations and local doings may prove to be the firmest foundation for the systematic unmasking of propaganda.

ENDNOTES

1. *San Jose Mercury News*, 9/22/89: 14A.

2. Cf. Christopher Hanson, "Mr. Clinton's Neighborhood," *Columbia Journalism Review*, May/June 1993, p. 21; and Aristotle, *The Rhetoric*, 1.1 and 2.1.

3. Maureen Dowd, *San Jose Mercury News*, 5/9/93: 20A.

4. *San Jose Mercury News*, 8/7/93: 1A, 12A.

5. Louisville, KY *Courier-Journal*, 7/3/85: A1.

6. See *New York Times*, 4/4/89: A10.

7. *San Jose Mercury News*, 4/2/89: 22A.

8. Harold W. Stoke, "Executive Leadership and the Growth of Propaganda," *American Political Science Review* 35 (1941): 490-500.

9. Jacques Ellul, *Propaganda* (New York: Knopf, 1965): 118ff, 181ff, 250ff.

10. Michael R. Beschloss, *May-Day* (New York: Harper and Row, 1986).

11. *Newsweek*, 3/3/86: 80; *New York Times*, 11/14/88: A9.

12. See David Halberstam, *The Powers That Be* (New York: Knopf, 1979): 490.

13. William E. Porter, *Assault on the Media: The Nixon Years* (Ann Arbor: University of Michigan Press, 1976): 44-46.

14. Spiro T. Agnew, "Television News Coverage," in *American Rhetoric: From Roosevelt to Reagan*, ed. H. R. Ryan (2nd ed.; Prospect Heights, IL: Waveland, 1987): 212-219.

15. Quotations from *Newsweek*, 4/5/71: 54.

16. Odessa, TX *Odessa American*, 2/17/74: 10.

17. Stanton in *Newsweek*, 4/5/71: 54; Porter, *Assault on Media*: 244.

18. Porter, *Assault on Media*: 268, 271.

19. *San Francisco Chronicle*, 4/9/88: A8.

20. *Chronicle of Higher Education*, 6/20/84: 11.

21. *San Francisco Chronicle*, 10/4/88: A7.

22. *New York Times*, 10/5/88: A1, A14.

23. Louisville, KY *Courier-Journal*, 6/29/78: A3.

24. General sources regarding secrecy practices of the Reagan Administration include the following: American Civil Liberties Union, *Civil Liberties Alert*, May 1983; Frederick W. Whatley, "Reagan, National Security, and the First Amendment: Plugging Leaks by Shutting Off the Main," *Policy Analysis* (Cato Institute), May 8, 1984; Louisville, KY *Courier-Journal*, 6/15/84: A3; 3/26/85: A5; 3/28/85: A3; Anthony Lewis column, 2/20/85: A9; *Chronicle of Higher Education*, 3/30/88: A1, A26.

25. William Safire, Louisville, KY *Courier-Journal*, 1/23/84: A7.

26. *San Jose Mercury News*, 2/10/89: 1A.

27. *San Francisco Chronicle*, 10/4/88: A14.

28. *San Jose Mercury News*, 7/13/90: 8A.

29. *New York Times*, 5/3/90: A14.

30. *San Francisco Chronicle*, 8/29/88: A7.

31. *New York Times*, 12/11/89: A15.

32. Robert J. Wagman, Palo Alto, CA *Peninsula Times Tribune*, 7/28/87: A11.

33. *Newsweek*, 12/16/84: 35.

34. Palo Alto, CA *Peninsula Times Tribune*, 10/19/87: A9.

35. *San Francisco Chronicle*, 10/2/86: 1, 17; *Newsweek*, 10/13/86: 43, 44, 46.

36. *San Francisco Chronicle*, 10/9/86: 1, 22; 10/15/86: C3.

37. Porter, *Assault on Media*: 41, 160.

38. *San Francisco Chronicle*, 3/24/88: A2.

39. *Denver Post*, 11/10/85:1.

40. *Chronicle of Higher Education*, 1/16/85: 25. See also *New York Times*, 6/1/89: A8.

41. Louisville, KY *Courier-Journal*, 2/26/83: A3; *San Francisco Chronicle*, 4/29/87: 8.

42. Palo Alto, CA *Peninsula Times Tribune*, 9/14/88: A6; *San Francisco Chronicle*, 1/6/88: A13.

43. *San Francisco Chronicle*, 10/7/86: 11.

44. *Newsweek*, 3/10/75: 84.

45. Louisville, KY *Courier-Journal*, 6/25/78: A14; Kenneth O' Reilly, *Hoover and the Un-Americans: The FBI, HUAC, and the Red Menace* (Philadelphia: Temple University Press, 1983): 200, 212.

46. Thomas C. Reeves, *The Life and Times of Joe McCarthy: A Biography* (New York: Stein and Day, 1982): 499-502.

47. *Hearings Regarding Communist Infiltration of the Motion Picture Industry*, Hearings, Committee on Un-American Activities, 80th Cong., 1st Sess., Oct 20-24, 27-30, 1947 (Washington: Government Printing Office , 1947): 10 .

48. O'Reilly, *Hoover and Un-Americans*: 6ff, 80ff.

49. Anthony Lewis, Louisville, KY *Courier-Journal*, 6/14/84: A15.

50. *Newsweek*, 5/30/77: 28.

51. *Newsweek*, 2/8/88: 29; *Chronicle of Higher Education*, 2/10/88: A1, A13; *USA Today*, 2/28-3/2/86: 3A.

52. J. William Fulbright, *The Pentagon Propaganda Machine* (New York: Vintage Books, 1970): 13-15, 27, 41, 46.

53. *Newsweek*, 12/31/84: 34.

54. *San Jose Mercury News*, 5/11/89: 2A.

55. Odessa, TX *Odessa American*, 5/22/75: 8B.

56. *San Jose Mercury News*, 12/13/89: 13A.

57. Louisville, KY *Courier-Journal*, 2/18/86: A6.

58. Louisville, KY *Courier-Journal*, 6/8/86: I5.

59. Odessa, TX *Odessa American*, 12/19/73: 11C.

60. Daniel C. Hallin, *The "Uncensored War": The Media and Vietnam* (New York: Oxford University Press, 1986): 126-134; Edward J. Epstein, *Between Fact and Fiction* (New York: 1975): 210-232.

61. Epstein, *Fact and Fiction*: 212.

62. Louisville, KY *Courier-Journal*, 12/3/83: A10.

63. Eric Boehlert, *New York Times*, 1/17/90: A19.

64. *San Jose Mercury News*, 1/25/91: 18A; 1/31/91: 12A.

65. *Newsweek*, 5/20/85: 79.

66. Theodore Draper, *New York Review of Books*, 1/19/89: 38ff, and Draper, *New York Review of Books*, 8/17/89: 54ff; New York Times, *The Tower Commission Report* [President's Special Review Board] (New York: Random House, 1987.)

67. Louisville, KY *Courier-Journal*, 6/10/85: A4.

68. Louisville, KY *Courier-Journal*, 2/21/86: A3.

69. Lars-Erik Nelson, Palo Alto, CA *Peninsula Times Tribune*, 8/27/87: A15.

70. Louisville, KY *Courier-Journal*, 3/7/86: A1.

71. Louisville, KY *Courier-Journal*, 4/16/85: A7.

72. *Newsweek*, 3/18/85: 32.

73. *Capitol Magazine* (of *Columbus Dispatch*), 5/4/86: 14.

74. *Capitol Magazine* (of *Columbus Dispatch*), 5/4/86: 11.

75. *Capitol Magazine* (of *Columbus Dispatch*), 5/4/86: 13.

76. Flora Lewis, Louisville, KY *Courier-Journal*, 1/16/86: A11.

77. Flora Lewis, Louisville, KY *Courier-Journal*, 12/4/85: A15.

78. *San Jose Mercury News*, 9/7/89: 1A.

79. Odessa, TX *Odessa American*, 3/27/75: 6C.

80. Louisville, KY *Courier-Journal*, 8/24/78: A11; 8/11/78: A1, A12.

81. *Tobacco Talk*, publication of Brown and Williamson Tobacco Co., August 1978: 6.

82. Louisville, KY *Courier-Journal*, 7/21/82: C4.

83. Louisville, KY *Courier-Journal*, 12/9/83: A23.

84. *San Francisco Chronicle*, 8/25/87: 15.

Esperanza

SOUTH BAY SANCTUARY COVENANT
St. Ann Chapel (415) 326-1903
1247 Cowper Street, Palo Alto CA 94301

"When a stranger sojourns with you in your land, you shall not do him wrong ...you shall love him as yourself; for you were strangers in the land of Egypt." Leviticus 19:33-34.

MAY - JUNE 1989

IS SANCTUARY LEGAL OR ILLEGAL?

This question was definitively answered by JIM CORBETT, one of the Tuscon co-founders of the Sanctuary Movement, when he spoke at Stanford on March 15. Jim gave the final lecture in the "International Refugee Crisis" class taught by LISE GRANDE and HERB SCHMIDT of South Bay Sanctuary Covenant. In his opinion, Sanctuary has remained vital despite government harassment because it has provided ordinary people with the means to uphold US law even when our own government has consistently broken it. Corbett is widely recognized as the author of Civil Initiative, the new strategy for organizing communities on the basis of the legal argument established during the Nuremburg trials that individual citizens and communities of people are obligated to uphold international standards of just behavior despite governmental orders to the contrary. Corbett applies the Nuremburg principles to US refugee law and concludes that Sanctuary volunteers are actually UPHOLDING US and international law whereas the US government is guilty of breaking it. This interpretation of Sanctuary's legality directly challenges governmental authorities who claim that Sanctuary volunteers break the law when they assist undocumented refugees. At the heart of this debate is the US's 1980 Refugee Act. The Act states that a refugee is one who: "owing to a well-founded fear of being persecuted for reasons of race, religion, nationality, membership of a particular social group or political opinion, is outside the country of his nationality and is unable or, owing to such a fear, is unwilling to return to it."

Corbett and other Sanctuary workers argue that many Central Americans seeking asylum are refugees according to the 1980 Refugee Act. The government on the other hand, claims that the vast majority of Central Americans are economic migrants who are coming to the US for better jobs and who therefore do not qualify as refugees. The government has been criticized for its treatment of Central American refugees by countless organizations, its Allies, and most importantly by its own Supreme Court. Despite this criticism, there are few organizations actively attempting to uphold the law. Of these, the most successful is Sanctuary.

Here in the South Bay, our local Covenant is in the process of creating an affirmative filing project in conjunction with lawyers in San Jose and San Francisco. The purpose of the project is to provide refugees with legal counsel so that they can make informed decisions about whether or not to apply for political asylum. By helping, refugees file for political asylum, we are simultaneously upholding the 1980 Refugee Act, responding to our international obligations under the Nuremburg mandate, and assisting people who desperately need our help.

Liberal Churches *vs.* Reagan on Immigration

CHAPTER 3

PROPAGANDA IN THE TWO RS: RESEARCH AND RELIGION

Science and religion represent systems of knowledge that, by definition, are connected to higher principles. It is no accident that both academic researchers and theological doctors are entitled to wear medieval robes signifying their initiation into institutions of a higher calling. The claims to infallibility of scholarly research are rooted in the scientist's quest for objective truth and knowledge. The elevated status of religion derives from alleged transcendent moral principles that arise from a divine dimension.

Research and religion both claim a level of independent integrity and purpose that would place them above sweaty politics and self-serving promotionalism. Yet, the historical record shows instances of scholarly inquiry and religious expression alike becoming channels of propaganda, serving the interests of administrators, partisans, and pressure artists. War often supplies the context linking both religion and research to political society. From the first time that someone prayed "praise the Lord and pass the ammunition," to the high-tech research for Star Wars, religion and research have become the right and left hands of societies battling outside enemies. In 1918, socialist Eugene V. Debs railed against religion's fidelity to the call to arms, proclaiming that "when Wall Street says 'war,' every pulpit in the land yells 'war.'"[1] Debs would not have been surprised to find physicists later spearheading a crash program to give America the atomic bomb. Even when they are subtle and hard to detect, propagandas based on the Two Rs represent important sources of social belief and political action.

PRESSURES ON RESEARCHERS

Our image of the independent researcher is of the academic engineer, scientist, social scientist, or humanist working in the antiseptic laboratory or ivy-wrapped tower. Faculty researchers at American colleges and universities are supposed to be independent. Academic tenure is defended as necessary to assure that researchers do not yield to political pressures to modify or hide the results of scholarly study. Because most academicians are pictured as floating above the fray, the mass media invariably turn to academics for expert comment on fast-breaking news developments. "When you're looking for an opinion that is trustworthy, you go to the campus because it is perceived as having credibility," said M. Frederic Volkmann, director of public relations at Washington University at St. Louis.In fact, scholars regularly appear on network news shows. Shortly after Rajiv Gandhi became the Prime Minister of India, a University of Chicago professor of political science, Susanne H. Rudolph, appeared on the MacNeil/Lehrer NewsHour to assess Gandhi's leadership abilities. During the 1984 presidential debate season, two academic debate coaches, J. W. Patterson of Kentucky and Thomas Goodnight of Northwestern, appeared on the CBS Morning News as commentators.[2]

The Problem of Sponsorship

Although highly-educated intellectuals and scientists are sought as independent experts, their freedom of inquiry is nonetheless buffeted from many directions. The most immediate limitation on the autonomy of researchers is their need for financial support. Research, especially in the natural and physical sciences, is expensive and requires sponsorship; this necessity ties scholars to outside interests. Granting agencies that commission and support investigations also may want to use the findings for political purposes.

The political philosopher Walter Lippmann was one of the first to recognize the danger that research information could be used for purposes of propaganda. Lippmann believed that administrative governments would increasingly apply political criteria in support of research, and he feared that biased data would distort reality and bring about disastrous policies. Lippmann proposed establishment of independent research bureaus to be organized around an "institutional safeguard" whereby "the staff which executes" would be kept separate from "the staff which investigates."[3] Since Lippmann's day, charges of tainted research have been leveled not only against government agencies but also against research sponsors from business and industry.

The first significant public recognition of propaganda in research came during the late 1920s when the Federal Trade Commission investigated efforts by the electrical power industry to manipulate public debate on power-plant ownership. The FTC found that national and state representatives of the National Electric Light Association (NELA) provided retainers to a number of college faculty members for study and consultation. The FTC believed that professors owed the public an "unbiased and scientific attitude of mind" when these academic researchers compared private versus public ownership of utility corporations. The FTC held that covert contacts between scholars and industrial organizations were inherently detrimental because politically motivated support could be expected to generate biased research findings.[4]

The NELA affair brought into public view the dilemma of the modern researcher. On the one hand, the investigator needs direct contact with real-world organizations and problems. On the other hand, when a researcher keeps close contact with outside interest groups, that person is less in a position to claim independence.

Prompted by the FTC investigation, the American Association of University Professors (AAUP) probed the growing link between academic researchers and outside sponsors. The AAUP acknowledged that contacts between college faculties and businesses were a natural and inevitable circumstance whenever professors conducted research work in the community. But the AAUP emphasized that contacts between investigator and sponsor should be open and honest so that the public would not lose confidence in the independence of scholars and teachers. For instance, the AAUP noted the risk posed by outside funding when the research dealt with politically-tinged questions such as labor relations and fair taxation of business. "If an individual knows that his investigations are being financed by a particular enterprise, it is only human nature to give it at least the benefit of any doubt."[5]

The Value-Laden Nature of Research

The impulse to look for suspicious connections between researchers and sponsors springs from an underlying recognition that research can never be value free. Even when researchers try to identify objective conditions and causes, their findings necessarily support some ideas and some perspectives in preference to others. The result is to tie the research, implicitly if not explicitly, to social and political values. The impact of policy assumptions on research may be observed in a survey of Black workers in South Africa conducted by a South African university and partially funded by the U.S. Department of State. The survey results showed that the workers rejected, by a considerable margin, the idea of withdrawing foreign investment in South Africa as a strategy to defeat *apartheid*. Supporters of divestment immediately attacked the study for its having been partly supported by the U.S. government, which opposed divestment.[6] Proponents of divestment were immediately suspicious of an alliance between the U.S. State Department and South African researchers, both of whom might gain advantages from propagandized findings.

Closer analysis of the South African disvestment survey reveals two further ways in which the results raised troubling political questions. First, the findings gathered by the survey could never have been "neutral" even assuming that they were accurate. Data showing that South African Blacks opposed divestment inevitably would become a useful weapon for the political opponents of divestment policies. Research findings always constitute a potential propaganda weapon.

Further, a critic of opinion polling might well argue that the inherent framework of the South African study was unfavorable to the leadership of Black workers. Use of a survey methodology presupposes that the true opinion of workers is best measured by having them respond individually to questions that are asked in a neutral frame of reference. Leaders of workers' organizations represent an alternate source of information about the opinions of workers. In this connection, the council of the Federation of South African Trade Unions earlier had taken a position in favor of divestment. Clearly one propaganda implication of the South African opinion study would be the underlying assumption that summaries of individual, spur-of-the-moment, context-impoverished responses by workers should carry more weight than the expressed, official positions of working-class leaders. The questions that researchers ask, and the methods they use, tie the scientist to one side or another of a social question.

How Sponsors Influence Researchers

Because scientific information has political uses, anyone who funds research prefers to know in advance what directions the data are likely to take. Institutions that sponsor research have an incentive to steer inquiry along certain lines and away from others. Sometimes the political agenda of those who support the research is explicit. For instance, Donald A. Hicks, Under- Secretary of Defense in charge of research, argued that scientists who publicly criticized the Reagan Administration's Strategic Defense Initiative program should not receive research money. "They are free to keep their mouths shut," Hicks said, and "I'm also free not to give the money." Hicks believed that he should discourage scientifically based public criticism of Star Wars because, as he said, "I'm trying to save the country from the Soviet Union."[7]

Other instances of research overtly politicized by the sponsor are abundant. In 1980, for example, the administration of Jimmy Carter pressured federal education officials to fund an $800,000 award to Atlanta University. After a conversation between Carter and Atlanta University trustee Martin Luther King, Sr., a White House staffer called Assistant Secretary Mary F. Berry and asked her to approve the grant. Without White House intervention, it is unlikely that education officials would have funded Atlanta University's grant proposal, inasmuch as the school had not given an adequate account of how earlier grant money had been spent.[8]

A similar incident of basing grants on political considerations took place in 1990, when Richard Nixon said that his new presidential library, administered by a private foundation, would use a political test in admitting researchers. Nixon stated that his library would not be open to "irresponsible journalists," such as Bob Woodward, whose articles on the Nixon Administration had helped expose the Watergate scandal. Although Nixon later reversed himself on the issue, the episode shows that politics and research are ever linked in the minds of institutional leaders.[9]

While overt political considerations sometimes affect which research gets funded, grant agencies normally exert a more subtle influence on research. Agencies steer researchers by making money more available in problem areas that policy makers currently view as most pressing. Thomas C. Greaves, dean of social and behavioral sciences at Trinity University, explained that "scholars, especially in the social sciences, follow society." He added: "During the Vietnam War, we talked about war and revolution; during the civil-rights era, about voting rights and integration. Now, because of problems in the economy, we are looking at work."[10]

Whether direct or indirect, the pressure placed on researchers seems to be almost a universal of modern life. Whether the impetus for research is war, voting, or efficiency in the work place, society's official funding agencies have an agenda in mind when they offer to support researchers. Research is loaded in advance with the viewpoints, interests, or ideologies of sponsors.

RESEARCHING FOR NATIONAL SECURITY

Ellul's paradox of the simultaneous need for, and danger of, propaganda[11] is nowhere more obvious than in research for national security. Few would deny the responsibility of government to fund studies to bolster national defense, but the service of scientists to national security still raises troubling questions of propaganda.

The Size of the Defense Research Machine

A researcher's idea of utopia might include funding available for every interesting question regardless of its immediate ideological, political, or practical implication. Historically, the strength of American research has been the availability of support for researchers to conduct what is called "basic " research, that is, research that seeks fundamental information not tied to immediate practical objectives.

Social critics worry that America's commitment to basic research will decline because of an increasing effort by research managers to channel money and talent into those problems viewed as having immediate political or corporate pay-offs. The issue of basic research versus administratively-managed research is not merely technical, argued Robert Crease, a science historian, and Nicholas Samios, Director of the Brookhaven National Laboratory: "At a time of widespread lamentations about the loss of U.S. technological competitiveness, it is ironic that we are destroying one of the most important means by which we established that technological competitiveness in the first place."[12]

Not only is scientific inquiry increasingly managed for immediate administrative purposes, but also an increasing amount of federally supported research is funded by the Defense Department. The Council on Economic Priorities (a New York-based non-profit research organization) reported in 1986 that "D.O.D. [Department of Defense] research accounts for 16 per cent of all federal spending for university research, up from 10 per cent in 1980."[13] More than anything else, the Star Wars program prompted concern about the weapons orientation of American research. For instance, Charles Schwartz, professor of physics at the University of California at Berkeley, expressed concerns about the growing militarization of the entire field of physics.[14] His views were shared by other physicists who, at a meeting of the American Physical Society, went on record to argue that research for space-based weapons systems was diverting money that could be better spent for other studies.

Government research directives are not the only way in which the increase in defense-related research has begun to control American scientific enterprise. Ofttimes researchers are not pressured so much as they are seduced by the availability of funding. The dependence of scientists on federal research dollars may cause them to volunteer support for political causes in the interest of bringing in research money. In 1984, several members of Congress charged that the Lawrence Livermore National Laboratory greatly exaggerated the feasibility of an X-ray laser in order to get millions of dollars of Star Wars research money. The foundation for this controversy was laid in 1982, when the Livermore Lab's former director, Edward Teller, testified that the X-ray laser was virtually ready to enter the engineering phase. This testimony helped establish the feasibility of a key component of the Reagan Administration's Star Wars missile defense system. However, later findings suggested that a feasible X-ray laser would not be ready for development for 15 or 20 years. U.S. Representative Fortney Stark argued that the lab "has sacrificed its most important asset—its reputation for scientific objectivity—in order to push its own projects."[15]

While some researchers seek defense dollars, others worry that <u>any</u> connection to the military establishment will make their research look like propaganda. For instance, in 1981, the Defense Intelligence Agency asked various university-based African research centers to bid for government contracts. Some scholars objected on the grounds that their research could become tainted with political objectives. Further, African-Studies researchers feared that African countries would become suspicious of those American scholars who were supported by the Pentagon.[16] The controversy over Pentagon funding for African-Studies research reproduced the debate during the 1930s over research funding provided by the electrical power industry. Would the Defense Department steer research findings? Even if not, would Pentagon funding stimulate the perception that the research findings were biased in favor of interests of the U.S. government?

Issues of Secrecy

Much discussion of the Defense Department as a research sponsor has to do with requirements for secrecy placed on Pentagon-supported studies. In 1986, the Massachusetts Institute of Technology undertook to review the impact of military research funding on the MIT faculty. The survey showed that 39 percent of MIT's faculty knew of situations in which military support for research led either to restrictions on the publication of research or to changes in the kind of research going on at the university.[17]

For their part, Pentagon officials deny that they are guilty of excessively restricting publication of academic research in science and engineering. Robert M. Rosenzweig, president of the Association of American Universities, also believed that complaints about the Pengaton had been exaggerated. He noted that Defense Department officials had agreed to restrict publication data only from projects having direct national security implications. Similarly, James A. Ionson, director of the Innovative Science and Technology Office of the Strategic Defense Initiative Organization, pledged that he would not impose restrictions on publications of research findings except those "critical to defense programs."[18]

Contacts between faculty and the Central Intelligence Agency have aroused concerns similar to those being expressed about Pentagon funding of research. Beginning in the 1970s, many academicians argued that CIA work was covert and therefore inherently injurious to the independent role of a scholarly inquirer. Because the CIA's support of research was disguised, readers had no way of knowing that some of the published material they used was covertly sponsored by the government. Further, contacts between the CIA and the researcher sometimes did not go through normal university channels. Therefore, CIA-sponsored research was more likely to bypass such customary academic rules as the requirement to review the impact of research on human subjects.

Another way that the CIA compromised the independence of scholars was to establish clandestine connections with faculty members who would report secretly on what they learned during overseas trips. For example, Michael Selzer, assistant professor of political science at Brooklyn College, came under fire from his colleagues for covertly gathering intelligence for the CIA while visiting Europe. The Brooklyn College political science faculty voted to disapprove of Selzer's secret work for the CIA because it "casts grave doubts upon his credibility as a teacher, scholar, and professional colleague."[19] This censure was based on a view that clandestine contacts with the CIA make a scholar more an agent for official government policy and less an independent investigator.

In response to widespread revelations of the CIA's covert contacts with American scholars and writers, Senator Daniel P. Moynihan (D., New York) proposed a ban on the secret use of academicians, journalists, and clergy as intelligence gatherers for the CIA.[20] Taking the opposite view, Stansfield Turner, CIA director under President Jimmy Carter, denied that the agency's contacts with faculty members "in any way compromise the integrity of the academic profession or infringe upon their official responsibilities to their institution."[21] Turner argued that professors act according to a natural spirit of public service when they agree to brief the CIA. Turner maintained, further, that prohibiting contacts with the CIA would violate the academic freedom of researchers. In contrast, Morton Halperin, a critic of the CIA, argued that the very covertness of the CIA program presented inherent problems. He pointed out that, until the 1970s, the CIA refused publicly to acknowledge that it used academicians for covert intelligence gathering.

Controversies continue to surface concerning the CIA's covert contacts with researchers. In 1988, H. Joachim Maitre, Dean of the Boston University College of Communication, disclosed that he might have unwittingly participated in a CIA propaganda campaign to influence domestic U.S. opinion on policies about Nicaragua and Afghanistan. Maitre produced a documentary on the Contra rebels in Nicaragua, and he also directed a program in Pakistan to teach refugees from Afghanistan to write newspaper articles about the Soviet-backed invasion of their country. Apparently, Maitre made his disclosure fearing that his reputation as a scholar could be tarnished if he were shown to have been even indirectly connected to covert propaganda activities being run by the National Security Council.[22]

RESEARCH FOR FEDERAL DOMESTIC AGENCIES

Agencies with national security responsibilities have a mission that combines constant vigilance with a need for discretion. The resulting effort to attain immediate results coupled with secrecy means that defense and intelligence agencies are vulnerable to accusations of sponsoring research for purposes of propaganda. It turns out that federal domestic agencies also are tempted to sponsor research for reasons of political advantage.

The Spread of Secrecy

As smoke signifies the danger of fire, secrecy should alert us to propaganda. In recent years, certain of the secrecy policies of the Pengaton and the CIA have become norms in the research-grant operations of other federal agencies. The CIA and Pentagon initiated the practice of placing the label of "national security" on research data. It is understandable that the CIA would want to protect the confidentiality of intelligence sources, and that the Pentagon would want to keep a lid on military technology and strategy. However, the CIA's and the Pentagon's practice of requiring pre-publication review of federally sponsored research has spread to other agencies of government that can claim little, if any, rationale for secrecy. Under the guise of witholding sensitive technical information, federal agencies sometimes refuse to publish research on domestic social issues that might embarrass the executive branch.

The issue of using pre-publication review as a device of propaganda apparently has become widespread. In 1985, John Shattuck, a Harvard University Vice President, complained that more and more federal agencies were requiring pre-publication review of research supported with U.S. funds. He believed that most efforts to restrict publication of research information had no clear relation to national security. Furthermore, during the 1980s, the federal government was pushing to extend its right of review to whole areas of research, such as nuclear power and cryptography (the study of codes), whether or not the research had been conducted with U.S. funds. Shattuck contended that claims of national security were a smoke screen to justify pre-publication reviews really designed to hide findings that contradicted official policy. In this case federal agencies asserted a power not only to review data but also to influence interpretation of studies on housing, health administration, education for the elderly, and cancer screening. Shattuck concluded: "Apparently, federal agencies believe that they can in this way insure that the research they fund is consistent with their view of their mission."[23]

The Politics of Educational Research

Although education in the U.S. is chiefly a concern of state and local governments, federally supported educational research can be a focus for issues of propaganda. One important executive agency that sponsors research is the National Endowment for the Humanities (NEH). (I myself have received four grants from this organization.)

In 1985, a number of historians complained that William J. Bennett, chair of the Endowment, was committed to classic master works in the humanities and that, therefore, he underfunded projects in such newer areas as women's history and Black history and other ethnic history. In this connection, Mary B. Norton, former member of the NEH's National Council, argued that the Endowment often chose not to fund proposals that had been favorably rated by outside review panels. "Recently the staff has been using the strategy of asking for additional reviews on panel recommendations, as a way of not funding proposals that have been strongly recommended by the panel." She also believed that "Bennett is stacking certain council committees," and that, "when all else fails, he is turning down proposals on his own authority."

Not all historians were unhappy with the back-to-the-basics orientation of William Bennett's NEH. Samuel R. Gammon, executive director of the American Historical Association, praised Bennett's approach which, he said, increased the "emphasis on history in general." Bennett acknowledged that proposals in Black studies and women's studies were supported at lower rates under his administration than previously. He contended, however, that this result was due to his fair treatment of the proposals in contrast to the preferential consideration they had received earlier. Bennett claimed: "I take the recommendations given to me by our panels of reviewers 99.38 per cent of the time." Norton countered that, although Bennett had denied only 46 proposals, he used political reasons for doing so. For instance, she said, Bennett rejected one proposal for having "a strong ideological bias highly critical of the government and the economic system," and another for an allegedly too narrow feminist perspective.[24]

Not all complaints about covert propaganda in NEH grants alleged a rightward political bias. A. M. Eckstein, University of Maryland historian, gave a critical eyewitness account of a conference on George Orwell's book, *1984*, sponsored by the NEH. Eckstein said Orwell would have been dismayed at the theme of most papers at the conference that "the totalitarian nightmare of *1984* has been, or at least is about to be, most fully realized in America." Eckstein expressed surprise that not one paper attacked totalitarian practices in Eastern Europe, Asia, or the U.S.S.R. He argued that participants lacked the critical ability to distinguish between totalitarianism and American "bourgeois democracy." Eckstein wondered why more attention was not paid to the irony that Washington was paying for all these papers attacking both the U.S. government and American culture for their allegedly oppressive characteristics.[25]

Reviewing the NEH's record, Morton Sosna of the Stanford University Humanities Center and John Gilkeson of Middlebury College jointly argued that the agency's vague mission rendered it particularly susceptible to political controversy. They found that, from the start, the agency tried to mix elitism and populism. The NEH sought to bring basic cultural knowledge to the masses through popular education at the same time that it supported sophisticated high-level humanities research. Because the NEH never had a clear mission to support excellence of scholarship, its grants have ever been subject to charges of political tampering.[26]

Propagandizing Our Culture?

Charges of rightward or leftward bias in NEH funding reveal common suspicions that government grants will be used to promote self-serving political agendas. Michael Mooney, an editor of *Harper's Magazine*, carried the point further in his belief that the entire program of federal grants to the arts and humanities has been problematic. Mooney argued that federal grants to the arts and humanities in effect constitute a semi-official cultural bureaucracy that has an undesirable impact on American life. According to Mooney, national cultural objectives are set through a large federal grant labyrinth. On the national level is the Federal Council on the Arts and Humanities that coordinates 300 national programs of the National Endowment for the Arts, the NEH, the Corporation for Public Broadcasting, the National Science Foundation, the Smithsonian Institution, as well as the Departments of Education, Interior, and Labor. Also included in the federal arts establishment are various programs based in the states, municipalities, regions, universities, and other foundations and corporations.

According to Mooney, the result of the official grant machinery has been to establish a "New Order" of culture, set in place by selective

grants that are subject to influences of cronyism and bureaucratic petti-
ness. Worse yet, he argued, the official cultural apparatus has been
shrouded in secrecy because many grant applications are treated as confidential for reasons of privacy. Another result of erecting an official culture through government grants has been to reduce private initiative,
Mooney contended. Artists who are unsuccessful in tapping into this de
facto Ministry of Culture simply give up. Many observers argued that
Mooney had vastly exaggerated a small problem; however, Joseph
Duffey, Chairman of the NEH, did respond to Mooney's book by opening to the public some meetings of the Endowment's National
Council.[27]

When government supports artistic creation, culture becomes a
political issue. One of the most significant episodes illustrating this principle is the ongoing controversy over grants by the National
Endowment for the Arts for allegedly obscene art. In 1989, the U.S.
House of Representatives reduced the $171.4 million appropriations of
the NEA by $45,000, which was the cost of two art exhibits featuring
works by Robert Mapplethorpe deemed obscene by some members of
Congress. "Is a picture of Jesus hanging from a cross submerged in a jar
of urine worthy of public funding?" asked Representative Dana
Rohrabacher (R., California).[28] The Senate's funding bill for the NEA
also contained a ban on grants to the two art institutes that had dis-
played the controversial artwork of Mapplethorpe.[29] The NEA later
asked grant recipients to pledge that they would not apply funds to
works considered obscene. Many academicians agonized over whether
the pledge was or was not a threat to academic freedom. Eventually,
most decided to take the money.[30]

The issue of federal funds for obscene art continued into 1990
when Congress held hearings on extending the charters of the NEA and
the NEH. Members of Congress debated whether or not to prohibit
support of certain kinds of art and research. For its part, the Bush
administration proposed that the NEA and NEH be rechartered with
no strings. The Senate concurred, but stipulated that any grant recipient
convicted of obscenity or pornography must return the grant money.[31]

Controversies over pre-publication review and over the grant policies of the Arts and Humanities Endowments alike show that federal
support brings political problems. The conflict of values seems inherent
to a democratic way of life. The public is served when scholarly research
and artistic expression are free from political censorship. At the same

117

time, the public rightly expects that elected officials will hold grant recipients accountable for the responsible use of public money.

HIRED GUNS FOR THE PRIVATE SECTOR?

The alternative to public funding is private funding; nevertheless, researchers cannot eliminate problems of propaganda simply by seeking private support for their research. Privatization of grants does eliminate the need for recipients to satisfy political officials about how the money was spent; researchers and artists find, nevertheless, that they must make similar accountings to private grantors who also want congenial findings and productions. The possibility that private groups will put research to use as a private propaganda becomes clear when we examine controversies over research funded by American businesses.

Industry's Brain Trust

Business organizations support the same kinds of research that the government does; nevertheless, commercially funded studies more often tend to belong to the category of applied research rather than to "basic" studies of fundamental physical or social processes. When researchers focus on applied, commercially relevant problems, they become vulnerable to the charge that their scholarly role is hampered by a conflict of interest with their role as business adviser. It is difficult to estimate the extent to which researchers actually compromise their independence when conducting studies to aid commercial interests. We may, nonetheless, point to many complaints feeding a general suspicion that researchers do sometimes serve as propagandists for businesses.

Charges of a pro-business propaganda of research surfaced in connection with payments by AT&T for expert reports and testimony. During the time when AT&T was trying to prevent the break up of the Bell System, the company paid $3.5 million to professors for consulting work, notably expert testimony to Congress and in courts.[32] This statistic naturally prompted a suspicion that researchers acted as hired guns for AT&T, although it is equally possible that researchers testified purely as to their honest scholarly opinions. Other situations seem to give a clearer indication that researchers are lured into functioning, at least in part, as propagandists. We may turn to instances in which industry sought in a variety of ways to skew research by means of grants and contracts to investigators.

By their nature, grants are designed to stimulate research on certain issues in preference to others. To take one case, grant announcements from the National Association of Broadcasters (NAB) have given the appearance that the industry wanted to initiate research to help in programming, selling advertising, and/or in fending off attacks from critics. In a 1988 announcement of grants, the NAB solicited proposals dealing with VCR use, the causes of heavy TV viewing among children, the relationship of media to consumers' purchase decisions, and choices by radio listeners. Proposals funded by the NAB in 1989 included studies measuring prime-time TV ratings, radio listening habits, and how closed-captioning affects children for whom English is a second language.

Commercial interests may influence the direction of research not only through grant announcements but also through research contracts. Critics in the field of archaeology express worry that contract archaeology will shift the kind of studies done in the field. Archaeological surveys often are required by law when sites are excavated in preparation for construction. One result of the estimated $100 million spent for contract archaeology by the mid-1980s was stimulation of the rise of private archaeology firms. These firms compete for research contracts with archaeological organizations that are affiliated with universities. Critics point to a potential problem that is inherent to the research-for-hire approach that has come to dominate archaeology. When conducted under a commercial contract, archaeological research is likely to provide what the developer wants, which is enough quick and superficial documentation to satisfy federal or state requirements. Critics complain, further, that commercial contracts produce bad training for graduate students when academic institutes conducted the contract work.[33]

Albert H. Meyerhoff, lawyer for the National Resources Defense Council, argued that increased research funding by industry might transform the academic world into a private brain trust for business. He called for Congress to enact federal legislation, similar to that already in force in California, to compel academic researchers to disclose any ties to industry. Congress, on the other hand, generally prefers to have each institution set up its own conflict-of-interest guidelines.[34] Many universities already have set guidelines about research sponsorship. Forty-six of 51 institutions surveyed in a study by the Association of American Universities reported that they had written policies in place to prevent conflicts of interest among academic researchers.[35]

Complaints sometimes seem relatively trivial about the potential conflict of interest in private research funding. Who cares whether businesspeople channel research into directions favorable to their own needs and away from the amassing of independent research data? So what, if business gets a benefit—they paid for the studies didn't they? These questions are interesting to consider in light especially of challenges now being made about research in the area of public health.

Research and the Public's Health

Nowhere are conflicts of interest potentially more serious than in the area of public health. If commercial needs distort research in archaeology, the impact may be nil as regards the public's daily life; in contrast, the effects can be serious when research funding skews inquiries into matters of health. An early criticism of industry-sponsored research came during the late 1960s when TV broadcasters were given veto power over social scientists selected to participate in the Surgeon General's massive study of the social effects of violence on TV. The broadcasting industry blackballed two researchers, Albert Bandura and Leonard Berkowitz, who had already done work suggesting that TV violence is harmful.[36]

In the 1980s, a controversy about propagandized health research emerged in connection with studies conducted at chemical testing labs. Critics argued that scientists in these labs had been pressured by chemical manufacturers to certify new products as safe for sale. In 1983, federal prosecutors charged that the Industrial Bio-Test Laboratories doctored test records to enable manufacturers to get federal approval for certain chemical and drug products.[37] Charges of this kind have brought demands for more explicit disclosures of contacts between researchers and business organizations. In 1990, *The New England Journal of Medicine* began to require that authors of review articles and editorials must not have a financial interest in the products treated in the material being reviewed.[38]

No health controversy has been more strident than that concerning the effects of tobacco. One component of the controversy concerns the tobacco industry's uses of research on cigarette smoking. In the mid-1980s, Antonio Cipollone sued three tobacco corporations (Philip Morris, Liggett, and Lorilard) for his wife's death from lung cancer. Cipollone's lawyers obtained documents indicating that cigarette companies tried to support and/or publicize favorable research in order to minimize the link between cigarette smoking and cancer. In 1981, the Tobacco Institute took out full-page newspaper ads to publicize an independent researcher's article suggesting that the hazards of second-hand cigarette smoke might be small. The researcher, whose later work showed major adverse health effects from second-hand smoke, publicly objected to the tobacco industry's use of his report. The researcher was unhappy that his article was employed to discredit a larger, Japanese study that found dramatically higher cancer rates for women married to smokers. A 1965 tobacco industry report recommended a more direct way of gaining political advantages from research. The report suggested that the industry set up a panel of scientific experts who could serve as spokespersons against the view that cigarette smoking was harmful.[39]

Evidence that propaganda may contaminate health research has led two Federal agencies—the National Institutes of Health and the Alcohol, Drug Abuse, and Mental Health Administration—jointly to propose guidelines to stem conflicts of interest among researchers who receive grants for health research. The proposed health research guidelines were developed in response to various problems identified in Congressional hearings on grants. In 1988, Congress heard testimony about various suspicious episodes, including a case in which physicians researched an experimental drug and, at the same time, held stock in a company manufacturing the drug. During tests of the drug, the researchers did not tell drug recipients that the medicine might cause fatal strokes. In another case, a pediatric researcher was paid by a drug company to give presentations about the company's products at medical schools and professional meetings.[40]

SUPPORT FROM THE CHARITABLE FOUNDATIONS

Federal tax laws allow individuals with available funds to deposit some of their resources in a tax-exempt charitable foundation as an alternative to paying inheritance taxes to the government. In exchange for the license to distribute wealth privately, foundations agree not to undertake activity that might influence legislation. Many, if not most, foundations are relatively noncontroversial, either because of their lack of activity or because they concentrate their grants on medical research. Nevertheless, grants by foundations sometimes become a focal point for controversies about propaganda in research, particularly when the research concerns major social problems.

Inoffensive Social Research

Some critics argue that the effort of foundations to avoid controversy can become a kind of propaganda for conserving the status quo in society. On the one hand, foundations want to support projects that delve into social problems that are currently of concern to the nation. On the other hand, foundations would prefer to avoid funding any research that could bring into question their tax-exempt status. The solution to this dilemma first adopted by major foundations (Carnegie, Rockefeller, and Ford) was to support well-established social researchers at elite universities. According to observers of foundation funding, this formula tended to produce sophisticated academic theorizing that was largely silent about specific changes necessary in American society.[41]

Foundations have learned that the dangers of supporting controversial social research are not merely hypothetical. In 1954, for instance, a House committee under Congressman B. C. Reece inquired into why foundations "do not support projects of a pro-American type."[42] Reece was particulary unhappy about grants of the Ford Foundation to study civil rights and to investigate tactics used in Congressional hearings on communist infiltration. Later, in the 1960s, Congress took another swipe at the ability of foundations to use social science research grants to promote innovation and change. The Tax Reform Act of 1969 further tightened the ban on grants construable as having a political purpose. The provision seemed to be aimed at the few foundations that were making grants in the areas of civil rights, the urban crisis, and government reform. Whitney M. Young, executive director of the National Urban League, complained that the new policy was set in place just in time to keep African-American organizations from securing beneficial foundation grants.[43]

Since World War II, therefore, foundations influenced by a social conscience have found themselves torn between their commitments to reform and their instincts for institutional survival. The predictable result has been a balancing act in which foundations grant money for social research of a fairly safe kind. On the one hand, foundations support research that is innovative enough to show good faith and that attracts prominent social scientists. On the other hand, foundations prefer grants that avoid unnecessary controversiality that might attract hostility from conservatives.[44]

Contradictory objectives render foundations ever-tentative about the undertakings they will support. For instance, the Rockefeller Foundation withdrew support for the Kinsey Institute for Sex Research during the 1950s when Kinsey's data about rampant premarital sex upset orthodox views of American moral life. Kinsey found himself occasionally labeled a "communist" because of claims by right-wing critics that his reports cast aspersions on American morality.[45] It is not difficult to find evidence that the social ambivalence of private foundations has remained a constant. In the mid-1980s, Albert Camarillo, director of Stanford University's Center for Chicano Research, reported his impression that those foundations that underwrote his institute "do not want anything controversial."[46]

Corporate Funding

Foundation money has typically originated from the estates of such deceased private capitalists as Andrew Carnegie, John D. Rockefeller, and Henry Ford. In addition, private funding for research also may come directly in the form of grants by profit-making businesses. If the trustees of foundations are reluctant to support controversial social research, active businesspeople are even more so. It is not surprising that businesspeople who control private corporations are wary of supporting research that might give aid and comfort to their ideological and political opponents. Albert Camarillo of Stanford observed that "whatever is true of foundation funding is doubly true of corporation money. It takes a long time to establish relationships with corporations, and they are usually unwilling to fund anything except very applied research."[47]

When businesses do make grants for social research, they tend to favor studies that support the general aims of the profit-making corporation. This proclivity may be seen in the case of the Ameritech Foundation, financed by Ameritech, the parent corporation of several Bell telephone companies in the Midwest. Ameritech's first grant was to Northwestern University for research in government regulation, a subject of great interest to media companies. The president of the Ameritech Foundation, Leighton C. Gilman (who was also a Vice-President of Ameritech Corporation), affirmed that his organization would be active in finding and funding projects of interest to the Foundation. Gilman explained that his organization would be "proactive, initiating and conducting philanthropic programs rather than reacting to unsolicited requests."[48]

Private Think Tanks

Another issue in the propaganda of research accompanied the dramatic rise of the private think tanks. If some of the major foundations have practiced a generalized, non-partisan liberalism in grants for civil rights and social reform, several of the new think tanks have abandoned the effort to downplay their engagement with political causes and parties. In the 1980s and 1990s, think tanks became more active in directly bolstering particular factions in socio-political controversies. Paralleling the upswing of political conservatism during the period 1975-1990, private research institutes catering to the political Right enjoyed particular growth.[49] The Reagan years were good for established conservative think tanks, with the Hoover Institution and the American Enterprise Institute increasing substantially in staff size and endowment. Even the smaller rightist research foundations fared quite well between the mid-70s and the mid-80s. For instance, the Heritage Foundation rose from two staff persons in 1973 to an annual budget of $11 million in 1986. Other think tanks enjoying a dramatic expansion included the Cato Institute, the Hudson Institution, and the Center for the Study of Public Choice.

The rise of the research-oriented think tank has given political conservatives a new ability to win increased attention for their views, not only when these savants testify before Congress but also when their conclusions are reported by the news media. In 1984, the Heritage Foundation published "more than 200 books, monographs, and legislative analyses."[50] Heritage researchers discovered the advantages of sending their material directly to the nation's 1,600 daily and weekly papers instead of focusing exclusively on the big media. The Heritage Foundation's widely-circulated publication, *Mandate for Leadership* (1980) provided a vast number of policy recommendations for the early Reagan Administration. Heritage's detailed proposals included a variety of free-enterprise approaches to social problems such as more competition in health care and private management of wilderness areas.

By means of direct links to policy makers and media outlets, conservative writers and researchers during the 1970s and 1980s began to compete successfully with liberal-leaning elite universities in providing high-level, policy-oriented research. Notable was the work of the Center for Strategic and International Studies (CSIS) which arranged for more than 2,500 TV and radio appearances in 1985 for its research fellows. The CSIS was able to capitalize on the media's appetite for political bigwigs, providing a large number of attractive big names, including Henry Kissinger (former Secretary of State), James Schlesinger (former Secretary of Defense and of Energy), and Zbigniew Brzezinski (Jimmy Carter's national security adviser). The CSIS cultivated a reputation for expertise on subjects such as terrorism.

One factor promoting the expansion of conservative think tanks was the feeling of business leaders that they had lost ideological control of the major foundations. For instance, in 1977, Henry Ford II resigned from the board of the Ford Foundation, contending that the foundation was taking an anti-capitalist orientation in its grant funding. More recently, William E. Simon, former Treasury Secretary, criticized grants by corporate foundations to liberal groups, arguing that "the leaders of the free enterprise system . . . are financing the destruction of their own system and ultimately of our free society."[51]

A related motivation for business leaders to support the rightist think tanks was the success of several left-leaning research organizations that sprang up during the decade of social protest after 1964. Ralph Nader became a major promoter of leftist research groups when, beginning in the early 1970s, he spearheaded establishment of Public Interest Research Groups (PIRGs). In 1990, the California PIRG reported about 130,000 members who had contributed between $15 and $5,000. Cal-PIRG focused on such causes as environmentalism.[52] Some of the Nader-oriented PIRGs benefited from built-in funding from college students, and in 1985 some 500,000 college students were PIRG members.[53] PIRG membership was boosted by the negative check-off system used by some colleges whereby the PIRGs would get funding from student fees, unless a student specified otherwise. PIRGs have proved to be major irritants for conservatives. One rightist columnist, James J. Kilpatrick, argued that it was unAmerican to compel students to support an outside research group that "lobbied for the Equal Rights Amendment, supported tenants' rights, advocated a freeze on nuclear weapons and worked for 'social change.'"[54]

Concerned about the political drift of research scholarship during the 1970s, more and more businesses funneled money into research organizations with direct links to conservative politics. These rightist think tanks represented a relatively safe haven for corporate money because researchers at the think tanks were more likely than university scholars to favor military and business interests. Partly on this account, critics sometimes charge that the right-leaning think tanks practice a kind of ideological paternalism. For one thing, these think tanks may place explicit restrictions either on research topics or findings. The Cato Institute frankly acknowledges that it will not publish any commissioned study that calls for establishing a government program.

Another bone of contention is the alleged willingness of think tanks to accommodate the wishes of their ideological allies. For instance, the Department of Defense once publicly objected to certain conclusions in a study of military reform published by the Heritage Foundation. The Foundation thereupon stopped publicity on the study, eliminated references to it in other Foundation literature, and gave no more research commissions to the author. Furthermore, critics argue that think tanks frequently tailor their studies to the interests of their major corporate backers. For instance, the Heritage Foundation once published a study that severely criticized federal subsidy programs. This study avoided criticizing one major federal subsidy program of the Carter administration, the Synthetic Fuels Corporation, which provided grants to companies that, in turn, were major donors to the Heritage Foundation itself.[55]

Although research presents itself as objective and independent, scholarship and science clearly can function as propaganda. We may point to a proven tendency for research conclusions to favor whatever governmental or private agency controls research funding. Sometimes the propaganda of research is subtle, as when a scholar soft-pedals criticism that would offend the sponsor. Sometimes the propagandizing of scholarship is explicit, as when a research sponsor knowingly distributes grants to persons likely to report favorable findings. Alert citizens need to look behind the conclusions of research, asking whether any self-interested motives may have distorted the information.

RELIGION AND POLITICS

Just as witch doctor and village chief cooperate in primitive cultures, modern Western societies sometimes exhibit the alliances of throne and altar between religious and political leaders. The political tangent of Christianity in the West may be inevitable, given that the Bible prescribes ideal ways of social ethical behavior. In their efforts to make scripture relevant to life, American preachers have clearly trodden on political ground. The colonial pulpit was one of the most important channels for building sentiment in favor of the American Revolution. Pious preachers of abolition played as great a role as hot-headed

Southern states-rights advocates in moving the nation toward the Civil War. Preachers played an important role in rallying support for World War I by minimizing the pacifistic elements in Christianity and by proposing the image of a warrior Jesus. In an about-face during the post-World-War-I years, American religious leaders expressed embarrassment over the previous use of the Gospel for the purposes of war. Nonetheless, in the final decade of the twentieth century, the occasions are as numerous as ever before to wonder whether preachers are rendering greater service to Caesar than to God.

Religion shows signs of becoming propaganda whenever clergy are swept up by social issues such that they merge tenets of religious faith with fashionable political policy or ideology. Given that Christian preachers feel a duty to apply the Gospel to contemporary life, religion will always be an ambiguous source of modern propaganda. For one thing, how can one separate the religious from the political motives of religious leaders? No one can claim infallibility in marking off the divide between divine inspiration and self-serving propaganda. All a propaganda analyst can do is to be aware of the linkages between religion and politics, watching for any questionable mixing of godly insight with worldly politics.

Separation of Church and State?

The American tradition of separating church and state makes for many ambiguities in the political reach of religion. On the one hand, scholars point out that an "American civil religion" has been dominant since Colonial times. Religious piety in American civic life finds expression in the ceremonial speeches of civic leaders, especially U.S. presidents, and in such mixed civil/religious ceremonies as White House prayer breakfasts.[56] Although the religious and political feelings of Americans are often intertwined in speeches, ceremonies, and public symbols with religious implications, an opposing American tradition stands for separation of the institutions of church and state. During his quest for the presidency in 1960, John F. Kennedy uttered one of history's strongest calls for a total separation of church and state:

> I believe in an America where the separation of church and state is absolute—where no Catholic prelate would tell the President (should he be a Catholic) how to act and no Protestant minister would tell his parishioners for whom to vote . . .

I believe in an America that is officially neither Catholic, Protestant, nor Jewish—where no public official either requests or accepts instructions on public policy from the Pope, the National Council of Churches or any other ecclesiastical source—where no religious body seeks to impose its will directly or indirectly upon the general populace or the public acts of its officials . . . .[57]

We must keep in mind that Kennedy's extreme presentation of church/state separation was motivated partly by his effort to reassure Protestants that it was safe to cast a ballot in favor of a Catholic candidate for president. Further, Kennedy's call came during a period of relatively great social consensus that predated such religiously-sensitive social issues as abortion and nuclear-arms control. The line between religion and politics has become murkier in the years since the Catholic Kennedy's address to Protestant ministers in Houston, Texas.

During the 1960s, liberal clergy became involved in the civil rights movement and, later, in efforts to stop the Vietnam war. In the 1980s, many liberal clerics felt called to support a freeze on nuclear weapons and to oppose aid to the *Contra* rebels in Nicaragua. In like manner, conservative clergy have taken up leadership in the political campaign to curtail abortion-on-demand and to eliminate federal educational programs that promote a so-called "secular humanism," i.e., the notion that morality is not necessarily based on a divinely-inspired code. Notwithstanding the American tradition of church/state separation, both the Left and the Right in America look for religious sanction for their struggles, and they welcome the support of friendly clergy.

While religious leaders have ever been familiar participants in political debate, we must recognize the inherent danger of propaganda when clergy state or imply that socio-political conclusions are ordained by God. The entry of religion into the political fray inevitably means that adherence to controversial political positions may be recast as simple fidelity to godly truth. Conversely, opponents of clerically-sanctioned positions may be demonized. Furthermore, when advocates employ a religious basis for their political arguments, they sometimes claim a higher level of insight that belongs to them alone, and which cannot be morally opposed. Claims of this kind may be worrisome in a democracy where political debate is supposed to be based on rational argument, and where political truth is seen as residing in majority rule.

Religious leaders correctly sense their right—even duty—to enter the public forum. How can we ask the clergy not to oppose publicly what they believe to be evil and advocate what they affirm as good? Nonetheless, the definition of propaganda offered in chapter 1 calls our attention to the covert partisanship that may ensue when political argument is recast in terms of religious truth. When religion becomes a channel for political argument, propaganda is likely to emerge. Because religion and politics are proven partners in socio-political affairs, democracy may be strengthened when critics apply principles of propaganda analysis to invocations of religious sanction. For instance, it may be useful to explore situations in which politicians bolster the legitimacy of their policies by reference to religious leaders. Since George Bush's own Episcopal minister was opposed to the Persian Gulf War, the president may have had politics partly in mind when he invited Billy Graham, the world-famous evangelist, to the White House on the eve of commencing the air attack against Iraq.

Like Bush, President Ronald Reagan turned, in the mid-1980s, to religion as a prop for war policies. Reagan tried to associate his efforts to defeat the Sandinista government of Nicaragua with religious truth. Reagan claimed that the Pope backed "all of our policies in Central America," including, by implication, the effort to aid the military rebellion in Nicaragua. Subsequently, the Vatican issued a statement saying that the Pope would "exclude the possibility of his support or endorsement of any concrete plan dealing, in particular, with military aspects."[58] Later, in 1987, on the rebound from the Iran-*Contra* scandal, Reagan appeared before a convention of the Conservative Political Action Committee with conservative preacher Jerry Falwell at his side.[59]

If religion can serve politics, the reverse is also true: politics can be a help in legitimizing religion. One incidental result of the Cold War in America was to increase acceptance of Roman Catholicism as a creed. Anti-Catholic feeling is an old tradition in America—one that John F. Kennedy labored mightily to overcome in his run for the presidency in 1960. Because no organization is more anti-communist than the Catholic Church, however, the church gained religious legitimacy from its political stand. It seems, therefore, that by espousing mainstream political values, a non-mainstream religious group can gain acceptance.

Because the Roman Catholic Church is the largest single religious denomination in the U.S., the political empowerment of Catholic politicians may have been relatively easy compared to the situation faced by members of smaller sects. A more eccentric instance of the political legitimization of religion took place when the Unification Church of

Reverend Sun Myung Moon sought to improve its image. "Moonies" were frequently stigmatized as belonging to a dangerous cult; however, Reverend Moon's staunch anti-communist politics won him friends among many denominations and gained him an invitation to Richard Nixon's White House. One of Moon's organizations sent pastors of various Christian churches to all-expense-paid three-day anti-communism seminars,[60] and after the fall of the Berlin Wall, Moon felt comfortable in arguing that he had been the true prophet of the fall of communism, after all.

Religion and Television

The increasing appearance of religion on television has made the issue of religious propaganda increasingly salient. During the 1950s and 1960s, TV stations often provided limited coverage of religious services on Sunday in the interest of "license insurance." That is, by televising religious services, a station could show the Federal Communications Commission that it was serving all segments of the community and, therefore, deserved to retain the coveted license to broadcast.

The earliest TV coverage of religious services chiefly included the so-called mainstream Protestant denominations, as well as occasional Catholic and Jewish services. Evangelical preachers and marginal sects tended to be frozen out under the system of religious TV programming that prevailed during the first twenty years of television. As a result, evangelicals developed their own independent media during the 1970s and 1980s,[61] set up their own television channels, and televangelism was born. As religion became more directly wedded to mass media techniques, the evangelical churches—and later the mainstream Protestants—began to use an advertising approach formerly associated with business and politics. For example, in the mid-1970s, Baptists in Texas developed the Good News Texas campaign with commercials for Christ on television and radio, and ads in newspapers. One ad in the campaign showed Eldridge Cleaver, the former African-American militant, who stated that his former "Communist philosophy" did not work in practice, and that he had turned to Jesus: "Can He be trusted to untangle a fouled up life? I'm living proof of it."[62]

The most obvious potential vehicle for a religiously oriented propaganda are the programs of the powerful TV preachers who command millions of viewers and possess great this-worldly political power. The most visible impact of religion on media was the rise of the powerful television preachers during the 1970s and 1980s: Jerry Falwell, Jim Bakker, Jimmy Swaggart, Oral Roberts, Robert Schuller, and Pat Robertson. These major conservative preachers became controversial because of their constant appeals for money and their amassing of great wealth. In the heyday of Jim Bakker's ministry, his PTL organization reported annual revenues of $126 million.[63] Jimmy Swaggart's ministry took in around $150 million in 1987.[64]

Even before television expanded the audience for "the old-time religion," many critics were suspicious of the promotional tactics of revivalists such as those unmasked in Sinclair Lewis's novel, *Elmer Gantry*. By magnifying the Gospel of Prosperity, television associated religion with materialism more closely, and it contributed to an image of celebrity preaching as a gravy train for pulpit stars. Like Hollywood personalities and Washington politicans who had been alternately envied and pilloried for living the lifestyle of the rich and famous, televangelists became popular celebrities only to fall inevitably in scandal. Towards the end of the 1980s, Jim Bakker was tried and imprisoned for financial improprieties. Bakker's conviction provided food for those who criticized televangelistic preaching as a guise under which holier-than-thou hucksters amassed fortunes. Similarly, Jimmy Swaggert went down under a hail of media fire for sexual escapades that proved as evocative as had been his earlier dramatic crusades for Jesus.

Not only were televangelists controversial during the 1980s for amassing wealth but also they seemed poised to shape the direction of American politics through their access to the broadcast audience. The most prominent of the great political preachers was Jerry Falwell, a Baptist preacher in Lynchburg, Virginia. Falwell founded the Moral Majority organization in June 1979 to campaign against abortion, homosexuality, drug use, and pornography as well as to support a strong national defense.[65] Falwell exhibited a confrontational political style that drew criticism like a magnet, and he soon became controversial for his pronouncements on sensitive political issues. For instance, in 1985, Falwell opposed the growing and ultimately prevailing sentiment in favor of severing U.S. financial ties with South Africa. Falwell commented that he would invite "millions of Christians to buy Krugerrands [the South African gold coin]," and reinvest in South Africa.[66] The South African government, almost universally despised abroad, appreciated Falwell's support.

In pursuing his vision of a moral America, Falwell rejected the view that his actions were an inappropriate imposition of religious views on a secular society. Falwell took the position that his liberal critics were hypocritical in opposing his religiously oriented politics:

> Of course, there was nothing wrong, so far as liberals were concerned, with "imposing" their own views, whether those views had to do with civil rights, the Vietnam War, busing, the eradication of voluntary school prayer or the extermination of unborn babies through abortion. Liberals could impose their views because liberals were right! And they call us arrogant![67]

Falwell was not the first to apply religion to contemporary politics, but he remained the most prominent, prompting concerns about a confrontational mixing of religion and politics. When sanctified by the symbolic trappings of religion, political action seems to brook no challenge or debate. Citizens of a secular state become concerned when religious leaders take absolute, uncompromising positions, such as when Pope John Paul II prohibited teachers of theology from publicly contradicting official Catholic Church doctrine.[68] Religion has standards of truth more rigid than majority rule, hence it is not easily reconciled with the rational-majoritarian traditions of American politics that were forged during the Enlightenment.

The absolutism of a religion-based politics remains a source of concern both for politicians and the general public. For instance, by 1986, Republican party leaders were becoming nervous about the efforts of Pat Robertson, a TV preacher, to win the GOP presidential nomination. "For every two new people he might draw into the party, we'll lose four," commented one top Republican party strategist to *Newsweek* magazine.[69]

Pat Robertson's quest for the presidency marked a milestone in the ever-winding road that leads from religion to propaganda. Robertson did well in recruiting supporters in the Michigan precinct delegate selections in 1986, although he eventually faltered in the ultimate campaign for the Republican nomination of 1988. Whereas Robertson's campaign drew much attention, but realized little success, other evangelicals elsewhere were quietly offering themselves as replacements for regular political candidates who did not make religion an issue. Christian organizing activity paid off in Indiana, where Don Lynch, a Nazarene minister, won a GOP congressional primary after spending only $4,000 in campaign funds.[70] Episodes of this kind began to worry

Republican party regulars who feared losing control of the party to born-again Christians who, during the 1980s, had moved increasingly into the GOP coalition.

RELIGION IN POLITICAL MOVEMENTS

Major televangelists serve to focus concerns about religious propaganda; however, campaigns by church groups frequently provoke discussions of the role of religion in politics. On the one hand, religious leaders enjoy common American citizenship rights that clearly imply responsibilities to offer opinions about social and political conditions. On the other hand, when political speakers stress their role as religious advisers, they arouse fears that politics will lose its give-and-take qualities. Whenever speakers cite religious tenets as proof for political views, they raise the specter of political programs becoming direct extensions of religious dogma.

The dilemmas of religion-based politics can be observed in controversies over TV content, the curriculum of public schools, abortion, and various other political issues.

Religious Influence on TV Content

Religious spokespersons have been active in several political efforts to change the content of American television. In the early days of television, the Standards Departments of the broadcasting networks were quite vigilant in policing the language used in TV shows and the moral behavior of TV characters. With the onset of the more relaxed 1960s, however, TV executives began to allow more sex, violence, and profanity onto the screen. The result was to prompt conservative religious leaders into action. The Rev. Donald Wildmon, an obscure rural minister, began to mobilize fundamentalist congregations, helping them mount letter-writing campaigns against such shows as ABC-TV's *Soap*, a spoof of the sexy TV soap operas. The leading commercial sponsors of TV shows were not particularly happy about threats by Wildmon and others that fundamentalists would boycott products advertised on offending shows. Nevertheless, sponsors did begin to watch more closely the moral content of the programs on which their commercials were aired.

The incipient fundamentalist campaign against TV accelerated in 1981, when Jerry Falwell's Moral Majority organization joined with Wildmon and others to found an organization called Coalition for Better Television (CBTV). The Coalition evaluated TV shows for excessive "skin scenes," implied sexual intercourse, profanity, violence, and general "sexual innuendo." CBTV threatened to boycott the products advertised on offending TV shows.[71] CBTV scored a notable success when Owen B. Butler, Proctor and Gamble's Chairman of the Board, publicly accepted the general validity of the boycott approach. Butler told the Academy of Television Arts and Sciences that watchdog groups such as CBTV had legitimate complaints about "gratuitous sex, violence and profanity." For their part, broadcasters and civil libertarians objected to the CBTV boycotts, characterizing them as a form of undesirable censorship.[72]

Religious Influence on the Public School Curriculum

Another notable political campaign begun by religious groups was the effort of fundamentalists to promote "scientific creationism" as an alternative to the theory of biological evolution. Beginning in the 1960s, certain fundamentalist Christian groups successfully persuaded a number of school boards in California, Arkansas, and Louisiana either to recommend or require that the story of a six-day creation in *Genesis* be given "equal time" alongside the Darwinian theory of evolution. The idea of equal time for religiously-oriented theories of creation seemed plausible to many citizens. In fact, a survey taken among students enrolled in science courses at Ohio State University showed that a majority expressed support for equal time to creationism.[73] The public's willingness to apply the equal-time concept to Biblical creationism alarmed scientists, prompting leaders of American science to produce a large number of readable, popular works explaining evolution.[74]

The conflict between evolution and creationism moved into the courts as well. Creationists generally enjoyed less success in the courts of law than in the forums of general public opinion. For instance, in 1973, a U.S. Circuit Court of Appeals dismissed a suit filed in Texas that called for a prohibition on the teaching of evolution in the state.[75] In 1982, Judge William R. Overton declared unconstitutional an Arkansas law that required giving equal time to creation science (as an alternative to evolution) on the grounds that creationism was a thinly-veiled version of the Biblical account.[76] To this day, legal traditions and precedents favoring church/state separation have worked against having scientific creationism presented as an alternative to scientific theories about the physical origins of life.

The Churches and the Abortion Controversy

Among the various political campaigns mounted by religious groups, none has been more intense than the crusade against abortion on demand. Since the Supreme Court's 1973 decision, *Roe v. Wade*, grass-roots groups and major religious institutions have cooperated in an effort to undo the Court's opinion that an implied Constitutional right to privacy limits the power of the government to ban access to abortions. The Catholic Church's hierarchy became increasingly active in pressing Catholic politicians to support anti-abortion laws consistent with official church teachings. In 1990, John, Cardinal O'Connor of New York put Catholic politicians on notice that they risked excommunication for continued support of pro-choice laws. One implied target of O'Connor's threat was New York Governor Mario Cuomo, who, nevertheless, refused to budge from his position that the public had a right to choose liberal abortion laws.[77]

One interesting twist in the evolving religious propaganda against abortion took place in 1990 when the U.S. Roman Catholic bishops announced that they would sponsor advertisements against abortion. The bishops chose Hill & Knowlton, a public relations firm, and the Wirthlin Group, a polling firm, to coordinate a church-sponsored anti-abortion media campaign.[78] Of course, the Catholic bishops had as much right as any other group to employ modern techniques of mass persuasion, and the bishops' nemesis, Planned Parenthood, was already spending $1.5 million on advertising in 1989 to advance sexual mores directly opposite to Catholic policy.[79] Here again, however, the mixing of traditional religion and avant-garde persuasion prompted consternation among some commentators.

In particular, the mass-mediated anti-abortion campaign of the Catholic bishops raised issues of propaganda. Eugene Kennedy, a college professor and former Catholic priest, argued that the bishops tarnished their moral authority by embarking on the kind of "maneuvers and manipulation of opinion" that corporate CEOs and politicians regularly employ to dress up their actions.[80] Fighting fire with fire, Cardinal O'Connor argued that the Church's use of the media was a "reasonable response" to "a torrent of propaganda against human life."[81]

Religion and Liberal Agendas

Political crusades from the Right by fundamentalists against school curricula and by pro-life clerics against abortion have attracted most of the attention in debates about religious propaganda. Leftist political agendas, however, can be served equally well by the channel of religious propaganda. Religious fervor sustaining liberal causes is as old and as venerable a political tradition in America as the similar efforts of conservative religionists. Liberal clergy in the 19th century underwrote the Abolition Movement, while moralists across the theological spectrum in the early 20th century weighed in for Prohibition.

History shows that church groups, particularly the National Council of Churches, made significant contributions to the success of the civil rights movement in the 1960s. Churches put together an important grass-roots network to help promote civil rights demonstrations and political lobbying.[82] As they had been on the forefront of racial integration in the 1960s, religious groups were a major source of opposition in the 1980s to the Reagan administration's effort to aid the *Contra* rebels in Nicaragua. In 1986, for instance, several hundred religious protesters formed a human cross on the steps of the U.S. Capitol to oppose U.S. policies that encouraged civil war in Nicaragua. Speaking for the protesters, Roman Catholic Bishop Thomas Gumbleton of Detroit read this declaration: "In the name of God, stop the lies, stop the killing."[83] The anti-Contra campaign by church people stirred up government attention in the form of FBI scrutiny (see above, pp. 79-80).

Religious groups joined with the political Left in the U.S.A. to support a number of other political causes, as well. For instance, Left-leaning American churches sustained the sanctuary movement that helped Central American war refugees gain residency in the U.S. In doing this, the churches worked against the efforts of the Reagan and Bush Administrations to label the refugees as economic migrants ineligible for asylum in the U.S.

In addition to weighing in for the Left in important political debates, American churches, in their internal dynamics, have mirrored certain leftward ideological trends in secular politics. For instance, church people imbued with feminist thinking have been wont to label traditional Christian policies and practices as "sexist." This flirtation with feminism suggests that liberal Christian churches might become vehicles for diffusing avant-garde leftist political ideology, and this would be a new chapter in the propaganda analysis of religion.

In the 1970s, the National Council of Churches fully accepted a major tenet of feminist linguistics that certain traditional uses amounted to "sexist language."[84] The Council set out guidelines to minimize uses of the generic "he" and references to God as "He." A religious-based movement to change traditional translations in favor of "inclusive language" has continued unabated to the present day in liberal denominations. The words of familiar readings and the lyrics of old church songs written in pre-feminist times are routinely changed according to the view that sacred words are not merely modes of expressing humanity's devotion to God but also should be considered weapons of social and political empowerment. It is no small feat to change people's linguistic habits almost overnight. With a boost from liberal denominations, however, feminist linguistics has been able to make such new usages as "chairperson" become the accepted standard.

The increasing tendency for well-educated clergy to be unrepresentative of their typically more conservative congregations fuels concern about whether churches are becoming too willing vehicles for leftist political machinations. In a major review of seminaries in the 1990s, Paul Wilkes found that an increasing number of students enter divinity schools because they are out of sync with society. Some seminarians find the authority role of a religious leader attractive in gaining relief from a tortured background of family alcoholism or substance abuse. Wilkes contended that many others turned to religious training in search of acceptance for their non-mainstream views or life styles. As a result, radical feminist and Marxist opinions have found favor in many seminaries, with the ironic result that seminarians have been taught to view traditional religion as a force of oppression! Wilkes predicted that Christian congregations increasingly would find their ministers moving them in directions that went against the traditional religious grain.[85]

Religion remains a broad and muddy channel for a flood of political commentary and action. Judged from the standpoint of competitive democracy and the free market of ideas, we have little grounds to fault the churches for speaking out on issues of war, peace, social justice, and human equality. Religious groups have no less right than do secular organizations to spread their vision of the ideal moral world. Nevertheless, religiously-oriented political persuasion will always make Americans nervous. American political institutions were forged during the Enlightment period when memories of various European wars of religion remained strong. The marriage of religious dogma and political ideology inevitably raises the question of whether this cohabitation is one of convenience more than for the social good. When political views are presented in religious terms, the opposing side is almost certain to suspect that an advocate or group seeks a quick or easy victory by subordinating the logical merits of its claims in favor of invoking the sanction of transcendence. Used as a major vehicle for politics, religious communication will ever be worrisome in a secular society. Citizens in a democracy will want to scrutinize religious communication to separate what must be rendered to Caesar and what to God. Similarly, they will want to look twice when politicians benefit from godly symbols as when campaign strategists weighed how much Bill Clinton's and Al Gore's Southern Baptist roots might appeal to voters.

The academic podium and the religious pulpit represent two potential channels of propaganda in American society. Scientists and members of the clergy often are individuals of exceptionally high moral integrity who express their beliefs and findings honestly and with genuine conviction. Nonetheless, both the academy and the church are subject to ideological and political currents flowing in society. When the clergy and religious laity carry their godly beliefs and values into the political fray, they risk transforming religion into a covert vehicle for secular ideologies and policies. The dangers of research-based propaganda are even greater. For one thing, researchers are more subject to outside sources of funding, which means that the pressures of propaganda probably will be greater on scholars and scientists than for people of the cloth. Further, the propaganda of research is more hidden and subtle than that of religion. If the careers of Jerry Falwell and John O'Connor prove anything, infallible political statements from religious leaders seem to evoke more suspicion than do the subtler persuasions of less-well-known scientific researchers and their fallible findings. In any event, the links between politics, research, and religion deserve continued and careful scrutiny in a political democracy.

ENDNOTES

1. C. R. Miller, "Debs Urges Aid for Bolsheviki from America," *Cleveland Plain Dealer*, June 17, 1918: 1.

2. *Chronicle of Higher Education*, 11/7/84: 25-26.

3. Walter Lippmann, *Public Opinion* (New York: Macmillan, 1922): 384.

4. *Utility Corporations; Summary Report of the Federal Trade Commission to the Senate of the United States*, No. 72-A (Washington, D.C.: U.S. Government Printing Office, 1935): 816.

5. Edwin R. A. Seligman, "Propaganda by Public Utility Corporations," *Bulletin of the American Association of University Professors*, 16 (1930): 365.

6. *Chronicle of Higher Education*, 11/21/84: 29.

7. *Chronicle of Higher Education*, 6/4/86: 12.

8. Louisville, KY *Courier-Journal*, 1/27/80: A18 .

9. *San Jose Mercury News*, 7/13/90: 4A.

10. *Chronicle of Higher Education*, 3/12/86: 6.

11. Jacques Ellul, *Propaganda* (New York: Knopf, 1965). See chapter 2, p. 54.

12. *Atlantic Monthly*, 1/91: 82.

13. *Chronicle of Higher Education*, 2/5/86: 22.

14. *Chronicle of Higher Education*, 5/7/86: 9.

15. *San Francisco Chronicle*, 4/13/88: 1, 6.

16. *Chronicle of Higher Education*, 11/7/84: 7, 13.

17. *Chronicle of Higher Education*, 6/4/86: 4.

18. *Chronicle of Higher Education*, 9/25/85: 1.

19. *Chronicle of Higher Education*, 1/24/77: 2.

20. *Chronicle of Higher Education*, 5/12/80: 14.

21. *Chronicle of Higher Education*, 9/5/78: 9.

22. *Chronicle of Higher Education*, 10/12/88: A2.

23. *Chronicle of Higher Education*, 1/9/85: 13-17.

24. See *Chronicle of Higher Education*, 1/9/85: 8; 4/24/85: 38.

25. *Chronicle of Higher Education*, 10/17/84: 72.

26. *Chronicle of Higher Education*, 4/18/90: A6-A8.

27. *Chronicle of Higher Education*, 11/24/80: 13, 15.

28. *New York Times*, 7/13/89: A13.

29. *Chronicle of Higher Education*, 8/2/89: A14.

30. *Chronicle of Higher Education*, 7/11/90: A1, A18.

31. *San Jose Mercury News*, 3/22/90: 16A; *New York Times*, 9/13/90: B2.

32. *Chronicle of Higher Education*, 6/16/82: 2.

33. *Chronicle of Higher Education*, 1/18/84: 6-7.

34. *Chronicle of Higher Education*, 6/23/82: 15.

35. *Chronicle of Higher Education*, 3/6/85: 7.

36. John P. Murray, *Chronicle of Higher Education*, 5/8/85: 35.

37. *Newsweek*, 5/30/83: 83.

38. *Chronicle of Higher Education*, 7/25/90: A4.

39. *Newsweek*, 4/11/88: 66.

40. Congressman Ted Weiss (D., New York), *Chronicle of Higher Education*, 10/4/89: A56.

41. Edward H. Berman, *The Influence of the Carnegie. Ford, and Rockefeller Foundations on American Foreign Policy: The Ideology of Philanthropy* (Albany, New York: State University of New York Press, 1983): 105-111.

42. Thomas C. Reeves, *Freedom and the Foundation: The Fund for the Republic in the Era of McCarthyism* (New York: Alfred A. Knopf, 1969): 56, 74-75.

43. Waldemar A. Nielsen, *The Big Foundations* (New York: Columbia University Press, 1972): 18-19.

44. Irving L. Horowitz and Ruth L. Horowitz, "Tax-Exempt Foundations: Their Effects on National Policy," in I. L. Horowitz, ed., *The Use and Abuse of Social Science* (New Brunswick, New Jersey: Transaction Books, 1971): 170-195.

45. Herman Wells (former president of Indiana University), *The IU Newspaper*, 4/18/86: 2; Daniel J. Boorstin, *The Americans: The Democratic Experience* (New York: Random House, 1973): 243.

46. *Chronicle of Higher Education*, 9/3/86: 7.

47. *Chronicle of Higher Education*, 9/3/86: 7.

48. *Chronicle of Higher Education*, 3/6/85: 24.

49. Gregg Easterbrook, *Atlantic Monthly*, 1/86: 66-80.

50. *Atlantic Monthly*, 1/86: 72.

51. *San Jose Mercury News*, 2/10/90: 1B, 4B.

52. *Palo Alto Weekly*, 8/8/90: 13.

53. *Chronicle of Higher Education*, 3/20/85: 17.

54. Louisville, KY *Courier-Journal*, 10/17/85: A7.

55. *Atlantic Monthly*, 1/86: 78-79.

56. Roderick P. Hart, *The Political Pulpit* (West Lafayette, Indiana: Purdue University Press, 1977).

57. John F. Kennedy, "Speech to the Greater Houston Ministerial Association," in J. Michael Sproule, *Speechmaking: An Introduction to Rhetorical Competence* (Dubuque, Iowa: Wm. C. Brown, 1991): 418.

58. Louisville, KY *Courier-Journal*, 4/18/85: A1, A12.

59. *San Francisco Chronicle*, 2/21/87: 7.

60. Louisville, KY *Courier-Journal*, 7/28/85: B1.

61. *Newsweek*, 2/9/81: 101.

62. *Texas Monthly*, 2/77: 84.

63. *San Francisco Examiner*, 8/30/90: E1, E3.

64. *People*, 3/7/88: 35.

65. Jerry Falwell, *Newsweek*, 9/21/81: 17.

66. *Newsweek*, 9/2/85: 30.

67. Jerry Falwell, *Newsweek*, 9/21/81: 17.

68. *Chronicle of Higher Education*, 6/5/90: A1.

69. *Newsweek*, 6/2/86: 27.

70. Louisville, KY *Courier-Journal*, 6/2/86: A1.

71. Todd Gitlin, *Inside Prime Time* (York: Pantheon, 1985): 247ff.

72. *Newsweek*, 6/29/81: 60.

73. *Chronicle of Higher Education*, 4/3/85: 8.

74. *Chronicle of Higher Education*, 12/15/82: 33.

75. Odessa, TX *Odessa American*, 10/11/73: 5A.

76. *Newsweek*, 1/18/82: 75.

77. *Vanity Fair*, 8/90: 160; *Newsweek*, 6/25/90: 64.

78. *New York Times*, 4/6/90: A1, A10.

79. *New York Times*, 4/6/90: A10.

80. *New York Times,* 4/19/90: A19.

81. *New York Times,* 8/14/90: 1A.

82. *Chronicle of Higher Education,* 8/8/90: A7.

83. Louisville, KY *Courier-Journal,* 3/5/86: A4.

84. Odessa, TX *Odessa American,* 3/12/77: 6A.

85. *Atlantic Monthly,* 12/90: 59-62, 64-66, 70-72, 74-75, 78-81, 84, 86-88.

Corporations Crashed Earth Day's Party

CHAPTER 4

PROPAGANDA IN THE NEWS

The news of the day as it reaches the newspaper office is an incredible medley of fact, propaganda, rumor, suspicion, clues, hopes, and fears, and the task of selecting and ordering that news is one of the truly sacred and priestly offices in a democracy. For the newspaper is in all literalness the bible of democracy, the book out of which a people determines its conduct. It is the only serious book most people read.[1]

Separating legitimate news from self-serving propaganda is a delicate matter. For one thing, news always is incomplete. News tells us, or shows us, what is happening—not what it all means. Commentators aside (exactly who grants them their newpaper columns and television studio seats, anyway?), most of what Americans recognize as journalism amounts to a rather disjointed patter about daily events, people, and places. In this confusing symbolic welter, self-interested parties are able to employ a variety of techniques to insinuate their biases into both the print and the electronic media.

Although problems of propaganda in news are vexing, we may turn to a long tradition of popular-press criticism, beginning with the muckrakers. Press criticism has grown to be a fruitful branch of academic study as well. Manipulation of news has been a more consistent interest of social critics than co-optations occurring in any other of the several channels of propaganda. I begin this chapter with a review of news and news practices, turning then to special problems of propaganda that abide to trouble the house of contemporary journalism.

NEWS: THE MODERN RHETORIC

The institution of news reporting has brought changes to the climate of public communication in America. Understanding the propaganda of news requires that we take a look at the transition from oratory to news.

News versus Oratory

The rise of news reporting changed the complexion of public communication in the United States. Communication was more direct and partisan in the nineteenth century than today. In the rhetorical climate of the 1800s, orators directly addressed their remarks to important audiences. The great orations were then diffused to the masses, not only by word of mouth but also by widely-circulated pamphlet reprints. The social importance of oratory in the early nineteenth century is nowhere clearer than in the fame won by the great legislative orators of the American Congress such as Daniel Webster, Henry Clay, Thomas Hart Benton, and John C. Calhoun. Until the Civil War, Congress had little trouble challenging the power and prestige of the executive branch. Oratory's power vis-a-vis the administration is shown by the relatively more lasting fame of the nineteenth century's great congressional speakers as compared to their less-well-known contemporaries in the White House: John Tyler, James K. Polk, Zachary Taylor, and Franklin Pierce. Further reinforcing the power of direct oratorical democracy in the nineteenth century was direct participation in the political parties. Millions of people took part in the great torchlight parades that marked political campaigns.

In contrast to communication via oratory and pamphleteering, the institution of news has made today's public communication more indirect. Communication today is less the feisty orator addressing a presumed whole public, and more the large institution reaching several segmented publics (e.g., Blacks, Whites, and Hispanics) through spokespersons. In national politics, the executive branch has become preeminent partly because of its greater facility in providing centralized communication. We observed in Chapter 2 that federal press-relations practices during World War I solidified the position of the departmental press spokesperson. Thereafter, news about the government fundamentally was a carefully channeled phenomenon. At the same time that press liaisons were helping to give an institutional spin to news, public-relations experts, such as Edward Bernays, were discovering that inaugurating organizations and staging events were better ways to get good coverage than merely sending out press releases. For example, to promote a line of automobiles that engineers claimed had better ventilation, Bernays set up a group called the Metropolitan Committee on Better Transportation Ventilation. This committee, formed in 1932, consisted of various scientists and engineering experts who, through the auspices of Bernays's office, grabbed newspaper space with announcements about the importance of ventilation in automobiles. General Motors followed up this free publicity with a promotional campaign declaring that "their 1933 cars assured the ventilation the committee was agitating for."[2]

Individual orators such as Jesse Jackson may seem to defy today's norm that communication comes to the public through an alliance between large institutional persuaders, such as General Motors, and the communication professions, such as public relations. However, most of what we hear from, and learn about, Jesse Jackson still comes not from direct observation but through snippets selected by news professionals and diffused through media channels. What is news, if not a collection of items deemed newsworthy less by society's partisans and more by professional journalists, broadcasters, and their producers?

Norms and Practices of News

Journalism represents a retreat from the old direct marketplace of political disputation in which the public was privy to whole messages prepared by opposing advocates. Because journalists do not function directly as advocates, they attempt instead to simulate a public forum by seeking to "balance" the news. In national politics, balance often means to report the official position of the Administration, and then to select one opposing mainstream position for representation, often by quoting spokespersons of the other major party in Congress. Given that TV must compress the news to a larger extent than do newspapers, electronic journalism tends to fall back on the formula that a controversy has two sides *and only two sides.*[3] In the case of the Vietnam War, for example, the two-policy positions receiving major media attention were (1) the official statements of the Administration that the war was necessary and that we were gradually winning it, and (2) the comments of leading Democrats in Congress that the war was not quite such a good idea and that we should pursue negotiation more eagerly. Although the antics of protesters also received attention, news of the war did not fully represent the wide spectrum of opinion, which at the time ranged from immediate withdrawal to the use of nuclear arms.

Because news reporters construct society's important lines of theoretically-balanced argument artificially, instead of letting the partisans speak for themselves, journalistic practices give an official cast to news. Journalism's folkways also tend to channel news in a mainstream direction because views held by a minority are less likely to receive air time or paper space. The advent of TV has solidified the advantages that institutions and administrative spokespersons enjoy in communicating with the public. Traditionally, national TV networks employed only a dozen or so film crews, stationing them in big cities where news could be expected. Network cameras were more likely to appear at scheduled briefings than at spontaneously occurring events. Modern news has been biased toward predictable people and expected occurrences, so that film crews could set up operations. The early progressive critics of the mass media recognized that the transition from speechmaking and pamphleteering to news reporting posed a significant problem for democracy. According to traditional democratic theory, citizens are able to obtain directly the information needed for rational political decisions. The mass-mediated marketplace of ideas becomes problematic, therefore, because people increasingly must rely on others to certify the purity of information. Instead of measuring what the orator said against a more-or-less known reality, today's audiences are in the position of reading, watching, and hearing about events that they cannot directly experience or judge.

"The protection of the sources of its opinion is the basic problem of democracy," wrote Walter Lippmann. "Without protection against propaganda . . . the living substance of all popular decision is exposed to every prejudice and to infinite exploitation."[4] Lippmann's concern for protecting news from propaganda became the mission of the early progressive critics of the press (see pp. 18-19). Progressive criticism offers citizens of today a framework for examining whether the norms of professional journalism are sufficient to protect the vitality of democracy in the electronic age.

The rhetorical climates of oratory and news pose different problems for democracy. While oratory encourages a more direct and participatory form of democratic life, speechmaking carries with it the problem of demagoguery. Aristotle pointed out that democracy is the form of government most vulnerable to demagogues because they flatter the audience.[5] By charming their audiences, unethical charlatans temporarily may fool the public with appealing proposals that lead to disastrous policies.

Plato, on the other hand, seems to have exaggerated the problem of oratorical demagoguery such that idealistic philosophers have been poisoned against rhetoric ever since.[6] The triumph of demagogues in classical times tended to be temporary, for opposing speakers checked the authority of the dishonest or ignorant speaker. Nevertheless, the prejudicial antipathy of philosophy toward rhetoric no doubt contributes to today's tendency to ignore the positive value of political speechmaking. After all, if oratory leads to demagoguery, why should we bemoan the passing of the pre-Civil War oratorical age?

Yet the replacement of political oratory by political news reporting is by no means the story of a passage from wilderness to promised land. News is a problematic form of rhetorical communication in which the responsibility for keeping the public forum honest is taken from advocates and is given to expert journalists who synthesize speeches and debates according to principles of "news value." At the same time that news reporters successfully digest the welter of messages from governors to the governed, journalistic communication also makes the public more vulnerable to propaganda. Just as the dark side of speechmaking is demagoguery, so also is news a kind of rhetoric whose characteristic downfall is propaganda.

To understand how propaganda enters the news, we must confront a number of questions about the modern practices of journalism. What are the norms and practices of professional news reporting? What are the implications of media organizations as profit-oriented businesses? How do social institutions and groups interact with news organizations?

News versus Truth

When Walter Lippmann distinguished between news and truth, he laid out the basic problem that journalists face in keeping the news free from the taint of propaganda.

> News and truth are not the same thing, and must be clearly distinguished. The function of news is to signalize an event; the function of truth is to bring to light the hidden facts, to set them into relation with each other, and make a picture of reality on which men can act.[7]

If we may liken the public to a jury, the old-style orators and pamphleteers of the nineteenth century acted as trial attorneys, putting different visions of truth before public jurors who were asked to render a judgment. So long as oratory served as the basis for public opinion, the public could keep in direct contact with the raw facts and opinions of society and politics. However, when the news replaced oratory, the public's view of society began to be colored less by direct contact with partisans and more by the professional mediation of journalists. The opinionated orators of pre-Civil War America functioned as advocates; in contrast, reporters and editors have taken on the role of judge. In preparing news messages for the public jury, the journalist-as-judge uses professional standards for news value as the criteria according to which to select what will be called "news," as well as where and how news will be reported.

Modern democracy depends heavily on the ability of today's journalists to separate fact and solid opinion from inaccurate propaganda. Journalists try to be responsible to what they view as the truth, the public interest, and social necessity. At the same time, they strive for a detached view of the people and events unfolding in society. But is the profession of journalism up to the task of making democracy safe from propaganda? One sign of journalism's progress against propaganda is that the crude ideological censorship that reporters faced during the Progressive Era has now declined. Today, editors and publishers rarely intervene to censor or alter news, especially in the larger media organizations.[8]

If outright news censorship has declined, does it then follow that journalism has reached its ideal expression? We need to explore whether the practices of professional journalists are an adequate bulwark against propaganda's infiltrating the news through such tactics as leaks, pseudo-events, and hoaxes.

PRACTICES OF OBJECTIVITY

Today's journalists shrink from the pretentious claim that they are objective; nevertheless, the key principle of professional journalism is fidelity to factual information coupled with a detached viewpoint. However much they dislike the word, journalistic professionals strive for objectivity. At the same time, however, news people are required to sort out rumors, reports, and confusing claims—and to do so quickly. Faced with a daily avalanche of ambiguity and confusion, journalists have developed a number of conventions to make their job easier. Paradoxically, these conventions complicate the effort to attain a factual detachment; like everyone else, news reporters and the organizations that back them, are subjective.[9]

Official Spokespersons

One conventional way to get objectivity is to report the official material. A classic case in point was when, in the infancy of TV news, broadcasters based coverage of the Korean War on film supplied by the government. Official sources may act responsibly, but news people can get in trouble when authorities use the news as a conduit for distortions or falsehoods. For instance, accepted journalistic practices made the media into virtual accomplices of Senator Joe McCarthy as he spread unfounded charges of rampant communist subversion in America.[10] Journalistic strictures of the day prevented Washington correspondents from putting into print the common thinking of reporters on Capitol Hill, namely, that McCarthy's charges were absurd. Media workers and executives had little reason to buck the prevailing norms of "who-said-what"-type reporting, for McCarthy's claims always made for tantalizing headlines and interesting copy. Nevertheless, McCarthy's short career amply illustrated the problems that may ensue when journalists simply transmit news obtained from an official source.

Journalists similarly are in danger of exaggerating the truth or significance of facts when they rely on advocacy-group spokespersons. Illustrating this problem is the controversy surrounding press attention given to the Reverend Al Sharpton, a would-be general spokesman for downtrodden African Americans on the East Coast. Like Joe McCarthy, Sharpton performed as a fascinating, but ultimately troubling, public figure. Sharpton's persistence and courage as spokesperson in the Tawana Brawley and Yusef Hawkins cases won him considerable press coverage and support from some African Americans, particularly disaffected youths. On the other hand, critics focused on Sharpton's shoot-from-the-hip charges and physical antics as evidence that he attached himself to controversies involving Black Americans chiefly for the purpose of promoting himself. For instance, on the eve of Nelson Mandela's visit to New York City in 1990 (after his release from years of imprisonment in South Africa), Sharpton appeared on the scene demanding to be jailed for a previous minor conviction. His picture behind bars duly appeared in the *New York Post*.

Because Sharpton appeared to have neither a significant organization nor a major following, some reporters and editors wondered why his appearances reliably generated significant press coverage. Attention to Sharpton was particularly troubling to journalists because he seemed not to distinguish between legitimate grievances (the murder of Yusef Hawkins by a mob in Bensonhurst) and media hoaxes (Tawana Brawley's apparently faked abduction and assault). The solution to the riddle of Sharpton's media mastery seemed to be that, like Joe McCarthy, Al Sharpton tailored himself to fit the norms of journalism, thereby mitigating against his lack of credibility as a responsible leader. Jerry Nachman, editor of the *Post*, reflected, "If he is a monster, then we are the Dr. Frankensteins who created him. He is an assignment editor's dream come true, and not just because of his flamboyance and provocative statements. He knows about deadlines. He knows about photo opportunities. He knows how to use a phone beeper for radio. He understands us cold."[11]

By 1990, Sharpton's antics had begun to wear thin on mainstream media, resulting in some unfavorable coverage focused on his own persona. Then the attempted assassination of Sharpton later that year generated new sympathy that acted to improve his general press image. At the same time, Sharpton seemed to appreciate the value of moderating his claims in the interests of securing a wider audience. Nevertheless, a few months later, there was Reverend Sharpton in London calling the Queen a "racist" and delving into British ethnic relations without seeming to know any of the facts.

Balance in Coverage

The cases of McCarthy and Sharpton highlight the vulnerability to demagoguery of the news, a democratic art form. The irony of press coverage of McCarthy and Sharpton is that professional news reporting, for all its standards and self-scrutiny, seems no more resistant to demagoguery than is oratory.

The pro/con, or balanced, model of coverage is journalism's common solution to merely reporting single versions of news from a government official, such as McCarthy, or from a spokesperson, such as Sharpton. While the effort to report two sides of a controversy corrects some obvious abuses in relying on a single perspective, the balance approach has its limits, as shown by the Watergate episode of the early 1970s.

The pro/con angle actually helped to slow the flow of news on Watergate because the norms of journalism initially helped the Nixon administration to keep Watergate off the front pages during the months of the 1972 campaign. Stories dealing with the break-in at the Democrats' headquarters in the Watergate Hotel had to be treated as part of the general presidential campaign. Accordingly, there was a tendency to hold back Watergate-related stories until a denial could be presented by the White House to "balance" an unfavorable story that connected the break-in to either Nixon's White House or the Committee to Re-Elect the President.[12] Only when U.S. Senate hearings changed the context of Watergate from a political clash to an official investigation, could the press step around the limits of the balance approach.

Another problem with trying to attain objectivity via the two-sided dialectical balancing act is that a story prepared according to this norm may leave out the third, fourth, and other positions. Ernest Lefever, a conservative media critic, complained that CBS-TV News inappropriately limited its coverage of national defense matters to official spokespersons, who maintained that Cold-War-era military and diplomatic efforts were sufficient, and to leading Democrats, who often called for less military spending and more diplomatic concessions. Lefever argued that the alternate rightist position was essentially ignored. This viewpoint, which Lefever argued was the correct one, held that the U.S. needed more military spending and tougher diplomacy vis-a-vis the Soviet bloc.[13] Pacifistic positions were similarly slighted.

Another limit of the pro/con model is that it encourages the press to focus on the two major political parties to the exclusion both of alternative political organizations and critics of the major parties. In covering elections, the mainstream press regularly ignores votes cast for American third parties. Overlooking the third-party vote became systematic when the major networks and press services set up the News Election Service, a joint company that reports vote totals. The NES has followed a policy of ignoring votes not cast for a Democrat or Republican. This policy is bad in principle because attention to third-party ballots reminds voters that other parties exist as alternatives.

Ignoring the minor parties is even worse in practice than in principle because the procedure can lead to atrocious situations. For instance, in one New York City Council district, the left-wing New Alliance Party candidate came in second with 40% of the vote. Due to NES practices, this total was not reported. In the 1988 presidential election, NES ignored third-party votes so it could round out the Bush and Dukakis numbers to 100%. This practice overlooked the real possibility that voters picked the minor candidates for the explicit purpose of protesting the candidacies of Bush and/or Dukakis.[14] In a *1984*-esque fashion, these votes disappeared on television.

GETTING THE IMPORTANT NEWS

In addition to journalistic norms focused on the ideal of objectivity, what Americans read in their newspapers or see in TV news originates partly in a journalistic notion of significance. Journalists always seek to make sure that they emphasize the *important* news.

The Cult of Celebrity

One way that news people guarantee that they focus appropriately on important goings-on is to attend to powerful and famous individuals. News is partial to celebrities, to the hero of the day. This means that high-level corporate executives, such as Lee Iacocca, are always prime candidates for press attention. The focus on the visible hero contributes to a publicity cycle in which the already well-known figures get coverage, while their equally-important colleagues may be ignored. Lee Iacocca, Ted Turner, Victor Kiam, Frank Bormann may be shoo-ins for press attention while equally significant and well-paid no-name executives receive less or no coverage.[15]

Christopher Lasch, a social critic, described the disproportionate attention to the already-famous as reflective of our contemporary "cult of celebrity."[16] A preoccupation with celebrity has become a matter of convenience for media channels and managers. It is easier for mass media to present a few megapersonalities than to search out unknown spokespersons or experts. Hollywood was among the first to learn this elementary principle of modern publicity. The earliest movies did not always indicate the names of the players. Soon, however, the identification of particular movie stars became the emphasis itself, when Hollywood finally understood that the public craved familiar faces.

When journalism becomes beholden to the cult of celebrity, news coverage becomes part of a covert, propagandistic process of manufactured social reality. Norms of celebrity set in motion a sub rosa alliance between self-serving individuals and journalistic convenience. Hype often signals the journalism of celebrity. Surrounding national and local news programs is an implicit, and often explicit, plea to "look at me!" and "watch this!" Who would be surprised to hear a local news teaser such as "World to end tomorrow—details at 11!" It is easier to keep viewers interested when familiar celebrities predominate on news. Media deference to the chosen few then confirms the importance of these media sages and, implicitly, the truth of their messages.

Nowhere is the blending of news and celebrity promotion clearer than when Hollywood stars tour the country to promote their latest films. For instance, in 1986, Paul Newman and Tom Cruise teamed up to promote their film *The Color of Money*. This duo appeared on the covers of the *The New York Times'* Sunday magazine, *Life, USA Today*, and dozens of other newspapers around the country. Newman and Cruise also received exposure on "The Today Show" and "Entertainment Tonight" as well as other electronic outlets. The attention paid to Newman and Cruise resulted from work by various publicists for the two stars, for director Martin Scorsese, and for Walt Disney Studio. This whole engine of "news" production was coordinated by the vice president for publicity at Disney.

Angling for press coverage can be a risky business, however, because the coverage might become unfavorable. One way to minimize the risk is to make the publicity undertaking a cooperative effort between propagandist and journalist. Both can benefit from the alliance, as when the editors of *Newsweek* saw in the Newman/Cruise combination a perfect eye-catching cover for their magazine. David Anson, a senior writer for *Newsweek*, commented that "with that combination you'd have to be an idiot not to think of it as a cover."[17] *Newsweek* eventually bounced the two stars from the face of its domestic issue, but they remained on the overseas covers.

For its part, *Life* magazine had Newman and Cruise pose together atop a pool table at Newman's home. Such a striking cover of two hot stars would pay obvious publicity benefits to *Life* at the same time as it boosted movie attendance. Hollywood insiders observed that Newman's willingness to pose for photographs was somewhat amazing, given his reputation for avoiding interviews. Old hands in the industry speculated that Newman's acquiescence in the staged publicity shots was motivated by his interest in winning an Oscar nomination. So the photographs benefitted everybody—except, perhaps, members of the public who did not recognize the covert mutual back-scratching.

The People-and-Pictures Story

The people-and-pictures approach is another device to make the audience sit up and take notice of important news. Journalism habitually relies on pictures and accompanying interviews rather than deeper investigation. Today's press people typically recoil from documentary research; they much prefer the interview.[18] From a propaganda analysis point of view, however, the interview poses problems. Documentary research facilitates attaining multiple perspectives in contrast to interviews where the journalist is in no position to compel truthful testimony.

Given that the press hates assignments that require dull investigation, it is not surprising that the press did not break the Watergate story. Notwithstanding the heroics of Bob Woodward and Carl Bernstein, as recounted in *All the President's Men*, the press only began to get really close to the truth of the Watergate scandal when the FBI and the courts compelled truthful testimony from key defendants.[19] Press scoops amounted to little more than scraps from investigators with power to punish untruthful talk.

I. F. Stone, the legendary investigative journalist, held that news people who seek inside dope from interview sources eventually become dependent on cultivating good relations with their special sources. In this scenario, journalists become enmeshed in a climate of mutual back-scratching in which they get news scoops in exchange for putting across a biased "inside dope." News derived from "exclusive sources" becomes a conduit for a self-serving propaganda of, by, and for these sources. Stone believed so strongly in forsaking interviews for documentary research that he sometimes resisted granting interviews when he himself later gained celebrity status. Stone once told me that I should not waste my time (and his) learning about the history of journalism by interviewing him. "Young man," he told me, "you should get into the documents."

One reason that the press missed the savings-and-loan scandal of the late 1980s may have been that this story of massive financial fraud was too much a numbers tale instead of a more easily grasped people-and-picture story. The story of fraud in the savings industry not only required fidelity to dull details but also a special initiative on the part of journalists who found no dissident voices complaining about easy loans and insider benefits. Both Republicans and Democrats were riding comfortably on the gravy train, so politicians were not eager to raise the issue. The victims of this polite crime were not complaining either, for S&L deposits by citizens were covered by federal insurance.[20] Only later did the saga of Neil Bush, the president's son, help to focus greater attention on the Savings and Loan story. Now, news organizations were able to personalize the scandal with pictures of young Bush, who could be variously presented as the president's feckless offspring and/or a greedy manipulator from the me-generation.

A particularly useful kind of picture for getting audience attention is the action shot. Action pictures function propagandistically by promoting a perceived objectivity based on the assumption that pictures do not lie. (The advent of computer-generated images eventually may change this inaccurate perception.) Journalists know that the best kind of photo is not the dull line-up of people as in a high school yearbook, but the real action photograph that symbolizes or makes the point dramatically. Pictures are usually at the center of the journalistic action story. Rioting, violent conflict between opponents, and police "head busting" all make for good visual news.[21]

The Gulf War of 1991 will be remembered by all those who stayed behind as a mélange of pictures. Tanks crossing the desert, airplanes taking off and landing, artillery firing at unseen targets, SCUD missiles streaking overhead. Ironically, the most compelling picture story of the Gulf War may never be seen. Denied the ability to interview soldiers spontaneously and to accompany front-line units, the U.S. media played into the hands of military public-relations officers who prevented unrestricted filming of actual combat. TV audiences had to be satisfied with selected releases from military camera operators or benign shots of behind-the-front equipment.

The effort to infuse action-type objectivity into the news via pictures extends even to still photography. In 1985, for instance, *People* magazine did a story on the rejection by the California State Board of Education of all textbooks submitted by publishers in the area of junior-high-school science.[22] Accompanying the story was an obviously-posed photograph of Bill Honig, California Superintendent of Public Instruction, standing with one foot on a stack of books giving the thumbs-down sign with both hands.

Propaganda in the news means more than legendary press magnates forcing their ideological biases on unwilling reporters or the wealthy and powerful seducing craven press people with baubles. The norms and practices of journalists themselves can become linchpins of a propagandized news. Knowing that certain kinds of people, particular kinds of events, and special facets of situations are more likely to become news, propagandists work to attach their biases to the folkways of journalism. Propagandists know that favorable news coverage is more likely if they can package their own slant to look official or to appear as a credible *mainstream* alternative to the official. Cagey publicists are ever ready to trade on celebrity name-recognition in order to embed their biases in filmed action or in evocative still photographs.

NEWS AS A BUSINESS

However much the norms of journalism become targets of opportunity for propagandists, there remains still more to tell about about how manipulators infiltrate the news. The propaganda-makers also take full account of the economic conditions of the journalism business. They look to the business side of the news for additional options to influence the content of news programming.

Ideological Censorship

In the good old days of journalism, the business end was likely to be under the control of an opinionated owner of the type made famous in Orson Welles' movie, *Citizen Kane*. The classic press lords laid down rules about what was and was not fit to print, as when William Randolph Hearst would send his editors a "Chief says" memorandum. Hearst once ordered his papers to use the term "Reds" or "Communists" when referring to the government of Spain during the Spanish Civil War.[23] Hearst favored the fascist rebels led by General Franco. Journalists chafed under the corrupt system in which owners and powerful editors explicitly enforced their biases. Between 1940 and 1950, George Seldes filled the columns of his *In Fact* newsletter with items of suppressed news sent to him secretly by outraged or disillusioned reporters.

While today's reporters rarely complain of oppressive ideological censorship, we still may find occasional glaring episodes. For instance, John McGoff, president of the Panax newspaper chain, apparently maintained a practice of ordering his papers to print favored stories that sometimes reflected low journalistic standards. In 1978, he ordered his papers to print a report that President Jimmy Carter was grooming his wife for the vice presidency. The editor of Panax's *Escanaba [Michigan] Daily Press* refused to print the story as news, offering instead to run the piece as editorial opinion. Fired for insubordination, the editor was compelled to accept part-time work as a broadcaster.[24] The McGoff episode was criticized by the National News Council as "a gross disservice to accepted American journalistic standards."

Explicit ideological censorship is the most dangerous manifestation of the gatekeeper's role undertaken by America's editors and publishers. Even though overt censorship is less frequent today, the gatekeeper connection remains an inherent defect of a democracy that relies on news for its intellectual nourishment. Even the most respected editors and publishers are human beings who have a stake in what is printed or shown. Where the marketplace of democratic debate depends on gatekeepers rather than free-wheeling orators, problems of self-interested reporting will inevitably crop up.

Even the most honorable of the gatekeepers are wont to influence the stream of ideas from time to time. One example was the pressure placed on Harcourt Brace Jovanovich when that publishing house was on the verge of releasing *Katharine the Great,* a biography of Katharine Graham, owner of the *Washington Post.* This book contained unflattering material not only about board chairman Graham but also about Benjamin Bradlee, the *Post's* famous executive editor. Both Graham and Bradlee complained to HBJ officials that the book was inaccurate. For his part, Bradlee denied the book's charge that he had compromised his journalistic integrity by writing stories that undermined French communists at the behest of the CIA. Although the author stood behind his documentary evidence, HBJ withdrew the book in deference to the complaints.[25]

News as Product

However well-intentioned they may be, instances of from-the-top ideological censorship constitute a by-definition kind of propaganda because they skew the news along self-serving lines. The business dimensions of news can be equally troubling from a propaganda analysis point of view, even when commercial practices do not lead to direct ideological censorship. A business-based propaganda of news takes place when, in the interests of economic advantage, news becomes less democracy's tribune and more a marketplace commodity.

Because media organizations are businesses, they necessarily are interested in packaging what happens in the public realm into a saleable product. Journalism corporations need to make news attractive in order to provide advertisers with an audience. Advertising is all-important in the media business: In 1979, seventy-five percent of the income of American newspapers came from advertising. Newspapers frequently use market research to find out what kind of news is most saleable. This kind of audience research has helped produce a shift from political news (which nourishes democratic life) to lifestyle features on entertainment, sports, recreation, travel, food, and such items of personal interest as parenting, relationships, and home maintenance.

The requirement to make news profitable produces an ever increasing business-based packaging of news reports—particularly on television. This intrusive packaging for reasons of profit may be acting to lessen the coherence of political debate. A striking example is the shorter average length of time that major political candidates are shown speaking. In 1984, news networks gave major presidential candidates an average of 14.8 seconds to make uninterrupted speech arguments. These speech moments, usually termed "sound bites," declined in the 1988 campaign to a mere 9 seconds. In 1968, by way of comparison, sound bites for presidential candidates had lasted an average of 42 seconds.[26] TV journalism may be progressively retarding the political intelligence of the public. Never in the course of democratic life have so many depended so much on so little.

I challenge any reader of this book to make an intelligent, significant, and coherent argument about anything in 9 seconds. Perhaps this challenge is in vain, for we media consumers have become satisfied with one-line arguments:

> "How can anyone support the Democratic Party; after all, most Democrats in Congress didn't support President Bush and our men and women in the Persian Gulf." (a 9-second argument).

> "Bush's veto of the 1991 Civil Rights Act shows that the Republican Party supports racism." (6 seconds)

Although having some coherence, assertions of this kind provide little information, and they give scant perspective to either the events in the Persian Gulf or the debate over civil-rights legislation.

In contrast to the starvation diet provided by one-liner sound bites, we may turn to the speeches of the Lincoln/Douglas debates of 1858. Candidates Abraham Lincoln and Stephen Douglas gave detailed analyses of slavery and other pressing issues. Their speeches not only enriched the knowledge of the listeners but also helped audiences make sense of the welter of details—not that Lincoln's and Douglas's arguments are immune to criticism. For instance, both candidates made charges that went far beyond the facts, as when Lincoln accused Douglas of plotting to extend slavery, and when Douglas accused Lincoln of undermining the Constitution. At least the charges came in a pro-and-con context of information and analysis that helped the audience to make a sensible judgment.

Unlike the Lincoln/Douglas debates of 1858, which featured alternating whole speeches, news-conference norms, rather than principles of deliberative speaking, held sway during the 1988 Bush/Dukakis debates. Norms of packaged entertainment predominated even before the gavel sounded. Much speculation and excitement surrounded the choice of the journalist panelists. Jim Lehrer of PBS-TV was selected to moderate the first debate, with questions coming from Peter Jennings (ABC news anchor), John W. Mashek (correspondent for *The Atlanta Constitution*), and Anne Groer (political writer for the *Orlando Sentinel*). As a result of the news-conference format, the debate became somewhat of a disjointed event with each reporter pursuing a different line of questioning. The first question dealt with drugs. After a total of six minutes of speaking from the candidates—divided into four segments—the "debaters" were bidden to discuss the federal deficit, then national health insurance, and so on throughout the 90 minutes.

With the speeches limited to two minutes (with one minute rebuttals), a visitor from another planet might have expected that the post-debate news coverage would strain mightily to extract the maximum possible intellectual and political content from the brief responses by the speakers. Instead, the focus of news and commentary was on the strategic and public-relations value of the debates. For reporters, the key story seemed to be that neither candidate had said anything that could generate an intriguing furor. In his post-debate commentary, Tom Brokaw quickly commented that the clash between Bush and Dukakis produced "no knockout punch" by either contestant.

Lacking a convenient single newsworthy knockout to focus coverage of the debate's political strategy, commentary thereupon shifted to the second standard public-relations question of TV debating: Who won? These headlines appeared in the *San Francisco Chronicle's* page-long coverage of reactions to the debate:

"Naming a Winner in the First Debate." Brief comments from nine figures in the world of politics, high-school debate, or public affairs.

"Instant Poll Says Dukakis Won Debate." An ABC poll gave Dukakis the nod 44% to 36%.

"Dukakis Wins in 'Undecided' Group." Report of results from focus groups and from preference indicators (normally used to track responses to advertising spots) held by viewers during the debate.

News coverage of the 1988 presidential debates illustrated the effort of journalists to digest and package events into an easily-presented story. The search for news that quickly satisfies is extreme in television where executives assume that any uninteresting material in a story can lead to a sudden loss of viewers. The news-as-product orientation has produced a virtual preoccupation by reporters and editors with dramatic conflict, with the interesting tidbit, and with the pat story—all given in a "balanced" way. These foibles of news reporting make today's ideologically uncensored, but business-oriented, journalism vulnerable to manipulation by cagey partisans who know how to offer what will be snapped up.

Entertainment norms are most pressing in TV news because viewers may tune out at any time. TV journalists employ the dramatic theatrical forms to hold viewers with what seems interesting and important. As in a dramatic production, news is structured around conflict. There is a rising action that leads to a climax and, finally, a falling action. Moreover, TV news focuses on pictures to hold interest. Current tendencies in TV news favor those in a conflict who are able to generate the best pictures and the best drama. Large institutions and noisy dissidents are best able to stage spectacular events. In contrast, representatives of the middle ground of a dispute are usually less interesting and therefore less-well-covered.[27]

Television's organization to package content for maximum profit has heretofore discouraged major networks from seeking out and fully covering lively political debate, partly because news organizations have found "unscheduled news" (spontaneous public events) to be costly when it disrupts regular, paid-for programming.[28] From a business point of view, it makes more sense to digest or package an event for later summary than to cover speeches, debates, and ceremonies as they occur. Furthermore, what often passes as social and political debate is chopped up into small bites by a program moderator. The discussion format favored in television's panel shows also tends to rob single advocates of the opportunity to make extended arguments.

Columnist William V. Shannon argued that as a result of its edited-for-TV campaigns, "television subverts self-government." Shannon pointed out that TV news must "cut, edit, soup up and distort" a political contest to conform to entertainment values. He argued that these norms and practices forced television to bungle coverage of the 1988 national political conventions. As often as not, the networks did not cover the speeches, preferring instead to construct their own pseudo-events in the form of interviews. Furthermore, interviews were kept to less than three minutes to avoid boring an audience that was raised expecting TV to be pure entertainment.[29]

In connection with the political party conventions, Democrats and Republicans alike sometimes cooperate in the trivialization of political dialogue. For instance, leaders of both parties know that the news organizations want to make presidential nominating conventions easy to watch. The two parties oblige by staging pretty spectacles built around artificial exhibitions of party unity. The parties make sure that significant debate and business are conducted in the more private venue of the hotel suite.

Under today's television set-up, few people will encounter a robust point/counterpoint debate on crucial social and political issues unless they make Herculean efforts to do so. Even though certain specialty cable channels now televise routine Congressional floor action or various speeches and press conferences, this live coverage reaches only a very small audience. On the other hand, it is possible that the old broadcasting networks—NBC, CBS, ABC—might eventually find a new niche by looking for significant live events to be covered fully as they unfold. In other words, the economics of television in the multi-channel environment of the cable era may be different from the way it was in the first generation when there were only three major networks. Public events of social and political significance may offer opportunities to lure viewers away from 100 channels of scheduled entertainment fare and toward real-life, real-time happenings.

As evidence of a possible new trend away from pure packaging in political news, we may turn to the emergence of a "talk-show democracy" in 1992. During the presidential campaign of that year, candidates were featured for extended periods on such TV shows as "Larry King

Live," "Arsenio Hall," and "Phil Donahue." Many of campaign '92's memorable moments occurred in the context of TV interview shows: Bill and Hillary Clinton discussing their marriage on "60 Minutes," Ross Perot announcing his candidacy on Larry King's show, Clinton playing his saxophone for Arsenio Hall.

Reflecting the increased prominence of talk-show-style campaigning, innovations in the 1992 presidential and vice-presidential debates mitigated somewhat the news-conference format and winner-take-all coverage that had marked earlier TV debates. The vice-presidential debate saw a single moderator act as referee during what became a fluid free-for-all among Dan Quayle, Al Gore, and James Stockdale. Commentators noted the increased degree of clash among the candidates and the greater focus on particular issues. A similar format was employed during the early part of the third presidential debate among candidates Bill Clinton, George Bush, and Ross Perot. Most unusual, however, was the second presidential debate, during which the candidates, sitting on stools, responded to questions from members of a studio audience who were recognized by a moderator circulating up and down the aisles. A number of commentators believed that the forthright questions of uncommitted voters selected for this debate did better than veteran journalists in capturing the mood of the country.[30]

The single-moderator and audience-question formats used in the debates of 1992 had the effect of transforming these heretofore packaged encounters into less-predictable, live performances. Nonetheless, even if TV opens itself to spontaneous, somewhat unpredictable political encounters, the tendency for TV executives to treat broadcast minutes as units of profit seems more likely to increase than decrease. Due to rampant media consolidation, the ability of business norms to dominate the news becomes ever more pressing. Formation of newspaper chains and media conglomerates increases the context for lessened journalistic independence and diversity, and the fealty to profit is greater than ever. As Allen Neuharth, chairman of the board of the Gannett newspaper chain, once commented: "Wall Street didn't give a damn if we put out a good paper in Niagara Falls. They just wanted to know if our profits would be in the 15-20 percent range."[31] When the print and electronic forums are governed by such dollars-and-cents considerations, matters of improving the quality of public discourse may become secondary to the bottom line.

Foreign Connections

The business tangent of news reporting raises the specter that the news may be captured by overseas interests and agencies. For instance, the promoters of investment bonds can spread good news about foreign countries in order to steer investors to risky ventures overseas. In the 1920s, American bankers cooperated with Italy's fascist-censored press to promote a newspaper image of Italy as a stable country. That view helped the bankers float Italian loans on the American market.[32] In a number of more recent situations, the news has been similarly influenced by overseas interests and their American co-participants. In 1978, a former aide to Shah Mohamed Reza Pahlevi of Iran disclosed that he had made gifts to American and European reporters in exchange for their placing favorable stories about Iran in overseas media. These charges, however, were denied by the various reporters named.[33]

A clearer case of foreign influence in the news was registered in 1979. Investigators in South Africa reported that John McGoff, an American publisher, had received $11.3 million from the South African government to help him buy American newspapers.[34] Evidently, McGoff was supposed to encourage favorable coverage of South Africa. Several years later, the U.S. Justice Department charged McGoff with failing to register as an agent of the South African government, but the charges were later dismissed because the statute of limitations had expired. The investigations by the Justice Department and the Securities and Exchange Commission indicated that the subsidies to McGoff were part of a $37 million covert propaganda campaign mounted by South Africa.[35]

A slightly different twist on the foreign connections of American news occurred in 1986 when the Federal Communications Commission levied a $10,000 fine against KSCI, a Los Angeles television station. KSCI was fined for failing to disclose that its Korean programming had been prepared by South Korea's government-owned TV network.[36]

GETTING GOOD COVERAGE: THE ESTABLISHMENT

Propagandists are fully aware that they can take advantage of the practices and norms of the news, particularly by manipulating the desire of media managers to make news a saleable product. Some of the techniques for getting good coverage favor establishment groups, and others are better used by dissidents. Establishment groups are particularly able to exploit the desire of journalists for official statements, for leaks of inside dope, for helpful press-relations facilities, and for respectable-looking spokespersons.

Official Organizations

Official civic action groups carry legitimacy. Establishment interests are adept at hiding behind apparently spontaneous citizens' groups. In 1989, a coalition of health and environmental groups got enough signatures to put a measure on the California ballot to raise liquor taxes. Wanting to fight fire with fire, the liquor industry formed a group called Taxpayers for Common Sense. Backed with millions in industry money, this organization helped lead the fight against the new taxes.[37]

Another organization formed to influence the public mind in the direction of commercial interests, the Silver Balloon Association, sprang into action when the Public Utilities Commission of California made moves to outlaw metallic coated "silver" balloons. The PUC opposed the balloons because they caused power outages when, filled with helium and released, they settled on power lines and caused service interruptions. Claiming that the sale of metallic balloons was a $50 million business employing thousands of Californians, the Silver Balloon Association sent out material to the news media in an effort to weaken the PUC's case. The Association countered that animals, not balloons, were chiefly to blame for power outages.[38]

Official Spokespersons

Official spokespersons are also useful in capturing news attention for establishment causes. Getting official experts before the cameras can be a full-time job for such organizations as the Center for Strategic and International Studies in Washington, D.C. The Center, affiliated with Georgetown University, consists of 140 Fellows, including Henry Kissinger (Secretary of State under presidents Nixon and Ford), Jeanne Kirkpatrick (ambassador to the United Nations during the Reagan Administration), Zbigniew Brzezinski (foreign policy adviser to President Carter), and James Schlesinger (former secretary of both Defense and Energy).

The Center has been conspicuously successful in retailing its experts to the news media. This success has prompted criticisms that the Center's faculty spends more time before cameras promoting a conservative view of foreign policy and less time in classrooms. Complaints that the Center exists merely to issue press releases and interviews seem substantiated by the Center's lack of a library and the fact that some of its fellows never teach.[39]

Official Leaks

Oftentimes a better way to leverage one's official position is to use press leaks instead of official news conferences or press releases. Press leaks are endemic to Washington. General William E. Odom, Chief of the National Security Agency, once complained that "there's leaking from Congress . . . there's more leaking in the Administration because it's bigger."[40] Odom maintained that some official leaks enabled foreign governments to identify how the U.S. tapped their communications, thereby making his job more difficult. Odom favored a direct government attack on official leaks. On the basis of a 1950 law prohibiting disclosures of communications intelligence, he wanted to prosecute journalists who printed leaks.

We may assume that any effort to prosecute journalists for press leaks would run afoul of the Constitutional safeguards of a free press, but it easy to see why Odom and other intelligence officials want to turn the heat on journalists. The effort to stop leaks at the source perhaps may be likened to a futile effort to command that gossip cease. Government officials find it too tempting to use their insider's information to their own personal advantage. Anyone in Washington with information feels the tug to enlist the news as an ally. Even Nancy Reagan (the ultimate insider) turned outward to public journalism in her effort to get rid of President Reagan's White House chief of staff, Donald Regan. Nancy leaked to NBC news a charge that Regan had twice hung up the phone on her. Although the story was attributed to a source "very close to Mrs. Reagan," people at the *Washington Post* claimed that the tip came from Nancy herself as part of an effort to foment a climate in which Regan either would resign or be forced out.[41]

Official Press Relations

Not only may establishment leaders maximize their control of information but also they have several resources for packaging or orchestrating a story. The field of public relations experienced its first great spurt of growth when business leaders such as John D. Rockefeller discovered the usefulness of reaching the public through strategically-placed news stories.

The natural affinity of public relations for business institutions may be found in the Greyhound strike of 1990. Management's response to the strikers involved a close coordination between company executives and press-relations aides. When a sniper fired on a Greyhound bus in Florida, Greyhound chairman Fred Currey was on the scene within hours to be photographed boarding a bus at the very place where the gunman had opened fire. Curry's press aides also dispatched him to three Florida cities that day to meet publicly with riders and replacement drivers.[42] While management coordinated its news-skewing program, the Amalgamated Council of Greyhound Local Unions, which lacked an in-house PR team, hired a Washington public-relations firm to publicize the union's position that drivers' salaries had declined during the past decade.

Public-relations methods are useful not only for institutions with a message but also for leaders and celebrities who want to promote themselves. One public-relations firm, Publicity USA, specialized in packaging the message of an individual or institution, and placing the message in leading media outlets. The firm hired ex-reporters who were familiar with the norms of journalism. Publicity USA's president, Peter Jacobs, argued that his firm's fees (ranging in 1990 from $1,000 to $20,000) were a bargain because "a 30-second television spot goes for $300,000 and up."[43]

Another promotional firm, Primetime, charged clients on the basis of where the firm was able to place stories—instead of charging by the hour or by a standard fee. If Primetime placed an article favorable to the client in *USA Today,* for instance, the client paid Primetime $7,710; an article about the client appearing in the *Los Angeles Times* earned payment of $8,830; a spot on the *NBC Nightly News* netted Primetime $21,560. This payment-by-results plan has advantages for clients, but it only worsens ethical problems for professional journalists. The temptation for a low-paid reporter to take a kickback for writing up a Primetime client is worrisome, especially given estimates that up to half of the stories in American newspapers are the result of public-relations gambits.

Some publicists specialize in helping celebrities and would-be celebrities get into the news. For instance, Gustavus Ober of New York City, another ex-journalist, helped launch his clients into the social world by getting them invitations to New York's important parties and, from another direction, helping gather a prestigious guest list for parties hosted by his clients. Ober also provided specialized services in media exposure, for example, helping his clients get their apartments featured in *Architectural Digest*.[44]

Celebrity public relations may also work backwards. When a person has become infamous through accident, this individual may hire a publicist to channel his or her newly-heightened visibility in more favorable directions. In 1987, Fawn Hall, secretary to Col. Oliver North of Iran-*Contra* fame, gained her proverbial 15 minutes of fame during Congressional hearings, and she soon signed a promotional contract with William Morris, a prominent talent agency.[45]

The model for modern institutional press relations remains the Reagan White House. "Every president tries to use the press to his advantage," acknowledged Ronald Reagan at the annual White House Correspondents Association dinner in 1988.[46] The Reagan Administration became known for its particular adeptness in courting and coopting the press to get its point of view onto TV and into the newspapers. Members of the White House press corps worked hard at filing puff pieces that boosted the careers of various "confidential" sources. Reporters were so busy seeking after the crumbs from their coveted White House sources that they missed the truly large stories. The Iran-*Contra* scandal, for instance, was not broached by reporters stationed at 1600 Pennsylvania Avenue.[47]

It is difficult for White House reporters to forego the pleasures of access and the perquisites of proximity to power. William Safire, columnist for the *New York Times*, once explained why he declined an invitation to an intimate White House get-together with President Reagan. Safire, former speechwriter for President Nixon, learned that the event was to be strictly off the record—no tape recorders or pencils. He declined the invitation in small protest against the growth of "off-the-recordism," which Safire decried as a conspiracy to protect officials by enticing reporters to become insiders, thereby leaving the public outside.[48]

The evidence is tangible that Reagan's charming courtship of the press worked. Journalism researchers Elliott King and Michael Schudson compared Reagan's popularity, as measured by opinion polls, to his popularity as reported by Washington correspondents. According to opinion-poll data, Reagan's popularity lagged behind that of Jimmy Carter and other recent presidents for the first three years of his administration. The White House press corps, however, generally liked the personable Mr. Reagan. King and Schudson believed that Washington reporters spread a myth of Reagan's popularity that was not supported by the actual survey data. "Without meaning to, Washington insiders may have projected their friendly feelings toward Reagan onto the general public."[49]

New Technologies

By virtue of their material resources, establishment groups and individuals not only capitalize on information control and public-relations advisers but also their wealth permits them first access to new techniques for influencing the news. For instance, new-style video news releases (VNRs) cater to TV's need for pictures. Well-produced VNRs look like actual news stories prepared by local and national press organizations. Sometimes the VNRs are directly broadcast to the unsuspecting viewer who believes that the materials were gathered and put together by bona fide independent journalists rather than by press-relations aides of an organization.

One producer of video news releases, Armstrong Information Services of New York City, once prepared and sent out a VNR to promote Tetra-Briks, a box of water with protruding straw. Armstrong put together a story about how a "New Kind of Water Powers Marathon Runners." This video-commercial was produced to look and sound like a news story about the New York Marathon. It contained the standard TV-news-style opening that began with familiar pictures of New York, and then it cut to runners. A voice-over explained that runners could become dehydrated during the event. At the same time, the video showed runners getting cups to drink, spilling most of the water as they plodded along. The voice then explained how the Tetra-Brik cartons were a solution to the runners' problem.

Armstrong's Tetra-Briks voice-over was on a separate channel so that a news organization could replace it with their own anchor person who would read a script provided by the folks at Armstrong. This commercial-as-news-story was picked up by 32 stations with an audience of nearly 3,000,000 people.[50] Advertisers have been interested in the video news release approach because of the declining audiences for network TV shows. Armstrong Information Services claimed a 30 percent average success rate for each VNR that it shipped out to around 200 stations. They reported that the VNRs most likely to be picked up by stations are those having "great visuals" that can be used as a cheerful wrap-up at the end of the show.

170

While VNRs cater to the needs of local TV stations for great pictures, they find their way into national news as well. In late 1988, the CBS Evening News reported on the settlement of a federal investigation of the Drexel Burnham Lambert securities firm. The CBS story contained an interview of Frederick H. Joseph, the Chief Executive Officer of Drexel, that actually was prepared by Drexel itself. Ray Brady, CBS correspondent, defended use of the Drexel tape on the basis that Drexel released its story only at 5:30 P.M., precluding a CBS-conducted interview. Brady added that CBS edited the video interview to remove Drexel's self-serving puffery.

National TV networks are more likely than local stations to edit a video news release, thereby causing a problem for propagandists. However, Robert Kimmel, president of Audio TV Productions (another VNR producer), believed that 40 percent of stations that run a VNR run it intact. In such a case, viewers would have no reason to suspect that the pictures and accompanying story had been prepared and written by a propagandist rather than by a news organization.[51]

Establishment causes are able to infiltrate the news by projecting what seems to be a legitimate official version of reality. The news-control arsenal of elites includes not only official associations, spokespersons, and leaks but also press relations and new technologies to skew reporting.

GETTING GOOD COVERAGE: THE DISSIDENTS

Dissident individuals attain good news coverage chiefly through social dramas that win media attention. Actions and events leading to press attention can be initiated either by individuals or through mass organizing.

Flamboyant Individuals

The Rev. Al Sharpton's flair for the sensational (see above, pp. 151-152) illustrates the use of individual action to get media coverage. Flamboyant statements and activities, like Sharpton's, make for irresistible media events, but the arresting pictures and sound bites generated by charismatic individuals amount to an ambiguous form of propaganda. On the one hand, newspaper and TV people cannot afford to ignore sensational charges about a controversial issue, even when mainstream officials are vehemently denying them. Not only do flamboyant actions and charges generate captivating headlines but also the dissident view frequently turns out to be correct. In the early 1980s, for instance, U.S. peace groups insisted that the federal government was sending American equipment to *Contra* rebels in Nicaragua. Despite repeated denials from Washington, the dissident view eventually was proved accurate.

On the other hand, many charges by dissident individuals and many seemingly spontaneous events turn out to be hoaxes perpetrated in the interest either of getting attention or constructing a propaganda-of-action to favor some cause. Some sensational charges seem to be ploys consciously designed to get attention. A media hoax occurred during the Bensonhurst trial in which some young Whites were convicted of beating to death Yusuf Hawkins. A mystery witness emerged who made claims to newspapers and television stations that she had observed the defendants shoot Hawkins. Later, when the woman was unable to identify a picture of the defendant from a group of police photographs, she admitted that her story came to her in a dream.[52] In another propaganda-of-action case, two Israeli Jews admitted that they had desecrated hundreds of Jewish graves in Jerusalem in hopes that Arabs would be blamed. Their objective was to incite anger that would unite Israelis against Arabs.[53]

Collective Organizing

In addition to pursuing a propaganda of individual action, dissident groups may rely on their organizing abilities to mount major events of community or national scope. One example was Hands across America. This event was a promotional idea of Ken Kragen of Los Angeles, who built a nationwide demonstration to publicize hunger. The event proved irresistible to the media. Newspapers and television blanketed the country with pictures detailing every possible way that people had joined hands, including participants who held hands with animals.[54]

Earth Day '90—Sunday, April 22, 1990—was a national event that represented the acme of dissident-style mass propaganda. Coordinated by Earth Day 1990, an organization centered in Palo Alto, California, the event relied on the typical citizen's organizing efforts of dissident movements. Earth Day '90 eventually became a week-long campaign to get citizens to become part of a new environmental consciousness that would command political attention. Americans, both in their own lives and in community action, were bidden to participate. Nearly every locality saw efforts to promote recycling, energy conservation, and alternative forms of transportation.

News coverage of Earth Day '90 and other similar organizational actions is always problematic from a propaganda point of view. One never knows the extent to which the pictures are spontaneous or staged. Staged pictures, of course, pose the risk of foisting bogus news onto the media, even when the manufactured images are consistent with events actually happening elsewhere. During the violent clashes between demonstrators and police that accompanied the 1968 Democratic National Convention in Chicago, many complaints surfaced about reporters staging episodes for the cameras. For instance, U.S. Senator Gale McGee observed a TV camera team leading two young women over to where some National Guard troops were located. With the cameras rolling, one of the girls started to cry, "Don't beat me! Don't beat me!"[55]

One may sympathize with a camera crew that has missed spontaneous violence initiated either by demonstrators or police; nevertheless, when simulated news action is not labeled as such, the news becomes a covert propaganda. By staging, or acquiescing in, simulations, news people may be helping to exaggerate social action, or to cast it in an inaccurate light. Thorny distinctions between news and truth crop up even when all the pictures are accurate. For instance, after the San Francisco Bay Area's massive earthquake of 1989, fiber optics flashed around the country every possible picture of destruction, leaving television audiences with the false impression that the region was in complete ruin.

Earth Day '90 illustrated an additional problem of getting news coverage through organized dissident action. Propaganda-through-action is especially subject to cooptation by opposing groups. Business organizations used public relations to get on the bandwagon of Earth Day '90. For instance, shortly before the event, Roger Smith, General Motors Chairman of the Board, announced that his company would be mass producing an electrical car. Skeptical environmentalists pointed to earlier claims by the company that it was on the verge of selling electrical automobiles.[56] McDonald's fast-food restaurants announced that the organization would purchase up to $100 million in recycled materials for use in its buildings.[57] Although laudable, this announcement was timed for maximum impact, and it begged the questions of whether McDonald's initiative was likely to be realized or would be significant in scope.

A number of major corporations tailored their advertising campaigns during April 1990 to Earth Day themes. An Arco petroleum ad listed 10 ways that people could use their automobiles in a less-polluting fashion. The list was written on a removable scratch-and-sniff figure of a pine tree.[58] Denis Hayes, Chairman of the Earth Day '90 group, reserved judgment on what others had called corporate "Earth-hype." Hayes commented that, "If companies are going to make real improvements, that's great. If it is just for public relations, then I condemn it."[59]

Dissident groups that employ the propaganda of organized action frequently lack money, but they draw upon rich reservoirs of human commitment. They may find, however, that their propaganda of mass action becomes difficult to control. Just as corporations coopted Earth Day '90, so too can free news coverage become subtly detrimental to a dissident movement. Anti-establishment organizers cannot stipulate their image as it is conveyed in the news. A striking case in point occurred in connection with the Students for a Democratic Society organization of the 1960s. SDS found that it could overcome its obscurity by mounting a militant type of activity that was likely to get news coverage. However, media coverage of the SDS's antics made this rather intellectual and middle-class group look militant. Ironically, news coverage of militant SDS protests attracted a new, more militant type of recruit to SDS, thereby transforming the organization itself.[60]

Although dissident groups play up dramatic events to their advantage, dissenters may become so preoccupied with ideological enactment that they neglect other useful tactics for getting good media coverage. It probably is the case that establishment groups do a better job of staging fake grass-roots organizations than dissidents do of using mainstream public-relations techniques. Even when they have the resources, anti-establishment types sometimes have lacked appreciation of the advantages of using public relations and other behind-the-scenes media techniques. In the 1930s, George Seldes, the media critic, wanted to convince organized labor to establish a major labor-owned newspaper. Just when labor was finally getting the message that owning an important newspaper might be useful, World War II came along to distract attention from the project.[61]

While labor organizations share the disinclination of dissidents to use advanced techniques of public relations, the laborites occasionally can mount a limited foray of this kind. In 1988, unions in San Francisco cooperated to mount a pilot magazine-style television show called "California Working." With donations from labor and community groups, the series was designed to acquaint a non-union audience with workplace issues chronicled from a union point of view.[62] The first of these half-hour shows included a review of Cal-OSHA, California's occupational safety and health organization; a profile of a career waitress; and a comedy feature about airline deregulation. Costs often have deterred unions and other left-of-center organizations from promotional campaigns employing the news format. For instance, "California Working" was projected to cost $150,000 yearly.

The following case studies reinforce the perception that both establishment and dissident groups aim for favorable media treatment by adapting to the professional norms and business practices of news organizations.

PRESSURE GROUPS IN THE NEWS: CASE STUDIES

News coverage of pressure groups from left and right brings both opportunities and difficulties for journalists. On the one hand, reporters and editors are interested in the expressions and antics of movers and shakers. On the other hand, journalists fear that advocacy groups will transform the news into a self-serving vehicle for policies and ideological positions. The pressure campaigns of rightists against TV programming, and of leftists who derailed Robert Bork's elevation to the U.S. Supreme Court, together illustrate that dangerous liaisons may grow up between journalism and advocacy groups.

CBTV

The campaign of the Coalition for Better Television (CBTV) is the success story of how the small strength of a right-wing pressure group could be magnified by attention from the media. In 1981, CBTV, organized by Rev. Donald E. Wildmon of Tupelo, Mississippi, claimed that it represented 400 national groups and 1,400 Christian congregations,[63] including such groups as Jerry Falwell's Moral Majority. CBTV's claims and threats secured wide media attention, scaring not only TV executives but also TV sponsors with a threatened boycott by millions of consumers. Proctor & Gamble, which had spent $486 million for TV ads in 1980, withdrew sponsorship from 50 TV shows identified by CBTV as having too much sex and violence.[64] After meetings with advertisers, CBTV later called off the threatened boycott, but warned of its potential use in the future.[65] In 1982, CBTV announced a boycott of RCA products because the RCA-owned network, NBC, produced shows that were allegedly anti-Christian. Examples cited by CBTV included the appearance of the Playboy Playmates on a George Burns Christmas special.[66]

It is possible that media coverage exaggerated both the strength of Wildmon's CBTV and the extent of this organization's support, taking Wildmon's claims of a 400-group coalition at face value. Some of Wildmon's affiliated organizations appear, however, to have existed chiefly in the form of letterheads; others explicitly denied membership in CBTV.[67] Also, the considerable media attention given to Wildmon's office contributed to a bandwagon effect in which major advertisers, such as Gillette and General Foods, opted not to sponsor a greater number of controversial shows than in previous years. These businesses took pains to deny that outside pressure was the cause of their sudden sensitivity to issues of morality and taste.

Although Wildmon's crusade was receiving considerable publicity, the real threat of a CBTV boycott was hard to determine. Poll data available to advertisers indicated that barely two percent of Americans would support a boycott and that people who identified with the Moral Majority watched the same kinds of TV shows that other people did. The threat did encourage advertisers to scrutinize more closely the TV fare they were sponsoring. One important advertiser publicly embraced the aims of CBTV: Owen Butler, board chairman of Procter & Gamble (TV's biggest advertiser), surprised the industry by publicly praising CBTV for "expressing some very important and broadly held views about gratuitous sex, violence, and profanity."[68]

The flood of publicity about fundamentalist TV boycotts led to the establishment of an opposing organization. Norman Lear, producer of "All in the Family" and other TV shows, set up People for the American Way, a liberal advocacy group that opposed censorship of artistic expression.[69] Lear's group drew support from centrist and liberal religious organizations, such as the National Council of Churches and the American Jewish Committee.

The Balk over Bork

Leftist groups, too, use the news as part of their pressure efforts. In 1987, President Reagan nominated Robert Bork, a conservative jurist, for a position on the U.S. Supreme Court. Bork's nomination activated an opposition campaign by a coalition of liberal politicians and left-of-center pressure and advocacy groups. Women's groups, Black advocacy groups, and liberal pressure groups began to mobilize their constituencies. These lobbying organizations also worked with liberal senators and their staffs to dig up the record of Bork's opinions expressed in his many judicial actions, articles, and speeches. This research showed Bork to be at odds with the majority of Americans on such issues as use of contraceptives, forced sterilization, poll taxes, literacy tests, and court-ordered desegregation.

Alert to public-relations strategy, anti-Bork forces focused on those issues having the maximum potential impact. In a rare display of ideological restraint, the anti-Bork coalition avoided the divisive slogans of gay rights, feminism, and pro-choice advocacy. Instead, the anti-Bork campaign was organized around what was common to all these leftist groups: basic civil rights. Hence, the first witnesses called against Bork were spokespersons of African-American advocacy groups who portrayed Bork as a threat to fundamental civil-rights legislation. Senator Alan Cranston of California viewed this testimony as useful in weakening support for Bork among Southern senators who saw the conservative judge as likely to stir up old wounds in Dixie.[70] As a result of the propaganda against Bork, many senators came to feel that the only safe vote was an anti-Bork vote, and the nomination failed. In stirring up a publicity boom against Bork, the protesters applied a basic lesson of propaganda that communication practitioners have followed since World War I. Effective propaganda often influences elites (in this case, U.S. senators) by influencing their voting constituencies. The anti-Bork forces not only grabbed space on the news media by mobilizing women's groups and Black advocacy groups but also they successfully courted white Southerners with ads alleging that Bork would reopen old issues about voting rights and separate facilities, settled decisions that had become accepted practices. Norman Lear's People for the American Way ran commercials against Bork that enlisted actor Gregory Peck to complain that Bork "defended poll taxes and literacy tests which kept many Americans from voting."[71]

Senator Orrin Hatch of Utah criticized Bork's opponents for using what he termed a campaign of misleading "propaganda" to swing public opinion against the Reagan nominee.[72] Hatch's complaint was ironic. According to Christopher Matthews, a news analyst, the anti-Bork effort represented "a carbon copy of the media/lobbying campaigns often engineered by conservative groups."[73] According to Matthews, the campaign featured "a committed core of ideologues, total dedication to a single goal, smart use of polling data, a clear-cut message, and, most important of all, an ironlike discipline." In other words, the individual anti-Bork groups subordinated their own agendas and ego gratifications to the common purpose of defeating the nomination.

The moral restraint and media savvy reflected in the anti-Bork campaign is not typical of the work of left-leaning groups. These organizations and their spokespersons more often are seen and heard issuing shrill and narrow demands or indulging in high-pitched grandstanding. An illustration of narrow demands was the insistence by the Asian-American Journalists Association (New York Chapter) that Jimmy Breslin, a populist *Newsday* columnist, be suspended for his tirade against a Korean-American reporter.[74] The parallel tactic of getting coverage through dramatic grandstanding is illustrated by a rally mounted by Jesse Jackson in front of Harvard Law School. Jackson supported law professor Derrick Bell's demand that Harvard immediately add a Black female professor to the staff.[75]

BUSINESS AND THE NEWS

To whatever degree right-wing and left-wing organizing activity influences the news, it is likely that even more TV time and newspaper space are given over to items originating from the news-management methods of business organizations. No review of propaganda in the news would be complete without a close look at the work of publicity experts serving the business community. Business is so large a part of American politics and society that its efforts at news manipulation are an especially important feature of the current cultural scene.

Although business is central to American life and culture, representatives of American business frequently complain about hostile coverage by television and newspapers. Part of the explanation for this paradox may be that business executives are accustomed to deferential treatment by their subordinates, and so they are unprepared for the rougher handling they receive from journalists. Business leaders also have convinced themselves that they deserve a less critical treatment than the government routinely receives. Business people view their organizations as "private," in contrast to government which is "public" and therefore requires more scrutiny.[76] Nonetheless, many actions by private business organizations have public implications. Obvious examples include product safety and the impact of opening or closing a plant in a community. Business is the equal of government in deserving the critical scrutiny it will always receive through news reporting.

Business organizations respond to attention from the news media in a number of predictable ways. Like government officials, business people alternately pressure reporters and court them. At the same time, American businesses increasingly claim free-speech rights to speak out on social and political issues.

Pressuring the Media

The effort by business groups to influence news is as old as newspapers themselves. Before the emergence of today's familiar mass-circulation newspapers, many papers were entirely oriented to business concerns; they covered the coming and going of ships as well as other business transactions.[77] The emergence of general-interest newspapers seemingly diluted the orientation of mass media to commerce; however, because the general-interest papers were supported by paid advertising, these mass-circulation journals were subject to pressures from those who purchased the ads. Department stores were among the earliest businesses to employ advertising as a lever for influencing press treatment. Newspapers not infrequently suppressed items unfavorable to these large advertisers, including in-store robberies or scandals involving department-store owners.

Today, we find fewer and fewer complaints about advertising pressure distorting news coverage. For one thing, due to the consolidation of news organizations, the media enjoy a strong counterweight to threats of advertising boycotts. In a one-newspaper town, businesspeople are less likely to withdraw their ads than they were in the days when a large city might support eight papers. Nevertheless, as critics continue to point out, the financial influence of cigarette advertising, for one example, contributes to lessened press attention to the harmful effects of smoking on health. Two media researchers found that, even after the evidence had mounted that smoking is detrimental to good health, mass-circulation magazines have withdrawn stories that pointed up the health hazards of smoking in order to placate tobacco advertisers.[78]

Given today's large media monopolies and increased professionalization among editors and reporters, the influence of business on news content has become more subtle. Today's business community is more likely to court newspapers for good coverage rather than to demand favorable news.

179

Courting and Co-Opting the Media

The public-relations pioneer Ivy Lee preached the virtues of winning favorable coverage by taking a friendly and helpful attitude toward reporters. The idea was to make their job easier by providing amenities as well as helpful press releases that could serve as the basis for stories printed in the papers. For instance, during a bloody strike at the Colorado coal mines owned by Rockefeller interests, Lee brought in young John D. Rockefeller, Jr., to visit the mines and dance with the miners' wives at town functions.

The work of Lee and his successors amounts to a courtship-through-identification in which business leaders are presented as being just plain folk. Despite the complaints of today's capitalists about hostile newspaper stories, many media critics point out that businesses have one important advantage in news coverage of labor/management disputes: the tendencies are built-in for the press to give more attention to the management point of view than to labor. Reporters and managers both are part of the white-collar segment of society. Reporters not only have more routine contact with managers but also they find it easier to understand their white-collar brethren in management than to comprehend the world view of the blue-collar laborers.[79]

While overt advertising pressure is less common today than in previous eras, advertising continues to offer business a chance to mix pressure with courtship. Feeling constantly under siege from reformers, radicals, and impractical do-gooders, industry leaders have developed special expertise in rebutting, blunting, or turning around attacks by dissident groups. For instance, the business community embraced Earth Day with such an astonishing vigor that one almost looked for signs touting "Earth Day—*brought to you by* . . . ." The week preceding April 22, 1990, saw adroit press releases by businesses timed to coincide with environmental festivities. Major canning companies announced plans to stop buying tuna caught by fishing boats that used methods which also trapped dolphins. Coca-Cola trumpeted its efforts to help set up recycling programs. Conoco announced a new policy of acquiring only double-hulled oil tankers as a way to curtail oil spills. General Motors told the world that it would mass-produce an electrical car.[80]

The onset of Earth Day '90 also prompted institutional ads and advertorials (advertising in the form of editorials) in newspapers and magazines. The Chemical Manufacturers Association took a full-page ad to report on the industry's new "Responsible Care" program to promote safe use of chemicals and safe chemical waste disposal.[81] *Newsweek's* "Earth Day '90" issue contained a special advertising section on the environment. The section included features on such topics as industry's efforts to achieve energy efficiency. The section also attended to what individual people could do to improve the environment—e.g., to put a plastic bottle in one's toilet tank to reduce the use of water. In addition to news-type stories, *Newsweek's* special advertising section presented short pro-environment plugs by specific businesses. One ad by Toyota asked the owners of off-road vehicles to "go easy on the environment"; another by Phillips Petroleum described a bald eagle breeding program that the company supported.[82]

Earth Day '90 illustrated how business, its critics, and the press can dwell in a brief, artificial harmony. Notwithstanding episodes of good feeling, an inherent conflict exists between business, which wishes to keep its activities confidential, and the press, which wants to report any interesting business-related developments. News reporters and editors are nearly unanimous in the belief that if an interesting story about business is available, it eventually will be printed due to competition from other papers. The press generally believes that it would not be in the public interest for it [the press] to "work with" major corporations. Said one editor at a press-business symposium: "The day when hostility between business and the press vanishes will be the saddest day in our history."[83]

FREE SPEECH AND AMERICAN BUSINESS

In recent years, business organizations have begun to see themselves as just another advocate in America's idealized marketplace of ideas. Direct advocacy, so-called "business free speech," represents another way for business to circulate its views in news publications.

In 1978, the U.S. Supreme Court ruled that a state may not prohibit a business corporation from using corporate funds to propagate general political views unrelated to the corporation's business activities.[84] This decision was the culmination of a general trend to give bona fide free-speech protection to business organizations, thereby reversing an earlier tendency to see business speech as inherently dangerous. The earlier view had held that businesses were chartered to organize a private undertaking necessary for the general public interest. From this perspective, to allow a wealthy capitalist corporation free rein to speak would be to permit a private entity to manipulate the very public which it should be serving.[85] Now that the idea of business free speech is widely accepted, commercial organizations pursue direct advocacy in three ways: institutional ads, advertorials, and business advocacy groups.

Institutional Advertising

When the Depression of the 1930s brought business down from its pedestal, the captains of commerce turned to institutional advertising as a defense mechanism. Bruce Barton, advertising industry giant, told the National Association of Manufacturers in 1935 that big business needed to spread the word aggressively that large-scale commercial enterprises were using research and mass production to achieve low prices.[86]

The big-business press-relations campaign of the 1930s marked an early use of institutional advertising, that is, ads touting a business organization or industry in general rather than selling a specific product. Illustrative of business's institutional advertising in the 1930s were the two-page, four-color ads inserted by General Motors into magazines such as the *Saturday Evening Post.* The ads described the work of GM's labs, accompanied by a narrative text focused on the theme: "Who Serves Progress—Serves America."[87]

Once it became clear to media managers that corporations were open to buying institutional ads, publishers made overtures to secure this new advertising bonanza. The effort by media people to obtain lucrative institutional ads made them increasingly sensitive to the business point of view. Leaving nothing to chance, however, business leaders also turned to public-relations counselors such as Edward L. Bernays for direct help in injecting pro-business thinking into newspapers and magazines. Bernays and others coordinated the placement of speeches, events, and news releases that focused on actions by American industry. Further, the National Association of Manufacturers established a program to help local businesspeople make contact with local media for the purpose of emphasizing the management side of employment and production issues.

The form of institutional advertising changed little between the 1930s and the 1980s. An ad placed in *Sports Illustrated* magazine by the American Insurance Association illustrates institutional ads during this era.[88] The insurance industry ad touted air bags as a safety device to decrease death and injury from auto accidents. The ad further listed what the insurance industry was doing to control insurance costs, such as agitating for safer cars and highways, and lowering premiums for cars equipped with safety features.

Another variant of the institutional ad is the advertisement that touts a product that no consumer reasonably would anticipate buying. Why, for example, would an aircraft manufacturer choose to "advertise" in a major-circulation magazine? Most readers are not likely to go out and buy an F-15 airplane, so why advertise it to the public? Business people know that ads for nonconsumable products can have an impact. For one thing, ads of this kind remind consumers of the company's name and product. Similarly, this quasi-institutional advertising also shows industry's flag, reminding media managers and editors that the point of view of industrialists is not to be ignored.

Advertorials

More controversial than institutional advertising are today's advertorials, that is, editorials paid for by major advertisers. Today's advertorializing is best exemplified by Mobil Oil. Herbert Schmertz, a Mobil vice president, argued that the electronic news media ignore most significant stories about business because the stories are not simple enough or controversial enough to fit the requirements of television's short-attention-span format.[89] Mobil has therefore been a leader in advocacy advertising, presenting its point of view through paid editorials in newspapers.

In 1980, Mobil argued against government action in the area of energy supplies and conservation. After criticizing the Carter Administration for preaching about energy conservation, Mobil's ad asked: "So what's Washington actually *doing* about saving energy?" The Mobil ad then criticized the government for failing to practice energy conservation in federal buildings, as contrasted to "oil companies and other private industries" that were making notable progress. For Mobil, the ideal government action in the energy area was to do nothing, merely to sit back and let rising prices lead to greater production.[90]

While generally successful at inserting advertorials in print media, Mobil and other advocacy advertisers have had difficulty in securing time on national TV. Local stations often will run advertorials, but the networks have refused. For example, NBC's position has been that the public interest is better served when "partisan viewpoints on important issues, such as oil company profits, are presented in news and public affairs programs, produced by disinterested news professionals and not in paid commercials."[91] Advertorials have been widely criticized for their biases, for making free speech a matter of money, and for causing editors to lose control of the content of publications.

A more psychological objection to advertorials is that these propagandistic plugs take the reader by surprise. Art Buchwald once satirized the deceptive aura of a particular multi-page special advertising section that he encountered in a magazine.

> The other day I was reading a story in a news magazine about the king of Morocco. "This is some king," I remarked to Hyman Bixby, an editor of the magazine. "Your reporters think he's hot stuff."
>
> "Not our reporters. That's an advertorial," he told me. "It was paid for by Morocco. It says so at the top of the page."
>
> "I can't see anything at the top."
>
> Bixby handed me a magnifying glass and, after five minutes, I found the words `Special Advertising Section.' "By gum, it does say 'advertising.' It looks exactly like editorial copy."[92]

Business Advocacy Groups

In addition to institutional advertising and advertorials, business and industry may skew news coverage by forming citizens' organizations that impart a grass-roots aura to business lobbying.

In 1990, the alcoholic beverage industry in California spent millions to oppose a ballot initiative that would have increased the tax on liquor. The industry sponsored a group called Taxpayers for Common Sense as its agency to carry forth the anti-tax message.[93] Similarly, in 1986, major industrial manufacturers supported a "No on 65" campaign to defeat a California ballot initiative designed to control the discharge of cancer-causing chemicals. The business community argued that Proposition 65 would be disruptive to commerce, interfering with the use of such common items as aspirin and chlorinated water. At the same time, however, businesses also financed a billboard campaign that featured the confusing (and hypocritical) warning that the measure was *not stringent enough:* "No on 65. The Toxics Initiative. It's full of exemptions."[94]

Covert cooptation of the news is particularly dangerous when mounted by business organizations because commercial corporations control so much money. In the final analysis, however, business groups are only one of many advocates seeking to skew news in self-serving directions. Any number of social movers and shakers—establishment and dissident, liberal and conservative—are daily at work in the news. The tactics of news manipulation are legion, although not necessarily always successful.

The public's ambivalence about journalists supplies evidence that Americans are vaguely aware of the problem that propaganda poses for the news. Surveys report a general impression among people that the press tries to be fair and that it succeeds in being more even-handed than professionals in government, business, or labor.[95] At the same time, other polls reveal the public's suspicion that news media are more liberal than the average citizen. The public's innate sense that press people are opinionated, but strive to be fair, certainly captures the fundamental tension between propaganda and journalism. Knowing more about how propagandists infiltrate the news is a key to making sure that mass media—the Bible of American politics—play a constructive role in social democracy.

ENDNOTES

1. Walter Lippmann, "The Basic Problem of Democracy," *Atlantic Monthly*, November 1919: 622.

2. Edward L. Bernays, *Biography of an Idea: Memoirs of Public Relations Counsel Edward L. Bernays* (New York: Simon and Schuster, 1965): 543.

3. See, for example, Edward J. Epstein, *News from Nowhere* (New York: Vintage, 1973): 227.

4. Walter Lippmann, "The Basic Problem of Democracy," *Atlantic Monthly*, November 1919: 626.

5. Aristotle, *Politics*.

6. Plato, *Gorgias*; cf. I.F. Stone, *The Trial of Socrates* (Boston: Little, Brown, 1988).

7. Walter Lippmann, *Public Opinion* (N.Y.: Macmillan, 1922): 358.

8. George Seldes, interview with author, Hartland-4-Corners, Vt., May 12-13, 1984, and Stephen Hess, *The Washington Reporters* (Washington, D.C.: Brookings, 1981): 5.

9. S. Holly Stocking and Paget H. Gross, *How Do Journalists Think? A Proposal for the Study of Cognitive Bias in Newsmaking* (Bloomington, Indiana: ERIC/RCS, 1989).

10. Ben H. Bagdikian, *The Media Monopoly* (Boston: Beacon Press, 1983): 132 and Michael Schudson, *Discovering the News* (New York: Basic Books, 1978): 167-168.

11. *San Jose Mercury News*, 9/15/90: 1C.

12. Gladys E. Lang & Kurt Lang, *The Battle for Public Opinion: The President, the Press, and the Polls during Watergate* (New York: Columbia University Press, 1983): 39.

13. Ernest W. Lefever, *TV and National Defense* (Boston, VA: Institute for American Strategy Press, 1974).

14. San Jose, CA *Metro*, 12/14-20/89: 8.

15. Warren Bennis, *San Francisco Chronicle*, 10/20/86, 27.

16. Christopher Lasch, *The Culture of Narcissism* (New York: Warner, 1979): 55 and elsewhere.

17. *San Francisco Chronicle*, 10/25/86: 39,44.

18. Hess, *Washington Reporters*: 52.

19. Edward J. Epstein, *Between Fact and Fiction* (New York: Vintage, 1975): 19-32.

20. Ellen Hume, *New York Times*, 5/24/90: A25.

21. Epstein, *News from Nowhere*: 172-173

22. *People*, 10/7/85: 57.

23. George Seldes, *Even the Gods Can't Change History* (Secaucus, NJ: Lyle Stuart, 1976): 120-121 .

24. Louisville, KY *Courier-Journal*, 4/11/78: A9.

25. *San Francisco Chronicle*, 5/12/87: 21.

26. Marvin Kalb, *New York Times*, 11/28/88: A15 and *San Jose Mercury News*, 4/22/90: 6A.

27. See, respectively, Epstein, *News:* 172, 4-5, 241ff.

28. Epstein, *News:* 113.

29. William V. Shannon, Palo Alto, CA *Peninsula Times Tribune*, 7/31/88: A15.

30. *New York Times*, 10/21/92: A13.

31. Quoted in Ben H. Bagdikian, *The Media Monopoly* (3rd ed.; Boston: Beacon Press, 1990): xxi.

32. George Seldes, *You Can't Print That!* (Garden City, NY: Garden City, 1929): 93-94.

33. Louisville, KY *Courier-Journal*, 11/19/78: B14.

34. *Chronicle of Higher Education*, 3/30/88: A3.

35. *San Francisco Chronicle*, 11/1/86: 10.

36. *San Francisco Chronicle*, 7/17/86: 26.

37. *San Jose Mercury News*, 3/1/90: 9B.

38. Tim Goode, Palo Alto, CA *Peninsula Times Tribune*, 2/3/90: E1.

39. Louisville, KY *Courier-Journal*, 5/11/86: A9.

40. *San Francisco Chronicle*, 9/3/87: 16.

41. *San Francisco Chronicle*, 2/20/87: 14.

42. Palo Alto, CA *Peninsula Times Tribune*, 4/15/90: A6.

43. *Palo Alto Times*, 2/20/90: 3.

44. *San Francisco Chronicle*, 6/17/88: B4.

45. Palo Alto, CA *Peninsula Times Tribune*, 8/20/87: A2.

46. *San Francisco Chronicle*, 4/22/88: A1.

47. *Newsweek*, 5/23/88: 24.

48. Louisville, KY *Courier-Journal*, 8/17/84: A11.

49. *Psychology Today*, 9/88: 33.

50. *This World* (of *San Francisco Chronicle*), 10/25/87: 9.

51. *New York Times*, 1/2/89: 25.

52. *San Jose Mercury News*, 6/6/90: 6A.

53. *San Jose Mercury News*, 5/17/90: A3.

54. J. J. Kilpatrick, Louisville, KY *Courier-Journal*, 5/31/86: A7.

55. Daniel Walker, et al. *Rights in Conflict: Chicago's Seven Brutal Days* (N.Y.: Grosset & Dunlap, 1968): 201-202.

56. Palo Alto, CA *Peninsula Times Tribune*, 4/19/90: D1.

57. *San Jose Mercury News*, 4/18/90: 1A.

58. *Newsweek*, 4/16/90.

59. *San Jose Mercury News*, 4/18/90: 1A.

60. Todd Gitlin, *The Whole World is Watching: Mass Media in the Making and Unmaking of the New Left* (Berkeley: University of California Press, 1980).

61. George Seldes, interview with author, May 12-13, 1984, Hartland-4-Corners, VT.

62. *San Francisco Chronicle*, 1/27/88: A3.

63. Louisville, KY *Courier-Journal*, 3/5/82: A2.

64. *Christian Science Monitor*, 7/23/81: B15.

65. *Christian Science Monitor*, 7/30/81: 4.

66. Louisville, KY *Courier-Journal*, 3/5/82: A2.

67. Todd Gitlin, *Inside Prime Time* (New York: Pantheon, 1985): 250ff.

68. Gitlin, *Inside Prime Time*: 258.

69. *Christian Science Monitor*, 7/23/81: B14-15.

70. *San Francisco Examiner*, 10/4/87: A1.

71. *San Francisco Examiner*, 10/11/87: A1.

72. *San Francisco Chronicle*, 10/1/87: A18.

73. *San Francisco Examiner*, 10/11/87: A1.

74. *New York Times*, 5/10/90: B4.

75. *New York Times*, 4/26/90: A12.

76. Howard Simons and Joseph A. Califano, Jr., *The Media and Business* (New York: Vintage Books, 1979): xi-xii.

77. Schudson, *Discovering News:* 15-16.

78. William L. Weis and Chauncey Burke, "Media Content and Tobacco Advertising: An Unhealthy Connection," *Journal of Communication,* 36, No. 4 (1986): 59-69.

79. Michael Hoyt, "Downtime for Labor," *Columbia Journalism Review,* March/April 1984: 36-40.

80. *San Jose Mercury News,* 4/18/90: lA, 14A; Palo Alto, CA *Peninsula Times Tribune,* 4/19/90: D1.

81. *New York Times,* 4/11/90: A9.

82. *Newsweek,* 4/16/90.

83. Simons & Califano, *Media and Business:* 217.

84. Louisville, KY *Courier-Journal,* 4/27/78: A1.

85. See Candiss B. Vibbert, "Freedom of Speech and Corporations," *Communication,* 12 (1990): 19-34.

86. S. H. Walker and Paul Sklar, *Business Finds Its Voice* (New York: Harper, 1938).

87. Walker & Sklar, *Business Voice:* 17.

88. *Sports Illustrated,* 8/4/80: 39.

89. Simons & Califano, *Media and Business:* xv.

90. "Mobil Observations," Louisville, KY *Courier-Journal,* 1/6/80: 3.

91. Louisville, KY *Courier-Journal,* 1/31/80: B8.

92. Palo Alto, CA *Peninsula Times Tribune,* 2/3/90: B3.

93. Palo Alto, CA *Peninsula Times Tribune,* 6/28/90: A6.

94. *San Francisco Chronicle,* 10/17/86: 14; 2/10/87: 8.

95. Paul Janensch, Louisville, KY *Courier-Journal,* 9/8/85: D3.

Mobil Oil Corporation

150 EAST 42ND STREET
NEW YORK, NEW YORK 10017

THOMAS J FAY
GENERAL MANAGER
PUBLIC RELATIONS DEPARTMENT

May 4, 1977

Dear Professor:

Because we make an ongoing effort to communicate freely with the public on a wide variety of issues, Mobil has often been asked to discuss its public affairs programs—and the reasons behind them—to diverse audiences.

Recently, Herbert Schmertz, vice president, public affairs, described the problems Mobil faces communicating with and through the media before the Business International Chief Executives' Round Table. Mr. Schmertz's comments have been incorporated into a booklet comprised of five case histories, with exhibits, which we think will be of interest to everyone in the business of communicating.

If you would like a copy of "The Energy Crisis and the Media: Some Case Histories" for your own use, please fill in the enclosed reply card. We'd be most happy to send you one, and we would, of course, be interested in your comments.

Many thanks for your interest.

Thomas J. Fay

Everyone Wants to Help the Teacher

CHAPTER 5

PROPAGANDA IN THE CLASSROOM

Charles Lawrence is a popular professor. Voted best teacher by the Stanford Law School class of 1990, Lawrence is an expert on affirmative-action law. His seminar on "Constitutional Law: Minority Issues" is regularly overenrolled. Lawrence's courses, which require students to write reflection pieces and even participate in teaching, are oriented to a critical approach to legal education. In other words, Lawrence treats legal reasoning as something heavily influenced by the arguer's preexisting values and beliefs. A realist in his interpretation of the law, Lawrence does not shy away from the often hidden agenda of many teachers—to mold the minds of students. "Everyone sees themselves as trying to shape these minds," he says. "You never know that some student of yours isn't going to wind up on the damn Supreme Court."[1]

Lawrence's work shows that a single educator may embody the committed teacher, the effective teacher, and the influential teacher. A rich curriculum conveyed through probing dialogue and discussion cannot help but change the views of students. However, because education is not supposed to be a direct kind of persuasion, social influence through the classroom raises issues of propaganda. Whenever the teacher encourages students to challenge their own beliefs about vexing social issues, education teeters on the brink of becoming propaganda. How to handle the tension between education and propaganda is the focus of this chapter.

PROPAGANDA *VERSUS* EDUCATION

A clear distinction between propaganda and education is not easy to articulate; however, the difference between the two is well-expressed in a dictum of Kirtley F. Mather, Harvard professor of geology and leader in adult education. In Mather's view, the teacher should help people learn "*how* to think rather than *what* to think."[2] On tough issues relating to minority preferences, abortion, military spending, and flag-burning, the propagandist, unlike the educator, sees no need for exploration of ambiguities and ironies—all of which might arouse troubling notions and leave loose ends. The propagandist offers settled answers, preferably without too much exploration of the reasons for them, because giving reasons implies that an issue is open to debate. An interest in propaganda analysis draws one inevitably to an exploration of the distinction between propaganda and education as applied to elementary, secondary, and college teaching.

That education can serve as an important channel for propaganda is recognized by every totalitarian regime. Liberalizations in the Soviet Union during the late 1980s highlighted propagandistic features endemic to Soviet education. Soviet history books frequently ignored inconvenient facts, such as the millions killed in forced collectivization of the farms. Under the policy of *glasnost* or openness, however, some of the more blatantly propagandistic texts began to be removed from the shelves. In 1988, the lack of credible textbook treatments of Soviet history led to the cancellation of history exams for Soviet high-school seniors. In the interim, teachers substituted current newspapers and magazines for the old textbooks which some called "useless" because of their omissions and distortions. Some teachers in the former U.S.S.R reported that their classrooms had become home to freer discussions and fewer explicit curriculum controls.[3]

The hand of the educational propagandist is most easily detected in closed political systems, such as the former U.S.S.R, where one faction or party controlled a unitary state. Education can be a useful channel for propaganda in open systems, however, as well as in totalitarian regimes. Open socio-political systems, such as the United States, exhibit a different style of propaganda because different parties and pressure groups have space to compete. Although pressure groups of the Right and Left lack easy means to attempt to control the curriculum, they nevertheless try to influence the schools wherever possible. Competing to slant the

192

curriculum, today, are major interest groups representing business, religion, and various rightist and leftist causes.

For a hundred years, the American business community has taken a considerable interest in what goes on in America's schools. Modern businesspeople realize that educational materials can influence students' views of specific products as well as their grasp of important business concepts, such as competition and advertising. At the same time, American education since the 1950s has become more secular, and America itself more diverse in creed. These developments have caused religious pressure groups to become active in efforts to protect students from "offensive" beliefs, such as the theory of evolution and nontraditional perspectives on the family, e.g. single-parent families or homosexual marriages.

Business and religious pressures on the schools tend to blow in a rightward direction against social and political change. At the same time, especially since the 1960s, newer leftist pressure groups have come into play to steer the curriculum toward social transformations. For instance, feminists now comb the curriculum for materials offensive to their notions of what constitutes "gender equity." Feminists argue for purging educational materials of what they term "sexist language" and for ideas that smack of "patriarchy," i.e., the dominance of men.

Racial and ethnic pressure groups similarly work to make sure that the curriculum reflects what they deem to be a proper sensitivity to minority concerns. Dinesh D'Souza, a rightist political critic, described the move toward "multicultural education" as symptomatic of a leftward drift of the college curriculum that has resulted from agitation by ethnic group activists.[4] The wide range of pressure groups paying attention to the curriculum means that the issue of propaganda in American education is not simply a question of avoiding state control.

Most of today's propaganda battles in education seem to be fought around the marketing of textbooks and the implementation of curricula. To understand propaganda in the classroom, we must look at today's many struggles to control academic discussions of politics, society, and the economy.

BUSINESS PROPAGANDA IN THE SCHOOLS

Larger by far than any other pressure group in America is the business community that operates through individual corporations and trade associations as well as many national and local organizations, such as the National Association of Manufacturers. Business propaganda mixes the effort to achieve direct material benefits (e.g., making students into good consumers) with the effort to satisfy general ideological aims (e.g., defusing criticisms of advertising).

Issues of business propaganda became significant for educators as early as the 1920s when the National Education Association established a committee on propaganda in the schools. The NEA committee surveyed public schools, finding a variety of outside materials influencing the curriculum: essay contests sponsored by outside organizations, exhibits, films, book covers, and pamphlet study materials for teachers. The NEA warned its members that these self-serving materials provided by outsiders worked against the kind of curriculum in which the classroom "is open to all points of view."[5] The early battle over propaganda in the classroom was not without its casualties. For instance, W. W. Borden, Superintendent of Schools in South Bend, Indiana, was pressured to resign because of his criticism of a Women's Christian Temperance Union essay contest that had been placed in the schools without the OK of the Board of Education.[6]

The NELA's Power-full Propaganda

The single most important event bringing the general public's attention to propaganda in schools was the infamous campaign of the National Electric Light Association. Various committees of the national and state NELA covertly spread about the electricity industry's position that privately-owned power plants were best and that city-owned plants were "socialistic." Believing that the schools could help the NELA spread its views, the organization provided pamphlets for use in civics and English classes. The NELA's materials infiltrated a one-sided propaganda into the classroom, arguing that power plants owned by municipalities were too costly compared to privately-owned utilities, and that only private companies paid dividends to investors. At the same time, the NELA was able to induce some publishers to submit drafts of textbooks to the NELA for comment. NELA operatives also gave retainers to professors for study and consulting, and they helped set up college courses about utilities in which company speakers did some, or even most, of the teaching.[7]

Business propaganda is not always as directly connected to the interests of a particular industry as was the case with the NELA campaign. Business groups are often concerned with how the curriculum treats such general issues as free enterprise versus government regulation. In this connection, the NELA campaign also was designed to help squelch the idea of government regulation. The arguments against regulation sometimes were heavy-handed. Roy McGregor, assistant director of the Illinois Committee on Public Utility Information, advised his minions that in dealing with proponents of regulation, "my idea would not be to use logic or reason, but to try to pin the Bolshevik idea on my opponent."[8]

Free Enterprise *versus* Government Regulation

With the onset of the Depression, business leaders became alarmed about increased public support for regulation of free enterprise. The regulatory mood of the 1930s was enhanced both by Franklin D. Roosevelt's New Deal programs and the rising consumer and labor movements of the period. A major effort to combat the critics of business was coordinated by the National Association of Manufacturers and the U.S. Chamber of Commerce. These organizations set out a broad program of advertising and propaganda to sell the public on the merits of the private enterprise system as a whole. The NAM/USCC program employed standard advertising media such as billboards, radio, and films. In addition, business groups prepared pamphlets for schools, one example of which was *We Drivers*, a publication that mixed automotive information with propaganda touting the private automobile.[9]

An important goal of the business propaganda campaign was to counter the support for regulating business that frequently could be found in 1930s textbooks. Business leaders believed that if the schools began to preach government regulation, then the curriculum would become increasingly anti-capitalist. The National Association of Manufacturers therefore commissioned an economist, Dr. Ralph W. Robey, to scrutinize social-studies textbooks. Robey reported that a "substantial proportion" of the books were un-American in view of their derogatory presentation of the capitalist system. In Robey's view, the major problem was that the textbooks encouraged students to take a "critical attitude" toward society.[10]

Business Propaganda Today

Business propaganda of today shows the same mixture of promoting a particular industry together with advancing the business-oriented outlook on life. Educators find themselves faced with any manner of one-shot offers or long-range business partnerships. Illustrative of small-scale overtures by business was an offer by Mobil Oil to send teachers a booklet giving case histories of how the media have treated business.[11] Similarly, Atlantic Richfield contacted teachers to offer speakers who would address classes or meetings on topics relating to the wilderness, offshore drilling, corporate philanthropy, and conservation.

Sometimes the alliances between business organizations and the schools can be in the form of systematic "partnerships." A number of corporate foundations make grants to educational organizations. For instance, the Nabisco Foundation selected 15 schools to share in $8.5 million in grants in 1990. The U.S. Department of Education reported that the number of such business/education partnerships increased from 46,000 in 1983 to 141,000 in 1988, and that they took place in 40 percent of the nation's public schools.[12]

One factor making for the interest of businesspeople in the schools is the widespread concern about a coming labor shortage of well-educated persons. From a propaganda-analytical point of view, however, we need to inquire how much the particular interest of business coincides with the general public's interest. On the one hand, it is clear that upgrading the educational skills of the U.S. population is tied directly to the general public welfare. On the other hand, one can find possible one-sided benefits to business that might come from partnerships with education. As allies of business organizations, schools might feel constrained not to analyze commercial ethics or industrial advertising.

Inducing educators to moderate their criticism of business might occur *indirectly* through making the curriculum more vocational, or *directly* through self-censorship by schools and teachers. In any case, to accept money from corporate foundations is to lessen the autonomy of schools as a place for teaching critical analysis of society. The more that outside groups gain a hold on the curriculum, the more the schools will be vulnerable to the ideological and political demands of outsiders.

The admixture of business, politics, and education sometimes can be unfortunate. For instance, in 1989, a task force of the Kentucky General Assembly threatened the University of Louisville with funding cuts in response to the university's newly-implemented campus anti-smoking policies. Kentucky legislators found it irritating that a state university would dare discriminate against the tobacco industry, one of the economic mainstays of the Commonwealth of Kentucky.[13]

In addition to setting up loose partnerships, business interests sometimes explicitly work to modify the ideological currents in American education. For an example, we may turn to the "free enterprise" professorships established in nearly 100 U.S. colleges by the late 1980s through donations of corporate sponsors. Professors holding the free-enterprise chairs tended to focus their research and teaching on capitalism and entrepreneurship. In 1978, many of these chair holders and others formed the Association of Private Enterprise Education to help colleges establish free-enterprise chairs. Some in the association became embarrassed by the strident propaganda that occasionally emanated from certain of the free-enterprise policy centers. Supporters of private enterprise education argued, nevertheless, that most of their members fitted well with their host universities. Supporters further contended that free-enterprise chairs served a valuable role in representing the business point of view that otherwise might be missing from smaller liberal arts colleges.[14]

Business partnerships with education also may set in place direct commercial connections that raise issues of propaganda. For instance, Apple Computers has implemented a program to put computers in the schools. In 1990, the Apple program was in operation in 1,000 communities in 38 states. Whereas Apple's program has the effect of upgrading the computer skills of the public, the program also serves the economic interests of the Cupertino, California, company. When students used Apples in school, they became more likely later to become paying customers for Apple products.

The question of self-serving commercial propaganda arises any time a business organization provides its materials gratis. In this connection, we may turn to programs produced by news organizations to help teachers use newspapers and news magazines in the classroom. Clearly, programs of this kind mark an instance of a benign propaganda—something that meets the general interests of society in addition to providing a small boost to the newspaper industry.

Not all business promotions in schools are so benign, however. For instance, the liquor industry has been sharply criticized for the way it markets beer and wine on a number of large college campuses. Horror stories of chug-a-lug contests have become a part of the folklore at several large universities. In the 1980s, college officials and liquor industry representatives cooperated in establishing guidelines for on-campus promotions by liquor companies. These included prohibitions of giving free liquor as a prize, and a ban on portraying drinking as a solution to academic or personal problems.[15]

Channel One

Whittle Communications, Inc., a media company, has carried on such familiar promotions as the advertiser-sponsored health posters found in physician's offices. In the early 1990s, Whittle brought out Channel One, a TV network designed to broadcast a daily 12-minute program of news for high-school students together with four 30-second commercials. In return for agreeing to show the Channel One program to every student every day for three years, cooperating schools got a $50,000 package of TVs, VCRs, and other equipment. Whittle reported that, as of April 1990, some 2,500 schools had signed up, and that the company had sold $200 million worth of advertising contracts.[16]

Many educators opposed the concept of Whittle's Channel One. Among the teacher groups that came out publicly against the venture were the National Education Association, the National PTA, and the National Association of Secondary School Principals. Further, the states of New York and California essentially banned the Channel One program from their public schools. Bill Honig, California State Superintendent of Instruction, believed that Channel One would allow advertisers to exploit a captive audience of youngsters. Honig regarded the fight over Channel One as a "moral issue" and vowed to "fight this to the end."[17] He threatened to withhold two minutes worth of state money per student per day from schools that signed up for the service. A bill introduced in the California Assembly sought to prohibit schools from regularly showing TV programs that contained commercials. Nick Leon, an Eastside Union High School teacher, argued that the programs would take up the equivalent of eight days of instruction per year with a "*People* magazine type of curriculum."[18]

Not everyone in California education circles agreed with Honig's stand against Channel One. Stan Statham, California Assemblyman, regarded Whittle Communication's program as a valuable public/private partnership. With the objective of giving Whittle access to California schools, Statham introduced a bill to strip Honig of power to regulate audio-visual materials in the schools.[19] Evidently, some teachers also favored Channel One. For instance, teachers in Overfelt High school in San Jose, California, voted in favor of accepting Whittle's offer.

Clearly, the debate has been joined in California on the merits of Channel One. The Public Media Center, a San Francisco non-profit advertising agency, put together an ad published in California newspapers asking, "Should 10th Grade come with compulsory commercials?" The bulk of the ad was taken up with a letter from Honig asking what's next, "billboards in the halls? scratch'n'sniff ads in the textbooks?" In an effort to place advertisers on the defensive, the Public Media Center's ad provided letters addressed to Channel One's advertisers, including Pepsico, Warner-Lambert pharmaceuticals, and Nike athletic shoes. For its part, Nike argued that their ads would not sell sneakers but would feature sports stars, such as Michael Jordan, telling kids to stay in school.[20]

PRESSURE GROUPS AND THE SCHOOLS

When traditional American individualism and boosterism combine with the national love affair with voluntary associations, the result often has been the specialized pressure group. America is a land of lobbying and pressure that increasingly focuses on maintenance of a favorable public image. In an era of mass media, it is only natural that interest groups will be concerned about how their members or beliefs are portrayed in the forums of public communication. Since education is one of these forums, interest groups frequently seek to influence the curriculum.

Advocacy-group pressures on the schools frequently have manifested themselves through book-banning controversies. Recent instances of book-banning are useful to illustrate contemporary issues of propaganda in America's schools.

Texts for Texans

An important forum for complaints about textbooks has been the fifteen-member Texas State Textbook Committee that holds hearings to approve books for schools in Texas. The annual Committee hearings supply a forum in which various advocacy-group spokespersons report what they view as offensive material in the texts.

Of the 140 books presented by the State Education Commissioner to the Texas State Board of Education in 1973, 78 were protested for one or more reasons.[21] A highlight of the textbook hearings was the testimony by Mr. and Mrs. Mel Gabler, two of the nation's most outspoken textbook censors. Mrs. Gabler described *Psychology for You* as revolting because it "equates the Bible with a myth." The Gablers opposed *Psychology: Its Principles and Applications* for including works by B.F. Skinner on a list of suggested outside readings. The Gablers argued that citing Skinner was bad because his philosophy of deterministic behaviorism is "considered dangerous by many persons."[22] Some of the books were eventually approved, pending revisions, for example, deleting content and illustrations relating to the Christian religion, Jesus, God, and biblical events.

The Texas State Textbook Committee sessions of 1974 heard testimony from Mrs. R. C. Bearden, Jr., spokesperson for the Daughters of the American Revolution, who opposed several books because they contained pictures of, and/or references to, Dr. Martin Luther King, Jr. Mrs. Bearden contended that evidence compiled by the Louisiana Commission on UnAmerican Activities showed that King had associated with communists. In another complaint, Mrs. Bearden objected to a high-school speech text, *Patterns in Communication*, because of a discussion of symbols it contained. The textbook included pictures of unacceptable symbols, including the peace symbol, the "V" peace sign, and the clenched fist. Bearden maintained that the clenched fist was the salute of international communism, and that the peace symbols derived from satanic cults of the Middle Ages.[23]

Book Burning

Public schools are susceptible to pressure-group action because they are supposed to be accessible to ordinary citizens. The tensions inherent in democratic schools were well in evidence in the classic book-burning controversy that took place in Warsaw, Indiana. During the 1977-78 school session, the Warsaw School Board mounted a campaign to cleanse the school of "filth" found in textbooks. The board ordered removal of several books, including *Values Clarification*, a textbook on social problems, and *Go Ask Alice*, a diary of a young woman caught up in a drug habit. In addition, the board fired a number of teachers.

The books which precipitated the banning movement in Warsaw had been used in English classes. Teachers used *Values Clarification* because it treated contemporary topics such as premarital sex, abortion, and illegal drug use, encouraging students to think and write about their own lives. According to William Chapel, local Warsaw businessman and school board official, however, board members were concerned that the book "would encourage students to reject family values and those of the church and government."[24] The board sent a directive to teachers ordering them to avoid books that contained profanity, arguing that the staff had a responsibility to teach students not use bad language. *Values Clarification* eventually got the most media attention because a local group of senior citizens obtained forty copies of the book and then staged a public burning of them.[25]

The Warsaw book-burning incident was not one of a kind. In Drake, N.D., Kurt Vonnegut's *Slaughterhouse-Five*, used in English classes, was seized. The school board confiscated copies of the Vonnegut book and told the janitor to burn them.[26] The teacher who had assigned the book suffered vandalism and personal attack.[27] Although book-burning may not occur every day, the unsavory association of this practice with Nazi methods causes episodes like those in Warsaw and Drake to ring alarm bells among thoughtful members of the public.

More common than book-burning is book-banning of the kind that took place in Island Trees, New York. The affair began when three school board members attended a seminar in which a parents' group circulated a list of books that were held to be objectionable because of their "vulgar" language and "offensive" ideas. Numbered among these books were various of the usual suspects, including *Soul on Ice* by Eldridge Cleaver and *Slaughterhouse-Five* by Kurt Vonnegut, Jr. The school board ordered seven of the books taken off library shelves.[28]

The Case of Kanawha County

Perhaps the most infamous episode of book-banning in recent years occurred in Kanawha County, West Virginia. The Kanawha incident involved the same objections as the other burning/banning incidents cited above; however, the episode saw a greater community involvement because various local groups were active in fanning the fires. Particularly active were fundamentalist Christian clergy who made many well-publicized attacks on books authored by Eldridge Cleaver and other controversial writers. As is often the case, however, once the issue was joined, protesters began to uncover all manner of arguably objectionable content. One critic demanded removal of an illustrated version of the child's tale, *Jack and the Beanstalk*, because the story encouraged stealing and murder. The conflict soon escalated, and various efforts to harass teachers were accompanied by shooting and bombing incidents. The schools closed for a day because the superintendent believed the climate was unsafe for public education.

201

Torn between the needs to operate the schools and to placate public unrest, the Kanawha County Board of Education finally established guidelines for book selection. Books used in the Kanawha schools were required to recognize the sanctity of the home, to refrain from asking students to reflect upon personal behavior, to avoid profanity, to encourage loyalty to the nation, and to use traditional grammar. The board further established a screening committee to evaluate books for anything objectionable.[29]

Businesses and Minorities

Most efforts to ban school books seem to originate in the machinations of the religious or political right wing in America; however, business interests and minority groups, too, have become increasingly active in pressing their agendas upon the schools. In Laytonville, California, parents and school board members connected to the logging industry were able to secure removal from the second-grade core reading list a Dr. Seuss story that they described as offensive. Seuss's story, *The Lorax*, centers on greed shown by loggers who cut down all the trees in a forest. After protests by teachers, and after considerable media attention, the school board relented in its decision and allowed the book to remain on the basic reading list.[30]

In today's era of heightened racial sensitivity, it is not surprising to find minority groups turning to the tactic of book-banning. For instance, Black parents in Spring, Texas, tried to remove Mark Twain's *The Adventures of Huckleberry Finn* because they did not approve of the presentation of the runaway slave, Jim.[31] A human-relations committee of Fairfax County, Virginia, schools came to a similar conclusion that Twain's book was "racist." The school superintendent decided to keep the book in the school curriculum, however, noting that "it is the responsibility of the teacher to assist students in understanding the historical setting of the novel."[32] In a similar incident, three Black parents resigned from the Warren, Indiana Township School advisory council when a novel, *To Kill a Mockingbird*, was not removed from junior-high-school classrooms. In this classic story of racial tension in a Southern town, a Black man is falsely accused of raping a White girl.[33]

WHOSE PROPAGANDA IS IN THE TEXTBOOKS?

Walter Lippmann once remarked that politics is "the art of inducing all sorts of people who think differently to vote alike."[34] If we substitute the term "act" for "vote," this aphorism applies well to the situation of book-banning where groups ranged across the social and political spectrum have in common their ability to agitate over supposedly objectionable content in school books. What are we to make of claims that our textbooks are carriers of vicious religious, social, and racial propaganda?

To establish a basis for examining claims about religious and racial propaganda in the schools, I want to make a brief interpretive excursion into the nature of public discourse in an age of instant media. (This treatment previews certain themes to be developed later in chapters 7 and 8.)

The Victim's Perspective

Even minimal exposure to today's newspapers or TV journalism reveals that ours is an age of "identity politics." Senate Judiciary Committee hearings of 1991 supplied a powerful illustration of how citizens use social identities—sex, race, age, and other demographic characteristics—as lenses through which to interpret political events. A panel of senators heard charges that Supreme Court-nominee Clarence Thomas had sexually harrassed his former aide, Anita Hill. Both in expert commentary and in millions of casual conversations, the riveting televised event seemed to revolve more around lines of race and gender than issues of guilt and innocence. As the drama unfolded, the panel of senators (all of whom could be described in Affirmative Action terms as "White male") either listened passively or questioned aggressively a series of witnesses. The most notable testifiers were Thomas, a Black man, who described his plight as akin to being lynched in public; and Hill, a Black woman, who claimed that Thomas had subjected her to a barrage of unwanted sexual innuendo and demands.

Relatively few who watched the hearings saw them as a routine episode of conservative/liberal politics or interpreted them as a Watergate-like inquiry into the moral guilt and innocence of leaders. Instead, discussion of the Thomas/Hill hearings, both by journalists and by ordinary citizens, tended to employ racial and sexual terminology to decode the event. For some, the panel of senators represented the social dominance of Whites over Blacks, while others saw in the panel the patriarchy of men over women. Reflecting another line of thinking, some focused on the plight of Anita Hill, an everywoman who was forced to defend her honesty and motives against withering cross-examination by men. Taking a different tack, others maintained that the key to understanding the hearings was to accept as a given that only a Black man would be forced to suffer the indignities heaped upon Thomas. Almost forgotten were questions of evidence (what could be proved? what needed to be proved?) and precedent (how are nominees typically judged by Congress when questions are raised about them?).

The Thomas/Hill interlude supplies clues to help us understand motives that underlie episodes of book-burning and book-banning. As will become clearer in chapters 7 and 8, ours is an era when disputes often are quickly cast into terms of racial, ethnic, and gender victimization. Like the supporters of Thomas and Hill, who saw racial and gender-based victimization unfolding in the Judiciary Committee hearings, America's would-be textbook censors share a sense of cultural oppression. The result is a heightened sensitivity of these protesters to what they perceive is biased propaganda in the curriculum working against their moral or material interests. Parents who believe that their fundamentalist religious beliefs are under attack by secularized schools are not likely to be impressed by arguments that their children will benefit from values-clarification exercises that expose students to thorny real-world problems of drugs and sex. Similarly, those alarmed by unfavorable stereotypes about African-Amercans are quick to become concerned about negative impressions that may ensue when students are exposed to Jim, the ernest but uneducated runaway slave in *Huckleberry Finn*. Those committed to an image-based racial reading of Twain's novel are little assuaged by claims that *Huckleberry Finn* possesses literary merit. Nor are these readers much impressed by arguments that, in the context of the nineteenth century, this classic tale of boyhood exhibits a progressive view of race relations.

Just as many identified with Clarence Thomas or Anita Hill as heroic victims, the book-banning pressure groups are highly sensitive to image factors in public life and public communication. The significance of image factors has grown due to differences in the forms of discourse prevalent in the nineteenth and twentieth centuries. Before the twentieth century, Americans had more opportunity for public deliberation in which they and their neighbors could take the measure of each other's character through town meetings.[35] In contrast, as expressed through television and in today's metropolises and anonymous suburban neighborhoods, contemporary public contacts are quicker, more superficial, more sporadic, more media-based—and, hence, less deliberative.[36]

Where contacts between citizens are remote and impersonal, it is only natural for us to rely more on image and stereotypes. As illustrated by the Thomas/Hill imbroglio, today we often form impressions of people by patching together public images of them based on various demographic characteristics that can be apprehended at a glance, such as gender, age, or race.

We may contrast the quick and superficial nature of image-based interaction to a public world in which people respond to manifestations of each other's character expressed over a longer period of time. Knowledge of another person's human character requires that we obtain a large-scale portrait of an individual as that person directly expresses his or her humanity before our eyes and ears. Our knowledge of human character unfolds as we take note of uninterrupted episodes in which a person acts and speaks, either face-to-face or through television. Long-term perception of uninterrupted discourse may be contrasted to an image-based perception that emphasizes quick shapshots of a person's visual characteristics or known ideological beliefs. To describe a person as "a typical man" or "just another elitist" is far different from actually becoming acquainted with the individual's characteristic mood, personality, opinions, vocabulary, sense of humor, and aspirations.

An example of the difference between image and character is the public figure of former president George Bush. The image of Bush, or of any highly-visible person, would be essentially a matter of his known gender, race, facial appearance, and public position together with certain phrases that capture the essence of his policies, for instance, "Read my lips" (his anti-tax pledge). People could easily construct an image of Bush from afar by assembling relevant glimpses of his appearance. In contrast, knowing Bush's moral character is more difficult; it requires not only listening to his speeches but also keeping close track of his public actions. Only by specifically following Bush's statements and actions would we have a basis for judging his intelligence, his trustworthiness, and his quality as a human being.

Stability of perception is another distinction that may be drawn between image and character. Where image serves as the basis of perception, one blemish can tarnish, or even destroy, a public figure. Gary Hart's seemingly unstoppable presidential candidacy was derailed in 1988 once he became perceived as a womanizer. During the same period, Senator Joseph Biden and the late Martin Luther King, Jr., both suffered from charges that they had plagiarized their speeches or writings.

In these cases, many people acted as if Hart, Biden, and King should be completely reevaluated on the basis of single episodes or charges. In contrast, when we judge someone on the basis of character, we are not likely completely or immediately to revise our understanding of the person based on a single perception.

Just as judgments about leaders today are more superficially image-based, ordinary people themselves are often greatly concerned about the potential power of a single happenstance to place them in a bad light. Social conditions of our century tend to make one element of a person's image especially crucial at any given point in time. A record of military service was vital in the late 1940s when veterans (such as Richard Nixon and John Kennedy) campaigned for office on the basis of wartime participation. Marital status was crucial to perception during the 1950s, when divorce was scandalous and single people were seen as abnormal.

Since the 1970s, nothing has been more important in the image of Americans than gender and race. Americans are likely to compare their own gender and ethnicity to the faces seen on TV in a constant effort to monitor the effects and affects of the news on personal image, whether negative or positive. We want our own crucial demographic characteristics always to be presented favorably in order that we may enjoy the highest self-esteem. Hence, in 1992, some Black Americans fretted lest they lose face when U.S. humanitarian intervention in Somalia called more attention to the emaciated peoples and murderous gunmen of this failed African nation. At the same time, some American men fretted over the portrayal of their gender in the movie *Thelma and Louise*, in which two middle-aged women overcame a variety of uncaring, dishonest, letcherous, or brutal males.

In a climate of superficial, image-based public life, it is not surprising that interest groups spring up to protect the sanctity of various of society's demographic departments. In 1990, for instance, Asian-American groups demanded that columnist Jimmy Breslin lose his job for using the expression "slant-eyed" during a newsroom tirade against a reporter. As news organizations reported the Breslin Affair for the next few weeks, the public was treated to a contest of images between Breslin (seen in the image of an oppressor) and Asian Americans (the latest victims of image assassination).

The foregoing excursion into today's image-based politics suggests that book-burning and book-banning both represent an extreme form of an otherwise common preoccupation with identity politics. Educational censors appear to see themselves simply as victims who fight back.

Victims Who Fight Back

Textbook censors understand perhaps better than anyone else that image is everything in contemporary American public life. However exaggerated are their complaints over seemingly trivial words, labels, pictures, and statements, censorious protests make sense, given the superficiality of perception in the 1990s.

While claiming the status of victim of propaganda, America's textbook censors sometimes also appear as villains of either the comedic or sinister type. Many educators and citizens use the framework of comedy or tragedy in judging efforts to ban books from the schools. On the one hand, it is easy to laugh about certain of the banning efforts. The shrill, unsophisticated protestations of the book banners almost invite scorn. More often than not, the would-be censors have not read any of the books they rail against; usually, censors focus on selected passages lifted out of context. Further, the censors often make improbable charges. For instance, during the 1950s, some book protesters claimed that *Robin Hood*, the classic tale of a medieval knight who stole from the rich and gave to the poor, was part of a communist plot. From the perspective of the average citizen, book banners sometimes appear biased, uninformed, thin-skinned, petty—even paranoid.

At the same time, it is easy to become alarmed by the textbook protesters. Their vituperative language can be scary: "communist," "racist," "sexist," "un-American." Violence and vandalism sometimes accompany the protests. As charges and countercharges mount over books and films, citizens may wonder what kind of society America will become if the nation listens attentively to every noisy group that demands the right to censor the curriculum.

Whether we view textbook censorship as comedy or tragedy, citizens and educators alike need to be careful about taking an attitude of self-righteous superiority in the matter of school censorship. Educators are particularly susceptible to becoming co-conspirators in educational censorship. This is true not only because teachers are given authority to determine the curriculum but also because their political leanings are not representative of the general public. Espousing a disproportionately liberal reformist kind of politics, educators may be tempted to choose text materials with the objective of either provoking or propagandizing their students. Edward Jenkinson, the school censorship expert, says that primary-grade educators sometimes bring book-banning attacks upon themselves by occasionally using a book for its shock value. Further, he says, teachers sometimes make themselves liable to charges of propaganda by not giving a clear and convincing explanation of the purposes behind an educational program.[37]

Not only does the gatekeeping role of teachers cast the spectre of propaganda over the educational system but also issues of covert persuasion seem inevitable whenever school books contain discussions of social life. Both the history of a people and the current events of a society serve to highlight conflict and strife. Strife in society, then and now, inevitably spills over into the portrayal of society in the curriculum.

For instance, how can teachers help students learn about the Vietnam War without alerting them to disagreements about whether the security of America was at stake or whether the side in that civil war which America supported was democratic? Similarly, how could students of 1991 have discussed the Persian Gulf War without mentioning disagreements reported in the news or expressed by family and friends over the necessity for, and the tactics of, the war? Seemingly it is inevitable that someone may take offense when teachers address the specifics of yesterday's and today's struggles. Also, when teachers assign classic older books that reflect the values and expressions of former eras, the reading list will inevitably fail to pass muster with all the sensibilities of present-day audiences.

If discussions of social questions are inevitably controversial, then it follows that the schools cannot be neutral either, even if they wanted to be. Further, in considering issues of propaganda in the primary grades, we confront the argument that schools have the responsiblity not to be neutral, that educators have a duty to establish moral standards. Defending the effort of the Island Trees, New York, school board to ban *Soul on Ice, The Naked Ape* (and five other titles), attorney George Lipp, Jr. told the U.S. Supreme Court that "the transmission of moral values is a primary function of the school board."[38]

For a variety of reasons, then, we may expect that disputes over textbook censorship will not soon pass away. Professor Edward B. Jenkinson estimated that some 400 to 600 book-banning groups (or groups criticizing teaching methods) were active in the 1980s. The American Library Association reported about 300 book-banning incidents per year through the decade, and Jenkinson estimated that 50 incidents went unreported for every one that received attention.[39]

PROPAGANDA OF THE MARKETPLACE

While textbook censors claim to be the victims of offensive propaganda inserted into the curriculum, the censors together have become instigators of a system of market-driven propaganda. To understand the market-based censorship of school materials that is prevalent in the U.S.A., we need to compare the diversified American educational system with the more unitary programs in other countries.

Unitary *versus* Market-Based Propaganda

Localized conditions of American textbook propaganda vary from those of other countries in which a central Ministry of Education holds responsibility for textbooks. In some countries, the national ministry specifies one book for all students in a given grade. Bias induced by censorship becomes systematic when one official political unit controls all school materials. For example, in discussing the 1962 Cuban missile confrontation between the U.S.S.R. and the U.S.A., a 10th-grade world-history book mandated by the Soviet Ministry of Education left out one especially important detail—the fact that the Russians had placed offensive missiles in Cuba.[40] Lacking this crucial piece of information, Soviet students probably wondered what the U.S. was so upset about. In similar fashion, Korea and China frequently have complained about history textbooks approved by the Education Ministry of Japan. Korean and Chinese educators argue that Japanese textbooks ignore or obscure Japanese aggression and atrocities during World War II.[41]

In contrast to the U.S.S.R. and Japan, U.S. textbooks are adopted locally or through state committees. Accordingly, issues of textbook propaganda and censorship relate less to government action and more to marketplace pressures exerted on textbook publishers by various religious, ethnic, and ideological pressure groups.

Faced with tender sensibilities ranging across the social spectrum—from fundamentalists to feminists, from preoccupation with racism to manias about communism—the solution chosen by textbook publishers has been one of making books blander. Anxious to satisfy all pressure groups, publishers prefer to avoid real social issues altogether, believing that the easiest way not to give offense is to omit mention of controversial topics. Another way to escape the ire of pressure-group leaders is to present social issues without delving into their complexities. By avoiding the often controversial specifics of a social dispute, publishers defuse potential charges that they are telling students *what* to think. At the same time, however, by replacing detailed history with a noncontroversial blather, many textbook authors also fail to give students material necessary for learning *how* to think about their society. Students find it difficult to think intelligently about social issues without knowing the details of controversies. A glance at some examples of controversial text material in history and science sets the stage for a closer look at the operation of market-based textbook propaganda.

History without Content

Critics of today's textbooks sometimes complain that market-driven textbook censorship has produced boring history books. Paul Gagnon, Professor of History at the University of Massachusetts at Boston, reviewed five widely-adopted high school history textbooks in a study sponsored by the American Federation of Teachers. Gagnon argued that the books he read "leave the story of democracy largely untold." He found the books dull because they did not focus on "the compelling story of people's struggles for freedom, self-government and justice on Earth."[42] The result was a condescending kind of inoffensive history that passed by the struggles, the pros and cons, that were so important to the people who actually lived during the historical periods under study.

Religion is one chief issue that today gives fits to text marketers. Paul C. Vitz, New York University psychologist, reported an example of the great lengths to which text writers sometimes go to strip away references to religion in the interests of avoiding controversy. In one 30-page discussion of the Puritans, Vitz found that the social-studies textbook omitted the fact that the Puritans had emigrated to America because of their conflict with the Church of England.[43] For the Puritans, the religious motive was crucial to their emigration and their early life and government in America. In another such example, Isaac Bashevis Singer, a Nobel prize winning author, complained that Macmillan publishers deleted all references to God when reprinting his story *Zlateh the Goat*. For instance, Macmillan's editors changed the phrase: "We must accept all that God gives us" to read: "We must accept all that is given us." Not only is the edited version blander but also it carries the danger that students will lose a sense of what is, and has been, important in their history and society.

Like religion, war also raises controversial issues that can make textbook writers squirm. Terry Anderson, Associate Professor of History at Texas A & M University, cited a survey of high-school textbooks in Texas that showed a clear effort to avoid mentioning anything specific about facts and opinions concerning the Vietnam War. Not one text mentioned that the war "might have been considered a civil war; that the United States used Agent Orange and bombed nonmilitary targets; that our ally, South Vietnam, collapsed; and that America lost the war."[44] Publishers have good reason to tread lightly on the matter of the Vietnam War. Bill McCloud, a social-studies teacher and Vietnam veteran, once wrote to various diplomats, scholars, and soldiers in an effort to find out what they believed was the lesson of Vietnam. McCloud's survey of participants or commentators on the war turned up a wide variety of opinions about the meaning of the war. According to Gen. William C. Westmoreland, who commanded American forces in Vietnam, the "war was lost by congressional actions." In contrast, Clark Clifford, former Secretary of Defense, argued that our whole Vietnam intervention had been a mistake since "we should not have sent American troops to fight in this war."[45]

Congressional stupidity? A mistaken war? American students may never have the chance to think through these issues of Vietnam. If textbook authors, hoping to avoid the wrath of pressure groups, omit complex conditions, unpleasant facts, and conflicting opinions, what will be the effect on students? Will students be able to understand their world after a diet of sanitized readings? If students are unaware of controversies over the Vietnam War, can they ever be fully prepared intelligently to discuss the pros and cons of future wars? Terry Anderson argued that children are cheated when "wimpy school board members" cave in to vocal groups that zealously guard images and ideologies.

Neutralized Science

Critics complain that our science textbooks routinely fail to treat the civics of science and technology. In other words, students rarely have an opportunity to consider that America has made political choices about technology. For instance, professors J. L. Heilbron and Daniel Kevles argued that science books could help students understand the citizen's role in decisions about nuclear technology by explaining how the

Atomic Energy Commission has acted as both a promoter and a regulator of atomic energy. They argued, further, that textbook authors should not be afraid to tread on such issues as which groups opposed and which groups favored the Star Wars missile defense system—and why.[46]

No issue of science has been more controversial in American education than the subject of evolution. Since the early part of the century, educators, religionists, and politicians have argued whether textbooks should present human life as something that evolved slowly over the eons or whether schools should give credence to the Biblical account of a divine creation in six days.

In 1985, the debate over evolutionary theory in science textbooks came to a head in California. The California Board of Education rejected all 7th- and 8th-grade science books submitted by publishers because the books "systematically omitted" a thorough discussion of evolution. Because the giant California textbook market is a bellwether for U.S. publishers, the books were quickly revised. However, in 1989, the Board agreed to delete its requirement that evolution be treated as a scientific fact.[47] The 1989 guidelines further encouraged authors to mention the importance of respecting the views of those who, for religious reasons, rejected evolution. The final wording of the 1989 guidelines was a political compromise engineered by Bill Honig, California Superintendent of Public Instruction, to placate conservative members of the State Board of Education. Conservatives had been dissatisfied with the forceful directive to teach evolution given in the 1985 guidelines.[48]

Two lobbying groups have been particularly active in the area of evolution versus creationism. One group, the Traditional Values Coalition, wanted schools to teach "scientific creationism" along with evolution. The other, People for the American Way, wanted more attention paid to evolution with no concessions at all to religious fundamentalism.

How do the students fare in the debate? In the view of some critics of science education, a consequence of the creationism-versus-evolution dispute has been to weaken the treatment of genetics in the public-school science curriculum.[49] Alleging that high-school biology teachers are cowed by creationists, critics argue that, as a result, schools fail to provide the public with necessary scientific knowledge. To the extent that genetics education is stunted, people have less background to interpret proposals about genetic alteration and screening of parents for such diseases as cystic fibrosis, sickle-cell anemia, and hemophilia.

Boycotts and Bandwagons

Textbook publishers today face not only boycotts and court challenges from outside pressure groups but also the latest educational fads and bandwagons driven by educational insiders. The result is a complex process of marketplace propaganda that works itself out daily in many schools around the nation.

"Purists could put us in the poorhouse," said Randall Marshall, a McGraw-Hill publisher, commenting on the work of outside textbook pressure groups.[50] Publishers know that bad publicity generated by critics can undermine large adoptions by school districts or by state textbook committees. Publishers pay particular heed to states in which a single committee reviews books for the whole state, such as in California or Texas. To be financially viable, school books simply must make the list of approved texts in key states. Not only must textbook publishers run the gauntlet of pressure groups and school boards but also they may find their offerings challenged in the courts. For example, in 1986, U.S. District Judge Thomas G. Hull ruled that the Hawkins County, Tennessee, schools must excuse children from reading classes that require material deemed offensive by parents. The Court ruled that families had a right to avoid books that parents believed promoted feminism, pacifism, and other themes held to be anti-Christian.[51]

The Hawkins County ruling (later overturned on appeal) was part of a general attack by fundamentalist Christians on what they call "secular humanism," that is, a human-centered, instead of a God-centered, view of life. For instance, the Hawkins County parents objected to having their children assigned to read *The Wizard of Oz*. They argued that the book portrayed a witch as good, and also that the book presented character traits as being personally developed rather than God-given. During the last twenty years, the largest number of complaints about textbooks has come from fundamentalist Christians who believe that their faith is undermined by humanistic educational material. Some, such as Tim LaHaye, a San Diego minister, talk of a humanist conspiracy to control the schools, government, and the media.[52]

Fundamentalists, however, are not the only advocacy group that seeks to shape the content of textbook material. Recent years have seen an increase in efforts by feminist and ethnic groups to influence the tenor of educational content. American educators tend, as a whole, to be more sympathetic to the protests of the liberal minority and women's groups than to those of conservative religious fundamentalists. As a result, demands for ethnic and gender balance in curricular materials frequently come more from educational insiders than from outsiders. "The first thing we look for is ethnic and gender balance, even above educational considerations," commented Tony Magales, head of the Institutional Materials Committee for the Seattle School District.[53] As a result, publishers sometimes use a rule of thumb that stories in school readers should include 50 percent women, 20 percent minorities, and 10 percent handicapped.[54] Authors find that they may need to change the names of story characters to achieve this balance.

Guidelines from publishers to promote gender and ethnic diversity represent an arguably benign kind of propaganda. Here the goal chiefly seems to be that of promoting a diverse, harmonious society, an objective that is in the general public interest. Authors and educators will nonetheless chafe under a system in which critics, publishers, and educational administrators enforce guidelines that equate human character and experience with gender and race formulas.

Irene Trivas, an artist, stopped accepting commissions to illustrate children's readers because of her frustration over the increasingly constricting demographic directions she faced. In one story, Trivas was told to make the hero an Hispanic boy with Black, White, and Asian friends. The White girl was to be physically handicapped. The dog was to be female. The boy's family was not to be shown eating cheap iceberg lettuce but something "nice" like endive. The senior citizen in the story was to be shown jogging.[55]

A danger arises when textbook adoption committees judge materials according to public-relations standards in preference to educational ones. Good stories and illustrations are often the result of a happy coincidence of creative powers that are not reduceable to formula. We have reason to worry about a system in which the creativity of writers and teachers is made to conform to "P.C." (politically correct) social guidelines, however well-intentioned they be. Criteria appropriate for selecting clothing models in a Sears catalogue may not be equally well-suited for educational materials.

The tendency of publishers to make explicit public-relations demands on authors has helped foster the committee system of textbook composition. The shift from single-author books to committee-managed school texts has become prevalent, especially in elementary and secondary-school publishing. Unfortunately, books produced by the committee approach have tended to be the most boring, for the creative process is subordinated to guidelines, formulas, and heavy editing. Critics contend, further, that the committee approach is part of a general "dumbing down" of American texts in which school books are stuffed with dull, inoffensive, contentless blather.

Dumbing Down

During the 1960s and 1970s, some educators began to adopt the view that educational material should not challenge students—that challenges made our schools too difficult and therefore excessively elitist. Complaints about a resulting "dumbing down" of American textbooks became commonplace during the 1980s.

One manifestation of the dumbing down of books was the obsessive attention sometimes paid to readability formulas that measure sentence length and difficulty of words. As author Frances FitzGerald explained, a publisher might use a computer to assure that there were no more than one four-syllable word per 35 words.[56] A preoccupation with readability considerations sometimes produces curious effects on school materials. The Virginia State Board of Education once discovered that textbooks used in the state deleted the word "inalienable" from the Declaration of Independence because the word was deemed too difficult for students.[57]

Another part of the dumbing-down process in educational materials occurred in connection with a focus on skills versus content. For instance, in reading classes, drills frequently were substituted for reading actual works. Carol Elie Gray, a sixth-grade teacher in New Orleans, found that students in her English class were tiring of skill drills. As a change of pace, she gave one student a science fiction story by Ray Bradbury. The student later commented: "I like this much better than reading." Somewhat taken aback, Gray explained to the student: "This *is* reading." The reading drills that Gray's students found so boring reflected the educational approach of breaking reading into separate steps to be mastered one at a time. This kind of skills-hierarchy approach may be contrasted to the holistic approach to reading, increasingly common today, in which words and grammar are taught in the context of a whole story. Educators term the new method a "whole language" philosophy.

Bill Honig, California Superintendent of Public Instruction, became a nationally-noted critic of bland educational materials. His argument was that "textbooks are like television. They aim at the lowest common denominator. The marketing people, not educators, are running the show."[58] For instance, the California State Curriculum Committee found that publishers routinely altered the language of classic children's stories in order to make the books easier. As the publishers substituted bland language for the original content, the porridge prepared by *The Three Bears* became fish. *The Little Engine that Could* no longer "puffed along merrily" but now "went along very well."[59]

It seems unfair to blame publishers exclusively for the failings of America's textbooks. After all, textbook companies merely want to provide books that achieve a profitable level of sales. Watered-down books are a rational response to the difficulties that publishers face in the murky and quirky politics of textbook adoption. If the bland books become educational best-sellers, does not the ultimate fault lie with the educators and school board members who are preoccupied with appearance over content?

Calls for Better Books

During the decade of the 1980s, Americans heard many calls for better teaching and better school materials. The effort to tighten educational standards was reflected in action by the State of California, mentioned above, to refuse science books that avoided the word "evolution." Toward this same purpose, the National Council of Teachers of Mathematics published a new model curriculum for elementary and high-school math that placed more attention on statistics and problem solving. New York, California, and other states revised social studies curricula to place more emphasis on real historical events and controversial social conflicts. California's new standards for English required inclusion of classic literature, and they no longer required routine application of readability formulas.

By the late 1980s, an increasingly broad consensus held that American textbooks had failed to tell the story of how people enjoy freedoms and attain rights in a democratic society. Albert Shanker, president of the American Federation of Teachers, saw a new "rediscovery of the fact that content is important."[60] In this connection, Bill Honig of California called for more real stories of American life and classic legends that would capture the interest of students and give them a tangible sense of history.[61] The American Federation of Teachers sponsored a document entitled *Education for Democracy* that was endorsed not only by

People for the American Way, a liberal group, but also by the National Association of Evangelicals.[62]

As educators strengthen the content of the curriculum, they would do well to avoid deluding themselves by thinking that problems of propaganda come only from outsiders. The California Teachers Association publication, *Action*, once included a useful article on how the "Right-Wing Attacks Textbooks." The article encouraged teachers to "fight back." Ironically, however, the previous month's issue of *Action* included a article entitled "Textbook Reviewers Needed."[63] The article solicited volunteers to "review history-social science materials" for "depiction of male and female roles, cultural and racial diversity, and other social issues, including representation of the aged and disabled." To be sure, sensitivity to diversity has a public interest value in contemporary American society; however, conservative groups would make the same claim for their demands that the curriculum be focused on family and patriotic values. As noted earlier, parents and educational activists committed to "traditional values" might regard "social issues" tinkering as furthering various propagandas of secularism, feminism, and ethnicity. How to "screen" materials without becoming a propagandist became a matter of great importance for educators of the 1990s.

The best way for educators to avoid the role of propagandist is to make sure that a large number of people are involved in screening school materials. When educators take on the job alone, they have much to fear from their own well-intentioned efforts because, owing to the institutional character of propaganda, the most dangerous instances of manipulation have come from within organizations or professions. Only when all points of view are expressed can the public have the utmost confidence that teachers are making good judgments about what should be read. If the review process is sufficiently public, the pro/con debate will expose the biased perspectives and half-thought-out arguments that are characteristic of the book-burners on all sides.

PRESSURES ON TEACHERS

No one ever said it was easy to be a teacher. As the book banning controversies show, teachers may face angry attacks or even physical threats from outside pressure groups and organizations. Attack also may spring up from the inside when fellow educators accuse their colleagues of being variously "elitist," "sexist," or "racist." By the early 1990s, the ironic expression "politically correct" had emerged as a label for overzealous true-believers in education who demanded that their colleagues immediately adopt a progressive socio-political view stressing gender and racial sensitivity. In today's society, teachers remain at the center of a wide debate about social propaganda.

Outside Political Pressure

Kevin John McIntyre, a former colleague of mine, once became the focus of a brief controversy over the proper political orientation for a faculty member of a public university in Texas. McIntyre, who was Associate Professor of Government at the University of Texas—Permian Basin (UTPB), was quoted in the Midland, Texas, newspaper as having stated at a public meeting that "the capitalist system of this country has never worked. It has produced only atrocious policies under the guise of a free enterprise system." The *Midland Reporter-Telegram* not only reported McIntyre's alleged remarks but also ran an editorial stating that local people would resent having "a person like this" on the faculty of a state university.[64] The matter was officially investigated by the assistant to the president of UTPB who carefully listened to tape-recordings of the meeting to assess McIntyre's disavowal of what the professor claimed were inaccurate attributions. Soon, McIntyre's case was being monitored at the highest levels in Texas higher education by the chair of the University of Texas Board of Regents and by the University of Texas system chancellor.

Fortunately for McIntyre, the evidence supported his claim that the controversial statements attributed to him had been distorted and presented in an out-of-context fashion by the Midland newspaper. But suppose the young professor of government had believed that the capitalist economy was a failure? He might have faced a fate similar to that which befell Bertell Ollman, a Marxist-oriented scholar, whose appointment as Chair of the Department of Political Science at the University of Maryland was vetoed by John S. Toll, president of the university. Toll denied that Ollman's political view had anything to do with the cancellation of his appointment; however, Toll offered no other reasons as to why Ollman was unfit for the job.[65]

A teacher does not have to advocate Red economics to get into political trouble; it may be enough to advocate less red meat—if you are on the agriculture faculty at Iowa State University. Suzanne Hendrich, Assistant Professor of Food and Nutrition, was interviewed for a public-service message prepared by the university for local radio stations.

During the interview, Hendrich suggested that one way to avoid cancer was to adopt a diet of less red meat and more vegetables. Soon, the university began to receive outraged phone calls from area farmers, and the school pulled the radio spot. Then, state legislators weighed in, holding hearings on Professor Hendrich's views. Legislators were mollified when they heard the full tape-recording of the Hendrich interview which university officials contended had been tendentiously edited to highlight the comments on red meat.[66] Nevertheless, Iowa State's president, Gordon P. Eaton, expressed his concern lest the criticism be taken as "intimidation."

One does not have to search far to find similar instances in which fears of legislative pressure have caused teachers to tread lightly on political questions. The Dean of the Indiana University Medical School, Walter J. Daly, once warned his faculty against making public comments on abortion. Pending state legislation would have prohibited (with a few exceptions) public employees from performing abortions at public facilities. In a time when banning abortions was the reigning sentiment in the legislature, Daly believed that public remarks by the faculty would threaten the University's effort to get extra funding for its hospital operations.[67]

Educator *versus* Educator

Sometimes the complaints about ideological manipulation and propaganda come from educators themselves. For instance, Marxist critics attack sociobiological researchers who teach that genetic factors account for many social developments. Marxists argue that sociobiology acts as a propaganda for those who currently hold power in society because this social theory teaches that social problems may be natural and not due to policies of social oppression. For their part, sociobiologists contend that their critics are ideologues willing to bend scientific results to favor their pet ideological positions.[68]

One increasingly frequent instance of scholars branding each other as propagandists occurs in connection with the political situation in the Middle East. Scholars who study the Middle East find themselves under pressures from the large pro-Israel lobbies and smaller pro-Arab groups. For instance, in late 1983, the New England Regional Office of the B'nai B'rith Anti-Defamation League sent out a list that labeled certain researchers and institutions as being "anti-Israel" and "pro-Arab."[69] The Joint Near-Middle East Committee of the Social Science Research

Council and the Middle East Studies Association condemned this action by B'nai B'rith as a kind of political blacklisting based on flimsy evidence. The list apparently included persons whose sole offense had been to speak at public forums on the Middle East.

Accuracy in Academia

The controversy that surrounded the emergence of Accuracy in Academia (AIA) represents one of the best examples of political pressures placed on academicians to follow a political line. AIA was founded in 1985 by Reed Irvine as a spin-off of his Accuracy in Media (AIM) organization whose mission was to expose so-called left-wing bias in American news media. From the first, however, AIA had difficulty in deciding whether it was an educational service group or a right-wing political pressure group.

Sometimes, Accuracy in Academia seemed to work in the tradition of humanistic media critics. On occasion, Irvine argued from the generally-accepted principle that the problem of propaganda arises in education when educators force their political perspective on students. In this case, Irvine accepted the premise that educators permissibly would have their own views on society and politics, but would accept the "responsibility to present other points of view."[70] AIA executive director, Les Csorba, further stated that his group would ferret out bias across the political spectrum: "We're committed to working on any complaint that comes in."[71] AIA pointed to documented complaints by conservative students that their views had been ignored or even deprecated in college classes. For instance, one senior at Midwestern State University in Texas, contended: "I have been a victim (grade-wise) for standing up for what I believe to be true, and for pointing out what I believe to be an inaccurate statement by my professors."[72]

While Accuracy in Academia claimed to be defending conservative students against tyrannical leftist professors, the group seemed equally dedicated to making right-wing political points regardless of fairness. Equating "pro-American" with the right-wing side, Csorba claimed that his group went to bat for students who were "persecuted for their pro-American views in the classroom." More inflammatory was the charge by Malcolm Lawrence, retired U.S. foreign service officer and first president of AIA, that some 10,000 Marxists were teaching on American campuses.[73] Numbers aside, the undefended implication was that a Marxist social critic represented a subversive danger.

Scan, a publication of the Council for Liberal Learning, contended that the AIA approach invited abuse. *Scan* cited the case of Cynthia McClintock, associate professor of political science at George Washington University, who was accused by AIA of egregious bias. According to *Scan*, AIA's charge itself was demonstrably distorted, for the assigned readings for McClintock's course on Latin American politics included publications by the U.S. government and by conservative groups.[74]

As the publicity about AIA mounted in 1985, the heads of nine higher-education association organizations declared that AIA's critical approach would have a "chilling effect" on classroom discussions and would lessen the academic freedom of teachers and students to explore controversial views.[75] The American Association of University Professors (AAUP) sent a letter to members decrying AIA as an organization that aimed "to impose one particular group's single ideology as 'objective truth.'"[76] Even William Bennett, notable conservative spokesperson and (at the time) Secretary of Education, faulted the AIA approach as a "bad idea" that brought outsiders into sensitive matters that would be better handled within a particular academic department or university.[77] Irving J. Spitzberg, executive director of the Council for Learning of the Association of American Colleges, expressed the fear that AIA represented a revival of 1950s-era McCarthyism, a style of political oppression that caused professors to be fired or to suffer vigilante-style attacks for taking controversial positions.[78]

Early issues of AIA's *Campus Report* publication seemed not to warrant the cries of alarm that were characteristic of higher education's first response to the organization. Much of the material was defensive, with conservative students and conservative ideology portrayed as victims of campus liberalism. For instance, the lead article of the January 1987 issue reported on comments by Dave Emery, host of a student radio interview program at Foothills College (Los Altos, California). Emery apparently accused the U.S. government of plotting to cause liberals, affirmative-action advocates, and minority spokespersons to die of cancer. Emery argued that his charge was plausible given the "facts" that the U.S. "national security establishment" assassinated John and Robert Kennedy as well as Martin Luther King, Jr. Certainly, charges that "the government" assassinated King and the Kennedys are not widely accepted historical fact. Perhaps AIA was reasonable when it asked Tom Clements, Foothill College president, whether he found it disturbing that such comments were aired on the radio station of his campus.

The lead article of the October 1987 *Campus Report* represented more of the attack orientation that AIA's critics seemed to have expected. The article focused on complaints about one particular course: History and Journalistic Studies 370, Contemporary American History, offered at the University of Massachusetts by Dean Albertson. According to students cited by AIA, Albertson termed Ronald Reagan a "racist" for approving tax credits for private schools, and he pronounced capitalism to be "wasteful, stupid, futile." This article further reported an interview between Albertson and *Campus Report,* in which the professor admitted his biases which he justified on the basis that "all people are inherently biased." AIA was disturbed that the professor did not explicitly present opposing views. Albertson was quoted as follows:

> I offer them my point of view, the Marxist point of view, and the point of view of the books I assign. Other points of view I figure they can get out of *Time* magazine, out of anybody else that they want to. . . . [This] is not a course that is going to give them both sides of every question, because there's a lot of questions that don't have two sides . . . Such as Vietnam. Such as racism. Such as the environment. There's no two sides to those issues.

AIA did acknowledge that students evidently were free to bring in other points of view in their written assignments.

Although AIA's analysis of Albertson's course conveyed a polemical, rather than a reflective, tone, the charges were not unreasonable. AIA did at least give the professor a chance to respond. Certainly, the AIA approach of having outside polemicists intervene in various campus situations represents a thorn in the side of higher education.

Accuracy in Academia might become dangerous if the press, the public, leading citizens, and legislators ever were to accept its analyses and conclusions uncritically. If AIA's bulletin triggered reflexive responses by powerful rightist groups, then we might in fact witness a reprise of the 1950's witch hunts. So long as AIA's partisan orientation and intent are recognized, however, this pressure on professors does not, in and of itself, seem to threaten the integrity of the academy. Actually, the group may become part of a useful dialogue over the meaning of higher education. My own review of a year's worth of the AIA *Campus Report* (1986-87) convinced me that an alarmist view of the organization was not justified. AIA may be just another partisan group that gives a truculent, but reasoned, comment on its ideological enemies.

REFORM, IDEOLOGY, AND EDUCATION

The history of American education reveals frequent episodes in which businesses and advocacy groups put pressure on teachers, sometimes prompting intervention by government. We must not, however, overlook the ever-present temptations for teachers to become propagandists. Dean Albertson's cautionary note rings true that "all people are inherently biased"—teachers included. To say teachers have socio-political preferences is not, however, to say that they inevitably must function as propagandists. How can teachers remain true both to their own commitments and to their responsibilities to help students learn how to think about contemporary social controversies?

Liberal Ideologues on Campus?

Accuracy in Academia has complained that the typical college professor is a liberal ideologue who aggressively promotes his or her leftist views in the classroom. Thomas Sowell, fellow of the conservative Hoover Institution, further argued that college campuses have become places where free speech is suppressed whenever it calls into question favored liberal causes such as feminism, affirmative action, and Gay rights. Have we reason to worry about leftist propagandas in American higher education?

To bolster his argument about propagandizing professors of the Left, Sowell cited an example at Tufts University where a student was suspended on grounds of "sexual harassment" for wearing a T-shirt that listed fifteen reasons why "Beer is better than women at Tufts." He also cited a case in which an editorial cartoonist at UCLA was suspended for publishing a cartoon deemed "racially insensitive." In the controversial panel of this cartoon strip, one character asked a rooster how he had been admitted to UCLA, and the rooster replied "affirmative action."[79] According to Sowell, campuses such as Stanford University had become all too willing to mete out academic suspensions on grounds of "homophobia" when students expressed a personal opposition to homosexuality.

Sowell argued that the instances above bespoke a rampant double standard in higher education that was based on double talk. In Sowell's view, leftists demand free speech to burn the flag or shout down opponents with epithets, but they want to curtail free speech whenever they encounter opponents of their own sensitive causes. Sowell's criticisms

223

raise three questions that are useful in assessing whether college teachers function as propagandists. First, who are the college teachers—what is their ideology? Second, do faculty members typically set a one-sided propagandistic tone in their classrooms? Third, to what extent are the reformist efforts of college teachers oriented to the general public interest?

What is the political orientation of college faculty? A poll taken in 1984 showed that 40% of American faculty identify themselves as highly or moderately liberal versus 35% who identify themselves as moderately or strongly conservative.[80] An earlier poll indicated that 57% of faculty register with the Democratic Party versus 20% with the Republicans.[81] While one finds more Republicans in the professions—business, law, medicine, engineering—more Democrats are to be found in the humanities and social sciences. However, if American faculties are liberal, they do not seem to be radical. In one poll, 81% of faculty members agreed with the statement that "the private business system in the United States, for all its flaws, works better than any other system devised for advanced industrial society."[82] If the intellectual climate of the college campus is only slightly left-of-center, do a few professors nevertheless magnify the tilt to the Left by fostering a propaganda that spreads their ideology? Conservatives worry over findings that students frequently change their opinions during their college years. Conservatives fear that undergraduates are socialized into liberal views because they absorb the liberal line of thought that predominates on some campuses. James J. Kilpatrick once sounded an alarm about findings from a Gallup poll that 41 percent of students believed that their political attitudes had been influenced by their college courses.[83] If students are influenced by professors, and if this influence is more leftward than rightward, does it follow that professors are propagandists? Not necessarily, for the attitude change may point less to propaganda and more to self-conversions that result from serious and probing discussions of social problems. Causing students to think deeply about social problems clearly contributes to the general interest of society although these discussions may cause students to change their opinions.

Conservatives are convinced, however, that college students are liberalized less by self-conversion and more by deliberate propaganda. Many rightists believe that behind every liberal professor lurks a propagandist ready to exploit the vulnerability of undergraduate students. The Accuracy in Academia organization has featured letters from students who complain of college courses designed to indoctrinate. For instance, a student at the University of North Carolina (Chapel Hill) wrote that his course in Women's Studies did not accept any viewpoint other than the feminist ideology around which the class was built.[84] In addition, conservatives frequently claim that university administrations show hostility toward students who dissent from liberal views. R. Emmett Tyrrell faulted Dartmouth University for suspending rightist students after they knocked down anti-apartheid shanties. The university was biased, according to Tyrrell, because Dartmouth merely gave verbal reprimands to leftist students who had forcibly resisted the university's effort to remove the shanties.[85]

If the examples cited by Sowell and other conservative critics of academe are representative, then perhaps educators might examine whether they are part of a system that occasionally forces political ideologies on unwilling or unwitting students. Are certain members of the professoriate telling students exactly *what* to think about social questions instead of helping them learn *how* to think about the issues? Because perceptions of exclusion are personal, it is impossible completely to dismiss complaints from conservative students that they feel out-of-place on many campuses. However, the distinction between serious discussion and propagandistic pressure is subtle and difficult for young students (or outside commentators) to make. Discussion of controversial social issues such as peace, disarmament, and racism, only make the problem of propaganda in the classroom more intractable.

Education for Peace

Few teachers would disagree with Richard J. Barnet's argument that teachers can play a helpful social role by explicitly dealing with issues of the nuclear age.

> The teaching profession has failed to prepare young people to live in the nuclear age. We do not have courses that explain the most important fact of our era—that ours is the first generation in human history with the theoretical capability to end human history.[86]

Barnet recommended courses in the history of warfare and courses that probed the premises of the current national security system. Barnet wanted college teachers to help engender an attitude of peace that would replace the more common attitude that accepts war. "For a peace ethos to replace a war ethos, individual citizens need greater insight into

225

their own aggression and greater awareness of the private uses of patriotism and nationalism." Other commentators, however, might argue that peace studies are inherently propagandistic because they channel the thinking of students into an attitude of "peace at any price."

William J. Rewak, President of the University of Santa Clara (California) once struggled with the issue of education versus propaganda in the realm of national defense. He argued that universities cannot expect to treat issues such as nuclear arms in a completely "neutral" fashion. He maintained, however, that taking a position was not the same as spewing propaganda. "We need never worry about exposing students to ideas as long as we avoid propaganda, allow for free discussion and honest investigation, and help students develop the capacity for mature judgment."[87] In other words, the peace-studies educator teaches students *how* to think about nuclear war; the peace propagandist indoctrinates students in *what* to think.

In Rewak's view, the teacher need not hide his or her viewpoint nor must the teacher pretend that pro and con arguments always are in balance. Educators must, nonetheless, allow students the freedom to explore fully various points of view. When teachers punish or stigmatize the expression of certain views, they cause some students to tune out, which makes it difficult for the class as a whole to compare alternative positions.

Teachers who want to have their students confront difficult social issues might well take the approach of the debate coach, who assists students to formulate positions on various sides of a question, helping students to evaluate the strengths and weaknesses of opposing facts and arguments. When the coach is doing his or her job effectively, the students give little or no thought to what might be the instructor's personal position because what counts is finding and evaluating good reasons. The atmosphere is one of frankness—let the best argument win. The class easily tolerates dissent without any artificial efforts to balance the discussion and without a patronizing attitude that certain ideas should be avoided for reasons of sensitivity. Students build mutual respect through the process of stating, supporting, and critiquing their own and other's views.

Education for Cultural Diversity

The attitude of partisanship without propaganda that underlies a sound moral education has proven difficult in connection with issues of cultural diversity. The United States is in the midst of another period of demographic change similar to that caused by earlier waves of immigration in the mid-nineteenth century and early 1900s. Because many of our new citizens now come from non-Western cultures, college administrators, staff, and teachers are rightly interested in making sure that the college atmosphere and curriculum responds to the nation's growing cultural diversity. Many campuses are putting into place required courses on minority issues, third-world studies, women's studies, and cultural pluralism. Educational reforms of this kind can be part of the general public interest to build a just and tolerant society.

However, critics have raised the specter of propaganda in connection with multicultural education. The dilemma is reflected in proposals by William Damon, chair of Clark University's Department of Education. Damon argued that courses on cultural diversity are part of a socially useful moral education. Accordingly, he recommended "mandatory racial-education programs" in which "trained instructors explored students' beliefs concerning racial diversity and its social implications." So far, so good. If students change their views after a wide-ranging and searching examination of facts and issues of race relations, few would term the result propagandistic. However, Damon's ideal course arguably straddled the line between propaganda and education. This equivocation emerged in Damon's argument that racial diversity programs "should cover, and provide clear justification for, any racially or ethnically sensitive admissions or hiring criteria that students may see on campus."[88] Here teachers are not to be permitted freedom to deviate from the official line on affirmative-action matters; hence, they would be forced into a propagandistic role.

Will our campuses be able to provide a moral education in cultural diversity without straying into propaganda? This is a vital question, for many colleges are putting in place mandatory courses in race relations, and others are debating whether to require students to choose from a range of ethnic or women's studies courses. The debate is not an easy one. At U.C. Berkeley and the University of Michigan, the faculty were reluctant to put minority-relations courses or requirements into place. This reticence probably stemmed in part from a fear that the courses would become a propaganda of indoctrination. At Berkeley, these suspicions were fueled by several rallies at which minority activists demanded that the courses be required.[89] If the courses were established as a political concession to minority group leaders, then one might reasonably expect that the course content would be tinged with a definite political hue.

Another factor complicating the institution of minority studies courses is the fear of some students that the classes will be dominated by a strident ideology that condemns Whites as racists and that dismisses American history and Western culture as uniquely oppressive. Elaine McCrate, who taught a section of the University of Vermont's required course on Race and Culture, reported that White students (who made up the bulk of the enrollment) entered thinking that she was "going to spend five weeks telling them they were racist." Eventually, however, she found that the students became less sullen and more open to discussion.[90]

Some of the controversy over education in cultural diversity has arisen in connection with the textbooks chosen for the courses. Paula S. Rothenberg's anthology, *Racism and Sexism: An Integrated Study*, widely used in courses on cultural pluralism in the early 1990s, came under fire for its stipulative, politically-tinged definitions.[91] She defined racism as "the subordination of people of color by white people" and sexism as "the subordination of women by men." In this scheme, only Whites could be racist and only men, sexist. Persons of color who discriminated on the basis of race were deemed to be merely "prejudiced," as were women who exploited men.[92] Because "racism" has been one of society's most damning terms since the 1960s, projecting the term solely on Whites and the West arguably made it difficult for students to think critically about cultural diversity. Rothenberg's definitions were politically weighted with the effect that Blacks, Whites, and students of other racial classifications had much personally at stake when using the terms.

Educators clearly have difficulty in dealing with issues of cultural diversity. Other controversial issues, such as war and peace, are similarly taxing to the teacher who wants to pursue moral matters without becoming a propagandist. Keeping propaganda out of education, however, does not require that teachers pretend to be neutral about cultural diversity, nuclear weapons, and the like. Nor does avoiding propagandistic teaching necessitate that teachers refrain from stating or otherwise indicating their own points of view. Education on tough issues of social morality does require, nevertheless, a certain detachment in which the instructor allows students the freedom to probe issues fully and to decide for themselves. When a teacher blocks avenues of discussion, stacks the cards to favor one view over another, or stigmatizes students for their beliefs, that teacher risks becoming a propagandist. On the other hand, no teacher who requires all students critically to examine the reasons behind their beliefs need worry about whether some students may, as a result, change their views.

Propaganda in the classroom is not simply a matter of outside forces thrusting their ideologies into the curriculum. It is true that educators of today face a diversity of outside pressures from businesses, religious groups, conservative watch-dog groups, and leftist advocacy-group activists. At least half of the problem of propaganda, however, has to do with the practices of educators themselves. To what extent do educators tolerate or even foster the market-driven kind of propaganda in which publishers water down the curriculum to avoid controversy? To what extent do teachers take the short cut to moral education by pressuring students to accept certain views and to reject others? We may assume that these and other issues of propaganda in the classroom will be with us for as long as human teachers stand at the center of education.

ENDNOTES

1. *West,* (of *San Jose Mercury News*) 6/24/90: 14-23.

2. See comment by Mather in New York *Herald Tribune,* August 5, 1937, in Scrap Book No. 9, Papers of Kirtley F. Mather, Denison University Archives, Granville, Ohio.

3. *New York Times,* 10/20/88: A1, A6.

4. Dinesh D'Souza, *Illiberal Education* (New York: Free Press, 1991).

5. National Education Association, *Report of the Committee on Propaganda in the Schools* (n.p.: NEA, 1929).

6. *Elementary School Journal,* 31 (May 1931): 642-644.

7. Ernest Gruening, *The Public Pays: A Study of Power Propaganda* (New York: Vanguard, 1931): 28-65, 100-112.

8. Gruening, *Public Pays:* 147.

9. On the Depression-era business campaign, see S. H. Walker and Paul Sklar, *Business Finds Its Voice* (New York: Harper, 1938).

10. See *Publishers' Weekly,* 139 (March 1, 1941): 1023-1024 and J. Michael Sproule, "Whose Ethics in the Classroom? An Historical Survey," *Communication Education,* 36 (1987): 321ff.

11. Letter of Thomas J. Fay, general manager of public relations, Mobil Oil, May 4, 1977.

12. Palo Alto, CA *Peninsula Times Tribune,* 4/17/90: C9.

13. *Chronicle of Higher Education,* 5/3/89: A23.

14. *Chronicle of Higher Education,* 6/24/87: 10.

15. *Chronicle of Higher Education,* 2/6/85: 15.

16. Joan Beck, Palo Alto, CA *Peninsula Times Tribune,* 1/22/90: B4.

17. *San Jose Mercury News,* 4/27/90: 4B.

18. *San Jose Mercury News,* 6/21/90: E1.

19. *San Jose Mercury News,* 7/2/90: 5B.

20. *San Jose Mercury News,* 6/19/90: 4B.

21. Odessa, TX *Odessa American,* 10/28/73: 4A.

22. Odessa, TX *Odessa American,* 10/14/73: 17A.

23. San Angelo, TX *San Angelo Standard,* 10/2/74: 1A.

24. Louisville, KY *Courier-Journal,* 7/9/78, Indiana Section: 2.

25. Louisville, KY *Courier-Journal,* 1/12/86: B10; *Newsweek,* 11/10/80: 75.

26. *Newsweek*, 11/26/73: 36-37.

27. *Chronicle of Higher Education*, 1/4/84: 8.

28. *Newsweek*, 3/15/82: 82.

29. Edward B. Jenkinson, *Censors in the Classroom* (New York: Avon, 1979): 17-27.

30. *Action* (of California Teachers Association), 11/89: 4.

31. *Newsweek*, 3/15/82: 82.

32. Louisville, KY *Courier-Journal*, 4/13/82: B7.

33. Louisville, KY *Courier-Journal*, 11/23/81: B2.

34. Walter Lippmann, *Public Opinion* (New York: Macmillan, 1922): 197.

35. Cf. Alexis deTocqueville, *Democracy in America*, trans. George Lawrence, ed. J. Mayer (Garden City, NY: Doubleday, 1969) and Robert N. Bellah, et al., *Habits of the Heart* (New York: Harper and Row, 1985).

36. See Kathleen H. Jamieson, *Eloquence in an Electronic Age* (New York: Oxford University Press, 1988).

37. Louisville, KY *Courier-Journal*, 10/12/80: A24.

38. *Newsweek*, 3/15/82: 82.

39. All these estimates in Louisville, KY *Courier-Journal*, 10/12/80: A24.

40. Louisville, KY *Courier-Journal*, 2/25/80: B1.

41. *New York Times*, 4/19/90: A6 .

42. *San Francisco Chronicle*, 7/30/87: 14.

43. *This World* (of *San Francisco Chronicle*), 11/15/87: 10.

44. *New York Times*, 12/28/87: 18.

45. *Newsweek*, 5/16/88: 40.

46. J. L. Heilbron (professor of history, University of California, Berkeley) and Daniel J. Kevles (professor of humanities, California Institute of Technology): *Chronicle of Higher Education*, 2/15/89: A48.

47. *New York Times*, 11/10/89: A14.

48. *San Jose Mercury News*, 11/7/89: 8B.

49. *New York Review of Books*, 5/18/89: 35.

50. *Newsweek*, 12/17/79: 103.

51. *San Francisco Chronicle*, 10/25/86: 1.

52. *Newsweek*, 7/6/81: 48, 50.

53. *This World* (of *San Francisco Chronicle*), 11/15/87: 11.

54. *Newsweek*, 12/17/79: 102.

55. *New York Times*, 1/17/90: B7.

56. Louisville, KY *Courier-Journal*,12/18/77: D3.

57. *This World* (of *San Francisco Chronicle*), 11/15/87: 10.

58. *This World* (of *San Francisco Chronicle*), 11/15/87: 10.

59. *Los Angeles Times*, 9/8/88: 1, 26.

60. *This World* (of *San Francisco Chronicle*), 11/15/87: 11.

61. *San Jose Mercury News*, 2/28/89: 12B.

62. *San Francisco Chronicle*, 5/20/87: 21.

63. Cf. *Action* (of California Teachers Association), 5/90: 1 and 4/90: 27.

64. Odessa, TX *Odessa American*, 5/25/75: 1D.

65. *Chronicle of Higher Education*, 7/31/78: 5.

66. *Chronicle of Higher Education*, 3/9/88: A1, A22.

67. *Chronicle of Higher Education*, 2/21/90: A28.

68. *Scan*, 11-12/85: 5-6.

69. *Chronicle of Higher Education*, 3/27/85: 5.

70. Louisville, KY *Courier-Journal*, 11/28/85: H10.

71. *Chronicle of Higher Education*, 10/16/85: 28.

72. *Chronicle of Higher Education*, 10/16/85: 28.

73. Louisville, KY *Courier-Journal*, 11/28/85: H10.

74. *Scan*, 11-12/85: 7.

75. *Chronicle of Higher Education*, 11/27/85: 21-22.

76. Ernst Benjamin, General Secretary of AAUP, to members, Nov. 1985.

77. *Chronicle of Higher Education*, 11/20/85: 2.

78. *Scan*, 11-12/85: 11.

79. *San Jose Mercury News*, 6/24/89: 5B.

80. *Chronicle of Higher Education*, 12/18/85: 25.

81. *Chronicle of Higher Education*, 1/16/78: 9.

82. *Chronicle of Higher Education*, 1/16/78: 9.

83. Odessa, TX *Odessa American*, 6/5/75: 8B.

84. *Campus Report* (of Accuracy in Academia), 5/87: 7.

85. *Campus Report* (of Accuracy in Academia), 5/86: 7.

86. *Chronicle of Higher Education,* 12/24/82: 25.

87. *Chronicle of Higher Education,* 2/16/83: 64.

88. *Chronicle of Higher Education,* 5/3/89: B1, B3.

89. *Chronicle of Higher Education,* 12/7/88: A16.

90. *Chronicle of Higher Education,* 3/28/90: A20.

91. Paula S. Rothenberg (ed.): *Racism and Sexism: An Integrated Study* (New York: St. Martin's, 1988).

92. Rothenberg, *Racism and Sexism:* 6.

A Musical Salute to Our Russian Ally, 1943

CHAPTER 6

PROPAGANDA IN ENTERTAINMENT

Neil Postman, a critic of contemporary discourse, has described today's world as an age of amusement. According to Postman, the chief threat to democracy is not some totalitarian Big Brother who uses force to bully the public. Rather, Postman believed, free public opinion now is threatened by a host of pleasant diversions that distract people from their own best interests. Postman turned his critical eye to today's fast-paced and unreflective TV news, to today's sloganistic and picture-oriented politics, and to the effort of teachers to ape the educational approach of television's "Sesame Street."[1]

Today's merging of entertainment and public communication can be studied from two perspectives. On the one hand, we may examine how entertainment techniques have become commonplace in commercial and political discourse. At the same time, we may look at how propagandists infiltrate self-serving messages into such entertainment media as film, television, sports, and art. For a people who wish to retain democratic values, both trends are worrisome. One reason for concern is that people let down their critical guard when they are being entertained. Like a kitten mesmerized by a dangling pocket watch, citizens are likely to miss much of what is happening to them when they are focused on commercial spectacle or political amusement. Further, when citizens are fed a steady diet of charming but empty public communication, then the nation's collective economic and political intelligence may be cumulatively weakened.

One may object to this pessimistic view of entertainment-oriented contemporary communication by noting that amusement is a fundamental human need. Selling, promoting, and political persuading have always carried elements of entertainment. The patter of Harold Hill, the stereotypical traveling salesman in *The Music Man*, exemplifies the seductive power of promotionalism: "You've got trouble, my friends, trouble, right here in River City!" Like Hill, the great orators of yesteryear knew full well how to engage the interests of their listeners. After a windy opponent in Congress asserted that he would rather be right than be president, Thomas Reed replied: "The gentleman need not be disturbed; he will never be either." The amusements of traditional salesmanship and oratory, however, were of a more thoughtful sort in which entertainment was closely connected to the commercial or political content. Today's merging of entertainment and content produces a species of public communication in which self-serving messages are obscured or hidden behind a charming and essentially irrelevant facade.

A survey of propaganda in film, TV, sports, and art demonstrates the increasing power of entertainment-oriented thinking during a time when entertainment values have come to dominate public communication. If We the People have come to expect constant diversion and amusement, then we are increasingly less likely to pick out the self-serving propagandas that persuaders insinuate into entertainment fare.

THE ENTERTAINMENT NORM IN PUBLIC COMMUNICATION

A survey of the last one hundred years of public communication shows that entertainment values gradually have taken greater hold. The process began when techniques of circus promotionalism and theatrical press agentry spread to the commercial and political arenas.

Circus and Theater

P. T. Barnum, the circus promoter, originated many techniques for using the press to spread sensational and self-serving claims. An example is the furor that Barnum created over Joice Heth, a aged former slave whom Barnum claimed had nursed George Washington one hundred years earlier. To stoke the public controversy, Barnum even planted stories that denounced his own claims as fraudulent.

The use of staged events and sensationalism in public communication sprang not only from the circus but also from theatrical press agents who labored to get newspaper attention for their clients. For instance, the press agent might entice newspapers to print an interesting story about the jewelry worn by the leading lady of a touring company just arrived in town.[2] According to Edward L. Bernays, a founder of the field of public relations, press agentry quickly spread from its beginnings in the world of circus and theater to become a staple of corporate communications. By the early 1870s, railroads were staging publicity stunts to influence the public. A notable example occurred when railroads provided free transcontinental excursions for prominent citizens in trains equipped with printing presses to issue news releases.[3]

Promotionalism in War and Politics

The emergency of World War I opened the door of politics to the entertainment-oriented press-relations techniques of circus and theater promotionalism. In 1917, the U.S. government established the Committee on Public Information (described on pp. 16-18), which employed posters, expositions, films, and other tactics on a nation-wide scale. Edward L. Bernays, who had done theatrical press agentry before the war, was one of many young promoters whose CPI work alerted them to the vast potential of twentieth-century press relations. Bernays recalled that "my wartime experience showed me that press-agentry had broader applications than theatre, music or the ballet."[4] One of Bernays's first clients was the Lithuanian National Council, a group working to promote the idea of restoring an independent Lithuania in the aftermath of the collapse of the Russian Empire. Bernays's promotional campaign for Lithuania included sending stories about Lithuanian athletes to sports fans, and sending examples of Lithuanian amber to American jewelry stores.[5]

By the early twentieth century, the promotional approach to public communication was becoming well-established. Entertainment and spectacle were increasingly familiar components of modern politics. For instance, Bernays helped humanize the dour President, Calvin Coolidge, by arranging a well-publicized White House breakfast in which "Silent Cal" was surrounded by famous stars of the screen and stage.[6]

At the same time that the field of public relations was adopting techniques honed by circus and theater promoters, advertisers were developing the image approach to selling merchandise. In the late 1800s, most advertising amounted to a description of the product in words. By the 1930s, however, advertising professionals were using photography and art to display vivid layouts that arrested the attention. Advertising research showed that striking and attractive images often conveyed a "selling argument" more effectively than words. In addition, advertisers found that they could "attract and disarm readers by offerings of entertainment and human anecdote."[7] Developments in public relations and advertising together contributed to a cultural shift towards an increasingly less thoughtful business and politics. Political speech-making and descriptive advertising gave way to amusing events, exciting spectacles, interesting anecdotes, and vivid images.

The contemporary American scene is one in which entertainment values have insinuated themselves into business and politics through an alliance between institutional persuaders and professional promoters in public relations and advertising. If contemporary Americans make commercial and political judgments according to standards of the circus and theater, then how resistant can they be to propaganda that is embedded in the very media of entertainment? What could be a more effective vehicle for propaganda than entertainment through film, television, sports, and art?

FILM: A LIVELY PROPAGANDA

Films give an image of social reality that has visual punch and power. However, films can show only part of any situation, meaning that the movies provide an inherent background propaganda on social questions. As seen through the vehicle of film, a social question takes the particular perspective of its leading characters. Choices of character and dramatic action make for a tempting kind of propaganda.

Propaganda in Early Films

An early recognition of the propaganda power of film took place when D. W. Griffith produced his classic silent epic, *The Birth of a Nation.* Griffith's film, which premiered in February 1915, was significant in the transition from small nickelodeon shorts to the larger cinematic story played out on a vast silver screen. Three times longer than the typical film of its day, and involving the soon-to-be proverbial cast of thousands, Griffith's saga of the South gave a sweeping portrait of the Civil War and Reconstruction periods. At the same time, the film used innovative camera angles to convey the personal stories of the characters.

While *Birth of a Nation* was visually exciting, the film's story became controversial from the time of its first appearance. Stressing the horrors of post-Civil War Reconstruction, the film included scenes of violence and attempted rape that presented Black leaders as basically evil. One

238

subtitle projected during the film argued that, as a result of the failure of Reconstruction, Whites of the North and South were "united again in common defense of their Aryan birthright." The racial and political ideology communicated by the film outraged many African-American leaders and White liberals. Although the film played to vast audiences across the United States, opponents made a number of largely unsuccessful efforts to ban the film in the interests of good race relations.[8]

Critical responses to *Birth of a Nation* showed that films could convey a powerful ideological message about society and politics by means of their plot action and visual imagery. World War I further showed the ideological usefulness of entertainment films in getting across political positions. Shortly after the American declaration of war on Germany, D. W. Griffith traveled to London with the aim of making what Lillian Gish, his leading lady, later described as a "propaganda film" about the war.

Subsidized by the British War Office, Griffith's *Hearts of the World* was supported by Allied officials who allowed him to use destroyed French villages as movie sets. It is no wonder that Gish recalled the film as having "inflamed audiences," for the picture presented exaggerated scenes of abusive and raping German soldiers running amok in a captured French village. The film played to good houses in the USA until the Armistice of November 1918, "when people lost interest in war films." "This picture was our contribution to the war effort," recalled Lillian Gish, but in the atmosphere of postwar disillusionment, D. W. Griffith regretted having made a wartime hate film. "I don't believe that Mr. Griffith ever forgave himself for making *Hearts of the World*," Gish later wrote.[9]

Griffith's *Birth* and *Hearts* films were not alone in raising issues of propaganda through film entertainment. The hallmark World War I hate film remains *The Kaiser, The Beast of Berlin*, a silent classic that focused on a peaceful French blacksmith and his daughter who are shown to suffer through the brutal German occupation. The film showed the boastful Kaiser reduced to a prisoner whose jailer, by an ironic twist, turns out to be none other than the French blacksmith.

Like D. W. Griffith, who regretted his wartime film, Carl Laemmle, who helped produce *The Kaiser*, later expressed sadness at the "poisonous rubbish" communicated by the film. Laemmle regarded his later, anti-war film, *All Quiet on the Western Front*, as an act of atonement for his participation in the World War I anti-German mania. Laemmle hoped that *All Quiet* would stir up a hatred of war.[10] Evidently the officials of Hitler's Germany agreed, for *All Quiet on the Western Front* was banned by the Nazi regime.

Studies of Film Propaganda

Film producers were hardly the only ones during the 1930s who expressed misgivings about cinematic propaganda. The progressive propaganda critics of the 1930s (see pp. 21-22) paid attention to several dangers of mass persuasion through film imagery. Representative was Edgar Dale, media educator, who conducted a content analysis for the Payne Fund in which he noted a number of ominous social currents of propaganda in films of the period.

Dale found that film characters were disproportionately likely to be taken from the wealthy class. Only 13 percent of the films that Dale studied were set in a poor household. In addition to this "overemphasis on the ultra-wealthy and wealthy classes," Dale complained about the tendency to depict foreigners as humorous characters, and the virtual absence of Blacks—except in an occasional role as servants. Further, Dale argued that American films not only gave unrealistic portrayals of marriage but also made crime, vulgarity, and alcohol seem disproportionately prominent in life. Finally, Dale drew attention to the small percentage of characters whose motives were collective or social. He found that only nine percent of the goals pursued by movie characters were social in nature, for instance, oriented to social reform or scientific discovery.[11] Edgar Dale's study drew attention to the possibly unconscious life-style propaganda that resulted from an effort by film makers to portray interesting characters.

Other critical studies of film propaganda focused more on the deliberate use of movies as a vehicle for covert persuasion. In the 1930s, Hollywood studios were experimenting with short "sponsored films" that were disguised advertising for particular products. Warner Brothers, Paramount, and other major film companies were offering not only to make advertising films but also to release these films in their theater chains. Critics argued that this kind of film was unfair because viewers frequently did not realize that they had watched a feature designed to sell a product. On the defensive during the Depression, American industries produced many films that were shown in industrial plants, before civic groups, and sometimes in theaters. Two examples were *A*

Car Is Born, produced by Chevrolet, and *America, Yesterday, Today and Tomorrow* prepared by the National Association of Manufacturers.[12]

New Issues of War and Peace

While cultural and social critics complained about commercial propaganda's infiltration of films, politicians, too, began to worry about the possible use of entertainment films to advance political agendas. When World War II broke out in Europe and Asia, isolationists, who opposed U.S. intervention in the war, feared that Hollywood films were speeding the nation toward involvement in war. Senator Gerald P. Nye of South Dakota held hearings on what he believed was interventionist propaganda in American films. Nye pointed to the appearance of many films focusing on the evils of Naziism or Nazi infiltration of the U.S., including *The Great Dictator* and *I Married a Nazi*. Nye argued that Darryl F. Zanuck and other movie moguls seemed to have no time for movie themes that would quiet passions and paranoia about overseas developments.

In testimony before Nye's Senate investigating committee, Zanuck, of Twentieth-Century Fox, claimed that his films merely dealt with timely subjects as reflected in the daily news. Zanuck argued that Nye focused on but a few of Hollywood's many films, and that Nye's proposals amounted to an impossible censorship over film subjects. Harry Warner, President of Warner Brothers, emphatically stated: "I deny that the pictures produced by my company are 'propaganda,' as has been alleged." Warner claimed that his company's only offense was to record current events as they were. In particular, he argued, Warner's *Confessions of a Nazi Spy* was based on actual events as documented in court cases.[13]

However much Hollywood shrank from the propaganda implications of its pre-Pearl Harbor features, the film industry consciously volunteered its image-making services during World War II. The Office of War Information (OWI), the U.S. government's wartime propaganda agency, encouraged film makers to keep asking themselves: "Will this picture help win the war?" The OWI wanted films not merely to "use the war as the basis for a profitable picture" but to use the picture to help people understand something new about World War II.[14]

The OWI was particularly impressed with the propaganda value of *Mrs. Miniver,* an MGM production of 1942. *Mrs. Miniver* was so successful in combining compelling drama and timely propaganda that the film won seven academy awards. In the course of relating how the Minivers, an English upper-middle-class family, coped with the war, *Mrs. Miniver* effectively made a number of propaganda points. For one thing, the film helped defuse the obviously undemocratic British class system. Personified by Lady Beldon, a superficially stuffy but actually warm and caring character, *Mrs. Miniver* presented the class system as often misunderstood and sometimes charming. At the same time, the film used the marriage of Mrs. Miniver's son and Lady Beldon's granddaughter to imply that the war would help bring about a more classless Britain. Another example of blending propaganda into plot was the film's presentation of the dangers of war, calculated to produce feelings of national solidarity. While Mrs. Miniver's son survived intense combat as a Royal Air Force pilot, his young wife was killed in a bombing raid. Thus, the film brought home a message that civilians and military people alike faced dangers due to war, at the same time suggesting that the men who went off to war would return safely.

The years of World War II saw many transparently propagandistic films that emphasized a variety of one-dimensional characters: Heil-Hitlering Nazis and bespectacled Japanese given to leering, ranting, and brutal aggression. Cartoons starring Mickey Mouse, Donald Duck, and other characters also were pressed into service to communicate wartime stereotypes. The nationalistic approach seen in some wartime cartoons is likely to prompt feelings of embarrassment today (especially given the lack of a sense of history that is common in our image-oriented, here-and-now culture). For this reason, the Disney film company is reluctant to show some of its wartime productions today. "It wouldn't be right to reproduce them on cassettes or to edit them for the public," said Peter Schneider, senior vice president of Disney Studios.[15]

However, not all of Hollywood's wartime propaganda was so obvious in its work. For instance, in *Casablanca*, Warner Brothers was able to tell the simultaneously interesting and propagandistic story of Rick, a cynical American expatriate played by Humphrey Bogart. Living in French Morocco in the days just before Pearl Harbor, Rick gradually turns from detachment to commitment about the war against fascism. Rick eventually sacrifices his prosperous nightclub and his life's true love (played by Ingrid Bergman) so that he (and she) can take their proper places in World War II, seen as an anti-fascist crusade. The film remains a classic today.

The Blacklist Period

Part of Hollywood's service to the war effort was presenting America's allies in what was deemed as a properly favorable perspective. Just as *Mrs. Miniver* played up British determination while minimizing the notorious class system, so too did film makers cooperate in setting out a favorable view of Russia, our major ally in the eastern theater of the war.

The premier example of the pro-Russian wartime movie was Warner Brothers' picture, *Mission to Moscow*, based on the memoirs of Joseph E. Davies, U.S. ambassador to the Soviet Union. *Mission to Moscow* presented the people of the Soviet Union as happy, united, loyal to their government, and sharing the same basic values as Americans. Further, the film excused many of the known evils of the Russian regime. For instance, Stalin's paranoia about foreign spies is made to seem a natural consequence of sneaky German sabotage efforts. Similarly, Stalin's infamous purge (and murder) of thousands of Russian officials and military officers is presented as a justified and rational preparation for the German invasion that the wise Stalin was anticipating.

The OWI lauded *Mission to Moscow* as "a magnificent contribution to the Government's War Information Program" because the film catered to the government's desire to build public trust in America's Russian ally.[16] The OWI seemed oblivious to the film's blatant blindness toward Stalinist totalitarianism. These omissions, however, probably seemed justified according to the politics of the period, inasmuch as the Soviet Union was then bearing the brunt of ground combat against Hitler's legions. Nevertheless, conservatives and anti-Roosevelt leaders condemned the film as propaganda favoring totalitarianism, if not communism. When the anti-fascist crusade of 1941-1945 turned into a Cold War with Russia, the politics of some wartime films seemed out of step with later events and therefore less easy to justify. Looking for ways to weaken the administration of President Harry Truman, the anti-Truman faction that controlled the House Un-American Activities Committee (HUAC) decided to turn its attention to the wartime pro-Russia films produced by the Hollywood studios, notably Warner Brothers' *Mission to Moscow*. In taking testimony from dozens of Hollywood's famous stars and producers, HUAC found a gold mine of helpful political headlines.

J. Parnell Thomas, HUAC's chair, began the hearings on the motion picture industry with the observation that films exerted "a powerful impact" on the "thoughts and behavior" of the movie audience. He added that "it is not unnatural—in fact, it is very logical—that subversive and undemocratic forces should attempt to use this medium for un-American purposes." Responding to Thomas, Jack Warner, the studio mogul, contended that "there is not a Warner Brothers picture that can fairly be judged to be hostile to our country, or communistic in tone and purpose." Warner specifically defended *Mission to Moscow*, arguing that the film served an important wartime objective at a time when "our country was fighting for its existence, with Russia as one of our allies." Warner added that "if making *Mission to Moscow* in 1942 was a subversive activity, then the American Liberty ships which carried food and guns to Russian allies, and the American naval vessels which conveyed them, were likewise engaged in subversive activities." Jack Warner bolstered the patriotic credentials of his films by noting various wartime offerings by Warner that boosted the image of the military, including *This Is the Army* and *Destination Tokyo*. Warner also observed that his studio had made films before World War II about the dangers posed by Germany and Italy "where we endeavored . . . to awaken the democracies of America and England and others to this terrible menace that faced them." Warner's claim of a conscious persuasive purpose behind *Confessions of a Nazi Spy* and other such movies was ironic because he contradicted his brother Harry's earlier disavowals about that film before the Nye committee.[17]

While vigorously defending his own Americanism as well as the films produced by his studio, Warner did provide a list of 16 writers who had been admonished by his studio for trying to inject what he believed was un-American writing into film scenarios. This concession marked a turning point in the hearings by which HUAC shifted from a focus on particular films and on the studio system itself, to an emphasis on individual artists. Projecting the onus of "subversion" onto individual writers was questionable, however, given the studio production system in which screen writers and their words were closely monitored and edited at many points. The political advantages of HUAC's shift, nevertheless, were unquestionable. Focusing the glare of bad publicity on just a few individuals allowed Hollywood's leadership to acquiesce in a scapegoating procedure that protected the reputation of the studios. Pressured by unfavorable publicity generated by the HUAC hearings, stars such as

Humphrey Bogart, who had initially publicly opposed the Hollywood hearings, backed off. For their part, the studios set up a blacklist of individuals who would not be hired. Hollywood began a program of symbolic reparations by making a large number of overtly anti-communist films.[18]

The most prominent of the blacklisted individuals were the so-called Hollywood Ten. Some of the Ten were moviedom's leading screen writers, such as Academy Award winners Dalton Trumbo and Ring Lardner, Jr. Although every one of the Ten probably had been a member of the Communist Party at least briefly, each refused on principle to testify either about his own political beliefs and memberships or those of others. Lardner argued that "there is only a minor difference between forcing a man to say what his opinions are and dictating what his opinions should be"; both actions required persons "to open their minds to government authority."[19] As a result, the Ten were cited for contempt of Congress and later were jailed on these charges.

It was not necessary to be a radical or to hold Communist Party membership to run afoul of the new order of conservative political correctness reigning in Hollywood. HUAC was in no mood to make fine distinctions between liberals, progressives, New Dealers, Popular Frontists (those liberals who wanted to cooperate where possible with communists), members of the American Communist Party, and pro-Soviet communists. HUAC was not concerned with distinguishing between persons who wanted social reform and individuals who sought to bring down traditional American institutions. HUAC's peculiar Hollywood adventures had only a coincidental connection to actual national security. The committee's leaders were satisfied merely to induce headlines that generated bad publicity for New Dealers and liberals. As the Cold War heated up during the late 1940s, conservatives saw an opportunity to settle a score with those who had placed them on the defensive during the Depression and during the time of America's alliance with the Soviet Union.

Because of the general anti-liberal spirit that animated HUAC and the associated blacklist apparatus, Hollywood figures could come under attack for merely having a reputation for liberal politics or for a record of public opposition to HUAC. Actress Myrna Loy, one of the stars who had campaigned against HUAC's foray into Hollywood, had not even dabbled in Communist politics, although she had been a vocal New Deal liberal. To her surprise, Loy found herself attacked in the *Hollywood*

Reporter as "part of the Communist fifth column in America . . . serving a possible treasonable purpose" along with such others as Edward G. Robinson, Orson Welles, Burgess Meredith, and James Cagney. Loy brought a libel suit against the *Reporter* and eventually won a retraction.[20] Victories of this kind, however, were few and far between during the period of the blacklist and the Red Scare of the 1950s.

The effort to ban talented writers on the basis of their past politics was as difficult to maintain as it was undemocratic in conception. Sometimes film makers secretly employed blacklisted writers who evaded their exile by using pseudonyms. For instance, Carl Foreman and Michael Wilson were not given public credit for their work on *The Bridge on the River Kwai* (1957). Foreman, a disillusioned former communist, admitted that he had dropped out of the party in 1942; but he was blacklisted anyway for refusing to name other communists. Foreman's and Wilson's widows received their Academy Awards in 1985.[21] The blacklist finally was publicly broken only in 1960, when Dalton Trumbo was credited for work on *Spartacus* and *Exodus*. Ring Lardner, Jr., who had won an Academy Award in 1942 for *Woman of the Year*, spent 15 years on the blacklist. Later he was able to adapt *The Cincinnati Kid* and *MASH*.[22]

Films and the Cold War

The early history of American film-making shows how filmdom's images of the world may shift abruptly because of changing political currents. The "crush the Hun" approach of World War I, typified by *The Kaiser, the Beast of Berlin*, gave way to a number of quasi-pacifist portrayals of war in the 1930s, for instance, *All Quiet on the Western Front*. During the late 1930s, Hollywood studios took an anti-fascist, interventionist position, while denying this aim publicly when criticized by isolationists. Studios turned to pro-British and pro-Russian themes in the early 1940s to accommodate the needs of the wartime alliances. When the Cold War congealed, however, studios obliged the new political realities by producing films based on the theme of the "communist menace."

The shifting political sands of movie imagery are particularly striking in the case of the Cold War era. Films of the early Cold War era frequently played up the Red Menace directly, as in *The Iron Curtain* (1948) and *I Was a Communist for the FBI* (1951). While most of the overtly anti-communist films were box-office duds, the indirect approach to

Cold War film making was more successful. Jimmy Stewart's film, *Strategic Air Command* (1955), more popularly glorified the dedication and heroism of the men and machines that constituted America's nuclear deterrent forces. Further, it is likely that the prevalence and popularity of alien invasion films during the 1950s, such as *Invasion of the Body Snatchers* (1956), owed much to the anxieties of the Cold War. These films treated the communist threat by way of an extended analogy to invading plants and other organisms that secretly possessed the minds and souls of ordinary citizens.

By the late 1950s, American and Soviet leaders were meeting in bilateral exchanges, and the Cold War had melted into a muddy stalemate. Film makers responded to the newly complicated currents of the communist/capitalist struggle. For instance, in the early James Bond films, the Soviets alternate as the enemy with a fictional terrorist group called SPECTRE. Bond's effort to obtain a secret Soviet decoding machine caused him to struggle against both communists and SPEC-TRE agents in *From Russia with Love* (1963). By the time *The Spy Who Loved Me* appeared in 1976, Bond's cooperation with a winsome Soviet agent seemed natural, given the increased US/USSR cooperation that was characteristic of the Nixon-era thaw. A later ambiguous presentation of the Cold War in *A View to a Kill* (1985) finds a renegade KGB agent planning to trigger an earthquake that will destroy Silicon Valley in California. Bond and Soviet agents cooperate to stem the threat.

The ambivalent relationship of the James Bond genre to the Cold War is interesting from a propaganda point of view. Ian Fleming, author of the Bond novels on which the films were based, had at first written his books around villains who were directly or indirectly in the service of the Soviet Union. Fleming later turned to the SPECTRE approach in which a group of self-serving and apolitical bad guys sought to exploit East/West tensions. Focus on the fictional SPECTRE terrorists allowed both Fleming and the produers of the Bond films to minimize the risk of appearing politically out-of-step during the 1960s, a period when Cold War tensions rose and fell variously.[23]

In the aftermath of the Soviet invasion of Afganistan in 1980, which derailed the Nixon-era detente, Sylvester Stallone's Rambo films played upon the new anti-Soviet turn. In *Rambo: First Blood II*, we find Stallone combatting the Reds in Vietnam, experiencing torture at the hands of the communists, and personally dispatching over 60 North Vietnamese soldiers along with 20 Russians. *Rambo III* finds our hero fighting the husky Ruskies in Afganistan. However, this latter film not only suffered a reported $30 million dollars in losses but also was roundly panned by critics as being too jingoistic.[24]

The Cold War struggle eventually entered Stallone's film series about Rocky, the prize fighter. *Rocky IV* finds Philadelphia's favorite pugilist deep in the Soviet Union boxing for his patriotic life against Ivan Drago, an evil bionic giant produced by Red scientists. Rocky's bout against the Red Machine mirrored the post-Reagan mood of a can-do America overcoming the limitations and self-doubt of the 1970s. As a *Newsweek* reviewer put it, "Rocky is the self-made champion of freedom, Drago the machine-made product of the state."[25] Sylvester Stallone was not unmindful of criticisms that his good-versus-evil dramas encouraged revenge, hate, and violence. By 1990, Stallone was expressing a desire to regain the respect of the liberal elements of society whom he lost with Rambo and with the transformation of the shy and oafishly charming Rocky into another Cold Warrior. During the filming of *Rambo III*, Stallone told interviewers that Rambo's next cause might be the environment. Stallone was giving thought to having Rambo appear as something like a game warden in Africa fighting ivory poachers.[26]

Rambo was not the only film character to play to the revival of aggressive patriotism that came with the more heated Cold War atmosphere of the early 1980s. For instance, we may cite *Invasion U.S.A.*, *Born American*, and *Red Dawn* with their theme of attack by sadistic Russian soldiers. But the 1980s also saw the return of the more traditional military story in which the misunderstood young hero loses military honor but then saves the day and gets the girl. Typifying the revival of military hero films was *Top Gun*. This box-office hit of the mid-'80s paid homage to the honor and courage of America's top fighter pilots. *Top Gun* was set at the Navy's Fighter Weapons School at Miramar Naval Air Station in Southern California, where the best are taught to be even better. In the climactic scenes, fighters from a U.S. aircraft are surrounded by a larger Soviet air patrol. The feisty hero, Maverick, comes to the rescue by destroying enemy fighters that had been poised not only to destroy the Navy planes but perhaps even to sink the aircraft carrier itself.

The U.S. Navy was quite happy with *Top Gun*. The film improved the Navy's image at the same time that it boosted recruiting. Stephen H. Clawson, public information director at the U.S. Naval Academy, commented that "a movie like *Top Gun* shows a renewed respect for servicemen. It can't help but make young people think this is an exciting career."[27] The cooperation between the Navy and the film's makers began early. *Top Gun* was based on an article that lauded the Navy's Miramar school, and Navy brass quickly recognized the potential public relations value of such a film. The Navy cooperated fully with the producers, in exchange for some control over the script. The Navy's assistance turned out to be considerable. The film producers were granted use of 20 fighter pilots, the aircraft carriers *Enterprise* and *Ranger,* the Miramar facility, and—for only the cost of fuel—a fleet of Navy jets. The alliance between Naval personnel and Hollywood film makers extended even to the promotion of the movie. *Top Gun* was premiered at the Kennedy Center in Washington as part of festivities for the 75th anniversary of the Association of Naval Aviation.

Aware of the image orientation of contemporary American culture, the U.S. military services have a long memory when it comes to how they look in films. For instance, James J. Webb, Jr., Assistant Defense Secretary in charge of reserves, recalled an Academy Awards ceremony in which an anti-Vietnam War documentary, *Hearts and Minds,* won the Oscar for Best Documentary. Webb regarded the film as "an unbelievable slam at American values and American military values." He noted further that Bert Schneider, the producer of *Hearts and Minds,* won applause when he read a telegram from North Vietnamese officials that congratulated the Academy.[28] The Pentagon wanted no return to the anti-military cinematic image making of the 1970s, and one way to nurse along a good military image was to be selective in support of film makers. Accordingly, the services have been choosy about what films they would support, offering cooperation only when the movie made the military look good.

The policy of exchanging Pentagon support for favorable film treatment is an old one. For instance, the Navy refused to lend a submarine to Stanley Kramer in the 1950s when he was producing *On the Beach,* a film that depicted the world's population annihilated by toxic fallout in the aftermath of a nuclear war.[29] The Navy objected that the film exaggerated the human losses that would result from atomic warfare. Similarly, the Navy refused to help with such films as *Cinderella Liberty* (1973) and *The Last Detail* (1973) which focused on the problems of enlisted men and therefore seemed to present a negative view of military life.[30] Navy officials considered allowing Mark Rydell, director of *Cinderella Liberty,* the use of a destroyer, a Navy base, a hospital, and sailors. In exchange for this cooperation, Navy representatives negotiated a few changes in the script. However, Navy support was abruptly withdrawn when a higher-ranking Navy officer took exception to the filmscript.

The top Pentagon brass are known to be cautious about military films because they can get into political hot water for helping with the wrong film story. For instance, the Navy suffered criticism for lending military property at low cost to the makers of *Tora! Tora! Tora!* (1970) which depicted the Pearl Harbor attack by Japan. Some Congressmen wondered why the Pentagon would aid in the cinematic treatment of one of America's greatest military defeats.[31] However, excessive caution sometimes has caused the military services to miss a propaganda bet. For instance, the Navy refused to cooperate with the producers of *An Officer and a Gentleman* (1982) because the plot seemed too dark and sexual. Later, Navy officials credited this romance between a young cadet (played by Richard Gere) and a working-class girl (played by Debra Winger) for triggering a 20-percent increase in officer recruitment.[32]

Film producers find it tricky and touchy to merge the art of cinema, the economics of movie-making, and the image of the military. For this reason, John K. Swensson, a De Anza College English teacher, found a niche in the film business as a go-between for film producers and the military services. A West Pointer, Vietnam veteran, and one-time Army recruitment officer, Swensson called himself a "packager." "I bring people together. I try to broker between the creative community and the military."[33] Swensson helped put together *Fire Birds*, a summer 1990 action-adventure picture about Army helicopter heroics against a South American drug cartel. Although having no previous film experience, Swenssen contributed significantly to the production of this *Top Gun* clone by smoothing relations between the film's producers, the Army, and the McDonnell Douglas Corporation, maker of the Army's *Apache* helicopter. In exchange for helping to reduce the film's production costs, the Army got assurances that the script would be technically accurate, would not portray the helicopter heroes as reckless, and would not show women in combat roles.

Critics are always ready to pounce on films like *Top Gun* and *Fire Birds* which seem to beckon young people with the messages "Let's fight 'em" and "Join now!" Just as Sylvester Stallone expressed some pangs of conscience about the violent and militaristic image of his Rambo character, Tom Cruise, the star of *Top Gun*, felt a need to repent of his gung-ho fighter pilot character, Maverick. "OK, some people felt that *Top Gun* was a right-wing film to promote the Navy," acknowledged Cruise in an interview. "But I want the kids to know that that's not the way war is— that *Top Gun* was just an amusement park ride, a fun film with a PG-13 rating that was not supposed to be reality. That's why I didn't go on and make *Top Gun II* and *III* and *IV* and *V.* That would have been irresponsible."[34]

In his later film, *Born on the Fourth of July* (1989), Cruise certainly reversed his *Top Gun* image. Cruise played Ron Kovic, an archetypal child of the Cold War. Raised on war toys and games, steeped in the anti-communist rhetoric of the 1950s and 1960s, and sent to fight in Vietnam, Kovic is convinced that his nation's survival is at stake. *Born on the Fourth of July* departed from the typical pro-war ideology of military films in which war appears as necessary, purposeful, relatively clean, and essentially successful. Conveying an anti-war counterpoint, Kovic, the would-be war hero, is crippled, then abused, then disillusioned, and finally radicalized.

Alternatives to Red-Bashing

The early '90s saw the '80s Red-bashing formula of apocalyptic struggle give way to one of U.S./Soviet cooperation. It is no accident that an anti-war film such as *Born on the Fourth of July* would appear at the twilight of the Cold War. American film makers have been consistently alert to shifts in the political and ideological winds, as evidenced by the twist from pro-war to anti-war films during the 1920s and 1930s, the turn from pro-Soviet to anti-Russian films between 1942 and 1947, and the brief cinematic thaw of Nixon/Brezhnev era of detente. Illustrative of glasnost-era Soviet/American cooperation was *Red Heat* (1988) in which Arnold Schwarzenegger played a Soviet police captain, Danko, who joined Art Ridzik, a fictional Chicago detective played by Jim Belushi, in a fight against drug smugglers. In contrast to the cynical, loud-mouthed, and lewd Ridzik, Danko appeared to be dedicated, straight-laced, and contemptuous of the physical and moral decay of the Windy City. For instance, in his shabby hotel room, Danko happened upon a pornographic TV channel, watched for a couple of seconds, and disgustedly spat out the epithet: "Capitalism!" In regards to Hollywood's need for military villains, we may note the pattern of the 1980s and early 1990s whereby the Russians were replaced as the enemy-of-choice for action-adventure entertainment. Middle Eastern terrorists fulfilled the villan's role in *Back to the Future* (1985), and South American drug smugglers served as heinous foils for James Bond in *License to Kill* (1989). It seems that film makers are wont to reinforce whatever enmity seems to be uppermost in public consciousness. The tendency for film makers to follow news headlines and political trends in selecting movie villains presents some dangers from the point of view of propaganda. Even if a film merely reinforces existing socio-political beliefs, a social critic may want to challenge a process by which film makers offhandedly show us whom to hate and whom to fear. Since war and peace are the most powerful choices a democratic people must make, the costs can be high when movies beckon us to revere Stalin or to fear Arabs. More generally, if Americans are becoming a people who think according to visual images, then the propaganda of film is a matter of the utmost urgency.

As is emphasized later (pp. 336-337), the chief method of detecting propaganda in entertainment films is to become an alert reader of contemporary newspapers. Leading feature films always are accompanied by movie reviews and news stories that, on the one hand, give commentary on who is portrayed favorably or unfavorably, and on the other hand, reveal who is pleased or displeased with the plot or characters. By noting these reactions, and comparing them to the responses given to earlier films, viewers may keep tabs on propaganda in movie-making.

THE PROPAGANDA OF PRIME TIME

Although the searing images of film make for a powerful propaganda, nothing figures more prominently in the propaganda of appearances than does television. An omnipresent feature of the contemporary American home, TV imposes a face on life that no one can escape. Even more than film and radio, the popular art of television is something Americans cannot turn off. Even when we tune out our own TV's images, our neighbors and contemporaries are watching. We ourselves are ever shaped by a society that is constantly under the influence of television.[35]

Propaganda of an Intimate Kind

Television is not only a more intrusive channel for propaganda but also it is a more intimate kind of visual imagery than film. Joshua Meyerowitz, a media scholar, underscored this generalization when he argued that the stereotypical TV families of the 1950s paradoxically led to breakdowns in traditional male/female roles.[36] If we consider the strong actresses of 1930s films—e.g. Katherine Hepburn and Joan

252

Crawford—then the women of television's golden age present a stark contrast to what clearly was possible for a female character. The women of *The Donna Reed Show, Father Knows Best, Ozzie and Harriet,* and *Leave It to Beaver* seemed almost deliberately cast in a mold to discourage the career gains that women had made during the World War II years of Rosie the Riveter. Yet, according to Meyerowitz, TV did not have the stereotyping effect that one might predict on the basis of a simplistic theory of role models. Meyerowitz argued that the chief impact of family shows on television was to bring the backstage behavior of men and women into fuller view. The effect was to demystify the social roles of men and women both in relation to career and to family. Scenes of confused men and women discussing their own problems and those of their children helped make rigid sex-role distinctions seem ridiculous. Neither father nor mother had a firm hold on what life was all about.

Still it was, and is, possible for TV to take an ideological line by steering society's images in one direction or the other, for example, in the way the Cold War was portrayed on television. In his examination of TV listings of the 1950s, J. Fred MacDonald, the media historian, found a not-so-subtle effort to conjure up images of the Red Menace. Television of the 1950s contributed at least nineteen spy shows consistent with the cloak-and-dagger feel of Cold War intrigue. The classic example was *I Led 3 Lives*, based on the career of Herbert A. Philbrick as an FBI agent posing as a Communist Party activist. Philbrick himself advised producers of the show to make sure that the episodes closely mirrored FBI interests and practices. Toward the same apparent end, the ABC-TV and CBS-TV networks presented a number of shows throughout the 1950s that either depicted the effects of Russian nuclear bombing or that detailed modes of civil defense.[37]

Other nods by television to the crisis atmosphere of the Cold War included at least 16 TV specials, documentaries, or series that had a military settings. These varied from *Victory at Sea*, a 26-episode documentary on the Navy's part in World War II, to *The Phil Silvers Show*, which found Sergeant Bilko giving a benign treatment to gripes by GIs against officers. As MacDonald's review of the 1950s demonstrated, even children's programming was not immune to the insertion of anti-communist themes. Science fantasy programs for kids included *Captain Midnight*, a story about a Secret Squadron that combatted enemy agents and diabolical plots for world conquest.[38]

However much television shows seem to cater to dominant ideological moods in American life, TV producers clearly do *not* see ideology as their aim. The never-ending objective of TV executives is to gain the largest possible audience for the purpose of justifying the largest possible advertising rates. According to Todd Gitlin, a television critic, TV marketers aim to profit by being accommodating, by finding what is most acceptable at a given point in time.

The effort to present pleasing characters, plots, and images means that television producers normally will mirror ideological lines prevailing in society. For instance, Gitlin discussed the emergence of anti-establishment programs in the early 1970s. Television executives at that time believed that American audiences were receptive to portrayals of flaws in American institutions and dominant beliefs. Resulting TV fare included *All in the Family*, a spoof at the conservative and prejudiced views of Archie Bunker, as well as *MASH*, which highlighted the absurdity and human costs of war. By 1980, TV producers sensed a rightward swing of public opinion, and they produced shows accordingly. Typical of the corresponding new entries in TV's lineup were *Strike Force*, a drama about a police tactical unit, and *Today's FBI*.[39]

Television seems to cater most to propaganda interests when the medium tries to tell the grander kind of story. In this connection, we may profitably examine three notable examples: *Roots* (1977), *The Day After* (1983), and *Amerika* (1986).

The Propaganda of *Roots*

Roots, the television docudrama, began as a novelized account by Alex Haley of his ancestor, Kunta Kinte, who was taken by slavers and sold into captivity in the United States. Haley's original book presented Kunta Kinte as a noble citizen of the strong and honorable Mandinka Empire in Africa. Haley showed the Mandinkas as having fair laws, a reverence for education, and well-established customs for benign treatment of their own slaves. In contrast to the Mandinkas were the White slavers, whom Haley presented as ugly, immoral, and easily fooled.

After surviving his journey to the New World in a horrid slave ship, Kunta Kinte experienced a panorama of brutality and injustice in the ante-bellum South. Haley's historical novel emphasized the physical and psychological cruelty of Southern slave owners, in contrast to the Blacks who dwelled in brotherhood and who intelligently employed a host of stratagems to resist their exploitation. With a sense of irony, Haley presented this early resistance by slaves as the original basis for racial stereotypes. To outwit White masters, the slaves variously pretended to be stupid, lazy, or docile, all of which led to stereotypes about Blacks.

Haley's novel was powerful and seemed to call out for visual presentation, although ABC-TV executives had their doubts about whether a long drama about African-Americans would draw much of an audience; however, the audience for *Roots* broke ratings-share records. An estimated 130 million Americans watched at least part of this 1977 mini-series.[40] *Roots* appeared at a unique moment in which nostalgia for the 1960s Civil Rights movement merged with lingering White guilt about segregation, all of which coincided with the liberal upswing associated with the election of Jimmy Carter.

Not that everyone applauded a twelve-hour-long look at the American South from the perspective of Black slavery. Given the national fascination with *Roots*, however, few mainstream social or political figures dared to criticize it. David Duke, then the Grand Wizard of the Ku Klux Klan, was virtually alone in complaining about the image-propaganda inherent in a television drama that carried a social message. According to Duke, not only did *Roots* overstate the mistreatment of slaves but also the series ignored the slavery practiced by African tribes as well as problems experienced by Whites in the post-Civil War period. Duke demanded that ABC-TV produce an entertainment show that gave equal time to the "historical perspective of a white Southerner" on slavery and Reconstruction.[41]

From the perspective of TV drama, Duke's demand was a bit ridiculous. No single series could possibly give equal portrayal of all the various injustices occurring in the world at a given time. Even if a dramatist were able to mix Kunta Kinte's story with various holocausts and oppressions in Ireland, China, or Latin America, the effect would be to siphon off the dramatic integrity and moral meaning of the particular historical facts that prompted Haley's *Roots*. From the standpoint of propaganda, nonetheless, Duke's complaint made more sense than most commentators of the time recognized. With the constant array of the strengths of Blacks contrasted with the evils of Whites, *Roots* was fodder for African-American advocacy groups as well as effective background propaganda for a variety of social policies such as Affirmative Action. The silence of liberal critics on this point highlights the difficulty of recognizing propaganda, especially popular propaganda, at the very time that it is working its greatest effect.

255

Propaganda in *The Day After*

Spurred by the surprising successes of *Roots*, the TV networks looked for vehicles to capture the same excitement and mega-ratings that were generated by Haley's drama of the slave South. The centerpiece docudrama of the 1983 season was *The Day After*, shown on ABC-TV on Sunday evening, November 20, 1983. *The Day After* was an attempt to portray the experience of nuclear war by ordinary citizens in Kansas. The TV movie began with a view of typical farmers, students, and physicians going through their daily schedules. Interspersed among these scenes of normal middle-American life, however, were ominous snippets on various radios and televisions about a crisis brewing in Europe. With increasing urgency, news programs and special bulletins detail a building military crisis between NATO and Warsaw Pact forces. The crisis gradually escalates from conventional to nuclear weapons, and the TV emergency comes home to Kansas as American missiles based there are launched from their silos to far-off Soviet destinations. As Soviet missiles begin to fall upon formerly placid Kansas, the landscape becomes a dark scene of destruction, chaos, and horror. Much of the power of *The Day After* lies in the movie's vivid scenes of postwar injury, destruction, despair, and basic hopelessness. Physicians desperately try to continue some kind of normal medicine in a world of radiation injuries and mass suffering. Farmers get few credible answers from federal officials about how they can raise healthful food on contaminated soil.

The political controversiality of *The Day After* became apparent even before the docudrama appeared. In the months and weeks before the TV movie was shown, various news stories appeared dealing with last-minute machinations of scheduling and editing. When *The Day After* was postponed from an original May 1983 air date, the press speculated that the network was caving in to pressure from the Reagan Administration.[42] Later, ABC cut a snippet from the drama in which a newscaster made a reference to U.S. missiles: "The Soviet Foreign Ministry claimed that it was the coordinated move of Pershing II missile launchers that had provoked the original Soviet attack."[43] Questioned about why they excised a sentence that implied some U.S. responsibility for the outbreak of nuclear war, the ABC network felt obliged to deny that White House pressure had prompted the cut.

Advertisers, too, were somewhat nervous about placing their commercial messages on a show containing so many negative images of the national future. As it turned out, ABC showed four-fifths of the commercials before the missiles were fired. If U.S. policy makers and advertisers found the message of *The Day After* to be worrisome, the war-is-hell tenor of the program delighted supporters of the nuclear-freeze movement. "All our meetings are just a teardrop in the bucket compared to the number of people who will see this film," commented Jo Seidita, a California nuclear-freeze advocate.[44]

Responding to the growing political storm about *The Day After*, ABC used Ted Koppel's interview program following the show to diffuse any tensions that might have lingered as a result of seeing American citizens and cities reduced to radioactive ashes. The program included various notables, including former Secretary of State Henry Kissinger, former Secretary of Defense Robert McNamara, and scientist Carl Sagan. The panelists contributed fairly predictable viewpoints, with Kissinger calling the program simplistic, and Sagan warning that the effects of nuclear war would be worse than those actually depicted.

Comment around the nation also followed established ideological and political lines. Conservative columnists and leaders, such as William F. Buckley, Jr., and Jerry Falwell, were vocal in their outrage at the pacifistic ethos of *The Day After*. Phyllis Schlafly, conservative activist, was one of many who dispatched letters to ABC demanding equal time for those who favored building nuclear weapons for military deterrence. "This film was made by people who want to disarm the country and are willing to make a $7 million contribution to that campaign," charged Schlafly.[45] Peace groups, in fact, did seize the moment to set up public forums for discussion of the movie. For instance, Peace Makers of Southern Indiana sponsored a discussion in the parish house of St. Paul's Episcopal Church, New Albany.[46] On the other hand, Daniel O. Graham, retired Army general and head of a group called High Frontiers, hoped that *The Day After* would increase public support for his group's plans for a laser defense system to destroy enemy missiles.[47]

As one might expect, the popular audience's response to *The Day After* was ambiguous. Telegrams to ABC ran two-to-one in favor of the show, but polls indicated virtually no change in the percentage of people believing that nuclear war was likely. The show actually seemed to have increased the expressed support for President Ronald Reagan. Educators reported that comments by students tended to mirror the reactions of their parents, and also to follow the political orientation of the community as a whole. Dennis Hall, teacher at New Albany High School in

Indiana, reported that students followed the generally conservative line of that southern Indiana small town. "Most of my students said they pretty much support the administration line that we have to continue with a strong defense system, but that we should continue to try to bring the Soviets to the table for arms talks."[48] At a nearby elementary school in Corydon, Indiana, sixth-grade teacher Gary Haub found that while some students saw nuclear war as the end of a liveable world, others thought they would be able to survive.

As was the case with *Roots*, *The Day After* became briefly an important focal point in contemporary culture. Just as ABC aired its unusual after-the-show discussion panel, so also did various community and religious groups sponsor local discussion meetings. If the movie changed few opinions, it did succeed in seeming realistic and not overtly propagandistic. Before the show, 40% of respondents expected the film to be politically fair, with 26% expecting political propaganda. After the movie, 63% of respondents reported that they found the film generally fair, with 21% branding it propaganda.[49] However, given the ability of entertainment programming to mask propaganda, it is significant that many people still used that label to describe the show. Perhaps TV viewers can become wary of aural-visual manipulation when the commentary surrounding a program raises issues of propaganda. If true, this finding would support the kind of propaganda analysis recommended below in chapter 8, that of monitoring entertainment programming by taking note of critical commentary on contemporary shows.

The Propaganda of *Amerika*

If *The Day After* were propaganda for nuclear disarmament, how might the ABC network atone for its foray into the symbolism of pacifism? How might ABC respond to concerns of the Reagan Administration that programming such as *The Day After* might place the policy of nuclear deterrence in jeopardy? Perhaps a program on the communist conquest of America (an old staple of TV dramas of the 1950s) would make amends. Given the logic of these speculations, what are we to make of ABC Entertainment's announcement in 1984 that it would produce *Amerika*, a 14 and 1/2-hour TV movie depicting life in the U.S. under Soviet domination?

The project to produce *Amerika* was noteworthy in consideration merely of its scope, if not its subject. According to *American Film*, ABC's drama of a Sovietized America constituted "the longest and most expensive original-material film project in television history."[50] Todd Gitlin, University of California media critic, believed that ABC's decision to undertake this $40 million series was prompted by a desire to placate right-wing groups who earlier had lashed out at the anti-war ethos of *The Day After*.[51] This striving to restore ideological balance would be consistent with general network thinking, and who can doubt that a nod to the Right would have seemed particularly adroit in 1984 during the heyday of the Reagan presidency? Brandon Stoddard, president of ABC Entertainment, evidently picked up the idea for the series from Ben Stein, a conservative columnist, who had dared the network to make a film about "what life in the U.S. would be like if we lived under Soviet domination."[52] ABC denied, however, that the network pursued a political objective in making *Amerika*.[53]

Whatever the genesis of *Amerika*, its shadow seemed long and dark to many social commentators. "O[hio] U[niversity] Professor Decries Series as Propaganda," screamed a headline in the *Columbus Dispatch* of January 16, 1987. On the basis of an advance script of the show, Professor Howard Frederick dismissed the ABC series as merely a slick packaging of right-wing anti-Soviet propaganda. For its part, ABC-TV articulated a different view: "We're simply telling a story," said Brandon Stoddard of ABC, the man who not only commissioned *Amerika* but also *Roots* and *The Day After*.[54]

But what a story! objected the critics. ABC's drama presented a nightmare vision of the United States in 1997, after its peaceful surrender to the U.S.S.R. The "land of the free and the home of the brave" dwelled in shabby Eastern-European-style captivity, ruled by Soviet overlords, their American collaborationists, and sinister-looking puppet troops supplied by the United Nations. In docudrama style, *Amerika* portrayed conflicting responses to the Sovietized America. Representing those who resisted the new order was a righteous ex-presidential candidate played by Kris Kristofferson. His opposite number was a pleasant opportunist, played by Robert Urich, who believed that collaboration could be helpful for all concerned. In the background loomed various harbingers of life after liberal capitalism: shabby cities, police raids, school brainwashing, staged rallies, and such strange ideological juxtapositions as banners of Lincoln held up next to those of Lenin.

Apart from its general line on post-surrender conditions in the United States, *Amerika* offered a centerpiece atrocity in which the forces of the regime destroyed an American settlement of resisters in a graphic scene of tanks flattening buildings and crushing helpless civilians. Jeff Jarvis, movie critic for *People* magazine, called the scene "the most manipulative, hysterical and violent scene I've ever seen on TV, one clearly designed to make you scream: 'Nuke Moscow.'"[55] Further ideological touches troubling to the left-liberal side of the American spectrum included the image of occupation troops marching under the blue-and-white insignia of the United Nations, and hints that the cause of the collapse of American independence was soft-headed liberals who negotiated America away to the Russians.

The political jockying about *Amerika* started well over a year before the appearance of this TV movie. In fact, after ABC announced the coming mini-series, the Soviet government complained that the film was designed to worsen relations between the U.S. and the U.S.S.R. The Russian government threatened to set up obstacles for ABC News operations in Moscow if the network proceeded with the program.[56] ABC acknowledged that the Soviet criticism had contributed to a decision to postpone production of the series temporarily, although network representatives insisted that financial considerations were primary in delaying the expensive mini-series. Conservatives in the U.S. thereupon sprang up to criticize ABC for allegedly caving in to Russian pressure. William J. Bennett, Reagan Administration Secretary of Education, complained that "this is a bad lesson for our children. The American people might be denied a television series because the Kremlin does not like it."[57]

But Moscow was not the only one complaining about the ideological content of *Amerika*. Many bootleg scripts were circulating, leading to considerable media comment on the program long before it was shown. Jeff Cohen, director of Fairness and Accuracy in Reporting, argued that the mini-series fostered an exaggerated fear of the Russians, amounting to a "12-hour commercial for Star Wars."[58] Former Defense Secretary Elliot Richardson wrote ABC to complain about the "apparently McCarthyesque" tone of the program. Javier Perez de Cuellar, Secretary-General of the United Nations, requested that all references to the U.N. be deleted.[59] TV's maverick mogul, Ted Turner, called *Amerika* a "hate film," and he scheduled five programs on his WTBS super station that might promote U.S.-Soviet friendship.[60] Responding to sundry demands for equal time to counter the viewpoint expressed in *Amerika*, several local ABC affiliates eventually did grant broadcast time for opposing views.[61]

Set against past examples of propagandistic programming, *Amerika* did actually mirror those propaganda films that have appeared in the wartime U.S.A. *Amerika* was similar in tone to the kinds of movies that have appeared when Hollywood producers and the U.S. government decided to cooperate in reinforcing a wartime morale. *Amerika's* story of an occupied U.S.A. echoed *This Land is Mine* (1943), a World War II-era film about a Nazi-occupied country in Europe, presumably France. To the delight of the World War II Office of War Information, *This Land is Mine* showed collaborationists in business and government profiting from the occupation in contrast to workers and intellectuals who resisted the Nazis. Reviewing the script, OWI representatives asked that the horrors of the occupation be even more graphically shown.[62] Another propagandistic precursor of *Amerika* was *Chicago, Germany*, a radio drama that appeared as part of the Treasury Star Parade in 1942. This program depicted the forced Nazification of Chicago after a German victory. In an atmosphere of mass murder and family disintegration, Americans eked out a degraded survival or were confined in German labor camps.[63]

Given the cinematic ancestors of *Amerika*, it is no surprise that, as the show-date approached, leading actors in the series expressed some misgivings about it. Kris Kristofferson acknowledged embarrassment about his role in the film. "It is propaganda," he said, "but I hope it will fuel debate."[64] Kristofferson subsequently taped a 30-second announcement for the United Nations discussing the work of the UN peacekeeping forces, 700 of whom had died in the line of duty. According to Christine Lahti, who played Kristofferson's sister, the actors got together early in the filming with director Donald Wrye to express concerns about the political drift of the film. "Almost daily we were changing and cutting lines. I know Kris Kristofferson worked very hard at changing things to suit him better."[65]

Profit, not Propaganda

For those who control TV, the medium does not exist primarily to reproduce ideology through propaganda. Todd Gitlin's comprehensive review of the folkways of the TV industry makes clear that ideology is not the driving force behind TV programming. TV exists first and foremost as a field for profit.[66] In television production, the logic of profit and the rhetoric of the hedging the bet reins triumphant, although propaganda still lurks in the corners as profit-minded TV executives watch which way the ideological winds are blowing.

The debate over ideology and propaganda in TV fare seems destined to dog the future of television just as it has the past. Was the *Cosby* show of the 1980s helpful or harmful to social progress in view of its focus on the Black upper class? Was Bart Simpson a desirable "role model" for American school children of the early 1990s who seemed to be falling behind their fellows in Europe and Japan? The mini-series seems particularly destined to serve as a lightning rod for complaints about TV propaganda. For instance, the airing of *Roe vs. Wade* (1989), a dramatization of the legal case leading to the Supreme Court's affirmation of abortion-on-demand, provoked protests and threats against advertisers, some of whom withdrew sponsorship.[67] News stories and TV reviews provide ample fodder for those who are interested in monitoring propaganda issues on the cathode-ray tube. With this commentary in hand, and on the basis of the viewer's own critical reception of TV scripts and images, each analyst of propaganda may decide for him or herself whether television contributes positively or negatively to social and political morality.

IMAGE PROPAGANDA IN AN AGE OF APPEARANCE

Walter Lippmann located the problem of propaganda in the situation of the twentieth-century urban metropolis in which Americans knew a decreasing portion of their world through direct experience. More and more, urbanites relied on the second-hand reports of newspapers and magazines for knowledge of the people and events that influenced them.[68] Compared to the small-town citizen, who was personally acquainted with key social and political figures, and who personally experienced the results of most town policies, the urban dweller relied upon impersonal, albeit sometimes gossipy, reports of remote people and places. Lippmann believed that a public life governed by second-hand stories and imposed images was particularly susceptible to the clever covertness of propaganda in news.

In an atmosphere in which public figures and policies are known chiefly by indirection, public action and human character frequently are judged according to shallow standards of surface attractiveness rooted no deeper than in whatever is immediately pleasing. Illustrative is a lawsuit brought by R. H. Macy and Company, a department store, against the State of California. Macy's sought to invalidate portions of California's property tax laws that allowed new property owners to be taxed as much as 15 times more for their land and improvements than owners of comparable property that had not changed hands. Macy's suit, which was taken up by the U.S. Supreme Court in 1991, argued that such disparities in taxation were an obvious violation of the Constitution's guarantee of equal protection under the laws. Principle, shminciple! Macy's, a huge, faceless corporation, found out that its invocation of a Constitutional principle counted for little when the company posed a danger to the pocketbooks of California residents. Tax opposition groups immediately called for customer boycotts against Macy's for daring to challenge the tax advantages enjoyed by long-time property owners. Macy's quickly withdrew its suit.[69]

In addition to avoiding image disasters such as that which befell Macy's, today's individual and institutional persuaders find that they must undertake something striking to break into a public consciousness numbed by the overload of daily news in the vastness of today's urban life. The politics of the striking image was discovered by early practitioners of public relations, such as Edward L. Bernays. Bernays specialized in creating news by mounting events that would dramatize the characteristics of a product, idea, or institution. His masterpiece was the massive national celebration, Light's Golden Jubilee, the fiftieth anniversary of Thomas Edison's discovery of the incandescent lamp in 1879, ceremonies in which President Herbert Hoover served as host. Bernays arranged for a national radio hook-up to broadcast the reenactment of the moment when Edison successfully produced light by passing current through a filament held in a vacuum. This public-relations effort by Bernays was helpful to the electricity companies who were under investigation at the time for their secret propaganda campaign against publicly-owned power plants.

Daniel Boorstin, American historian, has coined the term "pseudoevent" to designate striking and dramatic episodes conjured up by public-relations experts or political operatives.[70] While recognizing the shift to a public world known only indirectly through stereotypical impressions, Boorstin took a generally favorable view of advertising and other facets of our image-based culture. For instance, Boorstin pointed out that advertising has had a somewhat democratizing impact by making goods more widely known and therefore available.[71] Advertising does not, however, democratize the whole public—just that portion of the people that can be momentarily captured for purposes of profit. Thus,

263

when advertising began to cater to the mass audience (instead of whole-sale buyers), ads shifted from explanations to pictures and slogans.

As modern media practices spread from commerce to politics, society and polity came to be discussed in simpler terms. For persons having little interest in often-remote socio-political affairs, one-dimensional pictures and slogans were more than enough. The simplifying of public life through advertising, film, radio, and large-circulation newspapers ever widened the door for propaganda's penetration into public life. Jacques Ellul, leading French theorist of society, pointed out that today's public almost demands the simplified answers that are typically supplied by propagandistic communication. However, he argued that neither the inevitability nor the popularity of propaganda constituted a sufficient defense of its desirability. He labeled propaganda as inherently contradictory to democracy because propaganda's simple good-versus-evil images undermine both rational choice and tolerance of diversity.[72]

The Propaganda of Sports

Although proposals of today's leaders are less directly intelligible than before, professional sports teams have emerged to supply twentieth-century Americans with a comprehensible drama of struggle, trial, victory, and defeat. Few things are more precious to the members of modern societies than sports because athletic team contests have replaced small-town politics as the focus of popular attention and discussion.

At the same time that sports serve as surrogate for old-time local politics, professionalized athleticism enhances today's promotional culture through an alliance of journalists, who want to build circulation, and sports capitalists, who want free publicity. Sports-reporting was recognized early in the twentieth century as a useful device for building newspaper circulation. The explosion of sports-reporting in the first decades of the twentieth century paralleled other popularizing aspects of journalism, including an increased use of pictures and greater attention to sensational crimes.[73] Sports-reporting grew not only because it puffed up newspaper circulation but also because of the free publicity it provided for privately-owned professional teams. Individual athletes, too, learned that their economic value might be enhanced by the added publicity provided by newspapers.

Sports-reporting caters not only to the needs of newspapers and sports capitalists but also to the cities and schools that sponsor teams. A winning professional team helps to give a good impression of a city as well as to stimulate business. Schools and universities, too, recognize the dollars that come from increased recognition through sports.

The transformation of sports into a propaganda of image typically has been overlooked by the public, which either enjoys identifying with players and teams or ignores the whole thing. Sports news has become so familiar a part of mass communication that few today pause to question the propriety of all the free publicity for owners, star players, and schools. However, occasional episodes remind us of social oddities resulting from the promotional nature of sports-reporting. For instance, Frank Boggs, an Oklahoma sports writer, once had to summon police protection because of his reporting about the University of Oklahoma football team. Boggs received bomb threats after writing a story in the *Oklahoma City Times* exposing abuses in the University of Oklahoma's football program.[74] Many fans considered Boggs a traitor. In this, the fans may have understood the essential nature of sports-reporting better than did Boggs. Home-team reporters are expected to be boosters for the team and the school, not objective journalistic detectives.

Because sports-reporting is skewed in the direction of boosterism, business interests are frequently able to transform an athletic contest into commercial propaganda. As an example of a corporation's promoting itself through association with popular sports events, we may turn to the former Bing Crosby Golf Tournament. For forty years (1937-1977), Crosby hosted a celebrity professional/amateur golf tournament in California. Kathryn Crosby, his widow, later withdrew the Crosby name from the tournament, protesting that the corporate sponsors who footed the bills had "commercialized this yearly gathering of friends" excessively.[75]

Organizations sometimes benefit by associating particular products with successful sports players. When honored for his third Olympic gold medal in 1972, swimmer Mark Spitz raised his arm to acknowledge the crowd—and also held in that arm a pair of Adidas shoes. According to the Olympic rules of 1972, Spitz could have been stripped of his medals, had the Olympic Committee been able to prove that Spitz was employed by Adidas. A controversy continues to this date as to whether Spitz's commercial plug was intentional (and paid for) or not.[76] In any event, Spitz (who won a total of seven gold medals in 1972) soon signed a $5 million contract with the William Morris Agency and began making endorsements for milk products, razors, credit cards, and swimwear.

Today, the Olympics are more commercial, and a gesture such as Spitz's would cause nary a stir. In fact, since Adidas now supplies sportswear for the Olympics, athletes routinely carry its trademark to the victory stand.

Olympian Propaganda

Because of the intrusion of nationalism, Olympic events have become the globe's most notable forum of propaganda-through-sport. After the invasion of Afghanistan by the U.S.S.R., for instance, one of the most significant symbolic responses of President Jimmy Carter was his boycott of the 1980 Moscow Olympics. On January 4, 1980, Carter warned the U.S.S.R. in a televised speech that unless Russia desisted from its aggression in Afghanistan, the U.S. might withdraw from the summer Olympic games. Subsequently, Carter asked the U.S. Olympic Committee to support him in trying to get the International Olympic Committee to move the games. The boycott initially drew considerable support, as evidenced in opinion polls and in sports columns.[77]

Whatever second thoughts later lingered about the boycott idea, Carter's march from Moscow certainly prevented the Kremlin from enjoying the chance to outshine its American foe in communism's Olympic moment. Just what the Soviets were missing became clear in the 1980 Winter Olympics when, to the surprise of just about everybody, the American ice hockey team defeated the Russians. The sister of one of the American players observed that she had not seen so many American flags being waved in years, whereas "we were burning them then."[78]

Although Carter's boycott showed in bold relief how political propaganda intruded into international athletic competition, this action hardly was the first evidence of propaganda in Olympic sports. Just four years earlier, for instance, African states had mounted a boycott to protest *apartheid* and the playing of national anthems. After the boycotts of 1976 and 1980, sports commentators at the 1984 Los Angeles Olympics were becoming attuned to the propaganda tangent of the games. The Soviet Union did its part to keep the political tangent of Olympic competition in the forefront, returning Carter's favor by means of a communist-bloc boycott.

At home, many Americans seemed hardly to notice the absence of the hammer-and-sickle emblem, welcoming the resulting increase in victories by Americans. Billy Reed, sports columnist for the Louisville *Courier-Journal*, observed that the end of the games brought a kind of relief, for "a body can stand just so much of flag-waving."[79] Reed noted the occasional jingoism of American commentators, and he observed the confusion produced by America's self-preoccupied Olympic TV coverage. U.S. TV coverage so overemphasized home teams that foreign competitors became outraged, believing that their countries were receiving the exact same telecasts. Actually, ABC Sports taped everything and allowed the foreign TV services to choose what they wanted to show.

If sports reporters had become inured to the propaganda aspects of the '84 Olympics, it is not surprising that political commentators also found the Los Angeles games a fruitful subject. Writing in an ironic vein, David Broder observed that a number of U.S. athletes let down the Gipper, Ronald Reagan, by losing gold medals to foreigners; Broder added, the ABC commentators had put matters right by not showing those contests where the Americans lost.[80] The "Bloom County" comic strip parodied the spate of corporations paying for the privilege of calling themselves the official X, Y, or Z of the Olympics. "Bloom County" proclaimed itself "the official comic strip of the 1984 Olympics"—until halted by a court order.[81] The political gloss of the 1984 Olympics traveled worldwide when foreign correspondents began to send home their impressions that the U.S. was being swept by a wave of national patriotism signified by the vast number of U.S. flags being waved during events.[82]

The Propaganda of the Goodwill Games

An ironic result of the Olympic boycotts of 1980 and 1984 was the emergence of Ted Turner's Goodwill Games of 1986, held in Moscow. Watching the 1984 Olympics, Turner became angry about the Soviet boycott and its U.S. predecessor. He vowed to prevent future boycotts by teaming up with the Soviets to buy up the TV rights for the 1988 Olympics in Seoul, Korea. Instead, Turner eventually hammered out arrangements with the Soviets to start an entirely new event, the Goodwill Games, a 1986 adventure that made possible the first comprehensive U.S./U.S.S.R. athletic competition in a decade.[83]

The Goodwill Games also provided propaganda points, of course, both for Turner and the Soviets. The first event drew 3,500 athletes from 70 countries. Worldwide coverage of the games showed that Turner's maverick network could mount a world-class production, although the games were not in themselves a moneymaking operation (Turner lost $26 million).[84] Mikhail S. Gorbachev, the Soviet leader, was able to get into the act, welcoming the athletes with a call for the U.S. to respond to Russian proposals for arms reductions.[85] At one point, the card section in the Moscow stadium displayed a mushroom cloud crossed out with an X symbol. The card display also included the Russian letters for Hiroshima—just in case anyone forgot who had dropped the first atomic bomb.[86] Recognizing that the Turner games would likely provide a modest propaganda coup for the Soviets, the Reagan Administration weighed in with its own propaganda of athletics, denying permission for U.S. soldier-athletes to participate in the Goodwill boxing events. The Pentagon objected that the games were "political in nature and intent" and that they would provide selective profits.[87] By forsaking Ted Turner's top fun while embracing Tom Cruise's *Top Gun*, the Pentagon proved that propaganda often lies in the eyes of the beholder.

By nearly all accounts, the 1980s saw a growing recognition that sports could be a vehicle for propaganda. By mixing entertainment with a root-for-the-home-team mentality, sports contests supply a stage for getting across propaganda points.

Toys and Cartoons: Art Meets Propaganda

Artistry is a component of entertainment that can be turned to profitable commercial and even political propaganda. Contemporary artistry forms a growing context for commercial propaganda through the vehicles of cartoons, magazine photographs, toy figures, music, and the promotion of celebrities.

Perhaps the most infamous of the links between art and commerce are the TV cartoon shows designed to sell toys. The 1980s saw the emergence of cartoons that were little more than extended propaganda for commercial products. Columnist Ellen Goodman once advised parents that "if you want a sneak preview of children's television shows for 1986, do not delve into the imagination of the young, the dreams of the screenwriters or, heaven forfend, the hopes of the educators. Check out the annual toy fair."[88]

In the early years of TV animation, kids' cartoon characters frequently led to spin-off products, such as Mickey Mouse ears. In the early 1980s, however, a special form of TV-based propaganda began when broadcasters increasingly designed children's cartoon shows to be explicit commercials for toys. Examples of toy-sale-based programming included Masters of the Universe (He-Man and She-Ra), Transformers,

GoBots, Care Bears, Strawberry Shortcake, as well as Gummi Bears (a candy product). These cartoon-propagated commercials were creatures of the deregulatory mood that prevailed in Washington in the 1980s. The first commercial disguised as a cartoon show had appeared in 1969—a program called "Hot Wheels." At this time, the Federal Communications Commission invoked its regulations requiring that programming and advertising be kept separate. By the 1980s, however, the regulatory atmosphere had changed such that when the General Mills Toy Group brought out a TV special, "Welcome to the World of Strawberry Shortcake," they opened the door for a new covert approach to marketing toys.[89]

"What difference does it make if the toy comes first?" asked Lois Hanrahan, an executive for Tonka toys. "Our business is kids. You find out what the kids want."[90] Since, notwithstanding, the cartoon characters were based on a very limited number of approaches—violence or cuteness—parents had a basis for questioning the motives of the toymakers. Were toy companies interested in children's happiness, or were corporations more interested in finding out what kids easily could be induced to want for purposes of commercial profit? Getting a child to desire a toy is not difficult, and each of the cartoon-promoted toy groups came out with an ever-increasing list of figures to buy. Measured against a definition of propaganda as covert suasion, the approach of designing shows to sell toys was clearly propagandistic. The shows were not an explicit commercial, but rather they amounted to a camouflaged effort to sell. The creative process was covertly harnessed to profit. Peggy Charren, of Action for Children's Television, argued that the broadcasters took unfair advantage of children because adults would not tolerate a show that featured only products for sale.[91] Granting the fairness of Charren's basic point, she may have overestimated the adults as evidenced by the later popularity of *The Love Connection* dating show and the cable home-shopping channels of the early 1990s.

What about the social impact of TV's toy propaganda? Peggy Charren argued that the commercialized, product-oriented shows were "pushing the more creative kinds of programming off the air."[92] Further, an article in *American Health* magazine (December 1988) suggested that TV-show toys dampened children's ability to be imaginative because the toys came with "set personalities that define the themes of play." As a result, children "mechanically re-enact the scenarios seen on TV or depicted on the box." By 1985, Action for Children's Television had filed suit to curtail the practice of toy-based kids' shows. The group made no progress for five years until the U.S. Congress finally directed the Federal Communications Commission to study the problem of "program-length commercials."[93]

Program-length commercials are a problem not just for kids but also for adults who watch feature films. Toy-based TV shows are an obvious case of artistry turned into profitable propaganda; less infamous is use of film-making covertly to insinuate product advertising. Movie houses have long imposed brief commercial messages upon their patrons, and the practice remains typical of today's first-run theaters.[94] U.S. movie houses often show three 60-second commercials before the feature—plugs for automobiles and other products. However much these overt commercials irritate patrons, who have paid for admission, the ads are less objectionable, from a propaganda point of view, than advertising embedded in the films themselves.

Today's moviegoer searches neither long nor far to find examples of hidden advertising in feature films. In the film *Flashdance*, for instance, the heroine is shown dancing in a dream sequence holding a can of Diet Pepsi. Usually a plug of this kind comes not by accident but by explicit arrangement. Robert Kovoloff of Associated Film Promotions got Sylvester Stallone to put a plug for Wheaties cereal into the film *Rocky III*. Rocky counseled his son that, "You wanna grow up and be big and strong, you gotta eat the Breakfast of Champions."[95] Film producers sometimes solicit manufacturers with offers to show their product for a fee. Other times, promoters work to connect the filmmaker and the advertiser. However the deal be done, the results can be very profitable. The decision by Mars Candy not to permit E.T. to eat M&Ms is now the stuff of legend. As we know, the Extra Terrestrial turned to Reese's Pieces—and sales of the Pieces jumped 65%.

Popular Arts as Political Propaganda

Various of today's popular arts, such as advertising, dolls, and comics, may exhibit interesting mixtures of entertainment, selling, and political persuasion.

While we normally think of ads as straight commercial persuasion, they sometimes can be a vehicle for disseminating political propaganda. At the deepest level, all ads represent a kind of background propaganda for the consumption of goods and, by extension, for commodity capitalism. Ads can, nonetheless, advance specific ideological positions while at the same time helping to ring up cash-register sales.

One striking example of propagandized advertising was a Wendy's hamburger ad that helped reinforce Cold War stereotypes. The Wendy's spot pictured a supposed Russian fashion show held in a drab, dark auditorium. A single overweight model wore the same dumpy outfit time and again under the different headings of eveningwear, swimwear, and the like. With each appearance, a bored voice intoned, "Izz niiice." Another example was Miller Brewing's 1987 ad in college newspapers that featured a photograph of large, hirsute, and homely women—obviously men dressed as women. Festooned with wigs and dresses, with one smoking an old cigar, the "women" posed with their beer bottles at a bar. The caption: "Why 'Helga' Piscopo, Ex-East German Swimmer Drinks Miller Lite—'To Keep the Girlish Figure.'"[96]

Other connections between popular commercial artistry and contemporary politics include Barbie dolls and comic books. The Army, Navy, and Air Force once cooperated with Mattel Toys to design military Barbie dolls. "We wanted to help provide a role model for girls," acknowledged Pam Carter, an Army public-relations officer.[97] Comic-book figures, too, sometimes enter the world of contemporary politics. For instance, in the comic book *Veronica in Russia*, the Archie crew made points for detente with Russia. Veronica met Gorbachev and learned the virtues of cultural exchange.[98]

High-Culture Propaganda

The vulnerability of art to propaganda is not limited to frivolous popular artistic forms such as dolls and comic books. Serious and high-culture art shows, too, can function as propaganda. For example, the Central Intelligence Agency covertly supported an organization called the Congress for Cultural Freedom that sponsored art shows and exhibitions around the world. The idea was to send an implicit message to the world about the great diversity of expression that was permissible under democratic governments, in contrast to the static and regimented forms of art favored by the Nazi and Soviet governments. Abstract impressionism became the signature of U.S. art, and it made an important propaganda point abroad. The program was deemed a political success because art publications featuring the avant-garde spirit of Western art began to reach the Eastern Bloc.[99]

271

An additional advantage to the CIA's covertness in supporting modern art shows was to insulate the agency from U.S. Congressmen who were prone to criticize officially sponsored exhibits. For instance, right-wing groups attacked art shows sponsored by the U.S. State Department because they featured modern art, sometimes condemned by conservatives as degenerate, strident, and (ironically) helpful to the enemies of America.

The chief sponsor of art shows has come to be corporate America—again with propaganda often in mind. By 1985, corporations were funneling $30 million dollars per year into art museums to sponsor blockbuster shows under the banner of one or the other corporate donor. Sponsorship of high-culture art makes the corporation seem public-spirited and innovative. In addition, the corporations can benefit from useful marketing tie-ins. For instance, Mobil Oil sponsored a show on Maori art in connection with its plan to build a plant in New Zealand. Museum patronage by corporations also can pay off in the sponsor's ability to rent a museum facility for an impressive party. Mobil Oil once donated $500,000 for a special opening of the Metropolitan Museum's Islamic Galleries, during which time Mobil executives entertained a Saudi Arabian prince.[100]

Critics sometimes complain that the marketing orientation of corporations causes them to support only the crowd-pleasing forms of art that are currently in vogue. According to Phillipe de Montebello, director of the Metropolitan Museum of Art, the problem is not so much that corporations explicitly turn down new or controversial work of art. Rather, he says, art museums tend to censor themselves by not bringing up the currently obscure or overlooked art to potential corporate sponsors. Of course, high-culture art can become the focus for occasional furors. Controversial art became a public issue in 1989 when Senator Jesse Helms initiated efforts to restrict government funding through the National Endowment for the Arts for "immoral trash."[101] Government money always raises the red flag of propaganda because any group or individual may resent tax-supported sponsorship for offensive art.

Facets of Magazine Propaganda

The propaganda alliance of art, commerce, and politics may be observed in contemporary magazines as well as in the popular and fine arts. For instance, Herbert I. Schiller, the media critic, faulted *National Geographic* magazine for taking a conservative political line. According to Schiller, *National Geographic* presented a world of nations and peoples devoid of politics. Notable were issues on Vietnam in which the war was presented as a vague, incomprehensible event lurking behind the pretty pictures.[102] In the 1980s, a new editor, Wilbur Garrett, attempted to make the magazine more socially relevant, but he irritated the National Geographic Society's leadership with coverage of such politically-charged scenes as the Exxon *Valdez* oil spill, the spread of AIDS in Uganda, and the postwar reconstruction of Vietnam. Garrett was fired as editor.[103]

Magazines focusing on celebrities, such as *Vanity Fair* and *People*, represent another case of photo-journalism becoming a covert vehicle for money-making and image-building by celebrities, film stars, and their publicists. Needing to pull in sales at magazine racks, publishers are eager to get celebrity pictures for their covers. As a result, celebrities increasingly realize their power to negotiate with magazines for stories and interviews. Critics argue that the result is a trend by the nation's magazines to provide awe-struck, almost reverential, articles on the rich, the beautiful, and the famous.

An estimated one-fourth of all interviews (in magazines and also on TV) involve an informal deal about the kind of coverage to be given. According to *Newsweek*, "except for the news magazines, it is now virtually impossible to get a magazine interview with a big film star without promising a cover story."[104] More controversial is the matter of whether the celebrity or source has the right to approve quotations. Executives of Drexel Burnham Lambert, the investment company, cooperated with author Connie Bruck as she prepared her book, *The Predator's Ball*. When they realized the book would contain unflattering details, they regretted signing away their power to change the book. Drexel executives were limited to adding footnotes where they liked.[105] Not all authors, however, are able to retain that much control when getting material from privileged insiders.

Today's promotion of celebrities is a system based on scarcity that has had interesting implications for politics. Only a few artists or film stars make the big bucks. For instance, perhaps a dozen opera stars and a handful of concert pianists hit it big, and these few are carefully promoted. Promoters find it easier to make money by marketing a few big stars than by offering to the nation and world a variety of excellent, but essentially unknown, artists.[106] The mechanics of celebrity promotion reinforces a tendency to make the false assumption that the more famous an individual be, the better he or she is.

The marketing of mega-stars takes an interesting political tangent when actors are promoted as political sages. Ronald Reagan became Governor of California when a number of wealthy conservative businesspeople engaged a leading public-relations firm to market Reagan. Reagan's political experience had been limited to serving as a genial TV program host and as an after-dinner speaker. However, the PR campaign vaulted him to the front ranks of political figures, and he was elected governor.[107] Today, no one who knows anything about public-relations politics is surprised when actors are sought for political races. In 1986, for example, actors Charlton Heston (most famous for his role as Moses in *The Ten Commandments*) and Fess Parker (alias Davy Crockett and Daniel Boone) both decided after much soul-searching not to seek the Republican nomination for U.S. Senate in California.[108]

Propaganda and Images of the Arabs

In an era of image, every individual and group must carefully guard his or her or its public face and, if possible, even promote the outward persona through the artistry of entertainment and leisure. However, the propaganda of artistry sometimes seems to work against certain individuals and groups. Not all causes or peoples can be easily promoted when cultural forces cast a group in a negative light. Although every possible group today seems to have its own vocal activists who cry out at any real or perceived slight, sometimes one group lags notably behind. Such is the case with Arabs in the U.S. who continue to suffer from a bad image on TV and in film.

In 1984, the American-Arab Anti-Discrimination Committee (ADC) protested a Goldie Hawn film, *Protocol*. The ADC group objected to the characterization of an emir and a holy man. The emir was depicted as a rich Arab leader presiding over a multitude of wives and handing out Rolls Royces. The character of the Islamic holy man was seen chasing after women.[109] The Arabs have become one of the last groups (along with "dumb blonde" jokes and "white-male" bashing) that may be adversely stereotyped in the U.S. without serious political or boycotting repercussions. James Zogby, ADC director, claimed that a TV executive once told him: "Let's face it. Jewish groups come down hard, Blacks come down hard, Hispanics are starting to come down hard. You are the last guys we can do this stuff to and get away with it."[110]

From a study of hundreds of films and TV shows, Jack Shaheen, professor of mass communication at Southern Illinois University, claimed that only two basic categories of Arabs exist in the popular American media: "wealthy sheiks and grotesque, seething-at-the-mouth terrorists."[111] Further, he argued, "10 of the 11 feature films [of the 1980s] that focused on the Palestinian portrayed him as Enemy Number One." What's the harm of this? The ADC argues that negative stereotypes lead to hate attacks on Arab Americans in the U.S. such as those that followed the NBC-TV movie *Under Siege* that depicted Middle Eastern people plotting an attack against the U.S.[112]

Anti-Arab propaganda exists also in forms of popular culture other than television and film. For instance, the ADC induced Coleco, a toy manufacturer, to discontinue production of Nomad, a swarthy doll dressed in robes and desert-style headdress, who was one of the terrorist figures in the Rambo toy-soldier line.[113] Among commercial plugs showing Arabs in an ugly and hostile light was an advertisement for a charcoal briquette called "Burn Sheeks" which showed an Arab man in turban headdress above a fire. The ADC succeeded in removing the ad from circulation. Similarly, unfavorable anti-Arab stereotypes are frequent in fuel economy ads. For instance, an ad for one brand of wood stove presented a sinister-looking Arab man with the headline "Don't get burned. Declare your freedom today." According to Marsha Hamilton, an Ohio State University researcher, it was the 1973 Arab oil embargo that increased the negative image of Arabs in ads. Before that date, the image of Arabs tended to sensual and magical; afterwards, they were presented chiefly as barbaric and greedy.[114]

What are we to make of the welter of charges that propaganda is running rampant in our media of entertainment, in sports, and in our popular arts? If Postman was correct that intelligent public opinion drowns in a sea of amusements, then we have reason to worry about entertainment becoming a major channel for propaganda. For one thing, getting people to enjoy an image seems a more effective means of persuasion than directly preaching a message. We experience thousands of hours of exposure to the images of popular culture every year, and much of this exposure finds our critical defenses dulled as we settle in, expecting only to be diverted from the stresses of the day.

When embedded in forms of amusement, propaganda is difficult to detect if one pays attention only to a particular message in question. Fortunately, as is explored in chapter 8, the many propagandas of film, TV, sports, and visual arts draw fire from social critics whose complaints are registered in articles in the popular media. Granted, these articles often are not to be found on page one; however, the persistently alert newspaper and magazine reader will find ample means for keeping tabs on contemporary entertainment propaganda.

ENDNOTES

1. Neil Postman, *Amusing Ourselves to Death: Public Discourse in the Age of Show Business* (New York: Viking, 1985).

2. For various tales of this kind, see [anonymous], "Autobiography of a Theatrical Press-Agent," *American Magazine*, 69 (April 1913): 67-70. Continued in the May and June issues.

3. Edward L. Bernays, *Public Relations* (Norman, OK: University of Oklahoma Press, 1952): 38-39, 58-60.

4. Edward L. Bernays, *Biography of an Idea: Memoirs of Public Relations Counsel Edward L. Bernays* (New York: Simon and Schuster, 1965): 194.

5. Bernays, *Public Relations:* 80.

6. Bernays, *Public Relations:* 84.

7. See, for example, Otis Pease, *The Responsibilities of American Advertising: Private Control and Public Influence*, 1920-1940 (New Haven: Yale University Press, 1958): 33-36 and Walter D. Scott, *The Theory of Advertising* (Boston: Small, Maynard, 1903).

8. See Goodwin Berquist and James Greenwood, "Protest Against Racism: 'The Birth of a Nation' in Ohio," *The Rhetoric of the People*, ed. Harold Barrett (Amsterdam: Rodopi, 1974): 221-239.

9. Lillian Gish, *The Movies, Mr. Griffith, and Me* (Englewood Cliffs, NJ: Prentice-Hall, 1969): 188-201 .

10. Carl Laemmle, Sr. to G. S. Viereck, May 8, 1930, Viereck Papers, University of Iowa.

11. Edgar Dale, *The Content of Motion Pictures* (New York: Macmillan, 1935): 39-42, 54-55, 124, 174, 178-185.

12. Darwin Teilhet, "Propaganda Stealing the Movies," *Outlook and Independent*, 158, No. 4 (May 27, 1931): 112-113, 126 and S. H. Walker and Paul Sklar, *Business Finds Its Voice* (New York: Harper, 1938): 33, 42-44.

13. U.S. Congress, Senate, *Propaganda in Motion Pictures*, Hearings before a Subcommittee of the Committee on Interstate Commerce, 77th Cong., 1st sess., September 9-26, 1941, Washington, D.C.: Government Printing Office, 1942: 35, 45, 49, 339-340, 346, 411.

14. Clayton R. Koppes and Gregory D. Black, *Hollywood Goes to War* (New York: Free Press, 1987): 65-67.

15. *San Jose Mercury News*, 6/1/90: 4A.

16. Koppes and Black, *Hollywood Goes to War:* 193, 205.

17. U.S. House, *Hearings Regarding Communist Infiltration of the Motion Picture Industry*, Committee on Un-American Activities, 80th Cong., 1st sess., October 20-24, 27-30, 1947. Washington: Government Printing Office, 1947: 1-2, 9-11, 21.

18. See David Caute, *The Great Fear: The Anti-Communist Purge Under Truman and Eisenhower* (New York: Simon and Schuster, 1978): 490-502 and Larry Ceplair and Steven Englund, *The Inquisition in Hollywood: Politics in the Film Industry. 1930-1960* (Berkeley: University of California Press, 1983): 279-298.

19. Statement of Ring Lardner, Jr. at the time of his sentencing in Ceplair and Englund, *The Inquisition:* 349.

20. *American Film*, 12/87: 24.

21. Louisville, KY *Courier-Journal*, 4/7/85: I1.

22. *Chronicle of Higher Education*, 4/12/89: A10.

23. See Tony Bennett and Janet Woollacott, *Bond and Beyond: The Political Career of a Popular Hero* (London: Macmillan, 1987): 33ff.

24. *San Jose Mercury News*, 1/19/90: 10D.

25. *Newsweek*, 12/23/85: 82.

26. *American Film*, 1/90: 57.

27. *Insight*, 6/16/86: 7.

28. *Insight*, 6/16/86: 7.

29. *American Film*, 3/87: 17.

30. Odessa, TX *Odessa American*, 12/19/73: 11C.

31. Odessa, TX *Odessa American*, 12/19/73: 11C.

32. *Insight*, 6/16/86: 7.

33. *San Jose Mercury News*, 6/12/90: 1C.

34. *Playboy*, 1/90: 56.

35. Cf., Gilbert Seldes, *The Great Audience* (New York: Viking Press, 1950): 4.

36. Joshua Meyerowitz, *No Sense of Place: The Impact of Electronic Media on Social Behavior* (New York: Oxford University Press, 1985).

37. J. Fred MacDonald, *Television and the Red Menace: The Video Road to Vietnam* (New York: Praeger, 1985): 44-45, 48-49, 102-105.

38. MacDonald, *Red Menace:* 114, 122-123.

39. Todd Gitlin, *Inside Prime Time* (New York: Pantheon, 1985): 221-246.

40. *Newsweek*, 2/14/77: 97.

41. Odessa, TX *Odessa American*, 3/5/77: 8B.

42. *Newsweek*, 11/21/83: 70.

43. Tom Dorsey, Louisville, KY *Courier-Journal*, 11/8/83: C3.

44. *Newsweek*, 11/21/83: 66.

45. *Newsweek*, 11/21/83: 69.

46. Louisville, KY *Courier-Journal*, 11/22/83: B1.

47. *Newsweek*, 12/5/83: 62.

48. Louisville, KY *Courier-Journal*, 11/22/83: B1.

49. Louisville, KY *Courier-Journal*, 11/22/83: A2.

50. *American Film*, 1-2/87: 27.

51. *San Francisco Chronicle*, 2/13/87: 4.

52. *Newsweek*, 2/16/87: 21.

53. *American Film*, 1-2/87: 25.

54. *Newsweek*, 12/10/86: 92.

55. *People*, 2/87: 9.

56. Louisville, KY *Courier-Journal*, 1/10/86: A2; *Newsweek*, 12/10/86: 91.

57. Louisville, KY *Courier-Journal*, 1/12/86: A10.

58. *Newsweek*, 12/10/86: 90.

59. *Newsweek*, 12/10/86: 92.

60. *San Francisco Chronicle*, 2/13/87:4.

61. *Newsweek*, 2/16/87: 21.

62. Koppes and Black, *Hollywood Goes to War*: 294.

63. J. Fred MacDonald, "Government Propaganda in Commercial Radio—The Case of *Treasury Star Parade*, 1942-1943," in M. J. Medhurst and T. W. Benson (eds.): *Rhetorical Dimensions in Media* (Dubuque: Kendall/Hunt, 1984): 157-158.

64. *San Francisco Chronicle*, 2/13/87: 5.

65. *American Film*, 1-2/87: 26.

66. Gitlin, *Inside Prime Time*.

67. *San Jose Mercury News*, 5/12/89: 14A; Palo Alto, CA *Peninsula Times Tribune*, 5/16/89: A12.

68. Walter Lippmann, *Public Opinion* (New York: Macmillan, 1922): 3-32.

69. *San Jose Mercury News*, 6/8/91: 1A.

70. Daniel J. Boorstin, *The Image: A Guide to Pseudo-Events in America* (New York: Atheneum, 1961).

71. See Daniel J. Boorstin, *The Americans: The Democratic Experience* (New York: Random House, 1973).

72. See Jacques Ellul, *Propaganda* (New York: Vintage, 1965): 232-250, especially.

73. See Silas Bent, *Ballyhoo* (New York: Boni and Liveright, 1927): 42, 129.

74. John Laird, Odessa, TX *Odessa American*, 12/12/76: 2A.

75. Louisville, KY *Courier-Journal*, 4/23/85: D1.

76. *West* (of *San Jose Mercury News*), 12/10/89: 29.

77. *Sports Illustrated*, 1/28/80: 7-8.

78. *Sports Illustrated*, 3/3/80: 18.

79. Louisville, KY *Courier-Journal*, 8/13/84: A7.

80. Louisville, KY *Courier-Journal*, 8/13/84: A7.

81. John Egerton, Louisville, KY *Courier-Journal*, 8/12/84: D3.

82. Maura Dolan, Louisville, KY *Courier-Journal*, 8/10/84: A1.

83. Palo Alto, CA *Peninsula Times Tribune*, 7/17/90: D1.

84. *Newsweek*, 7/14/86: 62; Palo Alto, CA *Peninsula Times Tribune*, 7/17/90: D6.

85. Louisville, KY *Courier-Journal*, 7/6/86: C1.

86. Louisville, KY *Courier-Journal*, 7/6/86: C5.

87. *Columbus Dispatch*, 7/4/86: 1A.

88. Louisville, KY *Courier-Journal*, 2/15/85: A9.

89. *Atlantic Monthly*, 10/86: 72-73.

90. *Newsweek*, 5/13/85: 85.

91. Cited in Ellen Goodman, Louisville, KY *Courier-Journal*, 2/15/85: A9.

92. *Newsweek*, 5/13/85: 85.

93. *New York Times*, 10/18/90: C5 .

94. *New York Times*, 1/29/90: C12.

95. *Newsweek*, 7/4/83: 46.

96. *Spartan Daily* (San Jose State University), 1/28/87: 8.

97. *San Jose Mercury News,* 3/3/90: 18A.

98. *Newsweek,* 5/7/90: 74.

99. John S. Friedman, *In These Times,* 1/9-15/85.

100. *Newsweek,* 11/25/85: 96.

101. *Newsweek,* 8/7/89: 23.

102. Herbert I. Schiller, *The Mind Managers* (Boston: Beacon Press, 1973): 86-94.

103. *San Jose Mercury News,* 4/18/90: 5A.

104. *Newsweek,* 1/9/89: 58.

105. *Newsweek,* 1/9/89: 59.

106. See Richard Sennett, *The Fall of Public Man* (New York: Vintage, 1976): 287ff; *Newsweek,* 2/24/86: 74-75.

107. See Kurt W. Ritter, "Ronald Reagan and 'The Speech': The Rhetoric of Public Relations Politics," in H. R. Ryan (ed.): *American Rhetoric from Roosevelt to Reagan* (Prospect Heights, IL: Waveland, 1983): 290-298.

108. Louisville, KY *Courier-Journal,* 3/7/86: A2; Louisville, KY *Courier-Journal,* 3/8/86: A3.

109. *People,* 5/7/84: 187-189.

110. *People,* 5/7/84: 189.

111. *Chronicle of Higher Education,* 10/31/90: B1.

112. *San Francisco Chronicle,* 4/24/87: 28.

113. *San Francisco Chronicle,*12/3/86: 3.

114. *On Campus* (Ohio State University), 4/9/87: 1.

Special Invitation

to meet

WALTER F. MONDALE

on the steps of

Louisville City Hall

6th and Jefferson

12-Noon, Wednesday, October 31st

Special Entertainment with Stephen Stills
of Crosby, Stills & Nash
and a Surprise Special Guest Appearance

Paid for by Mondale / Ferraro Committee

 30

Today's Politics by Special Invitation

CHAPTER 7

THE ENVIRONMENT OF PROPAGANDA

What differences does it make if the public receives a few doses of propaganda from government, research, religion, news, the classroom, and entertainment? After all, there's nothing more American than hype. Competing propagandas, such as the pro-military *Top Gun* and the pacifistic *Born on the Fourth of July* cancel themselves out, do they not? Opinions that propaganda is natural or benign are most often expressed by communication practitioners who see nothing detrimental in the contemporary culture of orchestrated mass persuasion. Practitioners of public relations, advertising, and the media channels tend to view covert social influence as a non-problem, a mere outgrowth of traditional American boosterism. Given the demonstrated pervasiveness of propaganda, however, can we accept the assurances of the practitioners that clandestine influence is socially neutral?

The complacency of the practitioners is rooted in a view of the public as intelligently resistant to social influence. Advertisers and program executives experience directly the difficulty of inducing people to buy individual products or to watch particular TV shows. In actual practice, the advertising and television professions are dependent upon educated guesses and speculative assumptions about what does and does not work.[1] The folklore of these professions is replete with tales of ad campaigns gone awry and "sure" TV hits that bottomed out in the ratings. Considered in total, however, advertising and television blanket the nation to such an extent that proposals to curtail these cultural engines significantly are given scant serious consideration. So it is logical to raise the question, as did critic James Rorty in the 1930s: Does the alliance between advertising and mass media make the ostensibly independent public psychologically beholden to "our master's voice?"[2]

The essential danger of propaganda comes from the inability of people to secure direct information about the forces represented by the propagandists. Even highly-informed citizens have little *personal* experience of the people and events depicted in national, or even local, news stories. The separation of people from national and local affairs makes them vulnerable both to whatever trends are influencing and to whichever managers are controlling the channels of social communication. This generalization applies not only to news but also to government-agency action, research, religion, education, and entertainment. In this indirect communicative environment, we cannot assume that the public is *intelligently resistant* to propaganda-shrouded messages. A "marketplace of ideas," the underpinning of classic democratic theory, presupposes the ability actually to handle the intellectual merchandise. For this reason, a mass-mediated democracy may resemble a cable-TV shopping channel more than it does the lively town market of yore.

Granting that communicating to the public now requires expensive media productions and/or a scrambling for news coverage, what implication does the more impersonal scale of social influence have for democratic decision-making? Do we yet have a sufficient store of vibrant speakers and lively communities to render the public relatively immune to the tricky language, orchestrated campaigns, and self-serving ploys that are associated with propaganda? Or does the artificiality of contemporary public discourse make society increasingly vulnerable to the blandishments of the propagandists? To decide whether propaganda is a pressing problem, we must determine whether democratic forms of governance can establish an environment in which propaganda can be neutralized. What is the current condition of today's speakers and audiences?

INCAPACITATED SPEAKERS

The golden age of democracy in America sometimes is equated with the period of the great Congressional orators, when pressing national issues such as war and slavery were debated eloquently on the floor of Congress by Daniel Webster, Henry Clay, Thomas Hart Benton, John C. Calhoun, and others. The view that our relatively open political system continues to stymie propaganda's over-simplifications may be questioned if we examine the neutralized condition of contemporary America's public speakers.

PAC-Neutralized Speakers

One benchmark of today's arguably synthetic politics is the neutering of political speakers. In the nineteenth century, major political speakers relied for re-election relatively more on local political party operatives and opinion leaders. Today's national politicians depend increasingly on a few media outlets and on the political action committees (PACs) of national interest groups. With politicians competing for the same national media channels and the same funding sources, the result is a homogenizing of political discourse. George McGovern, former U.S. Senator and 1972 Democratic candidate for president, decried the blandness of today's mainstream politics, notably the tepid opposition given by the Democratic Party to the Bush Administration, 1989-1993. McGovern argued that the Democratic leadership in Congress was astonishingly reluctant to grab the $500 billion savings-and-loan scandal as a club to bash the Reagan/Bush forces for their deregulation of the economy. He noted the slowness of the Democrats to call for substantial military cutbacks in the wake of the collapse of the Warsaw Pact in Eastern Europe. "One answer, and a major reason for the lack of a genuine Democratic opposition today," McGovern contended, "is that the same PACs are financing both parties."[3]

Today, much of the energy of politicians is taken up with getting money for increasingly expensive media-based campaigns. Incumbent Senators and Representatives frequently spend one-third of their time on fund raising during the years before an election. After being reelected to the Senate, Ernest Hollings of South Carolina held a series of town meetings for his constituents. He acknowledged that "I didn't get much of a chance during the campaign" for direct speaking to constituents. "I was too busy raising bucks."[4] Naturally, politicians like to secure funds in the largest possible chunks, meaning that organized PACs will receive considerable attention from legislators. Between January 1989 and June 1990, PACs contributed $94 million for Congressional elections, the largest amount coming from PACs sponsored by business corporations and trade associations, followed by those of interest groups and labor organizations.[5] When campaigns are financed chiefly by large PACs instead of by individual contributors, we may expect that the interests of the PAC organizers will be first, with a resultant dampening of democracy. "Everybody in the system organizes themselves more and more to respond to people who've got money," acknowledged former U.S. Representative Buddy MacKay of Florida.[6]

PAC financing not only elevates the interests of the big contributors but also limits the range of political thought and action. According to former Senator James G. Abourezk, the PAC funding system narrows the range of politics so that everyone strives not to look dangerously out-of-step with dominant opinion. The PACs scrutinize candidates to avoid funding anyone who looks or sounds like a loser. As a result, members of Congress try not to say or do anything unconventional that would cause them to be written off by the PACs.[7]

Not only does PAC financing lead to a bland and unimaginative politics but also it perpetuates the status quo by favoring incumbents. In 1986 and 1988, 98 percent of House incumbents were reelected. In the 1990 elections for the U.S. House of Representatives, PAC contributions flowed to incumbents, as opposed to challengers, by a ratio of 19 to one.[8] Because PACs seek to win the ears of incumbents, regardless of party, the PAC financing method is one that encourages a blending of differences between the parties. In a study of seven elections, Common Cause, a civic lobbying group, found 150 instances of a PAC's having previously supported a losing candidate but then immediately switching after the election to give money to the winning opponent from the other party.[9] PACs seem to regard candidates as relatively interchangeable resources.

While PAC financing helps mute the political differences between Democrats and Republicans, the two parties do differ on the ideal solution to the impact of PAC money in national politics. Democrats have been reluctant to place a limit on how much PAC money a candidate may accept (this proposal was tabled in 1985 and was defeated in 1988 and 1990) because their party does relatively well under a system favoring incumbents. On the other hand, Republicans typically believe that their party (for ideological reasons) would take in a larger share of corporate PAC money if party organizations were given control of fundraising instead of allowing PACs to contribute directly to candidates. For this reason, the GOP is opposed to the other most frequently mentioned reform, that of having the U.S. Treasury supply the funds for election campaigns.[10]

Media-Neutralized Speakers

Not only do Congressional politicians spend a significant portion of their careers scrambling for handouts from the same national PACs but also they are dependent on a few national media outlets as well. In the nineteenth century, political communication chiefly took the form of popular speakers delivering their addresses in public forums and then personally arranging for the speeches to be reprinted as pamphlets for wider general circulation. Under this system, political speakers were more in control of what the public heard from them. Now, politicians must depend on others for access to the public, the most important group being the journalists who assemble the news coverage. Because speakers cannot control how they will come across to the general public through news reports, these speakers naturally strive to avoid looking eccentric, controversial, or out-of-step.

The norms of journalism also encourage brevity and blandness, which predisposes politicians to avoid making reasoned presentations of a non-mainstream view. Brevity is required, according to Kathleen Jamieson, a communication scholar, because the speaker who can capsulize a topic "in a clear, concise, dramatic statement that takes less than thirty-five seconds to deliver is more likely to be seen and heard on broadcast news than those who lack that talent."[11] Further, these dramatic capsules need to be abstract or obscure to discourage the news professionals from seeking out adverse comments from other politicians or advocacy-group spokespersons.

The desire of members of Congress to look safely conventional may help explain the lack of debate in Congress in the fall, 1990, about the possible use of U.S. forces in the Persian Gulf to mount an offensive against Iraq. In the four weeks before the November 1990 elections, the news media were reporting that the Pentagon planned a major military escalation in the Persian Gulf. These reports suggested that U.S. forces would not wait until a blockade forced Iraq to withdraw from Kuwait, but rather would mount an attack. As it was election season, Congressional leaders kept their concerns about Bush's military policy largely private. Columnist Thomas Oliphant called this absence of vibrant public discussion a de facto "bipartisan conspiracy."[12] Two days after the election in November, President Bush finally announced that he was doubling the size the U.S. military forces in Gulf in preparation for taking a military offensive against Iraq. Even so, Congress still shied away from a full debate. "Where is Congress on the Gulf?" editorialized the *New York Times.*[13]

When the U.S. House and Senate belatedly took up debate on whether to authorize the Persian Gulf War of 1991—just days before the war began—the Democratic leadership of the House and Senate explained that they had delayed debate until the war-versus-peace nature of the vote had become unmistakably clear. Equally clear was that the tardy timing of the debate had contributed to its outcome. Many members of Congress justified their vote to authorize military action after January 15, 1991, as necessary to avoid a last-minute repudiation of a presidential policy that had been in force for many weeks. Even most opponents of authorizing the war argued mainly about timing, accepting the idea that fighting might eventually be the best way to force Iraq out of Kuwait. Notwithstanding the frequent eloquence of the Congressional speakers, the political impact of the war debate was undercut by its eleventh-hour character, an understandable result of Congress's two-month deference to the President's military build-up.

THE PASSIVE *POLIS*

Not only are PAC-funded and media-oriented political speakers more bland and less decisive, the national audience whom they think they are addressing has become more artificial and passive. The great orators of the nineteenth century addressed a national audience consisting of a collection of vibrant local publics. In contrast, the chief political audience today is a presumed national group that exists in the form of opinion poll data. Many who grew up in the era of opinion polling now take for granted that poll data and public opinion are one and the same; nevertheless, critics of polls point out that surveys and polls manufacture an artificial public sentiment, one that tends to be uninformed, reactive, and unstable.

A Public of Polls

In the days before opinion polling, politicians had to estimate general public sentiment on the basis of specific expressions from opinion leaders, e.g., letters from constituents. Opinion leaders were citizens who followed particular issues closely; opinion leaders were regularly consulted by persons who had less interest in an issue and therefore were less prone to keep up independently. In that system, opinion leaders, interest-group leaders, and local politicians had a significant influence over the diffusion of public opinion.

Early students of public opinion, such as sociologist Robert E. Park, organized their theories to differentiate the two kinds of public sentiment. On the one hand, they observed that some kinds of public opinion arose through discussion. Opinion leaders listened and read the statements of public officials and then widened the sphere of opinion by discussing issues with less-interested citizens. Park and others contrasted this opinion-through-discussion with mass opinion, which he described as an unreflective common impulse triggered by some significant event.[14]

An understanding of the working of polls suggests that public opinion as constituted by surveys is more akin to unreflective impulses than to discussion-based views. In producing a national survey, pollsters select a sample of around 1,500 individuals chosen at random. In this random aggregate, the views of persons who have thought little about an issue are counted as equal to the views of opinion leaders (although persons obviously unfamiliar with the questions may be classified as having "no opinion"). Since polls homogenize opinions on an issue, converting them into static average numbers, polling obscures the specific insights accruing from any discussion that may already be occurring among citizens.

Merging the mass and the public (to use Park's terms) not only dampens the discursive texture of society but also this homogenizing of opinion has the further effect of lessening the political clout of general opinion leaders as well as leaders of advocacy groups. To understand why this is the case, we must remember that persons polled in an opinion survey are required to make snap choices to questions asked in a neutral frame of reference by a person whom they do not know. Normally, people seek to avoid making choices in this rootless fashion; instead, they talk to their friends and family as a way of formulating their own opinions. When poll-style, unanchored choices are tabulated into official poll data, the effect is to undermine any opinion leader or interest-group leader who actually does have a considered opinion and who has been expressing it.

As an example of polls undercutting opinion leaders, we may turn to the use of poll data by the Nixon Administration to argue for its support by a "silent majority" in relation to the Vietnam War. Nixon's numbers suggested that vocal critics of the Vietnam War were out of step.[15]

Out of step with whom?—with people who had not necessarily followed the course of the war nor had been particularly energetic in expressing their views. Regarding the Administration's commitment of one-half million men to warfare in Vietnam, public opinion was "articulated" by persons whose sole qualification to be counted was their ability to answer "yes" or "no" to an anonymous poll taker who neither asked for action nor pressed for details. Where public opinion and poll data are treated as synonymous, local publics and opinion leaders atrophy, further enhancing the opportunities for top-down, propagandistic communication.

Not only does political polling work against opinion leaders, but it also undermines the leadership of interest groups. A representative example of this situation was given by Benjamin Ginsberg, a political scientist, who pointed out that President Nixon undermined the leadership of labor unions. Leaders of organized labor strongly opposed Nixon's program of wage and price controls. In contrast, Nixon was able to display poll data showing that rank-and-file laborers "had no strong views on the programs." Because modern dogma holds that only polls reveal the true public opinion, it followed that labor leaders could be safely ignored as being out of touch.[16] Polls made the Nixon Administration seem more the friend of labor than labor's own leadership!

George Gallup and other polling practitioners have argued that it is "elitist" to suggest that mass opinion is less enlightened than that of opinion leaders. Further, Gallup contended that opinion polls are actually more democratic than elections because polls, not having to wait for the next election season, can follow shifts of opinion over time.[17] Nevertheless, a democracy of random polls is one highly vulnerable to propaganda. When public opinion is equated with poll data, distant national leaders are able to shape the presumed public mind by concocting alleged events. One of these was the reported second attack on U.S. destroyers in the Tonkin Gulf by North Vietnam in 1964, the dramatic incident that caused Congress to give Lyndon Johnson license to escalate the Vietnam War. Surveyers confirmed that persons polled strongly supported Johnson's military actions in the Tonkin Gulf. Similarly, national leaders can manipulate poll-style public opinion by controlling the release of information, for instance, when the CIA would leak new (high) estimates of Soviet military spending just before Congressional debate on the arms budget.

Nose-counting has its uses, but where survey averages are treated as synonymous with public opinion, these data serve to homogenize a bland and artificial unitary public opinion that contributes to the bland and artificial texture of contemporary politics. One evidence of the superficiality of poll-based national publics is their tendency to "shift" sentiment when the wording of a question is changed. When pollsters asked voters whether they favored or opposed a Constitutional amendment "prohibiting abortions," 62 percent were opposed. When the same respondents were asked about an amendment "protecting the life of the unborn child," only 39 percent dissented.[18]

Other oddities in poll data reinforce the danger of trying to address the artificial audiences conjured up by pollsters. For one thing, an overuse of polling by political and business researchers (and a rampant practice of disguising sales pitches as polls) had caused a situation in which one-third of those people asked to participate in polls flatly refused.[19] As a result, the claimed randomness of polling has been in decline. Not only that, but sometimes voters have given what they believed was the preferred answer—and then acted differently. For instance, during the election of fall 1990, David Duke, former Ku Klux Klan leader, was running for the U.S. Senate seat of J. Bennett Johnson in Louisiana. Duke eventually received 44 percent of the vote, much higher than that forecast by polls. Since Duke was widely attacked as a racist, voters attracted to him were apparently reluctant to confess their real intentions about Duke to someone whom they did not know personally.[20]

Even though polls may shift widely or miss the mark considerably, they routinely receive the greatest amount of news coverage focused on the public. This preoccupation with numbers arguably prompts a bandwagon effect according to which voters revise their choices by noting the apparent weakness or strength of candidates.[21] Poll averages, in any event, do not constitute real audiences that, necessarily, emerge from specific circles of people, specific places where groups gather, or specific events that precipitate listeners. Widespread acceptance of a poll-derived "public" allows speakers to claim that they are addressing a local, regional or national public without responding either to specific climates of opinion or to established associations. Focus on anonymous averages distances real people still farther from politics, thereby enhancing the opportunities for propagandists to grow more powerful.

Protest Interludes

The blandness both of PAC- and media-projected speakers and poll-created publics is obscured by the occasional rhetoric of protest. Those who came of political age during the 1960s often have a justifiably great regard for the benefits of protest demonstrations. Protest rhetoric helped the nation break through the oppressive political structure that enforced segregation in the South. Also, given the tentative and timid Congressional opposition to the Johnson and Nixon policies in Vietnam, only the politics of protest forced the nation to confront the consequences of misbegotten policies. These examples, however, do not so much justify a rhetoric of protest as they call for a vibrant town-meeting style of political deliberation in which opinion leaders address real audiences and are beholden neither to PACs nor to a few national media outlets. Had the issues of civil rights at home and war overseas been subjected to real debate, there would have been little, if any, need to break apart the stultifying status quo with angry protests.

Protest is an ambiguous corrective to mainstream synthetic politics. Whereas bland mainstream discourse gives us a technical politics that minimizes differences, protest rhetoric exaggerates differences and subordinates reasons and details to passion. The usefulness of the protest strategy *is* its passion—and passion is one ingredient of eloquent communication; however, a constant recourse to defiant attacks brings about two related problems. First, defiance undermines the ability of diverse peoples to live together in a political community based on mutual respect. Second, a diet of rhetorical denunciations prevents construction of a political coalition that would be able to act on commonly perceived problems.

We search neither far nor long to find examples of angry, vituperative communication that exaggerates differences and minimizes the common ground needed for political action. On the campus of the University of Texas (Austin), Toni Luckett, the 1989-90 Austin student-body president, angrily challenged "the system" on her campus with a confrontational style in which epithets such as "racist" became commonplace. For instance, Luckett led a crowd of students who shouted down the university president, William H. Cunningham, when he attempted to deliver a speech on the subject of racial incidents on the UT-Austin campus.[22]

A loud rhetoric of confrontation was in force when the Gay community attacked the medical establishment in San Francisco in 1990. During the Sixth Annual International Conference on AIDS in San Francisco, June 1990, AIDS patients expressed their frustrations by attacking their former allies in the medical establishment. Whereas earlier AIDS conferences had exhibited a spirit of mutual mission and hope, in 1990 the activists shouted down the researchers. AIDS patients, who formerly reserved most of their anger for the impersonal medical bureaucracies, now railed at all physicians who merely studied or treated AIDS without actually having experienced it personally. The anger was borne of the immediacy of suffering. AIDS victims were angry at testing; they were angry at the tedious pace of research; they were angry at the lesser ability of the poor to receive good treatment. Speaking of the physicians and researchers, Larry Kramer, founder of an activist group, Act Up, was heard to shout: "You are co-conspirators, though you think you are heroes."[23] Commentators wondered whether the San Francisco AIDS conference would be the last of its kind.

Protest communication demands a drama of hero and villain wherein cooperation and compromise—even basic politeness—are forsaken in an effort to confront and attack permanent enemies and their fellow travelers. If our goal be action for change in a democratic community, however, undiluted protest rhetoric has limits as an alternative to the artificial, media-contrived calculations of synthetic politics.

Society without Community

What synthetic politics and protest rhetoric have in common is their mutual lack of a strong sense of community. Synthetic PAC-financed and mass-mediated mainstream politics brings a top-down reformism in which power elites respond grudgingly to what they perceive to be the public's wants and needs. This approach is based on a plebescite mentality according to which the public is not much involved until election season crops up or until events trigger a mass public-opinion shift. With its money, media, and polls, mainstream politics requires little in the way of direct and continuing public participation.

Protest rhetoric, similarly, requires no links of community among people. Protesters tend to see society simply as consisting of heros and villains, of oppressors and victims. Protest politicians, and their intellectual allies, build careers by stressing what divides a society rather than by focusing on what are promising avenues for (re)uniting it. Where communication is based on disrespect for one's opponent, as well as hatred of an impersonal "system," the divisions existing in society are seen as absolute and irreconcilable. This yes/no view provides an infertile field for continuing public discourse. During the 1960s, columnist Robert L. Steinback argued, defiance was a useful tool, particularly for minorities. Defiance can be useful, he added, because it is preferable to passive submission—*if these are the only choices.* The downside of defiance, Steinback observed, is that it mitigates against a number of character traits useful in building community: "patience, cooperation, trust, adaptability, tolerance, and perseverance."[24]

Synthetic politics and the rhetoric of protest, two opposites, have together contributed to a general loss of a sense that real people can transcend their private worlds to have a meaningful connection with a real public. The tendency to treat publics as unknowable abstractions perhaps has been inevitable in a nation grown from 3,000,000 rural and small-town dwellers to a 250-million-member megapolis. While today's people may be acquainted with more information, they are less personally knowledgeable about people and events that directly affect them. In this perceptual environment, people understandably think of the public sphere as an artifice; in contrast, they treat as "real" that which can be directly known—one's private goals, beliefs (or ideologies), lifestyle, circle of friends, and career.

The reflexive tendency to devalue the public, and emphasize the private, crops up in the way people perceive today's leading figures. For instance, during the late 1980s, scholars collating the papers of Martin Luther King, Jr., discovered that King had plagiarized some of the material in his doctoral dissertation. This finding produced consternation among the scholars. "It was anxiety about the damage it might do to Dr. King's reputation," said Ralph Luker.[25]

Why did anxiety over King's complacency about sources mean that his status as one of the truly great men of the twentieth century might be diminished? Like most of us, the researchers studying King's papers assumed that the "real" King lay not in his public expressions but rather in his private acts of composition. Their anxiety about King's image was based on the current view of private actions as the essential mark of character. If we were living in an era when the public sphere were highly valued, the researchers probably would have considered the blemish of plagiarism as relatively trivial when set against King's public character which was already firmly established through his eloquent speeches and political genius. Judged according to the standard of beneficial public acts, Martin Luther King, Jr., is a great man because of his public work, regardless of what we happen to know about his private foibles.

Because of today's emphasis on private life as the key reality, individuals find it difficult to imagine that they are connected in a real and meaningful public world. The result is a view of public life as insincere shadow-boxing. People are wont to be silent in public; they save serious talk for private occasions and comfortable encounters with friends and fellow believers. Public life—politics—becomes something to be escaped. People retreat to private spheres of home, automobile, workplace, shopping mall, and rap session. Yet, the contemporary sterility of public life produces a paradoxical nostalgia for the older kind of society in which people knew their neighbors and acted together in a cooperative spirit.[26] At the same time that people flee from demands outside of their own family and career they seek a mythical community that is well-stocked with others who have the time and inclination to volunteer for community groups and activities.

A *public community*, by contrast, consists of all those persons who perceive themselves to be affected by a given event, message, or action.[27] For instance, if a state legislature has the power severely to curtail women's access to abortions, then the political community for that decision consists of all who perceive themselves to be both affected by the action and able (potentially) to influence it. All students and parents subject to a college's fee increase belong to an identifiable public community defined by that public action. All citizens affected by the toxic smoke from an oil-well fire represent a tangible public community drawn together by that event. From this definition and from these examples, it is clear that many communities exist simultaneously on the local, regional, state, and national levels.

A public community is activated through the ability of its members to air grievances and take common action constructively. When members of the community listen to opinion leaders, when they debate and argue, a community has a chance not only to vent hostility but also to change its condition. Repeated face-to-face expression and continuing mutual action together foster a context in which mutual respect and commitment may emerge. For one thing, when members of a community see their opponents genuinely as potential converts, they tend to be more tolerant of nonbelievers. From this it follows that wherever unresolved anger exists between factions in a polity, we shall find a less vibrant political community.

One may draw an interesting analogy between the anger within individuals and the anger of a disaffected group in society. After observing people who experience chronic anger, researchers at the University of Michigan found that long-term suppressed anger leads to premature death. This finding about individuals is sobering when considered from the standpoint of today's rhetorical climate that does so little to help people resolve social anger. On the one hand, synthetic politics offers little opportunity for people to translate anger into action. Protest rhetoric, in contrast, intensifies anger, often without providing for a constructive resolution of it. Both synthetic policies and protest rhetoric may contribute to the premature death of public life.

Today's tendency to gunny-sack social anger comes from the lack of a vibrant public sphere in which people might listen to others, express their own views, and hear opposing opinion leaders. Unable to confront opposed believers, unable to listen while opposed advocates eloquently debate matters of mutual importance, citizens store up their gripes about the people and policies in their social world. Just as the tendency to store personal grievances is harmful to one's personal health, it is unhealthy for societies to store anger. "People who often explode in hostile rages or who sit around fuming over every perceived slight may be doing more than making themselves unpleasant. They may be killing themselves."[28] Societies that behave in this manner are headed for a similar fate.

Pseudo-communities

A functioning, substantial, "true" community has certain recognizable characteristics that may be used to distinguish it from a group of people who merely experience affinity or who use the term "community" metaphorically. A true community is an aggregation of people who share responsibility for resolving an issue that affects them mutually, if not identically. A true community is not simply a subsidiary group having a vested or particular interest in the kind of decision that is made about an event or condition. To the contrary, the hallmark of community is bridging the diversity of situations and of thoughts by means of discourse. The aim is to effect common policies that satisfy many (if not most) of those involved and, where possible, to accommodate all. The leading edge of the true community consists in the attendance and participation of those affected in debates about the event or condition under question.

Archetypes of the true and literally political community are the early-nineteenth-century New England small town and the ancient city-state of Athens. In New England, taxes (even state levies) were collected locally, voters knew public officers personally, and the body politic met with functional frequency both to listen to and to instruct officials. Granted, voting in 18th and 19th century New England was often restricted along lines of income, gender, and race; however, small towns of the early Republic saw a relatively close match between citizenship (as then defined) and participation. (If voting in the early Republic seems unprogressive by today's standards, it remains a fact that large-scale electoral participation was unknown at that time in most of the world.)

If our memory of small-town America calls to mind the participatory aspect of mostly homogenous communities, the democratic politics of ancient Athens reminds us that diversity is an important marker of community interaction. Formed from a group of neighboring tribes, the city-state of Athens developed a democratic constitution partly because the conflicting traditions of the different tribes could not serve as implicit guides to action for the whole community. While in some cases the Athenian constitution apportioned offices by tribe, the norm was to transcend tribal loyalties by means of debate and election.[29]

Given the nostalgic longing for true community in contemporary American public life, it is ironic that people of the early 1990s most often have used the term "community" in a way that actually has hindered achieving a public life based on principles of acting in concert with others. Interdependence in necessary action is the mark of a common political world (a polity); however, the concept of community most frequently articulated today is that of subsidiary social blocks of identically-situated, like-minded, or visually-similar people who see themselves as estranged from others whose agreement or acquiescence would be, nevertheless, required for public action to be taken.

These pseudo-communities stand in contrast to the literally political community. We are familiar with protests by persons who claim to be representatives of various disaffected demographic communities, and we sense nothing inherently sinister in groups of like-minded or similarly-situated people getting together. A problem arises, however, when persons who perceive themselves thusly linked become preoccupied with treating themselves *and everyone demographically similar* as constituting an absolute, discursively-significant community that can make decisions or enjoy benefits apart from the influence of others who are expressly excluded from "the community." The result is to dichotomize and reify various abstract pseudo-communities that see themselves as necessarily and ideally separate from the other people whom they are affecting and by whom they are affected: e.g. People of color vs. Whites; women vs. men; the homeless vs. the housed; Gays, Lesbians, and Bi-Sexuals vs. Straights; and the list could be extended into a fragmentation—a Balkanization—of the body politic.[30]

It is no accident that a politics rooted in pseudo-communities of people-just-like-me has accompanied the death of a vibrant sense of political community among Americans. Opinion leaders generally do not see much opportunity in our synthetic public life to make an impact on the literally political community (those people who can and do affect each other directly through negotiated action) unless they have some private, behind-the-scenes, access to the centers of power. Some, such as defense contractors or trade association leaders, have a direct pipeline to the power elites in government and society. Other opinion leaders who lack this easy covert access to power find that they must recast themselves as leaders of some harassed community-within-the-community in order to get any attention at all.

The tendency to establish sharply defined pseudo-communities has proliferated to the point of parody. Take the case of Toni Cassista of Santa Cruz, California, who was turned down for jobs because of her weight (305 pounds). Cassista argued that she was a victim of job discrimination based on her size, and she demanded a ban on weight and height discrimination. In today's climate of entitlement communities, each with its own rights, the way for Cassista to get recompense for the discrimination she suffered as an overweight person would be to cast herself as part of an oppressed minority, the community of "full-sized" people. Then, if discrimination on the basis of weight and size were to become recognized as validating social reparations, our public life would have gained corresponding fat and thin people's communities. Not far behind would be short people demonstrating that they, too, had been disadvantaged. Perhaps the next step would be to organize the ugly person's community or the "four-eyes" community of people who wear glasses. Clearly, these latter suffer the demonstrable disadvantage of not attaining the lifestyles of the beautiful and well-sighted.

Today's parodies of the pseudo-community impulse risk deflation in tomorrow's newspaper headlines. On our progressive college campuses, we can find pamphlets undertaking the seemingly impossible task of discouraging college students, of all people, from practicing "lookism" (using physical attractiveness as a basis for perception). Simultaneously, the "nerds community"—the opposite of the good-lookers—may be organizing for action. In 1991, four men were denied entrance to a chic Los Angeles night spot because the clothes they were wearing were not trendy. The men filed suit in small-claims court against the Mayan Club for unlawful discrimination.[31]

As a result of the legacy of the Civil Rights and women's movements, Americans tend to associate the politics of pseudo-communities with ethnic and racial minority groups. The largest and most powerful pseudo-community, nonetheless, is that of retired persons who act through their lobbying arm, the politically active American Association for Retired Persons. Numbering 31 million members, most of whom not only regularly vote but also have spare time, the AARP lobbies effectively for health care and social security.

Another emerging large "community" is that of the Baby Boomers. Given the financial squeeze faced by many Americans raising young families, it is not really surprising to observe efforts by the American Association of Boomers to raise consciousness and to represent persons between 25 and 43 years of age. "When the Social Security crisis hit a few years back, AARP was at the table to voice their concern," commented Philip Longman, financial analyst. "But there was no one there speaking for the baby boomers."[32] Another pseudo-community was born.

It is not difficult to find examples of Americans treating abstract demographic groups as actual communities having an unquestionably objective reality. For instance, during a debate over government welfare benefits, Rep. Pete Stark of Hayward, California, called Louis Sullivan, George Bush's Secretary of Health and Human Services, "a disgrace to his race." It seemed that Sullivan, who is Black, did not support national health insurance and a policy of easy access to abortions.[33] Stark's attack not only followed today's tendency to personalize a public issue but also his remarks reflected the familiar cementing of a person to his or her appropriate pseudo-community. Stark assumed that there was something called "the Black community" so absolutely real that it included— automatically and completely—all Americans of African-American descent regardless of their place of residence, moral preferences, or political beliefs. The irony, of course, was that this reified Black community was so fragile that Sullivan could be expelled from it merely for articulating views inconsistent with the dominant African-American opinion leaders. Columnist Mike Royko poked fun at this tendency to endow abstract demographic communities with an aura of bedrock reality. Royko once acknowledged that he was part of "the middle-aged white man community," membership in which included liking Glen Miller records, big black Oldsmobiles, and sexist jokes.[34]

If Americans treat abstract communities of age, race, occupation, sexual preference or a dozen other options as frozen blocks of opinion, then the nation's political discourse necessarily must suffer. Democratic political discourse in America's national, regional, and local communities requires that those people who are linked as fellow citizens within the polity be able to work from a minimum degree of common ground. Where people sense their political interdependence, they look for transcending principles, such as common human rights or negotiated democracy, to bridge the gaps that divide them. When political discourse is rooted in these transcending principles, heated political debate does not preclude a mutual granting of respect, a desire to find a commonly agreeable course of action, an acceptance of the right of each speaker to form his or her own opinions, and the presumption that each person's views are based on legitimate claims (although not necessarily agreeable or well-proved reasons). By contrast, where reified pseudo-communities hold sway in politics, propaganda abounds, and most citizens opt to avoid the fray.

THE POVERTY OF NATIONAL DISCOURSE

What is the health of America's national political community? To what extent can Americans find transcending principles to bridge disagreement about issues? When the American recipe for discourse becomes four parts synthetic politics mixed with one part of protest rhetoric, the result is a breakdown in community. People who are actually interdependent satisfy their nostalgia for public community by organizing, or fantasizing, demographic pseudo-communities. The following examples demonstrate the prevalence of public discourse that is variously incomprehensible or pathological in its loss of focus on the truly political community.

Multiple instances of the poor state of contemporary public deliberation on important issues make clear that the breakdown in public
communication is not restricted to major national political campaigns.
The problem is wider and deeper, applying equally well to important
social and political initiatives that, often as not, are supported with nothing that approximates a body of eloquent expression. This absence of
eloquent writing and speaking erodes literally political communities
even further and enhances the power of propaganda in support of pseudo-communities. By marking out the weaknesses in today's national
public deliberations, we can make significant progress in finding anti-
dotes to propaganda's poisons.

Poisoned Political Campaigns

Much attention today is focused on the poor state of discourse in
political campaigns. "Couldn't we just call the whole thing off and start
over?" asked *Newsweek* magazine during the last days of campaign '88.[35]
The article laid out a panorama of unflattering snapshots of the waning
1988 presidential contest. The Bush campaign was shown continuing its
barrage of charges about Michael Dukakis's patriotism and Dukakis's
supposed support of rapists and murderers. Meanwhile, Dukakis was
busy carping about Bush's "lies," and finally slinging some mud of his
own. Political commentators pointed to the lukewarm loyalty for both
candidates among voters who agreed in the polls (which are unexcelled
for simple nose-counting) that each major party could have found a
stronger candidate. Almost uniformly, the political pundits dismissed
campaign '88 as trivial and depressing.

Nor was the 1988 situation atypical of recent views of political
campaigning. Breast-beating about the state of major political contests
has become a familiar ritual in American politics. Midway into the 1980
Reagan/Carter contest, for example, Saul Pett of the Associated Press
wrote an extended essay summarizing many dissatisfactions that could
apply to almost any recent political contest. Pett cited the growing
length of campaigns in which candidates announce their availability
years before the election and spend months on the first New Hampshire
primary. Then there was the high cost, for example, $1.2 million for
Senator Howard Baker in 1980 to secure a total of one delegate. Finally,
Pett mentioned the worrisome tendency of candidates to spend disproportionate amounts of time addressing special-interest lobbies or advocacy groups (i.e., pseudo-communities) such as gun groups or

pro-choice activists, and he cited the distorting influence of media exposure which is given sparingly, if at all, to candidates deemed minor by
the networks.[36]

Routine Incivility

It might be possible to ignore or excuse the rhetorical excesses and
failures of political campaigns in view of their brevity, urgency, or infre-
quency, but a related and more pressing problem is the routine lack of
intelligent discourse found throughout public life. Even America's highest elected leaders sometimes seem bent on discouraging reasoned talk,
as indicated in one brief dispute among U.S. Senators that surfaced in
spring 1990. On March 22, 1990, the Senate passed by voice vote without debate (there were 80 sponsors) a non-binding measure expressing
the sense of the Senate that Jerusalem was the proper capital of Israel.
This action drew fire from Arab nations because the status of Jerusalem
had never been resolved after the 1967 Arab/Israeli war when Israel took
over the formerly Jordanian half of the city.

Soon after the Senate vote, Senator Bob Dole (R., Kansas) said that
the Senate had made a mistake in passing the resolution. He further
stated in an interview that "the leaders of the pro-Israeli lobby are short-
sighted and selfish in their zealous efforts to protect Israel's aid levels at
any cost."[37] Dole's testy remarks touched off a storm of criticism not
only on account of his challenging a nation usually revered as an ally but
also for his having made "personal attacks" against Jewish leaders. Dole
defended himself by pointing to what he claimed to be his 26-year-long
record of support for Israel.

The ebb and flow of argument about Dole's remarks illustrated a
number of tendencies in contemporary discourse. First, comments evidently intended chiefly as a criticism of policy frequently become treated as illegitimate personal attacks. The individuals who were angered by
the criticism strove to win an insurmountable moral position by articulating outrage (with demands for an apology) rather than developing an
eloquent defense of the particular policy under question. The atmosphere of pseudo-community insures that the feelings of disputants will be
taken as more important than their reasons. At the same time, wanting to
sound reasonable more than simply petulant, disputants on both sides
instinctively grasped for catch-phrases such as "anti-Israel" or "Jewish
lobby" that drew attention away from their own failures to develop reasons.

In the case of Senator Dole's mild rebuke of pro-Israeli lobbyists, what otherwise might have been a dispute about public issues became, instead, a searching into the private sensitivities and proclivities of the Senator. Instead of asking whether the U.S. should recognize Jerusalem as the Israeli capital or whether the U.S. should give $4 billion per year to Israel, attention focused on whether or not Bob Dole was anti-Israel or even anti-Semitic. Writing about the trend for debate over public issues to devolve into expressions of private feeling and group solidarity, columnist Ellen Goodman observed that rampant charges of "anti" or "ism" had become "the Saturday-night specials of discourse. They are a part of a random civil violence."[38]

The Perverted Debate over Drugs

Perhaps we might overlook the poor quality of discourse about Senator Dole's remarks in view of the great brevity of the affair; however, even sustained public issues of major scope today are supported by superficial bodies of discourse that leave the public vulnerable to the images, slogans, and hasty answers of propaganda. A major case in point is the national discussion of policies on illegal drugs. As with many provocative national questions, the drug debate of the 1980s proceeded as if there were only one legitimate position to be expressed—total prohibition of mood-altering drugs. Since pleasure drugs had to be illegal, the only significant body of national discussion centered on the penalties to be assigned to lawbreakers, the various methods for speedily detecting violators, and the pace of constructing prisons to house drug criminals. By 1987, Attorney General Edwin Meese was calling for mandatory drug testing not only for public-safety workers but also for public-school teachers.[39]

Taking their cue from the Reagan Administration's call to *jump* on the matter of drugs, froggy Congressmen, as well as state and local officials, duly adopted the *how high?* point of view. Politicians competed to deliver the most decisive anti-drug statements and to devise the most draconian penalties for offenders. For instance, Governor Kay Orr of Nebraska proposed that college students convicted of two drug offenses be expelled from school.[40] Convicted on two, no college for you! An amendment to the federal highway laws provided that states would lose money if they did not mete out a six-months driver's license suspension for anyone convicted of minor marijuana possession—whether or not the offense had anything to do with driving.[41]

The foregoing examples were part of a root-them-out-at-any-cost, manic discourse about drugs. Citizens who dissented from, or were lukewarm toward, the new drug crusade kept prudently silent or they made ambiguous statements, not wanting to become anathematized for seeming to condone or support use of illegal drugs. In the frenzied atmosphere of ever-escalating anti-drug rhetoric, who would want to risk appearing "pro-drug?" The unopposed anti-drug enthusiasms proceeded in a manner akin to previous national manias against alleged pro-Germanism (World War I), suspected Japanese-American disloyalty (World War II), and supposedly dangerous leftists in government and education (the McCarthy era).

The nation's one-sided "discussion" of the drug problem escalated during the Bush administration under the exhortations of the new "drug czar," William Bennett. Head of the Office of National Drug Control Policy, Bennett went around the country calling for heavy crack-downs on all illegal drugs; even casual marijuana users were included in the dragnet. Further, Bennett demanded that states enact mandatory drug testing for their employees.[42] During a speech at Harvard University, Bennett excoriated the nation's academicians, arguing that "in the great public-policy debate over drugs, the academic and intellectual communities have, by and large, had little to contribute."[43] Bennett's notion of "public-policy debate" seemed to offer academicians a choice of two sides only: (1) agreement or (2) absolute, flag-waving agreement.

One academician who failed to climb aboard Bennett's bandwagon was Ronald K. Siegel.[44] Siegel, a UCLA psychopharmacologist, wrote a book arguing that animals and insects had a tendency to seek out narcotic plants termed "adaptogens," substances that helped an organism adjust to physical or psychological changes. Because of the evolutionary and genetic dispositions of humans towards narcotic substances, Siegel argued, it was neither possible nor desirable to win the war on drugs by eradicating their non-medical use.[45]

By early 1990, drug-czar Bennett had good reason to lash out at backsliders in the war on drugs because a real debate on drug policy showed signs of beginning. After a half-decade of keeping a low profile, a few brave souls were tentatively raising in public some real questions about the governing assumptions of the Reagan/Bush anti-drug crusade. On October 7, 1989, former Secretary of State George Shultz told a group of Stanford University alumni that legalization of drugs was a sound alternative to the Bennett approach, but that legalizing drugs for personal use was something "everybody is too scared to talk about."[46] Enlarging his remarks in a later public appearance in Cupertino, California, Shultz argued that controlled legalization of drugs would allow for a "free market" in which lower prices would eliminate much of drug crime and violence. According to Shultz, this approach would leave the nation free to concentrate its resources on treatment for drug users and prevention of drug abuse.

The White House quickly pounced on Shultz's remarks, seeking to trivialize them. Marlin Fitzwater, White House Press Secretary, commented: "Whoa, he's been out on the West Coast too long, hasn't he? The guy slips into retirement and right away he starts saying things that are strange."[47] Not everyone, however, thought that Shultz had slipped. In an appearance before a large crowd in Cupertino, Shultz received cheers when he claimed that "99.9 percent" of the letters he had received about his drug arguments were favorable.[48]

Seemingly, Shultz's remarks opened a floodgate of repressed public expression about the drug problem. In a speech delivered at the Cosmopolitan Club in New York, U.S. District Judge Robert Sweet called for repeal of the drug laws. "More money, more prisoners, more addicts—these numbers demonstrate to me our present prohibitive policy has failed, flatly, without serious question."[49] While Shultz's and Sweet's calls might have represented tips of an iceberg of thought among opinion leaders, mass opinion at this time (courtesy of the polls) was firmly rooted in the official view. Opinion surveys showed overwhelming popular opposition to legalizing drugs, usually by ratios of 9 to one. If, however, we adopt Robert Park's dual view of public opinion as consisting both of a discursive public, vitally interested in discussing an issue, and of a more passive group waiting to be led, then the emergence of a second side in the drug debate might herald a long-term shift of opinion away from Czar Bennett's position.

One sign of a shift in the views of opinion leaders on the drug question was that columnists began to weigh in against the Reagan/Bush prohibitionist approach. "For too long, 'soft on drugs' McCarthyism has silenced debate on drug policy. We don't talk. We don't think. We just pay for more cops, more courts, more prisons—and more crime," complained San Jose columnist Joanne Jacobs.[50] What prompted Jacobs's ire was the effort of California Attorney General John Van de Kamp's office to censor part of a report by the state's Research Advisory Panel which argued that "prohibition, as opposed to regulation, has not controlled drug use." In a similar spirit, Jefferson Morley, an editor of *Nation* magazine, identified certain "dangers of addiction to drug war rhetoric." Morley smoked crack cocaine so he could write about it, discovering that crack was "pleasurable" but brought "powerful and unpleasant side effects," including stupefaction and paranoia. Based on his subsequent appearances on radio talk shows, he reported speaking to a surprisingly large number of people outside Washington, D.C., who agreed with the proposition that crack should be legal.[51] "What came through most consistently," he reflected "was a sense of relief at hearing someone in the media say something—anything—besides the bogus rhetorical consensus of zero tolerance."

The first evidences of real public discussion over the national drug policy had the effect of quickly transforming the heretofore manic quality of official drug discourse (i.e., obsessions accompanied by exaggerated flights of ideas) to that of a *manic/depressive* condition (i.e., alternating periods of mania and melancholy). By fall 1989, Bennett was lashing out against defectors in the war against drugs. "I'm mad; I'm frustrated," Bennett acknowledged as he criticized federal and state leaders for a lack of zeal and persistence. Not only that, but the people were at fault, too. Complained Bennett: "People are saying: 'OK, Bennett, we're with you as long as you can get this thing wrapped up fast. But don't give us one of those three-, four-, five-year things, because that's not the way America works.'"[52] A year later, Bennett quit his job.

The quick emergence of reasoned public dissent on drug prohibition seemed to stem from such stubborn statistics as the estimated 50 million Americans who have used marijuana or cocaine at least once.[53] Recently, fewer people reported using illegal drugs than previously; 14.5 million Americans in 1988 versus 23 million in 1985 admitted to having used illegal drugs during the preceding months.[54] Nevertheless, it appeared that the Reagan/Bush anti-drug crusade enjoyed a greater success in stifling free discussion of the drug problem than in eliminating the use of drugs.

The first to speak out publicly against William Bennett were those least likely to be accused of being drug users or drug supporters, including Reagan's retired Secretary of State and a federal judge whose job included sentencing offenders. Otherwise, the pattern of timidity in discourse stems from the inability of either synthetic mainstream public discourse or protest rhetoric to focus on rational issues apart from personal scrutiny of the private lives of those who argue controversial cases.[55] The fear of talking thoughtfully about the drug problem resulted from an assumption fostered in today's public forums that a critic of drug policy must necessarily be either a self-interested drug user or a drug dealer—or at least a person so totally removed from morality as to be either dangerous or insane.

The contemporary practice of making discourse hyperpersonal—and unthoughtful—is the mark of a society having a weakened public sphere. In such an atmosphere, the nation must frequently wait for real debate until opposition to the politically correct position comes from exceptional sources. These wellsprings of dissent seemingly must be individuals whom one would expect (given their all-important personal characteristics) to support the conventional policy. This means, of course, that the dissenters will invariably be accused of being turncoats.

The manic character of the anti-drug discourse of the 1980s encouraged government agencies, schools, and other channels of public communication to outdo themselves in disseminating an essentially unexamined conclusion—that making drugs illegal was the only way to handle their use and abuse. In the atmosphere of an exaggerated anti-drug consensus, the withered, albeit formally democratic, political discussion tended to sustain, rather than dampen, propaganda. Was this abetment of propaganda by the political-discursive environment an exceptional case? Sadly, it was not.

Negative Debate on Affirmative Action

Another instance in which a vast social policy went unsupported by a body of intelligent public discourse is affirmative action. Civil-rights laws, court rulings, and administrative enactments together have made affirmative action an ubiquitous part of the hiring landscape in both the public and private spheres. Millions of Americans have become familiar with the practice of marking (or declining to mark) their preferred ethnic identity on a host of employment and financial-aid forms.

Given the pervasiveness of affirmative-action policies, they elicited remarkably little public discourse. Of course, the nation had seen vituperative and violent protests against court-ordered busing for racial balance; however, as regards affirmative action, per se, discussion in the public sphere followed the pattern of drug rhetoric. The one politically correct position was to celebrate affirmative action as good, and to call for more. In the public sphere, little else in the way of discussion could be easily observed, especially as regarded any possible downsides to gender- and race-based preferences in employment and in economic aid. For those committed to affirmative-action policies, the silence probably seemed natural. Like those who wanted to keep harmful drugs out of the hands of Americans, affirmative-action advocates wondered who would dare say anything against policies designed to operate against the obvious social problems of discrimination and segregation. Who could be so insensitive as to resent aid to groups who suffered historic disadvantages either by custom or by law? In particular, affirmative-action discourse on college campuses seemed to flow from a spontaneous consensus.

To be sure, a few early and vocal malcontents spoke out as part of the collegiate conversation about affirmative action. These included Jack Hirshliefer, economist at the University of California (Los Angeles), who thought it a dangerous precedent to have federal monitors intruding with national guidelines into every key decision-arena of a university. Another was Paul Seabury, Professor of Government at the University of California (Berkeley), who worried about the constitutionality of race-based preferences and who predicted that individuals would file suits to challenge them. A third was Richard Gambino, Professor of Education at Queens College (New York), who feared that affirmative-action programs would fuel "the drive toward ethnic tribalism," thereby spawning a destructive disunity.[56]

These early lamentations had a legalistic, fussy, or speculative aura when arrayed against the pressing problems of racial discrimination and inequality. Nevertheless, subsequent events lent a middling credence to the prognostications of the early affirmative-action malcontents. In 1978, Allan Bakke successfully sued the University of California (Davis) medical school for "reverse discrimination" because the school denied him admission in favor of minority candidates. In 1980, the Labor Department threatened to cut off $25 million in funds for U.C. Berkeley because the university refused to let the Department make copies of some confidential letters in an investigation of hiring practices.[57] The major reaction to incidents of this kind, both from Washington and from university administrations, was, however, a renewed commitment to make affirmative action work. For example, President Jimmy Carter issued a statement encouraging department heads to "make certain that, in the aftermath of Bakke, you continue to develop, implement, and enforce vigorously affirmative-action programs."[58]

Possible negatives of affirmative action were easy to ignore in the eagerness of colleges to prove their commitment to political equality and social equity (and to avoid embarrassing protests, federal investigations, and court suits). The absence of a free-flowing discussion among college faculties and student bodies also seemed natural because, if only a few old fussbudgets (or unreconstructed racists) opposed affirmative action, why was there a need to discuss it publicly? The easy consensus about affirmative action in academe led to a complacency among supporters of these policies. Given the conspicuous absence of cogent and widely-discussed objections to race- and gender-based preferences, what need was there among supporters either to develop their reasoning consistently or to entertain explicitly and intelligently rebut objections to affirmative action? Anyway, the issue was settled: the Feds (administrative agencies) and the courts mandated affirmative action. For devotees of social equity, the only discourse that seemed necessary was a rhetoric of moral renewal in celebration of the commitment to equity, accompanied by a few verbal barbs to spur the slow, the lukewarm, or the backsliding.

Conditions of the late 1980s supplied further evidences that seemed to sustain the dominant publicly expressed view on college campuses that affirmative action was an unalloyed good, and that more programs were needed. First, after two decades of equity efforts among the colleges, the actual results of affirmative action had proved modest. True, the number of minority students had risen sharply, but these students reported feeling alienated. During the 1988 hearings of the California State Senate, minority students testified to various slurs and insults they had experienced. For instance, a Filipina student at the U.C. Berkeley reported being told by another student to "go back to where you came from."[59] Not only were minority students not satisfied but also the growth in the percentage of minority faculty members had been slow. In 1988, non-whites accounted for 35 percent of students at the nine-campus University of California, but only 12 percent of the faculty.

Given the limited progress of affirmative action, it was not surprising to hear renewed exhortations in the early 1990s to make campuses more diverse and multicultural. Most faculty and administrators, who came to age during the Civil Rights struggle, found little reason to doubt that the inevitable response to slow affirmative-action progress was to put in place more special admissions policies, minority-aid programs, and ethnic-based support groups. At Stanford University, for example, a blue-ribbon panel acknowledged that the campus had "achieved unprecedented racial and ethnic diversity," but they nevertheless called for "a new commitment" to "interactive pluralism."[60] Around the nation, educators called for new contacts between colleges and high schools to seek out minority students who were not yet planning college work.[61]

Another spur to augmented affirmative action was the rise of racially-motivated altercations on college campuses. Between 1986 and 1989, 175 college campuses reported episodes of insulting graffiti, hate notes, and even brawls.[62] Further, at Temple University, a group of students established a White Pride group to balance what its 89 members believed to be a "pro-minority" stance by the university's administration.[63] White Student Unions were reported to have emerged at other universities, including Mississippi State.[64] The standard explanation for the increase in unpleasant ethnic incidents and racial polarization was that a lingering White racism had flared up again, a situation that demanded further and more intense efforts to promote acceptance of cultural diversity. For instance, Charles V. Willie, Professor of Education at Harvard, argued that campus racial tensions were the result of White males "finally losing an entitlement that they had thought they would have to themselves forever."[65] James E. Blackwell, Professor of Sociology at the University of Massachusetts at Boston, put the blame on the Reagan administration, arguing that during the Reagan era students "haven't seen leaders forcefully assert that racism is a disease that will not be tolerated."[66]

In the belief that residual White racism was essentially the sole cause of racial incidents, universities acted to beef up their minority-affairs offices. Sometimes, this action came at the administration's initiative. At other times, action resulted from minority-student protests like that at Connecticut College where students took over an administration building to demand more minority enrollment and more staffing for the minority cultural center.[67] To spur responses of this kind, the Ford Foundation announced a grant program of $1.6 million to support new or revised cultural-diversity efforts.[68]

In addition to augmenting existing equity and multicultural programs, universities took two major new initiatives aimed at stemming the rise of racial incidents. The first of these was an effort to establish official policies against racist and sexist speech. For instance, the University of Pennsylvania banned "any behavior, verbal or physical,

310

that stigmatizes or victimizes individuals" and "creates an intimidating or offensive environment."[69] While most such guidelines were apparently intended to prohibit overt insults and epithets—so-called "fighting words"—many prohibitions were drafted in so vague a manner as arguably to prohibit legitimate comment or humor, and certainly they discouraged discussion and debate. A federal judge struck down the code at the University of Michigan on just this basis.

The second category of responses to racial tension on campus was the effort to establish new, required workshops or courses designed to build acceptance of what was called "cultural diversity." At Middlebury College in Vermont, students were attending a new student workshop in cultural diversity that included a dramatic skit depicting Black students receiving subtle and not-so-subtle insults. Beginning in 1990 at the College of Wooster (Ohio), all freshmen were taking a course on "Difference, Power, and Discrimination," using one or two anthologies: *Racism and Sexism*, by Paula Rothenberg, and *From Different Shores*, by Ronald Takaki.[70] In 1988, at the University of Michigan, a group of faculty members put forth a proposed compulsory course on racism for students in the college of literature, science, and the arts (about half of the student body).[71] Stanford University revised its core curriculum to include more attention to minority writers and to issues of race and gender, and a University Committee on Minority Issues proposed a further requirement that students take an ethnic studies course.[72] In addition to explicitly curricular responses to diversity, many universities began to sponsor cultural/recreational programs with the same objective. The University of Toledo mounted a week-long program of cultural events that included a mock "massacre" in which students strung up an effigy that symbolized ethnic and cultural stereotypes.[73]

Although the rise of racial incidents acted as a spur to a more intense promotion of affirmative action, ethnic tensions on campuses also acted as a catalyst for the first major public debate about affirmative action. The enhanced programs of affirmative action and multicultural education were a natural outgrowth of one particular view of the campus racial climate, namely, that campus racial tension resulted from vestiges of White racism not yet rooted out.

Some campus opinion leaders, however, saw in the incidents a different cause; therefore, they offered solutions that not only went beyond the customary assumptions of discourse on affirmative action but also explicitly challenged them in some cases. For instance, William R. Beer,

Professor of Sociology at Brooklyn College, denied the conventional assumption that affirmative action reduces racial tension. Writing of Black students at the University of Massachusetts main campus who occupied a building to demand more minority enrollment, he argued that the administration's prompt agreement to preferential enrollment resulted in "increasing white students' resentment of minority-group students."[74] Beer further argued that administrations erred in allowing Black students to have separate housing, such as the New Africa House at Massachusetts, because these led to greater tensions among ethnic groups.

Other dissenting views of affirmative action included those of Kelley L. Ross, instructor in philosophy at Los Angeles Valley College, who argued that campus programs to celebrate group differences were more likely to lead to ethnic tension than to tolerance. Ross favored putting more emphasis on the elements of common ground as principles of American democracy.[75] Chester E. Finn, Jr., of Vanderbilt University, claimed that preferential programs are inherently divisive because they must be continually propped up with reminders that the beneficiaries are oppressed victims. As an alternative to having groups "celebrating their victimization," he recommended a common, multicultural but integrated curriculum that allowed students to view the full mosaic of American history.[76] Alan C. Kors, professor of history at the University of Pennsylvania, warned that non-curricular multicultural programs run by student-life officers were the most likely to force a single view on unsuspecting freshmen. These programs, he said, "establish an official history of America, an official agenda of moral priorities, an official view of race, gender, and class." Further, Kors charged that campus ethnic and women's centers are often dominated by an unrepresentative radical fringe whose pronouncements increase campus tension.[77]

Thomas Sowell of the conservative Hoover Institution weighed in with some of the most forceful challenges to the standard view of new ethnic tensions on college campuses. Sowell criticized faculty and administrations for responding to the new spate of ugly campus incidents with only a "more fervent reiteration of the unexamined beliefs and obligatory clichés about race that have prevailed on most campuses since the 1960s." Sowell argued that "vicious racial incidents have been most prominent where the prevailing liberal (or radical) racial vision has been most prominent. The new racism is not a vestige but a backlash." Sowell argued that the prevalent "body-count" approach to affirmative action only contributed to a rise in tensions. On the one hand, preferential admissions turned outstanding students into artificial failures by forcing Blacks at the 75th percentile to compete with Whites who scored at the 99th. On the other hand, he argued, not only did preferential admissions irritate Whites but also administrations worsened the situation by capitulating to minority-group radicals who demanded separate programs and accommodations.[78]

The newly emerging and tentative conversation about affirmative action in higher education began to spill out into the general society with the appearance of Shelby Steele's book, *The Content of Our Character*, published in 1990.[79] An English professor at San Jose State University, Steele wrote of his own experiences with discrimination and racial anger, culminating in his eventual rejection of affirmative action. Steele acknowledged that "blacks have been terribly victimized," but pointed to the irony that today's Black college students are more likely to view themselves as racial victims than their predecessors of the 1950s. Yet, the earlier generation of African-American students not only experienced more vicious discrimination but also they were not able to benefit from today's "preferential admission and other special concessions." Steele explained this paradox by claiming that today's sensitivity about victimization "too often amounts to a recomposition of denied doubts and anxieties they are unwilling to look at."[80]

Steele contended that victim-based entitlement programs, such as affirmative action, are a "Faustian bargain," providing short-run benefits at the expense of crippling students in the long run with an impoverished ability to exercise personal initiative.[81] For Steele, affirmative action is "more bad than good." By changing the concept of discrimination to "mere color rather than actual injury," affirmative action provided colleges with "cosmetic diversity" to obscure the blemish that only 26 percent of Black students were graduating within six years of admission.[82] Further, he maintained, the preferential aspect of diversity programs only enlarged the self-doubt that many Black students already carried as a result of studying in predominantly White institutions. Steele attributed the rise of racial tension on campus to the twenty-year-old policy of treating students according to their ethnic identities. Students are encouraged to see themselves first as members of an ethnic group such that "each group mythologizes and mystifies its difference." Hence, the groups are quick to take on the us-versus-them mentality that serves as a seedbed for race-based incidents. Black students see racism in every overt insult or perceived slight, and Whites resent the demands of Black student leaders as well as the concessions that these demands bring from administrators. In this climate, Steele argued, successful Blacks must frequently announce their racial solidarity or face being marginalized.[83]

If Steele's book was a harbinger of a coming political debate on the basic assumptions of affirmative action, William J. Bennett opened the season on the issue. In the fall, 1990, Bennett announced that the Republican Party would make race- and gender-based preferential hiring policies a matter for political attack. Bennett, the erstwhile drug czar, was at the time preparing to head the Republican Party, and his statement suggested that he saw political gold in stirring up what had heretofore been—on the surface at least—a settled issue. "I believe that the idea of affirmative action—giving people credit for a job in the absence of a prior showing of prior discrimination simply on the basis of their race—is wrong," Bennett asserted.[84]

What are we to make of the new public discord on affirmative action? Certainly, putting affirmative action into political terms would be jolting and possibly hurtful to persons accustomed to hearing only a one-sided public treatment of the issue. In a sense, the new debate could be said to undo a generation of progress in building support for the nation's growing diversity. Some have even expressed the view that it is inherently racist to oppose affirmative action. Jeffrey C. Chin, Assistant Professor of Sociology at Le Moyne College, articulated this position:

> It is no longer acceptable to be overtly racist. Now prejudice can be expressed in different ways. People can say, "I don't like busing, affirmative action, or welfare." But what they're actually saying is, "I don't like the people who benefit from those programs." In their minds, those people are black people."[85]

While we may long for the old days in which affirmative action was a relatively settled matter, at least in public expression, I believe we have reason to be optimistic about a full public airing of views on the issue. If we have any faith at all in the viability of democracy and the efficacy of public discourse, then we have little to fear from a vigorous debate that defies conventional pieties, goes beyond slogans, and eschews reflexive "-ist" and "-ism" accusations. The possible outcomes of a full debate over affirmative action are not necessarily negative. The debate could be expected to result in one or more of these not-unfavorable outcomes: (1) a deeper and wider support for present policies, (2) new policies with broader support, or (3) if nothing like a new consensus emerges, at least a constructive letting off of steam accumulated during the past 20 years.

This is not to say that attaining a new homeostasis on affirmative action will be easy or pleasant. Bill Bennett's attack on minority hiring programs was obviously politically self-serving and was unavoidably divisive. The utility of affirmative action as a political scapegoat became clear in Senator Jesse Helms's reelection campaign for the U.S. Senate in the fall, 1990. Campaigning against a Black man, Helms profited politically from accusing his opponent of favoring racial hiring quotas. One ad by Helms showed a dejected White worker tearing up a job rejection letter.[86] If we believe in a democracy that is sustained by public expression, we may nevertheless have reason to think that conditions will be better once issues of affirmative action have been aired. From the standpoint of propaganda, we have more to fear from a rhetoric that is unconsciously divisive than from a rhetoric in which controversial assertions are explicitly set out with evidence. Further, affirmative-action programs have been, up to this point, chiefly a matter of administrative action or court order. Because the concept was never gauged by full public debate over a sustained period, the public's commitment to equity programs is necessarily untested.

I have recently had occasion to observe directly the impact of an open, albeit small-scale, public discussion of affirmative action—and the results are not fearful. I have taught at least one section of the general-education course in public speaking or debate during most semesters since 1971. I cannot recall hearing, until recently, even a single speech on affirmative action. However, in the last couple of years, several of my students have addressed the topic; three of these speakers publicly expressed either their frustrations with, or opposition to, programs of affirmative action. Speeches against affirmative action are remarkable not only in view of the longstanding absence of public talk about equity programs but also because public-speaking students normally recoil from any controversial topic that might increase their already high level of stagefright.

The first classroom speech I ever heard opposing affirmative action was by a young woman who discussed her own working-class background and her difficulty in mustering the money to attend school. She argued that her needs were no less than those of ethnic-minority students, but that she received less help. The next semester, a young man argued that "strong affirmative action" was a form of reverse discrimination against White males that not only lowered efficiency in the economy but also did not necessarily benefit individuals in proportion to how much their own ancestors had suffered. In a third speech, a young woman began by describing a bulletin board she had passed by on which were listed all manner of programs, clubs, and scholarships earmarked for one ethnic group or another. She felt excluded from benefits that she herself might use to overcome her own problems. Each of these three speeches brought about a constructive, albeit tense, discussion among class members. The last-mentioned speech prompted two students—a native-born Hispanic male and a young woman from a Salvadoran refugee family—to deliver addresses in support of affirmative action. What is significant, I think, is how quickly students were able publicly to formulate and express their thoughts on affirmative action. The speeches neither set out ideas that were previously unknown to the students, nor did the addresses foment a situation of tension where consensus previously had dwelled. Rather, the speeches merely brought to light existing thoughts and feelings in a forum that both required and encouraged analysis, reasoning, and respect for opposing speakers. Unlike the official rhetoric of affirmative action, described above, this give-and-take atmosphere found students going beyond institutional slogans and unexamined educational jargon.

Pretending to Talk about Abortion

If affirmative action is just beginning to enter the public sphere as a subject for debate, the abortion controversy, ironically, is only a bit ahead. Abortion was a topic much debated during the 1960s, but with the Supreme Court's 1973 *Roe v. Wade* decision, the pro-choice side became inactive. Abortion supporters were satisfied to rely on the Supreme Court's grant of unfettered access to (first-trimester) abortion based on an implicit Constitutional right to privacy.

At the same time that *Roe v. Wade* met the needs of the pro-choice group, the ruling energized a new pro-life campaign by abortion opponents. The debate on abortion after 1973, however, was a curiosity. Unable directly to overturn a Supreme Court decision, pro-life campaigners were driven by frustration as they sought political support. Since the law allowing abortion was seemingly set in stone, politicians were inclined to mollify pro-lifers and, at the same time, take little or no specific action. Further contributing to the bizarre quality of the abortion debate was the tendency for pro-choice politicians either to keep prudently silent or to speak vaguely in an effort to avoid offending the vocal pro-lifers. The refrain went something like this: "I'm personally opposed to abortion, but the Supreme Court has spoken ...." What ensued was a split in the public personality: action was separated from expression, and political motion proceeded without actual results.

The sham ended when Supreme Court put abortion back into the public sphere in July 1989. In *Webster v. Reproductive Health Services*, the Supreme Court ruled that states could pass legislation restricting abortions.[87] Within weeks, the whole rhetorical scene changed in the politics of abortion. Both the pro-life and pro-choice forces geared up for political combat on the state level. Politicians were now faced with the need to match words with actions. Having the power to affect abortion law, legislators could no longer placate the pro-lifers while doing nothing constructive. At the same time, pro-choice legislators could no longer merely declare their personal distaste for abortion while standing safely behind the Supreme Court's ruling. Candidates for public office quickly responded to the newly enlivened abortion issue in the months after the summer of 1989. For instance, a pro-choice Democrat running for governor of New Jersey, James Florio, explicitly attacked his opponent for supporting restrictions on federal funding of abortion.[88] Pro-life Republicans now experienced a new political vulnerability because for the first time pro-choice voters had reason to act against them. The GOP, which had gained much political capital by feckless nods and winks to the pro-life position, now found itself needing to respond to the new political situation. Because pro-choice voters outnumber those committed to the pro-life position, the GOP became, if not pro-choice, at least less vocally pro-life. After losses in the 1989 midterm elections, in which pro-choice candidates did well, the party changed its tune. Lee Atwater, Chairman of the Republican National Committee, expressed the party's new openness on abortion: "I want to make sure that everybody feels comfortable as Republicans, regardless of what their position on abortion is."[89]

For those Americans who believe there should be no state-imposed limits at all on abortion, it may seem a merely academic point to argue that the nation's democratic health is well-served by putting abortion back into the public sphere. Whereas a pro-choice activist might argue that the *right* to have an abortion carries a higher moral weight than the power to give *speeches* on the subject, a dichotomy of rights *versus* rhetoric may be misleading. Constitutional rights—and, to a lesser extent, human rights—are a matter of everlasting argument and discovery. Few in the 1950s, for example, could have imagined a Constitutional right to abortion, but by 1973, this position had won sway in the Supreme Court. The new view of abortion rights was born of, and was nurtured by, discourse. We may not assume that the social definitions of rights are unchanging. The 13th Amendment to the Constitution (1865) overturned the Dred Scott decision which, a scant seven years earlier, had seemingly settled the question of slavery by extending the right to hold slaves to all states of the Union. Rights are sustained by a social consensus that is the product of deliberative discourse. Those who rely on today's court rulings for their rights may have cause tomorrow for regret of their lack of rhetorical acumen.

The recent move toward a new national debate on abortion seemed to make the nation healthier from the standpoint of democracy and public deliberation. No longer did the pro-choice majority sit back, smugly relying on the courts rather than on their own powers to develop and sustain a democratic public opinion. No longer did politicians make cynical overtures to pro-life groups. No longer did pro-choice politicians nervously temporize on their commitment. No longer were pro-life adherents put in the frustrating position of being alternatively patronized and ignored—a rhetorical position of irrelevancy that bred hatred and violence. The old rhetorical climate was a witch's brew of complacency, political opportunism, euphemism, and malaise. The new climate may be hot and occasionally ugly, but it is more likely to bring a wider understanding of opposing positions. Through open democratic debate, the opportunity exists to build a climate of mutual respect, though perhaps not agreement.

DEMOCRACY'S DILEMMA

Neither political advertising nor TV news nor protest demonstrations supply the kind of cogent discussion that is capable of connecting people and their communities to pressing issues. Although America retains every possible form of democratic politics—open political parties, freedom to organize, voting rights, and regular elections—the face of our democracy exhibits many fissures resulting not only from our PAC- and media-neutralized speakers but also from our dysfunctional political communities. During the last few generations, propaganda has been the cement that held the fractured political edifice together. In the cases of the drug crisis and of affirmative action, orchestration from government agencies and schools has been the order of the day. In the case of abortion, vague speaking in TV-news and news conferences held sway. The public sphere has been debased by the many faces of a propagandized public communication, from the manias of drug rhetoric to the clichés and euphemisms of affirmative action to the schizophrenic separation of talk and performance in the arena of abortion.

Meanwhile, the selective nature of propaganda's seductions has obscured the frequent debasement of genuine discussion. There is nothing that everyone falls for, yet everyone falls for something. Because propaganda's temptations are constant and omnipresent, they seduce some of the people all of the time on every issue. As a result, the real problem of propaganda is not a total control of public perception by Big Brother but, rather, an accumulative casting up of blind spots that, together, eventually cloud Americans' view of public life. As dialogue seems hopeless or even undesirable, the possibility emerges that Americans might retain the forms of democracy while gradually losing a genuinely democratic public life. Wherever the public agenda has been set before discussion begins, free speech becomes a technical right. Whenever public opinion is channeled, the free flow of communication represents an empty boast. To the extent that actual choices are absent, ignored, or obscured, free elections become bland public rituals.

The upshot of this chapter is to sober the too cheerful assurances of communication practitioners that the forms of democracy render propaganda socially neutral. The converse seems more the case, i.e., that the forms of propaganda neutralize democracy. Democracy's somnabulized speakers and impotent communities continue to create a false impression that all is well. The old, oratorical democracy of yesteryear exists in a new, improved form, but only in our nostalgia. The audiences for TV speakers are undeniably vast, but speakers only infrequently ply their trade in an uninterrupted, unedited, unpackaged manner. Local, state, and national electorates continue in existence, but the members of these groups enjoy few forums at which to meet in open, free, and public deliberation.

Today's absence of prior restraints on communication suggests, further, that Americans have become inured to the go-getter's view that our propagandized forms of communication still implement democracy's objectives. Many are so collectively skeptical of restraints on communication that freedom of speech has been applied to such content-free vehicles of political expression as nude dancing, aggressive panhandling, and corporate funds doled out to politicians. In a media age, however, scrupulosity about individual free speech may be irrelevant in the maintaining of democracy against propaganda.

What of the future, then? Was it possible that the "talk show democracy" of the 1992 Bush-Clinton-Perot campaign portended a fuller participation by citizens in public affairs? An affirmative answer would have required evidence of a new urge, both among leaders and major media channels, to abandon such entertainment material as saxophones and sexual trivia (both having been featured items in talk shows of campaign '92). Further, an affirmative answer would have required signs that electronic programs of political dialogue were breaking free from the old formulae of one-shot speeches, one-sided political ads, and interviews featuring a single guest, a grandstanding program host, and a few stage-struck citizen questioners.

Little in the early months of the Clinton era suggested the emergence of significant public forums in which advocates could pursue a point/counterpoint debate focused on an important topic, and in which viewers could ask questions, make statements, and register their collective responses. Clinton seemed to fall back on the old standbys of post-TV political communication: executive prerogative (in the form of national TV addresses) complemented by the out-of-the-mouths-of-babes approach (i.e., question-and-answer sessions with citizens). At the same time, Ross Perot, 1992's chief proponent of national town-meeting-style government, turned his first post-election nationally-televised "referendum" (March 21, 1993) into a kind of telemarketing. After steering his audience into several pat "yes" or "no" responses, Perot pitched subscriptions to his United We Stand America organization.

If more speeches, more interviews, and more political advertising do not supply a solution to public passivity, what forms of communication might help Americans become more resistant to propaganda?

ENDNOTES

1. See Michael Schudson, *Advertising, the Uneasy Persuasion* (New York: Basic Books, 1984), and Todd Gitlin, *Inside Prime Time* (New York: Pantheon, 1985).

2. James Rorty, *Our Master's Voice: Advertising* (New York: John Day, 1934).

3. *San Jose Mercury News*, 4/12/90: 7B.

4. *San Jose Mercury News*, 9/17/89: 4P.

5. *New York Times*, 8/31/90: A10.

6. *San Jose Mercury News*, 9/17/89: 4P.

7. Louisville, KY *Courier-Journal*, 2/23/86: D3.

8. *San Jose Mercury News*, 11/1/90: 4A.

9. *San Francisco Chronicle*, 3/20/87: 11.

10. *San Jose Mercury News*, 11/1/90: 4A.

11. Kathleen H. Jamieson, *Eloquence in an Electronic Age: The Transformation of Political Speechmaking* (New York: Oxford University Press, 1988): 91.

12. Palo Alto, CA *Peninsula Times Tribune*, 11/18/90: B6.

13. *New York Times*, 1/3/91: A14.

14. Robert E. Park, *The Crowd and the Public and Other Essays*, ed. by H. Elsner (Chicago: University of Chicago Press, 1972).

15. See Benjamin Ginsberg, *The Captive Public: How Mass Opinion Promotes State Power* (New York: Basic Books, 1986): 59-85.

16. Ginsberg, *Captive*: 75.

17. George Gallup and Saul F. Rae, *The Pulse of Democracy: The Public Opinion Poll and How It Works* (New York: Simon and Schuster, 1940).

18. Louisville, KY *Courier-Journal*, 8/20/80: A11.

19. *New York Times*, 10/5/90: A1.

20. *New York Times*, 10/8/90: A1.

21. *San Francisco Examiner*, 4/10/88: A20.

22. *Chronicle of Higher Education*, 5/16/90: A33.

23. *San Jose Mercury News*, 6/24/90: 1A, 13A.

24. Palo Alto, CA *Peninsula Times Tribune*, 11/3/90: B3.

25. *San Jose Mercury News*, 11/19/90: 10A.

26. See Robert N. Bellah, et al., *Habits of the Heart* (New York: Harper and Row, 1985).

27. Cf. John Dewey, *The Public and Its Problems* (Chicago: Swallow Press, 1927): 28ff.

28. *New York Times*, 12/13/90: B1.

29. Primary texts for the archetypal New England town and the Athenian city-state are, respectively, Alexis de Tocqueville, *Democracy in America* (various editions) and Aristotle, *The Athenian Constitution* and *The Rhetoric*.

30. The notion of pseudo-communities adopted here may be pursued further in Richard Sennett, *The Fall of Public Man* (New York: Vintage Books, 1977).

31. Palo Alto, CA *Peninsula Times Tribune*, 10/4/90: A10.

32. *San Jose Mercury News*, 12/11/89: 7B.

33. *San Jose Mercury News*, 8/4/90: 11A.

34. *San Jose Mercury News*, 8/28/90: 5B.

35. *Newsweek*, 10/31/88: 16.

36. Louisville, KY *Courier-Journal*, 9/7/80: D1, D4.

37. *New York Times*, 4/20/90: A8.

38. Palo Alto, CA *Peninsula Times Tribune*, 2/27/90: B4.

39. *San Francisco Chronicle*, 3/20/87: 11.

40. *Chronicle of Higher Education*, 2/21/90: A31.

41. *San Jose Mercury News*, 1/4/91: 6B.

42. Palo Alto, CA *Peninsula Times Tribune*, 6/19/90: A7.

43. *Chronicle of Higher Education*, 1/3/90: A1.

44. *Life in Pursuit of Artificial Paradise* (N.Y.: Dutton, 1989).

45. *San Jose Mercury News*, 5/7/89: 5P.

46. Palo Alto, CA *Peninsula Times Tribune*, 11/18/89: A10.

47. *San Jose Mercury News*, 11/7/89: 18A.

48. Palo Alto, CA *Peninsula Times Tribune*, 11/18/89: A10.

49. *San Jose Mercury News*, 12/13/89: 2A.

50. *San Jose Mercury News*, 8/20/90: 5B.

51. *San Jose Mercury News*, 11/26/89: 4C.

52. *San Jose Mercury News*, 11/7/89: 18A.

53. *San Jose Mercury News*, 11/26/89: 4C.

54. *Financial World*, 10/3/89: 35.

55. Is it relevant that I am *not* among the 50 million Americans who have used illegal drugs? I relegate this confession to the endnotes because I do not want to reinforce the dangerous idea that advocacy must be treated as a mere reflection of personality. To the contrary, my point is that *anyone* should be able to engage in discussion about the drug issue on the basis of rational discourse, regardless of his or her life history or lifestyle.

56. See Sidney Hook, Paul Kurtz and Miro Todorovich, eds., *The Idea of a Modern University* (Buffalo: Prometheus Books, 1974): 252, 181, 215.

57. *Chronicle of Higher Education*, 9/22/80: 4.

58. *Chronicle of Higher Education*, 7/31/78: 5.

59. *San Francisco Chronicle*, 10/5/88: A10.

60. *Chronicle of Higher Education*, 4/12/89: A17.

61. *Chronicle of Higher Education*, 11/8/89: B2.

62. *New York Times*, 5/22/89: A13.

63. *San Jose Mercury News*, 11/24/88: 2C.

64. *Chronicle of Higher Education*, 5/16/90: B5.

65. *Chronicle of Higher Education*, 4/26/89: A30.

66. *Chronicle of Higher Education*, 4/26/89: A30.

67. *Chronicle of Higher Education*, 3/22/89: A33.

68. *Chronicle of Higher Education*, 2/14/90: A27.

69. *Chronicle of Higher Education*, 10/4/89: A38.

70. *Chronicle of Higher Education*, 6/27/90: A32.

71. *Chronicle of Higher Education*, 11/16/88: A35.

72. *Chronicle of Higher Education*, 11/12/89: A15, A17.

73. *Chronicle of Higher Education*, 1/10/90: A33.

74. *Chronicle of Higher Education*, 4/27/88: B2.

75. *Chronicle of Higher Education*, 7/5/90: B4.

76. *Chronicle of Higher Education*, 6/13/90: A40.

77. *Chronicle of Higher Education*, 11/8/89: A22.

78. *San Jose Mercury News*, 5/28/89: 1P, 8P.

79. Shelby Steele, *The Content of Our Character: A New Vision of Race in America* (N.Y.: St. Martin's, 1990) .

80. Steele, *Content:* 61.

81. Steele, *Content:* 14, 111.

82. Steele, *Content:* 113, 115-116.

83. Steele, *Content:* 141, 136-137, 143, 147, 171.

84. *San Jose Mercury News,* 11/30/90: 4A.

85. *Chronicle of Higher Education,* 4/26/89: A30.

86. *San Jose Mercury News,* 11/30/90: 4A.

87. *San Jose Mercury News,* 10/18/89: 16A.

88. *Newsweek,* 10/8/89: 35.

89. *New York Times,* 11/10/89: A1.

Rapid Response Team Roll of Honor
NOMINATION FORM

To: Executive Registrar,   *From:* _____
      Rapid Response Team   *Rapid Response Team Captain*
      Honor Roll Fulfillment Center

Let it be known that as one of our earliest supporters, the above-named **Rapid Response Team Captain** has joined the Clinton/Gore team in the fight to restore the genius and greatness of America. As a member of the Clinton Pre-Convention Team, the above-named **Team Captain** was one of the first to make a commitment to change America with Clinton/Gore in 1992.

This early Clinton/Gore supporter has shown a steadfast commitment to change in America by submitting for certification the <u>**Rapid Response Team Member Nominees**</u> listed below.

Therefore, you are hereby officially directed, by the Team Captain named above, to inscribe on the **Rapid Response Team Roll of Honor**, the full names of the **Rapid Response Team Nominees listed below.** This document will be co-signed by President Clinton and Vice-President Gore, and will be unveiled on Inauguration Day, January 20, 1993, and thereafter will be kept permanently, first at the Clinton/Gore White House and then at Bill Clinton's Presidential Library.

Empowered by the leadership of the above-named **Team Captain**, each of the undersigned **Rapid Response Team Member Nominees** has fulfilled the true obligation of all Americans: **to always be prepared to recreate the strength of the American community and to reaffirm our belief that tomorrow can be better than today, if we have the moral courage to take personal responsibility and make it so.**

	Name	Address	City/State	Zip Code
1.				
2.				
3.				
4.				
5.				
6.				
7.				
8.				
9.				
10.				

Please use the back side of this certificate as needed to register additional names.

These **Nominees** are hereby named for certification and will be forever recognized by all who examine this document as true **agents of change.** They have given much of themselves to restore integrity to the political process and to renew hope in America. They have come together to defeat the radical Right-Wing fear-mongers and conservative character assassins, and they offer hope to America through their strong support of Bill Clinton and Al Gore's message of unity and their economic plan to "Put People First."

Let it be known that each of the above named **Rapid Response Team Member Nominees**, along with their Team **Captain**, has contributed to an historic mission to keep the focus of the 1992 Presidential election on the future of America.

    Signed by _____ Submission date _____
         (Rapid Response Team Captain)

IMPORTANT MESSAGE FOR RAPID RESPONSE TEAM CAPTAIN: Congratulations! To provide the Executive Registrar with ample time to make all inscriptions, do not delay! Please return this form to us at P.O. Box 8803, Little Rock, AR 72231-8803 immediately upon completion!

A Participatory or an Honorific Public?

CHAPTER 8

PROPAGANDA AND THE PUBLIC

When propaganda becomes controversial and even offends, it poses relatively little danger because the attempt to manipulate has prompted an opposing reaction. Propaganda is most vicious not when it angers but when it ingratiates itself through government programs that fit our desires or world views, through research or religion that supplies pleasing answers, through news that captures our interest, through educational materials that promise utopia, and through pleasurable films, TV, sports, and art. The episodes of propaganda reviewed up to this point suggest that the chief problem of propaganda is its ability to be simultaneously subtle and seductive—and to grow in a political environment of neutralized speakers and disempowered communities.

When covert social influence through propaganda threatens a well-informed and democratic way of life, what is the solution? Polemicists and political activists, the most alert exposers of propaganda, favor the purge approach to covert orchestration and manipulation. They alternately scheme or agitate to remove their ostensibly unenlightened opponents from key positions in the channels of communication. Coming from the Right, the urge to purge may been seen in William F. Buckley, Jr.'s, early call to Yale alumni to act against professors whom Buckley contended were indoctrinating their children with an agnostic and socialistic propaganda.[1] Coming from the Left, the purge mindset may be seen in the effort to ban or rewrite books that contain either references to religion or language that is deemed insensitive by spokespersons of women's and minority groups. An extreme form of the purge mentality took hold when rightist politicians of the House Un-American Activities Committee strove to blacklist writers and actors who had been active in liberal or leftist politics during the 1930s. A garden variety of the mindset on the Left is evident on university campuses among those forces that their detractors call the "P.C. Police" who act as sensitive gatekeepers in the efforts to stanch perceived harassments of various kinds. Political activists, whether they are moderates or extremists, leftists or rightists, long for a utopia in which the channels of propaganda are safely under the sway of their own brand of correct thinking.

NO PANACEAS, NO LIBERATORS

Aside from the anti-German manias of 1917-1918 and the Red Scare of the McCarthy Era, the polemical or purge approach to propaganda has won little support from the general public. This is fortunate because the impulse to ban disfavored communication can itself become a self-interested manipulation. Two more typically American responses to the specter of propaganda have been contributed by journalists and educators. These two classes of professionals are notable for their frequent claims to protect public opinion from propaganda. Arguing from Lippmann's position that the newspaper is the *bible* of democracy, journalists are wont to describe themselves as knights who skewer Demon Propaganda with verbal lances. Educators, particularly proponents of critical thinking, aver that they have discovered ways to immunize people from the allures of linguistic manipulation. What are we to make of the claims that education is a panacea against propaganda, and that journalists liberate their readers from symbolic intrigue?

Because education and news are leading channels of propaganda, we have reason to question the anti-propaganda credentials of America's teachers and journalists. Reviews of journalism and education given, in chapters 4 and 5 respectively, suggest that neither person nor profession may rightly claim an immunity from charges of using propaganda.

No Salvation through Journalism

Many commentators on today's poor state of discourse look to improved journalism as the primary route to restore the environment of vibrant political expression in which propaganda withers. The hopeful recourse to journalism is natural because today's public sphere is increasingly channelized by newspapers, radio, and television whose professionals claim the responsibility (and assert the prerogative) to mediate public discourse.

Suggestions abound as to how journalism might better promote democratic public opinion. One recommendation is for news organizations to give more coverage to campaign issues instead of focusing on political personalities, media events, or electoral horse races. Others call for more investigative journalism to reveal behind-the-scenes conditions, events, and operatives. A related plea is for more analysis stories to put the minutiae of news into perspective. Journalists constantly demand more news conferences in which they may put challenging questions to leaders. Still other commentators recommend breaking up media monopolies or using subsidies to permit diverse groups and organizations to publish newspapers.[2]

Notwithstanding many persuasive dissertations on the importance of a free press in building a responsible citizenry, it may be too much to expect that a single profession can undo the weaknesses of today's public communication. Press critics themselves point out some obvious limits to what journalism can do to energize public expression. A. J. Liebling once estimated that journalists uncover only half of the truth of a situation, and that the constraints of reporting a story allow the reporter to communicate only half of what he or she actually has learned.[3]

Liebling's comment raises the question of whether journalism ever could sustain its pretention to construct news that accurately speaks for society's opinion leaders. It seems unreasonable to expect that journalism's professionals, no matter what their degree of competence, could by themselves paint a panorama of news that fully represented important advocates, significant political positions, and emerging world views. In this view, it would be better to have journalism recede into the background and turn, instead, to the natural environment of discourse that emerges when society's spokespersons are turned loose to argue and disagree in open forums.

The Watergate scandal of the early 1970s highlighted the essential weakness of a journalism-simulated public forum in which reporting about advocates and events takes precedence over allowing speakers to express themselves. Investigative journalism turned out to have played a relatively small part in bringing to light the effort of the Nixon administration to use illegal wire-taps and break-ins against its political enemies. Having no power to compel truthful testimony—or any testimony at all—the press mainly reported leaks from prosecutors, courts, and various officials involved.[4] Until the Senate conducted hearings on Watergate, in which speakers had opportunity to make statements and respond to questions, the public remained largely in the dark about whether the Nixon administration or its critics had been making the better case.

The same distinction between the simulated public sphere of journalism and the natural rhetorical context of opposing advocates became evident during the 1992 presidential election campaign. Even though the so-called "talk-show democracy" of 1992 may have packed less weight than the archetypal Lincoln/Douglas debates, the ability of propagandists to skew the news with irrelevant personal innuendo was lessened when people actually heard the major candidates speaking and answering (or not answering) questions at length. Allowing candidates to speak at length, even in informal settings, seemed in 1992 to have reduced the influence of propagandistic slogans and images.

Even when news professionals attain the highest levels of independence and competence, media news itself always represents a pseudo-context (to extend Boorstin's notion of the publicity-seeking pseudo-event).[5] The news is a packaged forum designed to make public affairs easily digestible for the casual reader or viewer. Discourse as summarized in the news inevitably represents a synthetic concoction since, as press critic Edward Epstein noted, news is not something that occurs and then waits to be found.[6] News represents a fabricated model of the public world. Just as tourists' buses and Hilton Hotels supply a pale version of foreign living, the news-of-the-day conveys only a relatively colorless outline of society's strivings. Just as foreign travel can be homogenized in the interests of safety and comfort, so too is the news conveyed in routine formats that increase ease-of-understanding at the cost of lessening the full experience. Manufactured from various available story lines—including conflict, irony, action, nostalgia—the news is fleshed out with whatever materials (particularly pictures) are readily available to reporters and editors.[7] (See chapter 4.)

Although the norms of journalism help make the news of the day conveniently comprehensible, they introduce a certain artificiality. For instance, journalism's norm of conflict, i.e., the two-sided mode of treatment, helps make the public sphere somewhat of a synthetic construction that imperfectly reflects actual arguments and implications about a subject. To take but one instance, the mainstream U.S. press, to avoid seeming anti-Nixon, held off emphasizing the Watergate scandal during the 1972 Nixon/McGovern election.[8] News organizations would sometimes hold back a Watergate report until it could be "balanced" with a denial from the White House. The result was to allow the Administration to cast the scandal as a simple political brouhaha of no special significance. Had news about the Watergate activities continued in this vein, President Nixon never would have been forced to resign.

To expose news as an uncertain antidote to propaganda, we need not emphasize the demonstrated pressures placed on news professionals by powerful institutions and ideological groups. We have only to turn to the norms and practices of journalism themselves to find that the news is an uncertain ally of full and open political debate. The news supplies merely the skeletal outlines of public affairs into which propagandists may insert self-serving details. The news is an unreliable panacea against manipulation because the news itself is ever vulnerable to becoming a channel of propaganda.

Critical Thinking Is Not Enough

If journalism is no sure cure for propaganda, what can we make of the claims by educators that they have special anti-propaganda powers? Since the 1940s, the classic educational remedy for manipulative communication has been the curriculum of "critical thinking" taught in America's colleges and high schools. One of the most widely known approaches to critical thinking has been the Public Doublespeak program of the National Council of Teachers of English. The anti-propaganda approach favored by the NCTE is reflected in a quarterly newsletter published by the organization that contains exposés of misleading and propagandistic language.

A good summary of the NCTE program may be found in William Lutz's book, *Double-Speak*, based on a compilation of material from the NCTE's *Quarterly Review of Doublespeak*. Lutz focused on how persuaders manipulate language, for instance, by using inoffensive words to disguise reality, by employing insider jargon (technical language), by hiding hard facts with bureaucratic expressions, and by using inflated words to give an air of importance to simple things. As an example of the Lutz/NCTE approach, NASA won the 1986 Doublespeak award from the NCTE for referring to the *Challenger* shuttle explosion as an "anomaly" (disaster), the remains of the astronauts as "recovered components" (dead bodies), and saying that these were placed in "crew transfer containers" (coffins).[9]

The NCTE's Doublespeak program has focused on manipulative words and phrases. With this semantic approach to propaganda, one emphasizes the individual texts of messages and deemphasizes the larger social context in which the communication is prepared and diffused. Following the NCTE's anti-propaganda methodology, one pays relatively little attention to questions of who is trying to persuade whom, through what channels, and for what purposes. In this respect, the NCTE's pedagogy follows the tradition of critical-thinking instruction which has favored a relatively narrow examination of claims as connected to evidence and the emotional tone of words as affecting their reception.

The tradition of critical-thinking education has been to improve the sometimes faulty nature of human thought by teaching people an objective, quasi-scientific process of inference. (See above, pp. 32-37.) Since the 1940s, mainstream critical-thinking curricula have associated good thinking with the method of science: hypothesis, experimental observation, conclusion. At the same time, critical-thinking teachers have tried to expose emotionalism as something that clouds clear-headed thought.[10]

A survey by Nickerson, Perkins, and Smith demonstrated that the narrow, text-focused orientation remained dominant in critical-thinking curricula during the 1970s and 1980s. Emphasis continued to be placed on objective analytical operations including classifying, formulating hypotheses, generalizing, recognizing contradictions, relating causes to effects, finding errors in reasoning, and identifying emotional blocks to thought. The messages studied tended to be short texts in the form of hypothetical cases or student-written compositions.[11] Overall, the approach to critical thinking favored through the 1980s was an emphasis on the mechanics of inference, with relatively little said about the content of actual disputes going on in society. The instruction largely operated at a microscopic level, rarely looking up to assess the larger issues of society's propagandists or the covert cooptation of communication channels.

WHAT KIND OF PROPAGANDA ANALYSIS?

If we define propaganda to be the covert orchestration of key communication channels by self-interested persons and groups, then critical-thinking pedagogies are too focused on microscopic considerations of logical reasoning to capture the manipulations practiced by propagandists who influence government action, research, religion, news, education, and entertainment. Might it be possible to set in place an anti-propaganda curriculum to examine the cooptation of communication channels for private interests?

Before the critical-thinking format gained sway, *propaganda analysis* was in vogue in American intellectual and educational circles. (See above, pp. 22-23.) With this approach to mass persuasion, one sought to discover occasions in which particular channels of communication were home to messages inserted by self-interested groups. A representative case-in-point was the exposure of the channel of education in use by propagandists hostile to the idea of publicly-owned electrical power plants, when the National Electric Light Association (a trade group representing private power companies) had subsidized textbooks and college courses on power generation. As implemented by educators in that case, propaganda analysis represented a specific effort to combat large-scale covert manipulation of society's avenues of communication.

Anti-Propaganda Devices or the Discursive Context?

The nation's single largest educational effort against propaganda took place during the 1930s under the auspices of the Institute for Propaganda Analysis (IPA), an educational group chartered in New York City by leading progressive intellectuals and educators. Prominent until World War II, the Institute pursued a wide-ranging inquiry into propaganda's pollution of public opinion. Early issues of the Institute's bulletin, *Propaganda Analysis*, taught readers how to find propaganda in newspapers, radio broadcasts, movies, public relations, and advertising. Later issues provided detailed case studies of propaganda, for instance, the public-relations campaign by large retail chains, led by A & P, against legislation favoring smaller mom-and-pop stores. Another of the IPA's significant exposés was an investigation conducted by I.F. Stone of the Associated Farmers (a group comprising large farms and agricultural financiers) who impeded unionization by branding organizers of farm-workers as Reds.[12]

The IPA's bulletin provided a wide-ranging education against propaganda by covering important propagandists, propaganda channels, self-serving aims, and tactics of manipulation; however, American educators tended to seize on just one of the Institute's anti-propaganda frameworks, namely, the seven propaganda devices: name-calling, glittering generalities, transfer, testimonial, plain-folks, card-stacking, and bandwagon (see above, pp. 5-6). Taken individually or as a whole, the IPA's seven propaganda devices focused the attention of educators and students on the internal, verbal workings of persuasive texts. For instance, application of the name-calling device focused on emotion-laden words such as "fascist" or "Red." Similarly, focus on glittering generalities made clear that abstract concepts such as "democracy" and "freedom" might be employed without explanation by a writer or speaker.

Where propaganda analysis became synonymous with the seven propaganda devices, this pedagogy suffered from the same limitations as critical thinking. In other words, focus on manipulation by tricky words and evocative phrases represented a preoccupation with message texts, with a corresponding neglect of the social context of leading propagandists (e.g., the NELA), self-serving socio-political objectives (e.g., union-busting), and co-optation or control of major propaganda channels (e.g., textbooks). When preoccupied with message texts, propaganda analysis shared the inattentiveness of critical thinking to the big picture of who was trying to hoodwink the public, for which purpose, and with what general strategies applied to the propaganda channels.

Linguistic frameworks, such as the seven propaganda devices and the euphemisms of doublespeak, work best when applied to individual propaganda appeals found in advertising, bureaucratic announcements, and political speechmaking. Linguistic devices are less potent against propaganda when the manipulative intention is both sustained and buried in the practices and formulae of journalism, research, education, and entertainment. For instance, analysis of bureaucratic euphemisms in NASA's communications would miss that the agency capitalized on its reputation (before the *Challenger* disaster) and that its press-relations practices lulled reporters. In like manner, critical-thinking formats and anti-propaganda devices often are ill-equipped to deal with non-discursive appeals found in entertainment fare like *Top Gun*. In this film, a pro-military message was deeply embedded in visual settings, plot action, and character development, such that the film's propaganda was relatively immune to analysis of individual words and phrases in the script. To decode the propagandas of NASA and of *Top Gun*, one would need to pay less attention to explicit statements and give more scrutiny to control of information, to the needs and vulnerabilities of journalists, and to the power of dramatic pictures and heroic characters.

In addition to overlooking embedded and non-discursive characteristics of propaganda, critics who emphasize linguistic devices may miss the self-serving strategy that resides in agreeable appeals. Thus, a second limitation to the effectiveness of propaganda devices pertains to the heightened difficulty in detecting fallacies when the critic agrees with the conclusion of a message. The NCTE's Public Doublespeak program, for all its great value, nonetheless seems disproportionately attuned to dubious expressions of the political right wing. This tendency may reflect a political proclivity of teachers participating in the program who, like everyone else, are more sympathetic to material that supports their existing biases.[13] The focus on individual statements and claims only amplifies the chances that political preferences will blind critics to the propaganda of favored groups (such as reformers) and in places held sacrosanct (such as education). In contrast, when the focus is on groups diffusing their ideas through propaganda channels, there is less of a likelihood that a critic will overlook or dismiss propagandistic efforts that are personally agreeable. Attention to the propaganda channels demands that the critic recognize the strivings of every vocal individual and institution seeking to influence the channel.

A third limitation of a propaganda analysis based on critical thinking and linguistic devices has to do with the connection between individual statements and claims and the wider social reality of which these expressions are but a small part. Labeling a statement as "name-calling" or characterizing an argument as a "glittering generality" presumes a context of information that is not supplied sufficiently by the definition of the individual propaganda device alone. It is not mere name-calling to label Senator Joe McCarthy or Reverend Al Sharpton as demagogues when one explores their known political careers. Similarly, a glittering generality ("national security"), used in the argument "Star Wars is vital to our national security," may make perfect sense (or constitute nonsense) if the full socio-political context is understood. Whether or not the generality in this argument glitters distractingly is a judgment dependent on the critic's context of information, a composite of factors far more complex than the critical analysis of rhetorical devices.

The issue of context is central to the limitations of a devices-based propaganda analysis. No one who is informed about the full environment of a social dispute is going to overlook embedded manipulation or the effort by all kinds of groups to insert propaganda into communication channels. If by "propaganda analysis" we mean the uncovering of propagandists, the exposing of self-serving efforts, and the discovery of infiltration in propaganda channels, then propaganda analysis requires the scrutiny of the discursive context more than of individual texts. In an era of pressure groups, inter-group struggle, and mass media, propaganda analysis implies getting information about the environment of discourse rather than merely knowing how to dissect the rational relationship of statement and proof in an isolated explicit message.

Help from Journalism

The question of focus on the context of discourse is central to the power of educators and journalists to contribute to defusing propaganda. I offer the particular kind of propaganda analysis that I practice in this book as an example. In the chapters focused on propaganda in government action, research, religion, the news, education, and entertainment, I take a basic approach premised on the advantages in certain features of American journalism. Although journalism, too, is vulnerable to becoming a carrier of propaganda, and this has often happened, the profession of news-gathering nevertheless offers the critic of propaganda important resources for defusing covert manipulation. These tools pertain to the characteristic topics of news stories as well as to the typical sources of these reports.

Journalism facilitates a context-sensitive propaganda analysis, first, because news professionals pay great attention both to major propagandists and to key propaganda channels. Nearly all American newspapers and popular periodicals give copious attention to complaints about government, research, religion, education, and entertainment. It is true that stories centering on these propaganda channels do not always become front-page news; nevertheless, the alert propaganda critic may easily keep close track of major propagandists and propaganda initiatives simply by reading and clipping relevant articles that pertain to various propaganda channels. Granted, newspapers may be more likely to report abuses of power in propaganda channels *other than news*; compare, for instance, the far fewer number of scandalous exposés involving journalists as opposed to the steady stream of investigative journalism about politicians. Nonetheless, the critic of the news may compare news stories on the same subject in different organs, and the news critic may also turn to the great reservoir of books and op-ed articles by journalists analyzing their profession. In sum, no one who tries to keep up with one or more of the key propaganda channels will lack for material gathered easily from normal reading in the periodicals.

The sources of news stories represent a second resource that enables an alert consumer of news to practice a context-based propaganda analysis. Many stories originate from complaints by an individual or group about the efforts of others to manipulate or to take advantage of special privileges. Propagandists themselves help establish a journalistic context for propaganda analysis by undergirding an "inside-dope" journalism that exposes the ploys of competing socio-political actors. For instance, complaints by liberal groups about the ABC-TV production, *Amerika,* led to articles probing whether this mini-series did or did not privilege exaggerated anti-communist thinking. Similarly, when scientists complained about the Defense Department's pushy effort to funnel research money to Star-Wars programs, periodicals and newspapers pursued these accusations, thereby helping to set out the social context of this governmental propaganda of research. When journalists pursued complaints by rival ideologues in these two instances, the results were behind-the-scenes exposés of self-serving ploys in the channels of entertainment and research.

But even the contextual propaganda analysis suggested here may be too limited to solve the full problem of propaganda as an obstacle to the formation of public opinion in a democracy. Educational propaganda analysis tends by its nature to make people into political hobbyists rather than participating citizens. It is well for educators to encourage their students to collect examples and anecdotes about symbolic strategizing. If, however, propaganda is well-ensconced in society's major channels of communication, protecting the integrity of public opinion may require something more than an educational remedy.

The Limits of Education

Even when a context-sensitive analysis pierces propaganda's covertness, self-servingness, and irrationality, education shares the tendency of journalism to be a somewhat artificial and over-responsible solution to propaganda. We may not assume that high-school and college faculties have either the inclination, the resources, or the power to immunize their students from the full spectrum of social propaganda.

Teachers arguably become over-responsible when they undertake the duty to defuse society's propagandas. We may question whether educators have the inclination fully to survey propagandists and propaganda channels. Even the NCTE's respected probing of public doublespeak seemed in the 1980s to be preoccupied with analyzing right-wing propaganda to the concomitant neglect of the Left. Nearly all of the NCTE's Doublespeak award winners were drawn from military and industrial elites and from among conservative Republicans. Perhaps most doublespeak and most propaganda during the Reagan Era did come from institutions in which conservative thought prevailed, but lacking a full examination of the matter, we ought not to assume that this was the case. The examples that I cite in this book suggest that the Left may be as active as the Right in efforts to capture certain propaganda channels, particularly education. A society that depends on social-science and humanities educators to collect examples of propaganda, risks allowing certain advocates, institutions, and lines of thought to escape close propaganda analysis.

Even assuming that a classroom-based propaganda analysis confronted the full spectrum of contemporary mass persuasion, the debunking of propaganda by educators faces a second limitation, that of artificiality. A context-rich propaganda education is an effort to identify and critique today's important behind-the-scenes persuaders and lobbyists; however, just as journalism supplies but a skeleton of society's struggles, so too does a context-sensitive study of propaganda supply but an artificial environment for disputation. A further limitation is that even this skeletal anti-propaganda education would not reach the entire American public. In a nation of 250 million people, pedagogical propaganda analysis would require an effort at Continuing Education that presently is impossible.

The matter of artificiality goes to the heart of the limited power of an anti-propaganda education. Research suggests that students who are taught how to analyze propaganda nevertheless find it difficult to apply these lessons to comparably contrived material they encounter later.[14] In other words, the effects of propaganda education are difficult to transfer from one controversy to another, and they tend to wear off. Moreover, propaganda analysis does little to overcome the basic psychological desire of people to support, rather than to criticize, their existing beliefs.[15] Not even highly educated intellectuals are safe from propaganda, as Jacques Ellul explained: Intellectuals sometimes are more vulnerable than others to propaganda because they live in a world oriented to ideas rather than to action.[16]

In the final analysis, a program of anti-propaganda education represents a limited antidote to symbolic finagling because it tends to view the public as consisting of bystanders. Education in propaganda analysis represents no more a solution to covert persuasion than does showing TV football games suffice in training a championship team. Propaganda is language in action; in order to block this linguistic energy, students of

338

propaganda must take part in, as well as observe, the play of politics. Strengthening the *public sphere* to encourage participation in political deliberation, debate, and action could supply a response to propaganda that is deeper than journalism and more lasting than education.

The Public Sphere

The *public sphere* is that meeting of place and time where and when citizens directly observe the political process and/or directly take action within it. Public meetings and public debates—particularly if the event culminates in a vote—are the essence of a democratic public sphere. The direct opposite of a lively public sphere is a discursive format that relies upon TV news—that unreal space and time in which sound-bite and photo-op doings are digested in brief summaries. Televised political advertisements, even more opposite to the public sphere, are the commercial packaging of fast-food politics. The journalistic dissecting of public events and the public-relations packaging of political messages alike encourage the public to respond as passive bystanders.

How to make Everyman and Everywoman his or her own propaganda critic is a question broader than that of textbooks and formal education. Defusing the social impact of propaganda requires nothing less than strengthening the public sphere in America. A vibrant public sphere is characterized by compelling speakers; evocative and mentally challenging messages; and alert, involved, active listeners. In a word, the hallmark of a strong public sphere is the appreciation for, and the frequent occurrence of, *eloquence.*

RESTORING ELOQUENCE

If, as noted in chapter 7, America's current public sphere panders to propaganda more than it neutralizes symbolic chicanery, what can be done to bolster the health of public deliberation? Moreover, how might a healthier public sphere counteract the rhetorical poison of propaganda? The answer to these questions raised here is a call for revitalizing rhetorical traditions that predated the rise of modern political journalism. I argue that a goal of restoring eloquent speechmaking will lead to a vibrant public space that is more resistant than is journalism to the temptations of propaganda, and more informative about symbolic strategizing than are educational programs. This view marks a merging of the practitioner and progressivist points of view summarized in chapter 1. In other words, the communication practitioners may be right that the competition of ideas can lessen the danger of propaganda; however, in the competition, we must pit eloquent speakers against one another rather than listen to clever propagandists.

Eloquence dwells where great thoughts are presented with passionate words that are based on the best and highest values of a community. Our current political climate of PAC- and media-neutralized speakers, of superficial and sloganistic messages, and of apathetic audiences does not permit the kind of eloquence that would penetrate and neutralize propaganda. (See chapter 7.) A climate of eloquence incapacitates propaganda by inviting advocates to link their ideas to the aspirations of citizens, thereby supplying the political passion that converts passive audiences into active, alert citizens. At the same time, eloquence dissolves the power of unsupported conclusions by inculcating an appreciation for reasons. Moreover, eloquence negates the power of visual images by forcing people to think about society as well as to watch fragments of it on TV. How does this magic called eloquence actually work? What evidence exists that eloquence makes for a social environment in which propaganda withers?

Eloquence and Its Absence

With the definition of eloquence offered above, I stipulate that eloquence is a kind of communication that draws upon great ideas, passionate commitment, and the highest values of a society or culture. Democratic Athens and the early American Republic represented two historical periods in which eloquence was practiced and appreciated. Historical samples of eloquence drawn from these periods suggest the kind of communication necessary in the 1990s to shake up neutralized speakers, to energize verbally bland messages, and, as a result, to challenge apathetic audiences.

An enviable standard of eloquence was set in ancient times by Demosthenes who asked Athenians when they would be ready to stop the encroachments of King Philip of Macedon against Greece.

> When, then, men of Athens, when, I say, will you take the action that is required? What are you waiting for? "We are waiting," you say, "till it is necessary." But what must we think of all that is happening at this present time?[17]

The stakes were high when Demosthenes challenged those Athenian orators who advocated caution and accommodation with Philip. Eventually, the persistent and stinging questions of Demosthenes rallied Athenians against the mortal danger to their democracy posed by the Macedonian monarchy. Unfortunately for Athens, the city had tarried too long in opposing Philip, whose son and successor, Alexander, soon became master of the Mediterranean world.

Examples of eloquence may be found not only in the oratory of old Athens but also in the speaking common to eighteenth- and nineteenth-century America. In the early American Republic, a standard of eloquence was set by orators such as Patrick Henry, whose final words to the Virginia assembly are familiar even today:

> Our brethren are already in the field! Why stand we here idle? . . . I know not what course others may take, but as for me, give me liberty or give me death.[18]

Just as eloquence spurred on the War for Independence, so too did passionate reasoning sustain other early movements for equality and tolerance. Chief Logan was an early model of vibrant political discourse when he put these questions to the colonial Governor of Virginia:

> I appeal to any white man to say if ever he entered Logan's cabin hungry, and he gave him not meat; if ever he came cold and naked, and he clothed him not.[19]

As an example of eloquence in the service of women's equality, we may turn to the power of Sojourner Truth's address to a women's rights convention in 1851:

> That man over there say that women need to be helped into carriages, and lifted over ditches, and to have the best places everywhere. Nobody ever helps me into carriages, or over mud-puddles, or gives me any best place—and ain't I a woman? Look at me! Look at my arm! I have ploughed, and planted, and gathered into barns, and no man could head me! And ain't I a woman? I could work as much and eat as much as a man—when I could get it—and bear the lash as well! And ain't I a woman?[20]

The era of the Civil War produced much passionate speaking that married cogent reasoning to the best values of the community. We may turn to Lincoln's "House Divided" speech of 1858:

> If we could first know where we are, and whither we are tending, we could better judge what to do, and how to do it.
>
> We are now far into the fifth year since a policy was initiated with the avowed object and confident promise of putting an end to slavery agitation. Under the operation of that policy, that agi-

tation has, not only not ceased, but has constantly augmented. In my opinion, it will not cease until a crisis shall have been reached and passed. "A house divided against itself cannot stand." I believe this Government cannot endure permanently half slave and half free.[21]

In none of the instances above did eloquence purport to guarantee social and political utopia. Demosthenes moved Athens, but too late. The appeals of Logan and Sojourner Truth were but opening salvos in ongoing revolutions for equality. Lincoln's political prudence did not restrain war. But, for all their limitations, Athenian and nineteenth-century American political communities confronted forthrightly, if not always wisely, the issues that divided them. The era saw relatively less of the tortured silence, the analytic schizophrenia, and the manic-depressive tonality that have characterized recent American discourse about illegal drugs, affirmative action, and abortion. Propaganda was a relatively minor force in the lively public spheres of Athens and the early American Republic because, more than today, issues were thrust to the forefront of public consciousness by powerful speakers using rhetorically evocative and intellectually meaty language.

Speakers in ancient times and in nineteenth-century America lived in an era of public life in which success demanded that they find powerful reasons to support great ideas that were conveyed through a style ringing with passion. Moreover, these rhetorical artifacts were available to the entire membership of the political community. In Athens, the relatively small number of citizens could crowd into the city's agora, and in the early American Republic, the great orations were reprinted in pamphlet form and widely circulated throughout the land. In contrast, packaged by ghostwriters, edited into sound-bites by electronic techies, and given an interpretive spin by TV journalists, today's speechmaking rarely attains either the passionate reasoning or the wholeness in wide circulation required for adequate public deliberation on political eloquence.

Today's public has been raised on a diet of impoverished speechmaking. Never before in human history have so many speeches been delivered to so many listeners to so little purpose. Excluding John F. Kennedy, Martin Luther King, Jr., Jesse Jackson, and other of the contemporary era's few rhetorical virtuosos, contemporary speaking is often ghost written and/or packaged such that major speakers have little personal involvement with preparing their addresses. The kind of bland speaking that results is evident when one consults what routinely passes for eloquence in recent issues of *Vital Speeches*, a digest of contemporary oratory.

Admittedly, contemporary audiences sometimes encounter a speaker such as Ronald Reagan who, if his ghostwriter were gifted, could simulate eloquence through his ability to read with conviction the words prepared by others. For the most part, however, the separation of speaking and composing has made for a disembodied discourse that lacks every ingredient of eloquence save the patina of passion conveyed by interspersed applause lines. At the same time, just as interludes of vituperative protest have shaken us moderns out of political stupor, occasional demagogues have livened up TV-era politics with sensational accusations and claims. Although it may be evocative, today's protest rhetoric is not eloquent, however. The definition of eloquence specifies that the rhetorical passion be grounded on the highest values of the society rather than lower-level appeals to hate or fear or self-assertion.

Under the influence of TV news, we still may experience a synthetic eloquence in the form of 20- or 30-second oratorical sound-bites in the news. Because these moments are torn by journalists from the context of reason, however, the speechmaking available to most Americans is notable for its lack of thoughtful, coherent passion. Excerpts shown on television are extracts of some of the emotional commitment and a few of the ideas that might produce eloquence; nevertheless, because today's memorable speeches rarely occur in a context of point/counterpoint debate, today's pseudo-eloquence lacks a train of reasoning that nourishes understanding of the issues. Today's infrequent, nationally televised speeches are one-shot affairs in which speakers, struggling not to offend anyone, contribute a bland level of thinking and analysis. In the worry that audiences have no patience for reasons, the speeches are more often packed with conclusions and stocked with clichés than armed with strands of reasoning. Recent Inaugural and State-of-the-Union addresses by U.S. presidents illustrate the point. Further, on those infrequent occasions when the speaking format requires point/counterpoint debate, the speakers not only are at the mercy of ridiculous time constraints (one and two minutes in presidential "debates"), but also are required to speak to disjointed questions by jockeying journalists.

Finally, today's televised speeches are not prepared in the manner of the old orators who assumed a responsive audience of interested hearers. Addresses are given in a casual conversational style more fitting for dinner-time patter than for crucial public issues. Television replaces speeches with interviews or panel discussions—anything to allow the camera to move or to get the celebrity program host out in front. Quintilian observed that a speaker cannot be eloquent when speaking to an audience of one. Such is the environment of television's pseudo-intimacy that conceives of its audience as people sitting singly in easy chairs rather than as a group of opinion leaders poised to hear and respond to eloquence.

The Restoration of Eloquence: A Hedge against Propaganda

If we can restore eloquence of expression to American society, we will have done much to combat the dangers of propaganda. Propaganda flourishes in a climate of synthetic politics mixed with defiant protestations—where passion is ever separated from reason in the communications available to the public. The restoration of vibrancy to public life would not only encourage eloquence but also—by publicly linking reason, passion, and values—dampen propaganda's unthoughtful slogans, disconnected images, and hidden agendas. *How* to restore eloquence becomes an issue of some importance for a society that wishes to live by the reality of democracy and not merely by its forms.

We can begin by realizing that ancient orators and nineteenth-century speakers were not genetically programmed for eloquence any more than are today's leaders. Rather, the eloquent speakers of yesteryear worked in a public atmosphere that encouraged eloquence. Our contemporary rhetorical malaise, born of placid speechmaking punctuated with moments of rank incivility, owes much to our lack of a viable public sphere. If we act as a society to establish a viable public space for speakers and audiences, we shall prompt them toward an eloquence of memorable discourse that brings issues to the fore and connects them to important values of the community. What kind of public sphere gives birth to an eloquence that renders the public more resistant to propaganda?

Defining Public Space

The essential first step in a restoration of eloquence is to define a truly public space for speaking. In ancient times, the public assembly (in Rome), the agora (in Athens), and in early America, the town hall were real places where the citizens interested in an issue could gather to hear relevant speeches. Our society has yet to face the question of what public space means in the electronic age. At a minimum, an electronic public space would be a regular time—not during elections only but throughout the year—when speakers would have the opportunity to address an interested public (national, regional, and local) without interruption by commercials, handling by spin doctors, or intrusions by journalists. If these electronic spaces featured pro and con addresses given on a single issue for a sustained period, then orators would need to avoid bland, packaged discourse designed for anonymous audiences.

Today's thirst for an active public space breaks out occasionally, for instance, when a group sponsors a one-shot meeting that gets brief media coverage. On Sunday, January 6, 1991, the San Jose, California, First Unitarian Church sponsored a meeting on the Persian Gulf crisis. Two hundred people showed up to participate in a heated, point/counterpoint debate, complete with hoots and hollers from the audience, and featuring speakers from Jewish and Islamic groups alike, as well as presentations by a journalist and a Hoover-Institution fellow.[22]

Other meat for today's malnourished public discussions comes in the form of radio or TV call-in shows which, in the 1992 election campaign, seemed actually to have improved the quality of discourse by comparison to 1988. Further, commentary sections of newspapers, specialty newsletters, and computer billboards offer glimpses of a vibrant public space. Nevertheless, few people demand establishment of recognized national, regional, and local electronic spaces that would reproduce conditions that existed in the agora of Athens or the New England town hall. So modest are prospects in this direction that a commentator may be labeled a visionary for proposing that TV networks give presidential candidates a mere five minutes of speaking time on the nightly news.

The timidity found in many proposals to reform American political speaking is exemplified in Neil Postman's *Amusing Ourselves To Death*, where, after 157 pages of critique of a TV-based discourse, Postman described as "near insurmountable" his task of setting out solutions. After five desultory pages, Postman finally called for schools to teach Americans how to watch TV.[23] Such reticence about solutions may be frustrating but it is not imprudent because would-be reformers of discourse find themselves immediately beset by a host of objections.

Objections to the utopia of eloquent speechmaking proposed in this present book include questions of who would choose the issues and speakers that would fill up the newly defined electronic public space. In the interests of keeping public space public, it might be well either to elect a community speakers' committee to manage public space, or to have town councils, state legislatures, and Congress set the agenda of issues. Once issues were set, the speakers could be selected by consulting either those groups in society that closely follow the issue undergoing debate or those leaders who have developed a reputation on the topic. On the major public issues discussed in chapter 7—illegal drugs, affirmative action, abortion—it would not be difficult to identify spokespersons from groups concerned with these topics.

The kind of public space advocated here would resemble "America's Town Meeting of the Air," a program produced during the 1930s and 1940s by NBC that became a recognized national forum for discussion of timely issues. The format included a moderator, George Denny, who provided commentary and introduced up to four representative speakers espousing different points of view on the subject of debate. Questions from the audience were a frequent part of the agenda. Typical was the program of March 21, 1946: "Have Britain and America Any Reason to Fear Russia?" In this broadcast, H.V. Kaltenborn, a radio commentator, argued that America was appeasing Russia's threats to the peace, and foreign correspondent Jerome Davis countered that Russia's effort to secure friendly governments on her borders was a natural consequence of the great losses sustained by the U.S.S.R. during World War II. Two other speakers addressed the increase of world tensions and the postwar evaporation of the U.S. Army.[24]

Whatever the mode for selecting issues and speakers, a town-meeting-style electronic forum would free citizens from dependence upon an artificial public world squeezed into news programs on the basis of journalistic norms and story-lines. Also, by allowing speakers to pursue their positions without interruption in addresses of some decent length, a town-meeting format would improve upon the radio- and TV-based talk shows, where speaking is organized around questions from the program host or from listeners. Eloquence would be more likely to prevail if speakers were allowed time to develop their points comprehensively and to respond to one another in successive, extemporaneous rebuttals. Eloquence would flourish if the same topic were pursued over the course of several town-meeting programs, each time before a sizeable live audience, with further opportunity for radio and TV viewers to express themselves through interactive connections. Any plan for an electronic forum faces the practical necessity of inducing those who control local, regional, and national electronic media to provide public-access programming like that once contributed by NBC. Public TV is one option. The Corporation for Public Broadcasting has served as home for a number of specialty discussion or interview programs. Perhaps PBS would be willing to undertake programs of speech and debate patterned on "America's Town Meeting of the Air."

Even the commercial media networks might become home to electronic public spaces. Although America's airwaves and cable wires today are treated chiefly as conduits for corporate profit, television executives might be persuaded to find a place for public-forum-type programming. In other words, it might be possible to overcome the packaged-for-profit nature of electronic media without recourse to a public law that would allocate time for local, state, and national speakers. A less adversarial approach might be to take advantage of certain changes in television. As cable TV and video cassette recorders continue to erode the market share of the old broadcasting networks, the networks might discover live events as a unique niche. If America's electronic public spaces featured excellent speakers pursuing vital issues in hard-hitting, point/counterpoint speeches, then the "show" (to use TV's entertainment-oriented language) might draw a sizeable audience. After all, political commentators are frequently surprised by the large audiences gathered by presidential debates—and these disconnected joint press conferences are fairly barren as regards eloquence.

When given live television coverage, eloquent speaking might surprise news professionals, who assume that the content of public-affairs programming cannot attract viewers but can only lose them.[25] Admittedly, broadcast audiences today are increasingly tuning out the nation's chief speaker—the president. Whereas 79 percent of the TV audience was tuned to the speeches of presidents Nixon and Ford, the later speeches of President Reagan were drawing a mere 50%, as viewers turned to the many cable and VCR alternatives.[26] This is because presidential speeches suffer from certain limitations. They tend to be single episodes that are scripted, one-sided, and without audience response. The same listeners and viewers who tune out teleprompter speaking might return to eloquent extemporaneous oratory that was accompanied by rebuttals from opponents, and responses by the audience.

We should not assume that the for-profit communication industry would be hostile to local, regional, and national speaking periods. For one thing, electronic news itself was not originally profitable. Networks first provided news services to fill up radio space that had not been bought by advertisers. The early news programs also provided local radio stations with "license insurance," that is, a convenient way to prove to the Federal Communications Commission, which renewed the license to broadcast, that the station was acting in the public interest.[27] (These two factors also contributed to the emergence of Denny's "Town Meeting" program on NBC.) Only later did the news become profitable. In like manner, the networks may eventually find it profitable to emphasize live speaking events on television.

Restoring an Appreciation for Debate

Debate can be distressing, and the fear of unpleasant confrontation contributes to society's tolerance for avoiding eloquent probings of illegal drugs, affirmative action, and abortion. Society's level of tension rose when these seemingly settled issues began to be hotly debated in the late 1980s and early 1990s. However, explicit rhetorical action on these matters may be healthier for democracy than are silence, a bogus consensus, and mere shouting. If the nation wishes to minimize propagandized reflexes and to maximize intelligent action, then the eloquence of *rhetorical debate* is bound to be to the good.

"Rhetorical debate?" The word "rhetorical" is troublesome for us because it is derived from "rhetoric," a term now disparaged as signifying artificial or overblown speech. The decline in the prestige of the word "rhetoric" occurred after the Civil War at just the time when political speechmaking went into eclipse and propaganda was waxing. This coincidence suggests that we may profitably investigate the pre-Civil War meaning of "rhetoric," a term which had antecedents in the writings of classical authors.

Aristotle believed that rhetoric was based on the premise that truth prevails only when the several sides of an issue are cogently argued.[28] In contrast, we find that in many disputes today—such as over drugs, affirmative action, and abortion—the side that predominates in official policy hardly is argued at all. At the same time, the noisy machinations of protesters on the periphery provide color and interest that, unfortunately, does not translate into a real debate of competing views. This climate of impoverished discourse contributes little to accommodation among opponents or to general acceptance of social policies. Deprived of the opportunity to witness the higher-quality (although still imperfect) debate found in the agora of ancient Athens or the town halls of nine-teenth-century New England, citizens float in a limbo of apathy or alienation. As a result, the public is left more vulnerable to the hasty generalizations, irrelevant reasons, slogans, and unsupported accusations favored by propagandists. Eloquent debate atrophies in favor of acquiescence to superficially attractive ideas embedded in government agency action, research findings, religious dogma, news, classroom materials, and entertainment shows.

Today's climate of discourse is both rhetorically and psychologically unhealthy. The point/counterpoint of publicly stated and defended reasons promotes a hard but healthful fight over the issues. This may be contrasted to a climate of poverty-stricken discourse in which supporters of the prevailing policy exhibit a complacent smugness, and those who want change are silenced or ignored and therefore experience frustration or even paranoia. To this unhealthful climate we may add the occasional manic flights of discourse shouted by protesters striving to break up the false consensus. Perhaps even worse for sustaining intelligent debate is the manic-depressive melancholy that leads to charges of "Traitor!" when someone who ought to support the dominant view (given his or her demographic characteristics) challenges it instead.

In connection with today's tendency to discredit dissenting opinions by reference to the private lives or presumed purposes of opposing advocates, we have reason to believe that this practice further leaves the public vulnerable to propaganda. Rhetorical theoreticians generally hold that the public can recognize dishonest speakers only when they repeatedly hear these advocates making sustained extemporaneous addresses that are rebutted by opposing advocates. Aristotle described the speaker's character—the speaker's *ethos*—as being most essentially revealed by what the speaker says as opposed to the speaker's prior reputation.[29] A Latin rhetorician, Quintilian, similarly developed a theory of ethical speaking based on the idea that bad speakers reveal themselves through their performance. He believed that these speakers would be found out by the public because they eventually dropped their pleasing masks to reveal their essential ignorance of the issues and contempt for the public.[30]

Our current rhetorical climate runs directly opposite to that envisioned by Aristotle and Quintilian. Today, the nature of public discourse as performance under conditions of risk has declined. Citizens typically observe national opinion leaders through the vehicles of packaged presentations, staged events, photo ops, sound-bites, quick news clips, and disjointed question-and-answer sessions. If citizens now have less access to fully-argued and extemporaneous discourses by national opinion leaders, then we have less reason to be optimistic about the safeguards of a supposed marketplace of ideas.

Public Talk versus Private Therapy

Granted, the hard-headed eloquence advocated here might be perceived as socially divisive when contrasted to the discourse of studied silence or sensitive euphemism. Eloquence, however, encourages the tolerance of differences by bidding people to embrace what they share in common. In the view of Isocrates, an Athenian teacher of rhetoric, speakers in a lively public space are likely to employ eloquent discourse that emphasizes transcendence rather than separatism. Isocrates believed that when orators sought to persuade the general public, they tended to seek out those values that represented the best in a society. In other words, faced with the opportunity to address the entire national (or regional or local) audience of people interested in a particular issue, speakers would inevitably find themselves relying on more-fully developed arguments and also linking these claims to the best values of the community.

One noteworthy example of when eloquence promoted a thoughtful tolerance may be seen in John F. Kennedy's remarks before the Greater Houston Ministerial Association in 1960. In addressing the charge that a Catholic could not be trusted to keep government free from dictates of his church, Kennedy relied upon transcendent principles of democracy to bridge differences between Catholic and Protestant.

> For side by side with Bowie and Crockett [at the Alamo] died Fuentes and McCafferty and Bailey and Bedillio and Carey—but no one knows whether they were Catholics or not. For there was no religious test there. . . .

> But if this election is decided on the basis that 40,000,000 Americans lost their chance of being President on the day they were baptized, then it is the whole nation that will be the loser in the eyes of Catholics and non-Catholics around the world, in the eyes of history, and in the eyes of our own people.[31]

Another example of transcending eloquence came from Martin Luther King, Jr., in his address at the Lincoln Memorial in 1963:

In a sense we've come to our nation's Capital to cash a check. When the architects of our republic wrote the magnificent words of the Constitution and the Declaration of Independence, they were signing a promissory note to which every American was to fall heir. This note was a promise that all men—yes, black men as well as white men—would be guaranteed the unalienable rights of life, liberty, and the pursuit of happiness.[32]

King stressed the common democratic heritage of all the people who pressed together before him in that public space.

In their search for ways to address a national audience, Kennedy and King instinctively turned to transcendent principles to bridge the divisions between Catholic and Protestant and between Blacks and Whites. Today's characteristic response to social conflict is different. When discord breaks out, it is rare that officials set up discussions in public space as a way for group leaders to work out the troubles through transcendent eloquence. More familiar is the recourse to administrative solutions that separate the groups, giving each group a special therapeutic treatment to placate it. While isolating and treating groups separately does avoid messy public squabbling, the effect is to focus on what divides—with the concomitant impact of enhancing the psychological power of the divisions.

The therapeutic scenario plays itself out in how universities have responded to the recent increase of tensions between students on campuses. Universities tend to favor a quick fix for tensions by placating individually whatever group complains.

Concessions to one group are easily justified as necessary to send a soothing message of inclusion to that segment of the campus community whose needs are recognized as special and hitherto unmet. Separate concessions by the administration, however, invariably send out a contrary message of separatism to the other groups. By not being invited to a common negotiating table, the other students are told to please pretend that they are not affected when benefits are parcelled out serially. Cumulatively, these instances of privately greasing squeaky wheels help to convince students that there exists no campus public sphere where all parties—offended groups, acquisitive groups, non-involved groups nonetheless interested in equity, other students, administrators, and faculty—can come together for an open discussion of the issues.

Given the weakness of the public sphere in contemporary American life, who can blame university officials for sacrificing the idea of a campus community in favor of making each pseudo-community feel secure in its own private nook? The effort to make every group feel special flows logically from today's politics of sensitivity, according to which we are bidden to focus on the private feelings of members of the public rather than their public positions on issues.

An emphasis on sensitivity leads to a therapeutic approach to conflict, as seen in 1989 at the University of Santa Clara. Campus tensions rose when copies of a men's fraternity newsletter leaked out to the general campus public. The newsletter not only advised fraternity members to look under their dates' dresses but also referred to women, Jews, and Iranians in derogatory language. The incident led to a march on campus by 400 students protesting racism and sexism. From a rhetorical point of view, the incident sparked the rise of a lively and potentially eloquent campus community—those people who perceived themselves to be affected by the newsletter. In accordance with the therapeutic approach, however, the harried university administration dealt with each group separately. The fraternity's 90 members were admonished and required to attend workshops on sexism and racism. For the demonstrators, there was sympathy and respectful attention to the demand for more hiring of minorities and more campus services for the offended groups.[33]

Instead of workshops for the obnoxious and counselors for the insulted, Santa Clara's administration might have opened a public forum at which representatives of the campus groups could have spoken out, and where votes on actual resolutions could have been taken. But public solutions seem too messy for our over-sensitive era; better to get people to the sidelines for private admonishments or sympathetic counseling, after which, bureaucrats hope, all will be forgotten. The sensitivity approach treats a public problem as though it were a collection of private misperceptions subject to individual therapies.

Richard Sennett, in his commentary on the general decline of public life in the modern era, wondered whether the approach of asking everyone to be "sensitive" does not promote weak personalities in what will always remain a tough world.[34] To this we may add the probability that failing to bring public closure to incidents of community tension probably increases reservoirs of private rage. Where officials try to solve controversial public matters with private action, the members of the affected public community will never be satisfied so long as they themselves lack a chance to speak and act on the situation. As a result, despite Santa Clara University's previous sensitivity workshops and efforts to enhance minority services, women students there expressed great anger to news reporters over a perceived lukewarm response by the administration to sexism on campus.

The Democracy of Public Space

Even if opening electronic public space did lead to a more transcendent form of discourse, this alone would not be sufficient to restore life to our barren public forums. A necessary further ingredient is to enhance the competence of the audience by giving ordinary members of the national, regional, and local publics a chance to talk and act for themselves. Particularly on the local level, it would be useful to allow members of the audience to make brief speeches. The broadcast audiences might vote through interactive TV.

The nature and role of the audience in electronic public space poses a problem. Today's preoccupation with scientific opinion polling predisposes us to reject any non-poll audience as somehow unreal or illegitimate. Professional pollsters, for example, commonly object to the practice of having viewers "vote" by means of calling a 900 number. "It looks like a poll, it sounds like a poll, but it isn't a poll," commented Richard Kaplan, executive producer of ABC's *Nightline* program. He observed that opinions registered via telephone calls were not random. Warren Mitofsky, director of the CBS election survey unit, further argued that voting by 900 number is not real public opinion.[35] In other words, opinion expressed by persons who have watched a program and who actively have responded to it, constitutes a non-real, illegitimate opinion. In this view, only pollsters, they themselves say, provide us with bona fide opinion when they seek out spur-of-the moment choices from 1,500 random souls otherwise occupied at home. Random, perhaps; but bona fide? This kind of poll-based opinion is torn from any meaningful national, regional, or local community capable of debating and acting.

Poll-created audiences may be useful fodder for sophisticated mass marketers who want to know the total sales potential of their product. Political democracy may be better served, however, by audiences that actually listen and respond to speakers, especially if the speakers participate in a recognized public forum such as "America's Town Meeting of the Air." A specific, listening/responding audience experiences a concrete context of speaker and speech; therefore, the listening/responding audience is in a better position than is a phantasmagorial, poll-based audience to discriminate intelligent from unreasonable discourse on the subject under discussion. Kathleen Jamieson, a rhetoric scholar, made the further point that when people habitually listen to eloquent discourse, they become more eloquent themselves.[36] More participation in public forums would enhance the rhetorical capacity of the public for eloquence.

BUILDING CITIZENS

It may seem ironic that a book about analyzing propaganda has not offered propaganda analysis as the best answer to the problem of manipulative mass communication. No one doubts that it is useful to train students and citizens in the art of detecting covert persuasion in various spheres and channels of communication. Nevertheless, from the standpoint of building actual resistance to the seductions of propaganda, it is better to have citizens take back some of the public space that they have yielded to private broadcasting and cable corporations. Citizens would be less likely to fall for catchy slogans, simplistic visual images, and ideologies embedded in institutions and media, were our public sphere to be characterized by eloquent discourse addressed to audiences empowered to signal their opinion directly on matters that affect them. Eloquent speakers and competent audiences would remove much of the tangle of public confusion in which propaganda hides and on which it feeds. When people become closely connected to their political world, when they are personally conversant with social issues, propaganda's impact declines.

Propaganda, as Edward L. Bernays said, may be inevitable in societies, even democratic ones. Nevertheless, much of propaganda's power flows from the way we manage our democratic public life. Where people experience democracy chiefly according to its forms only (e.g., elections), and where neutralized speakers address artificial audiences, propaganda will have great power. Where the public sphere is strong, where eloquence prevails, and where opinion leaders are heard and questioned, there propaganda presents little danger.

ENDNOTES

1. William F. Buckley, Jr., *God and Man at Yale* (Chicago: Henry Regnery, 1951).

2. See, for example, Ben H. Bagdikian, *The Media Monopoly* (Boston: Beacon Press, 1983); Robert G. Picard, *The Press and the Decline of Democracy* (Westport, Connecticut: Greenwood Press, 1985); Robert M. Entman, *Democracy without Citizens* (New York: Oxford University Press, 1989).

3. A. J. Liebling, *The Press* (2nd ed.; N.Y.: Pantheon, 1964): 120.

4. Edward J. Epstein, *Between Fact and Fiction* (New York: Vintage, 1975); Gladys E. Lang and Kurt Lang, *The Battle for Public Opinion* (New York: Columbia University Press, 1983): 59ff.

5. Daniel J. Boorstin, *The Image* (New York: Atheneum, 1961): 11-12.

6. Edward J. Epstein, *News from Nowhere* (New York: Vintage, 1974): 152ff, 244ff.

7. Epstein, *News:* 152ff, 244ff.

8. Lang & Lang, *Battle:* 39.

9. William Lutz, *Double-Speak* (New York: HarperCollins, 1990): 1-6, 222-223, 273.

10. Robert H. Thouless, *Straight and Crooked Thinking* (New York: Simon and Schuster, 1932); R. Flesch, *The Art of Clear Thinking* (New York: Harper, 1951).

11. Raymond S. Nickerson, David N. Perkins and Edward E. Smith, *The Teaching of Thinking* (Hillsdale, New Jersey: Lawrence Erlbaum, 1985).

12. See the following issues of *Propaganda Analysis:* "How to Analyze Newspapers" (January 1938), "The Movies and Propaganda" (March 1938), "Propaganda on the Air" (June 1938), "The Public Relations Counsel and Propaganda" (August 1938), "The A & P Campaign" (December 1, 1938), "The Associated Farmers" (August 1, 1939).

13. Thomas M. Conley, "'Logical Hylomorphism' and Aristotle's Koinoi Topoi," *Central States Speech Journal,* 29 (1978): 94.

14. Roy V. Wood, James J. Bradac, Sara A. Barnhart, and Edward Kraft, "The Effect of Learning about Techniques of Propaganda on Subsequent Reaction to Propagandistic Communications," *Speech Teacher,* 19 (1970): 49-53 .

15. Conley, "Logical Hylomorphism."

CHANNELS OF PROPAGANDA

16. Jacques Ellul, *Propaganda* (New York: Knopf): 76, 111.

17. W. Robert Connor, ed., *Greek Orations* (Ann Arbor: University of Michigan Press, 1966): 44.

18. William J. Bryan, ed., *The World's Famous Orations* (10 vols.; New York: Funk and Wagnalls, 1906): 8: 67.

19. Bryan, *Orations:* 8:3.

20. James Andrews and David Zarefsky, *American Voices: Significant Speeches in American History, 1640-1945* (New York: Longman, 1989): 219. I have edited the text cited here.

21. Ronald F. Reid, ed., *Three Centuries of American Rhetorical Discourse* (Prospect Heights, Illinois: Waveland, 1988): 402.

22. *San Jose Mercury News,* 1/7/91: 2B.

23. Neil Postman, *Amusing Ourselves to Death: Public Discourse in the Age of Show Business* (New York: Viking, 1985): 158.

24. "Have Britain and America Any Reason to Fear Russia?" *Town Meeting,* 11, No. 47 (March 21, 1946): 1-24.

25. Epstein, *News:* 172.

26. *Chronicle of Higher Education,* 6/1/88: A4.

27. Epstein, *News:* 48-60.

28. Aristotle, *Rhetoric,* I. 1. 1355a.

29. *Rhetoric,* I.2. 1356a.

30. Quintilian, *Institutio Oratoria,* XII, i, 12.

31. In J. Michael Sproule, *Speechmaking* (Dubuque, Iowa: Wm. C. Brown, 1991): 420-421.

32. In Sproule, *Speechmaking:* 288-289.

33. *San Jose Mercury News,* 3/3/90: 1B, 5B; 3/9/90: 1B, 7B.

34. Richard Sennett, *The Fall of Public Man* (New York: Vintage, 1976): 260.

35. *San Francisco Chronicle,* 7/7/87: 42.

36. Kathleen H. Jamieson, *Eloquence in an Electronic Age* (New York: Oxford University Press, 1989): 25.

356

INDEX

To order additional copies of this book, contact

ERIC / EDINFO Press

Indiana University • P.O. Box 5953 • Bloomington, IN 47407
Ph: 1-800-925-7853 FAX: 1-812-331-2776

Qty.	Title	Price	Subtotal
_____	*Channels of Propaganda* (cloth)	$39.95	_____
_____	*Channels of Propaganda* (paper)	$24.95	_____

	Subtotal _____
*Shipping and handling: Please add 10%. Minimum charge is $3.00.	IN residents add 5% sales tax _____
	Shipping and handling* _____
	TOTAL _____

Method of Payment:

❏ check   ❏ money order   ❏ VISA   ❏ MasterCard   ❏ Discover

Cardholder _____

Card no. _____ Exp. _____

Cardholder's Signature _____

Ship to:

_____

Name

_____

Title

_____

Organization   Phone

_____

Address

_____

City/State/ZIP

**If you would like to receive
our catalog of publications
please call 1-800-925-7853**